KHRUSHCHEV
AND THE ARTS

The Politics of Soviet Culture, 1962–1964

KHRUSHCHEV AND THE ARTS

The Politics of Soviet Culture, 1962–1964

Text by
PRISCILLA JOHNSON

Documents selected and edited by
PRISCILLA JOHNSON and *LEOPOLD LABEDZ*

THE M.I.T. PRESS

Massachusetts Institute of Technology
Cambridge, Massachusetts

Preface

The editors would like to thank *Problems of Communism* and its editor, Mr. Abraham Brumberg, for permitting Miss Johnson's supplement to the July-August issue of 1963 to be used as the basis of her essay in this volume. We are heavily in the debt of Mr. Leo Gruliow and the *Current Digest of the Soviet Press* not only for most of the documents that are reproduced here but also for an impeccable editorial judgment. Miss Johnson would like to give special thanks to Mr. Gruliow for his advice on her essay. Thanks are due to the journal *Encounter* for Khrushchev's remarks at the Manezh on December 1, 1962, and its translation of his speech of March 8, 1963; and to *Commentary* for the speech of Mikhail Romm in the autumn of 1962 and the exchange between Khrushchev and Yevtushenko on December 17, 1962. Finally, and most especially, Miss Johnson would like to thank the Russian Research Center of Harvard University for extending to her the facilities which enabled her to write the introductory essay. While the Russian Research Center is in no way responsible for any of the opinions expressed here, Miss Johnson would like to acknowledge her gratitude to the Center, and to Professor Merle Fainsod and Professor Richard Pipes in particular, for their encouragement.

PRISCILLA JOHNSON
LEOPOLD LABEDZ

November 15, 1964

Profiles of the
Major Protagonists

The *Ancien Regime*

LEONID ILYICHEV — 58-year-old Central Committee Secretary who served in the latter years of Khrushchev's rule as his principal spokesman in ideology and the arts. Currently Chairman of the Ideological Commission of the Central Committee, he was formerly a deputy editor of *Pravda* (1949–1952), head of the Press Department of the Soviet Foreign Ministry (1953–1958), and head of the Department of Agitation and Propaganda of the Party Central Committee (1958–1961).

ALEXANDER PROKOFYEV — 64-year-old Leningrad poet and winner of the Lenin Prize for literature in 1961. As a Secretary of the Union of Writers of the Russian Republic and member of the Board of the U.S.S.R. Union of Writers, Prokofyev was an early, outspoken opponent of travel abroad by Yevtushenko and other young writers.

LEONID SOBOLEV — 66-year-old writer of stories, novels, and essays, most of which appeared during the 1920's, '30's and '40's. More recently he has been mainly occupied in bureaucratic activity. He has been Chairman since its founding of the Union of Writers of the Russian Republic, which was set up in 1959 to serve as a counterweight to the liberal Moscow branch of the U.S.S.R. Union of Writers. Although he is not a Party member, Sobolev's friendship with Nikita Khrushchev in recent years added cubits to his stature as a ringleader of the conservative camp.

VLADIMIR YERMILOV — 60-year-old journalist and literary critic who is famous for his insinuation in 1930 that the poet Mayakovsky was "playing the game of the Trotskyite opposition." During the Great Purges Yermilov is believed to have informed on scores of other writers and intellectuals as well. In 1928–1934 he was a Secretary of the Russian Association of Proletarian Writers. After World War II he served for a time as editor of *Literaturnaya gazeta*.

vii

The Liberals

VASILY AXYONOV — Thirty years old, with a lantern jaw and straw-colored hair, Vasily Axyonov has been described as a cross between writer Truman Capote and boxer Ingemar Johansson. His longish stories that are highly unusual in their use of slang — including many imported Western expressions — have made the young writer a favorite among Soviet young people. Like Anton Chekhov, Axyonov has worked as a doctor at Moscow hospitals for part of his brief career. Although his work suggests a skeptical attitude toward slogans of all kinds, he is reputed to be rather orthodox in his political views. [For some English translations, see *Encounter* (London), April 1963, and *Dissonant Voices in Soviet Literature,* edited by Patricia Blake and Max Hayward, New York, Pantheon Press, 1962.]

ILYA EHRENBURG — Russian-Jewish writer, born in 1891 in Kiev. After emigrating to Paris for the first time in 1908, Ehrenburg served on the Franco-German front during World War I as correspondent of the Russian "Stock Market Gazette." From 1921–1936 he was special correspondent of *Izvestia* in Belgium, France, and Germany; in 1936–1937 he covered the war in Spain. Ehrenburg returned to the Soviet Union to live after the Nazi attack on France in 1940. Thereafter he became one of Stalin's most valuable propagandists: as a rallier of Soviet Jews and prophet of wartime cooperation with Russia's European allies. Because he seemed to enjoy Stalin's protection and because he survived the purge of Jewish writers in 1952, Ehrenburg remains an ambiguous figure to this day. To detractors he is a cynic, an opportunistic double-dealer. To others he has seemed an ally of the liberals who has tried, by his memoirs and his other writings in the post-Stalin period, to give back to younger Russians at least some part of the artistic heritage of the 1920's and '30's at home and abroad, of which they had been cheated by Stalin.

YURY KAZAKOV — Stammering and bespectacled, the 37-year-old Kazakov is the very picture of self-effacing shyness — backed by a considerable pride in his own work. Unlike many of the younger Soviet writers, he is not drawn to formal experiment — or to what he calls "style-chasing" of any kind — being frank to admit that he owes much to the influence of Ivan Bunin and, to a lesser extent, Chekhov. His critics say that he owes too much to Bunin to this day. The subjects of his short stories often being drunkards, vagabonds, and outcasts of society, he has also been taken to task by Party critics for "degeneracy" and for his profound pessimism about the human condition. A protege of Konstantin Paustovsky, Kazakov spends much of the year living quietly in Tarussa, not far from the elderly writer. Every June, however, he travels to Karelia to stay with the fishermen in their huts during the northern "White Nights," which he loves. (See *Going to Town,* a collection of short stories by Kazakov, translated and edited by Gabriella Azrael, Boston, Houghton Mifflin, 1963.)

ERNST NEIZVESTNY — Dark-browed and heavy-set, the 40-year-old sculptor
works in an extraordinary variety of materials, ranging from bronze to
wood, granite to pig iron to plaster. Born in Sverdlovsk, in the Urals,
he learned metalworking in a factory. During the war he fought in the
Ukraine, was severely wounded, and later spent time in a Soviet prison
camp. He was graduated, after his release, from the Surikov Art Institute
in Moscow. In the late 1950's, his work had mostly to do with horror:
the horror of war and the horror of prison. More recently Neizvestny,
like other Soviet intellectuals in the humanist tradition, has become preoccupied with the relationship between man and machine in an age of
cybernetics. Attacked by Khrushchev and Ilyichev as an "abstractionist,"
he can more fairly be called an expressionist. The influences a Westerner
can recognize most readily in his work are those of the Russian ikons
and of the English sculptor Henry Moore.

VIKTOR NEKRASOV — Dark-eyed and animated, Nekrasov looks more like a
Georgian than the Russian-Ukrainian he is. He is 53 years old, but
looks 35. In 1947, he won the Stalin Prize for *In the Trenches of Stalingrad* (in English: *Frontline Stalingrad,* London, Harvill, 1962), which
many critics consider the finest Soviet novel of World War II. He has
also written a number of remarkably candid short stories about the war,
as well as *Home Town,* an account of a Soviet soldier's return from
the front, and *Kira Georgievna* (New York, E. P. Dutton & Co., 1962),
a study of a returnee from a Soviet concentration camp and one of the
more probing de-Stalinization novels. Nekrasov began writing for Tvardovsky many years ago, when the latter was an editor of *Znamya.* His
"On Both Sides of the Ocean," the work that has recently landed him in
trouble, is based on a visit to the United States in the autumn of 1961
and to Italy in the spring of 1962.

BULAT OKUDZHAVA — 40-year-old poet, short-story writer, and guitarist of virtually charismatic attractions, whose recordings are the rage of Moscow,
who once filled stadiums with his guitar concerts and who ranked with
Yevtushenko as idol of youthful poetry lovers. Son of a Georgian
father and an Armenian mother, Okudzhava was wounded at the front
during World War II, attended Tbilisi University and worked as a village
schoolteacher until 1956. Poetry editor of *Literaturnaya gazeta* in
1961, he is believed to have played a role in the publication of Yevtushenko's famous poem, "Babi Yar." He is said currently to be writing two major works of fiction.

KONSTANTIN PAUSTOVSKY — 72-year-old writer of short stories, novels, and
literary criticism who is highly respected for his independence of
thought. In the early years after the 1917 Revolution, Paustovsky lived
in the colorful world of Odessa writers. In the fall of 1956 he gave a
stalwart defense, unpublished in the U.S.S.R., of Dudintsev's *Not by
Bread Alone* at a meeting of Moscow writers called to condemn the
novel. Himself of mixed Polish and Cossack origins—anti-Semitism is
often found in persons of Cossack descent—he spoke strongly against

the philistinism and anti-Semitism of the type of bureaucrat portrayed in Dudintsev's novel. During the Third Writers' Congress in May 1959, Paustovsky published an unorthodox plea for greater artistic freedom. Perhaps because it was considered too outspoken for delivery at the Congress, this plea appeared only in *Literaturnaya gazeta.* A protector of young writers and a friend of Boris Pasternak, since Pasternak's death he has to some extent, largely because of his moral courage, taken Pasternak's place as hero of the younger liberals in literature.

MIKHAIL ROMM — At 63, Romm has been directing films in the U.S.S.R. for 30 years. A graduate of the Sculpture Department, Moscow Higher Art and Technical Institute, he began to work in films as a scenario writer, and he has worked on scenarios of almost all the films he has directed. His artistic talent brought him a prize at the international film festival in France in 1945. Romm's career began in 1937 with the sound film *Thirteen* which received full Party recognition. He produced a number of propaganda films in the 30's and 40's culminating in the film *Vladimir Ilyich Lenin,* released for the 25th Anniversary of the death of Lenin. For these he received the Order of Lenin and five Stalin Prizes. Romm has since publicly regretted his "shortcomings of the past" and has disavowed Stalinism.

VLADIMIR TENDRYAKOV — Born in 1923, Tendryakov fought in the war until 1943 and then worked for the Komsomol from 1944 to 1946. Earnest and not given to sociability, he now spends most of his time in the provinces, avoiding the turbulent Moscow and Leningrad literary circles. Tendryakov has published many novelettes and is probably best known in the West for his "Three Seven Ace" (see *Dissonant Voices in Soviet Literature,* ed. by Patricia Blake and Max Hayward, New York, Pantheon Press, 1962), a description of life in a Soviet lumber camp. In his writings Tendryakov is preoccupied with essentially moral questions, set against backgrounds that are grim and almost painfully realistic.

ALEXANDER TVARDOVSKY — Born of peasant origins in Smolensk Province in 1910, Tvardovsky spent much of the 1920's and 1930's as a newspaper reporter in Smolensk and Western Belorussia. Author of nearly a score of volumes of verse, he created a new type of comic soldier-hero in his "Vasily Tyorkin" (1946). Another long poem, "Distance Beyond Distance" (1953–1960) was a milestone of de-Stalinization. Editor in Chief of *Novy mir* from 1950 to 1954, Tvardovsky was dropped, apparently for publishing Pomerantsev's "On Sincerity in Literature" and Ehrenburg's "Lessons of Stendhal," both landmarks of the early post-Stalin "thaw." Reinstated in the summer of 1958, he has managed, despite various tribulations, to hold on as editor since. Tvardovsky is an alternate member of the Communist Party Central Committee. He was said to have had the personal respect of Khrushchev.

ANDREI VOZNESENSKY — A 32-year-old poet whose booming voice and considerable presence at poetry readings belie a frail physique. A descendant of a Georgian priest, Voznesensky spent part of his childhood in Vladimir. Trained as an architect, he has worked always as a poet. His verses, often a glittering play on rhyme and meaning, owe much to the influence of such poets as Khlebnikov and Tsvetayeva, as well as to Pasternak, to whom Voznesensky was almost a son during the last years of the older poet's life, and whom he had singled out in 1962 as "the only poet to whom, from my school days onwards, I showed my poems" (*Soviet Literature,* Moscow, Dec. 1962, p. 132). [For some of his verses in English, see *Halfway to the Moon,* edited by Patricia Blake and Max Hayward, New York, Holt, Rinehart & Winston, 1964.]

YEVGENY YEVTUSHENKO — Aged 31, is the most idolized and controversial of the young Soviet poets. A product of the Gorky Literary Institute in Moscow, he has been publishing poetry since he was 16. He first attracted considerable attention in Russia in 1956 with the publication of his long poem *Stantsiya Zima,* which portrayed the spiritual and political confusion and searchings of a young man in early post-Stalin Russia. For this he was expelled from the Komsomol and attacked by the official critics. Yevtushenko's poem "Babi Yar," published in *Literaturnaya gazeta* in September 1961, launched a bitter public debate on Soviet anti-Semitism. (The poem takes its name from the ravine near Kiev where some 34,000 Jews were shot by the Nazis in 1941.)

Although his poems have occasioned frequent Party rebukes for what is called "truth-seeking" and "free-thinking," he has at intervals been accorded unusual privileges by the Party, and has even appeared to represent the Soviet Union on his travels abroad. A change in the political tide and the unauthorized publication of his *Precocious Autobiography* in *L'Express* in 1963 brought him the strongest criticism of his career.

Contents

CONTENTS

The Politics of Soviet Culture
1962–1964

by

Priscilla Johnson

During the winter of 1962–1963, the leaders of the Communist Party of the Soviet Union launched an enormous public campaign to bring writers and artists more closely to heel. The campaign, waged on a vaster and more threatening scale than anything of its kind since the Stalin era, brought the Party into collision not with all the creative artists in the Soviet Union but with virtually all in every generation who were possessed of genuine talent.

At bottom, the issue appears to have been one of authority and control. By destroying the legend of Stalin the Party had, in fact, destroyed the myth of its own infallibility. It had disillusioned thousands of Russians, above all young Russians, who had not lost the capacity to ask questions. But the Party had done more than weaken its authority in the eyes of many of the Soviet people. By a series of episodes in the 1950's and 1960's, it had shown that it no longer had total control over the vast expanse of Soviet Russia. For the first time since the 1920's, spontaneity had begun to show its face in public, notably in the poetry readings that were beginning to draw crowds in the thousands. On occasion, the Party had even turned to the writers for half-voluntary support of its policies — especially the policy of de-Stalinization. To Soviet writers and artists, this new scope for volition was itself a signal occurrence. Little by little, they had begun to make use of it to express a slightly unorthodox thought here, and with greater eagerness still, to make the occasional experimental brush stroke or the impish, irreverent rhyme there. To a Communist Party long accustomed to total control, long accustomed to view every departure from the most literal-minded orthodoxy as a token of longed-for revolt, the yearning of a few

1

talented individuals to experiment somehow spelled a challenge to its authority.

The encounter between the Party and the intellectuals, then, was more than an affair of the arts. It represented a collision between the Party leaders and a crucial segment of Soviet society. This collision occurred, moreover, during what most people took to be the twilight years of Khrushchev's rule, years in which the struggle to succeed him was already going on behind the scenes. And it occurred at a moment in which other chickens were coming home to roost: an attempt to lodge Soviet missiles in Cuba had miscarried and the long-smoldering dispute with the leaders of Communist China was about to blow into the open. Thus, the struggle between the Party and the intellectuals did not spring a fully armed and spontaneous genie from the head of Nikita Khrushchev. It began as it ended, a function of political events within and without the frontiers of the Soviet Union — impossible to understand in terms of art and, like so much else in Soviet Russia, comprehensible, if at all, only within the framework of politics.

It is, then, as a window on Party politics at a critical moment in Soviet history that the struggle between the regime and the intellectuals is worthy of study. Let us look at events, step by step, as they led from the liberal successes of 1962 to a period of crackdown and reaction.

In April 1962, while their conservative hetmen were off on a tour of the provinces, a group of writers in Moscow skillfully wielded the secret ballot to elect eight of their young and liberal members to the board of the Moscow writers' organization. Two leading conservatives were blackballed and three others failed even to be nominated for re-election. Stung by their defeat, the diehards retired to Rostov-on-Don, seat of the most reactionary writers' organization in the U.S.S.R., to lick their wounds and contemplate revenge.

"Such pain has accumulated in my soul," said Leonid Sobolev, head of the Russian Republic writers' organization, "that I cannot help speaking about it." The conservative writers, he promised, would have their revenge, and would have it "from a Party position in literature." [1]

Less than a year later, in March 1963, it appeared that the conservatives had had their revenge. Yet precisely because they won it "from a Party position in literature" they, like the liberals, seemed doomed to perennial disappointment. For, as later events have made increasingly plain, it is the policy of the Soviet Communist Party to use first the left,

[1] *Literatura i Zhizn*, May 20, 1962. For a fuller account of this episode, see also *ibid.*, May 13 and 16, 1962; *Literaturnaya gazeta*, May 15, 17, 19, 1962; and David Burg, "The 'Cold War' on the Literary Front," Part III, *Problems of Communism* (Jan.–Feb. 1963), p. 57.

then the right, exploiting both, never giving up control, never wholly committing itself to either.

Surely, by the autumn of 1962, the liberals of both art and literature had racked up such a string of successes that they may well have suffered that Communist feeling of "dizziness from success." In the field of art, an article by the venerable critic Mikhail Alpatov had appeared in *Izvestia* on February 14, 1962, defending modern, even abstractionist trends in painting. A book called *Comrade Time and Comrade Art* issued from the pen of the youthful critic Vladimir Turbin, arguing that "the twentieth century is becoming an age of triumphant abstractions" in art as in science. And judging by the Benoises and Baksts, Mashkovs, and early Larionovs that newly adorned the Tretyakov gallery, it was apparent that the Soviet art bureaucracy was slowly creaking toward recognition of some of the experimental art groups that had flourished in the decades immediately before and after the Bolshevik Revolution.[2]

On the literary front the gains had been more spectacular and even more far-reaching. In 1962 the conservatives were foiled in at least two attempts to disband the liberal Moscow writers' organization. Yevgeny Yevtushenko and Vasily Axyonov, symbols of the spirit of youthful liberalization, were elected editors of the journal *Yunost*. At a plenary meeting of the board of the Moscow writers' organization at the end of September, the critic Alexander Borshchagovsky delivered a stout speech in praise of the young.[3]

The poetess Bella Akhmadulina sounded the note of hope that was now partly from sincerity, partly from tactical dexterity, being proclaimed by young writers: "I think that the time has become happy for us, that it now runs in our favor. Not only can my comrades work, but they are given every encouragement in their endeavor." [4] The cause of Akhmadulina's elation was not far to seek. From the speeches of Sobolev and others at the meeting it was clear that an amnesty had now been declared for an entire generation of writers who only a few months before had been under fire as moral and political corrupters of the youth. Under the terms of the amnesty, critics were free to write as they pleased about the literary merits of these writers. They were not, however,

[2] For several years, opinion in the Moscow branch of the Union of Artists had been more sharply divided on whether the Mir Iskusstvo group and other artists, such as Chagall, Malevich, Lissitsky, Tatlin, and Falk, should be recognized as part of the Russian art tradition and exhibited than on any other question. Until the work of these painters had been accepted, it seemed academic to discuss what official position, if any, should be taken toward the abstract artists of today. See *New Statesman* (London), Dec. 28, 1962.

[3] *Moskva*, 12, 1962. For accounts of this meeting, see *Literatura i Zhizn*, Sept. 28, 30, Oct. 3, 1962, and *Literaturnaya gazeta*, Sept. 29 and Oct. 2, 1962.

[4] *Literaturnaya gazeta*, Oct. 2, 1962.

openly to question their political motives in print. The meaning of the amnesty appeared to be that the Communist Party was now placing itself squarely in the liberal camp.

And yet there were signs all summer and fall that, chastened as it might be, the conservative impulse in the arts was anything but dead. In July 1962 the Party theoretical journal *Kommunist* published an unsigned article "On the Attitude Toward the Literary Heritage of A. V. Lunacharsky." Naming no names, the article seemed aimed against those, such as Ilya Ehrenburg, who had cited the views of Lenin's Commissar of Enlightenment to justify a lenient Party policy in the arts. During the same month, July, the literary journal *Zvezda* printed a scurrilous, politically motivated attack on the alleged "leftism" of the 29-year-old poet Andrei Voznesensky. When the first, liberal volume of the "Short Literary Encyclopedia" appeared in midsummer with Alexei Surkov as editor in chief, it was greeted by praise, then criticism, and then, strangely, by silence. Finally, Poetry Day, celebrated usually on the first Sunday in October, was mysteriously postponed and held only on December 16.

These conflicting trends in literature, one liberal, the other conservative, only reflected a far more fundamental split in the political sphere — above all, the struggle by bureaucrats left over from the Stalin era to hang onto their power and positions. On October 21, 1962, with scarcely any warning, *Pravda* published a poem by Yevgeny Yevtushenko called "Stalin's Heirs." In the poem, Yevtushenko called upon the Soviet government "to double, to triple" the guard at Stalin's grave "so that Stalin may not rise again and, with Stalin, the past." The poet added: "We carried him out of the Mausoleum. But how to root Stalin out of Stalin's heirs?!"

On the day "Stalin's Heirs" appeared, the newspaper *Komsomolskaya pravda* published still another poem by Yevtushenko, "Fears." This poem celebrated the end of the terror. Neither poem had been published before, although they had been known to exist for some time.

Then, in November, the literary journal *Novy mir* appeared, containing Alexander Solzhenitsyn's remarkable and powerfully understated story, *One Day in the Life of Ivan Denisovich*. A moving description of life in a Soviet prison camp under Stalin, the story was bound to stir a public sentiment that those responsible for the crimes of the Stalin era must now be brought to account. A few days later, five poems by Boris Slutsky, one of the most respected of the Moscow liberals, appeared,[5] recreating the mood of terror and celebrating its end under Khrushchev. Although the poems had been smuggled to the West and

[5] *Literatura i Zhizn,* Nov. 24, 1962.

at least two had already appeared there, it was the first time they had been published in Russia. Together, the publication of Solzhenitsyn's story and the verses by Slutsky and Yevtushenko seemed to be a signal that a new round of de-Stalinization — which had been promised at the 22nd Party Congress of October 1961, but had mysteriously failed to come off — was about to begin. The length and breadth of Soviet Russia, it appeared to mean that the jobs, and perhaps even the lives, of those who had assisted the terror, were now in peril.[6]

Meanwhile, an even more tangible threat to Stalin's heirs was rapidly coming to fruition. When the Central Committee of the Communist Party convened on November 19, it decreed a vast overhaul of the economy. Streamlining the entire Party apparatus into parallel industrial and agricultural units, the reform drastically reduced the power of the Party's agencies for ideological and political control.[7] Not only did the inefficient Stalinist economic manager appear to face loss of his position; so, too, did the ubiquitous ideological controller. The reform of the economy, which was aimed at higher production, was a brain child of Nikita Khrushchev.[8]

That his had been the leading role in reopening the anti-Stalin campaign in literature as well came to light at the same session of the Central Committee. In a speech on November 23, Khrushchev revealed that it was he who had authorized publication of Yevtushenko's "Stalin's Heirs" and Solzhenitsyn's short novel, *One Day in the Life of Ivan Denisovich*. Other members of the Soviet leadership, he disclosed, had suggested cuts in the story, but he had overruled them on the ground

[6] *Novy mir* reached the newsstands on Nov. 21. Evidently, however, publication of the story had been authorized at latest by Sept. 21, the date *Novy mir* was delivered to the printer. By mid-October, word was out in Moscow that the story was about to appear, contributing, along with Yevtushenko's verses, to a mood of euphoria among liberal intellectuals, and at the same time giving conservatives time to prepare a counteraction before the story was due to appear and the Central Committee to convene.

[7] The plenary session of November 1963 set up two Central Committee agencies for ideological control, both headed by Leonid Ilyichev: an Ideological Commission comprising Central Committee members active in the sphere of ideology, and an Ideological Department composed of full time functionaries, such as Dmitry Polikarpov, former head of the Cultural Section of the Central Committee. Apparently the two new agencies were designed to be relatively modest in size and scope. In this sense, the economic reform appears originally to have marked a trend away from ideological control.

[8] Even before the plenum, an old debate on the priority of economic versus ideological factors in a socialist society had been reopened, with Khrushchev on the side of those who believe that economic factors take precedence. See *Pravda,* Sept. 28, 1962, "New V. I. Lenin Document" and editorial; *Kommunist,* Nos. 14 (Sept.) and 18 (Dec.), 1962, pp. 3–14 and 3–12, respectively; speech by N. S. Khrushchev, *Pravda,* April 26, 1963; *Kommunist,* No. 7 (May), 1963, pp. 30–41; and speech by Alexei Adzhubei, *Pravda,* June 20, 1963.

that "no one had the right to alter the author's version." [9] Khrushchev's twin initiatives appear to have been intimately related, with a new round of literary de-Stalinization designed to pave the way for a purge of Stalinist holdovers from the creaking economic bureaucracy.

Khrushchev's speech of November 23 was never made public. Only a few days after it was delivered, he himself set in motion a dramatically reversed policy toward the arts. The last week of November was, in fact, one of those enigmatic periods, familiar to students of the Soviet scene, in which a trend that appears to be on the rise is, like a wave, actually at its crest, about to flow into swift and perilous descent.

Let us pause for a moment to consider the atmosphere of Moscow at that time, and especially to look at the factors that were to make painting and sculpture, of all fields, the takeoff point for a counteraction so political in purpose.

Let us first recall the Cuban crisis of October 1962, and with it the mounting criticism from China of Khrushchev's policies at home and abroad.

Let us next recall that economic unrest, sparked by price rises in meat, milk, and butter, is known to have been widespread in the summer and fall of 1962, culminating in outbreaks of violence among workers and young people in the North Caucasus, the Lower Volga region, and Kemerovo in the Kuznetsk Basin.[10] The apprehension aroused in the leadership by these disturbances can only have strengthened advocates of tighter political control over the population, the very people who were threatened by the November reforms and who, even in advance of the plenum, were on the lookout for issues with which to redress their position.

Let us recall that publication of Solzhenitsyn's novel had no sooner been authorized than a flood of literature on similar themes — the purges, life in the labor camps under Stalin, and even criticisms of present-day Soviet life — began pouring into the publishing houses of Moscow and Leningrad.[11]

Finally, let us recall that not only had the Moscow writers' organization passed into the hands of the liberals, but by the autumn of 1962, the conservative leaders of nearly all the creative unions of Moscow were under fire from younger, more liberal members. In the Union of

[9] *The New York Times*, Nov. 29, 1962, and *A Precocious Autobiography,* Yevgeny Yevtushenko, New York, E. P. Dutton & Co., 1963.

[10] *Ibid.,* Oct. 8 and Nov. 12, 1962. For a fuller account, see "When the Kettle Boils Over" by Albert Boiter in *Problems of Communism,* Jan.–Feb. 1964.

[11] Speeches by Leonid Ilyichev, *Literaturnaya gazeta,* Jan. 10, 1963, and by N. S. Khrushchev, *Pravda,* March 10, 1963.

Cinema Workers, for example, demands were openly heard for an end to all censorship. The Stalinist painter Vladimir Serov had been ousted as head of the Academy of Fine Arts. And, when Dmitry Polikarpov, head of the Cultural Section of the Central Committee, appeared at a meeting of the Academy of Fine Arts to present the official Party list of candidates for the forthcoming elections, he was hooted off the stage to jeers about his record under Stalin.[12] Even in the troubled year 1956–1957, Moscow had seen nothing like the scale of this revolt by intellectuals against the *ancien regime* in the arts.

By the time the Central Committee met to decree the economic reform on November 19, Stalin's heirs were ready to counterattack. At their initiative, the plenary session was presented with a petition from "a large group of artists" complaining of growing "formalist trends" in art and asking the Party to intervene.[13] This was the first link in a long chain that was to see Party conservatives destroy the recent liberal trend in art, then literature, in an attempt to halt the process of de-Stalinization and perhaps even upset the balance of power inside the Communist Party. The next link was a series of closely timed events that, together, had the effect of cleverly staged "provocation."

Art for the Party's Sake

On Monday evening, November 26, 1962, a semiprivate exhibit of art that by Moscow standards was avant-garde opened in the barnlike studio of a 38-year-old art teacher named Eli Belyutin. A handful of Western correspondents attended. So, too, did Soviet cultural officials and several hundred specially invited Muscovites. Hundreds more waited outside, hoping to get in. About 75 canvasses were shown, done by students of Belyutin in abstract or semiabstract style. So, too, was work by the sculptor Ernst Neizvestny. The exhibit, closed to the public, lasted only a few hours. In retrospect, however, it is a perfect example of why it has been the strategy of Soviet liberals in recent years carefully to weigh each new step forward, lest that particular step be the one to precipitate a reversion to the methods of the past.

On Thursday evening, November 29, a second exhibit of modern art was to take place in the Yunost Hotel. Hours before it was to open, the show was mysteriously postponed. Later, it was cancelled altogether.

[12] From an unpublished paper by Peter Benno delivered at an International Symposium on Soviet literature by the Institute for the Study of the U.S.S.R. at Bad Wiessee, Germany, Sept. 2–6, 1963.
[13] Speech by Leonid Ilyichev, *Pravda,* Dec. 22, 1962.

In the meantime, the work at the Belyutin studio was suddenly summoned to the huge Manezh gallery where a retrospective exhibit, "Thirty Years of Moscow Art," of 2000 canvasses and sculptures in now fashionable variations of the official, socialist realist style had been under way for nearly a month. The works from Belyutin's were not hung with the rest, but placed in three separate rooms. The Belyutin painters themselves had no idea why their work was summarily brought to the Manezh.[14] In the optimistic atmosphere of that time, some believed that their work was at last to be shown to the public. That hope was destined to cruel disappointment.

On Saturday afternoon, December 1, Nikita Khrushchev, accompanied by four Presidium members and several members of the Party Secretariat, paid a surprise visit to the Manezh. Khrushchev's reaction, with all its violence and crudity, is one of the documents in this volume. His remarks cast several illuminating sidelights. He rebuked Yekaterina Furtseva, the Minister of Culture, and Leonid Ilyichev, Chairman of the new Ideological Commission, for example, for being too permissive: "Comrade Ilyichev, I am even more upset by the way your section is doing its work. And how about the Ministry of Culture? Do you accept this? Are you afraid to criticize?" [15] Khrushchev was flanked, moreover, by the painter-bureaucrats Vladimir Serov and Alexander Gerasimov. As the group strolled past the work by Neizvestny and the modern painters, these two addressed negative asides to Khrushchev. The speed with which they took advantage of the visit suggests that they could well have had a hand in instigating it.[16]

Most fascinating of all is the fact that to certain high-ranking cultural officials, to say nothing of Neizvestny and the Belyutin painters who were also on hand, Khrushchev's negative reaction, let alone his violence, came as a total surprise. For hadn't Khrushchev authorized the release of a volume of liberal writing, *Pages from Tarussa,* in 1961, after his officials had confiscated it? Wasn't he said to have vetoed a monument to Marshal Kutuzov by the sculptor Nikolai Tomsky on the grounds that it was too conventionally socialist realist in style? And

[14] *New Statesman,* Dec. 28, 1962.

[15] At a later meeting of the Central Committee, Furtseva did, in fact, criticize herself (*Pravda,* June 21, 1963). Ilyichev at no time engaged in self-criticism. On the contrary, he associated himself with critics of Furtseva (*ibid.,* June 19, 1963).

[16] It was rumored in Moscow at the time that the immediate goal of those who staged the exhibit was to secure Serov's restoration to his old post as President of the Academy of Fine Arts. Indeed, on Dec. 4, he was elected to the post, replacing the more moderate conservative Boris Yoganson. Soon after, Gerasimov was elected head of the Union of Artists and another extreme conservative, Alexander Laktionov, became head of Moscow's Surikov Institute of Art.

weren't his words of praise on opening the glassily modern Pioneer Palace only the summer before on record? [17] There was, then, a myth of Khrushchev's "liberalism," and it seemed not altogether lacking in foundation.

As anyone who has trailed him on visits to Western exhibitions is aware, Khrushchev appeared genuinely to detest modern art, as distinct from functional architecture. Thus, those who instigated his visit to the Manezh no doubt counted on an outburst of profanity and were ready to use it for their own ends. In the post-Cuba atmosphere, with supporters of moderate policies on the defensive in every sphere, these conservatives were primed to carry the consequences very far indeed. They were lucky in their timing. The panic that seized them over *Ivan Denisovich* coincided neatly with an inner-Party recoil over Cuba.

Hours after Khrushchev's explosion at the Manezh, the campaign for "ideological purity" in art was under way. The papers came out with editorials demanding, among other things, that all unions of writers, artists, composers, and film and theater workers be banded into a single one to prevent nonconformity in the future. Several Stalinist bureaucrats were quickly restored to their old positions of prominence.

Yet the liberals took action as well. Undeterred by fear that criminal charges of "factionalism" might later be raised against them, at least three groups of intellectuals now sent protest petitions to the Central Committee. A group of young abstract painters declared in a letter that they were seeking their way in "socialist art" and that without such searches there could be no progress.[18] Seventeen eminent artists and scientists, in a message addressed directly to Khrushchev, pleaded with him "to stop the swing in the representational arts to past methods which are alien to the whole spirit of our times." [19]

The signatories of this letter included two Nobel-Prize-winning scientists, Igor Tamm and Nikolai Semyonov, the writers Konstantin Simonov, Ilya Ehrenburg, Kornei Chukovsky, and Veniamin Kaverin, the sculptors Konenkov and Favorsky, the composer Dmitry Shostakovich, the film director Mikhail Romm, and others.[20] A similar letter, but one that appeared to go even farther, calling for " 'peaceful coexistence' of all trends in art," was also dispatched.

The fact, which later came to light, that Alexei Surkov, former head

---

[17] As reported in *Izvestia* editorial, Dec. 4, 1962: "It's hard to arrive at a common opinion in judging a building like this one. Tastes differ, after all. You can't please everyone. Some like it, others don't. Myself, I like your palace. I'm expressing my own opinion."

[18] Speech by Leonid Ilyichev, *Pravda,* Dec. 22, 1963.

[19] Ilyichev, *ibid.*

[20] *Le Monde* (Paris), Dec. 28, 1962, by Michel Tatu.

of the Writers' Union and persecutor of Boris Pasternak, was one of the original signatories of this letter[21] is a sign how deep the dry rot of liberal ideas had penetrated even those on whom the Party had hitherto been able to rely as sturdy zealots of conformity.

In the early days after the visit to the Manezh, the reaction confined itself mainly to sculpture and painting. Apart from the general dynamic of Soviet society, there was no sign to show that it would spread to other art forms as well. On the contrary, on December 11, *Literaturnaya gazeta* printed a piece of fulsome praise by the liberal poet Pavel Antokolsky for the young poets Yevtushenko, Voznesensky, and Akhmadulina and the prose writers Okudzhava and Axyonov. The article was entitled "Fathers and Sons." [22]

Speeches and Discussions

On December 17, 1962, a meeting was held between Party leaders and four hundred writers, artists, and other intellectuals at the Pioneer Palace on Lenin Hills. On the eve of the meeting the mood of the liberals was hopeful. Despite the fiasco at the Manezh, they took Khrushchev's decision to meet with them again as the benevolent gesture of a gracious sovereign. He would listen to them, they believed, as he had listened a few months before to those who had urged that Solzhenitsyn's story be published.[23] Reassured as to their motives, he would ordain that things revert to their happier, pre-December 1 state. They were deceived as cruelly as the artists had been at the Manezh.

Khrushchev's address has not been made public. Identifying himself once again with the anti-Stalin issue, he presented to his audience the little-known Alexander Solzhenitsyn.[24] The main speech, said to have been ten hours long and originally scheduled for delivery by Khrushchev, was given instead by Ilyichev. Art, he said, must be militant. It must inculcate "Communist Party spirit." The artist has no right to a view of human nature that is his own. He has no right to forgive weakness or indulge in "abstract humanism."

A striking note in Ilyichev's speech was its defensiveness. "It is considered inconvenient," he complained, "and unfashionable to defend correct Party positions. One might get the reputation of being, so to say, a reactionary and a conservative." He revealed that the Party was

[21] See speeches by Ilyichev, *Pravda*, Dec. 22, 1962, and by Mikhail Sokolov, *Literaturnaya gazeta*, April 2, 1963.

[22] Attacked by Yury Idashkin, *Komsomolskaya pravda*, Jan. 18, 1963.

[23] Benno, *loc. cit.*

[24] Interview of Henry Shapiro with Alexander Tvardovsky, *Pravda*, May 12, 1963.

under what it considered intolerable pressure to allow greater freedom of expression. There are people, he admitted, who are asking for an end to all censorship: "Exhibitions without juries, books without editors, the right of the artist to display without an intermediary anything he wishes. 'Let us create as we ourselves wish,' these people say. 'Do not restrict us.' " Again and again, so that it was almost a leitmotif, he lamented the influence of the West on Soviet art. In so doing, he showed just how vulnerable the Party itself is to praise of its artistic exports abroad and how skillfully the liberals have used their renown in the West to bolster their standing at home. Compared with such speeches in the past, however, Ilyichev's tone — in the published text at least — was mild. Not only did he avoid aspersions on the motives of the modern-minded intellectual, he specifically granted that "he might have shed blood in the war and be guided by very good intentions."

Some of the informal exchanges at the meeting — the outside world only learned of them later — are remarkable, not only for what they tell of the intellectuals' resistance to Party interference in art, but also for what they reveal about Khrushchev's own feelings. Ilya Ehrenburg cited the cases of Picasso and Mayakovsky to show that modern artists need not, as the Party insists, be political reactionaries.[25] Lenin, Ehrenburg remarked, was tolerant in matters of art. He did not impose his tastes on anyone.[26] The sculptor Ernst Neizvestny reportedly said to Khrushchev: "You may not like my work, but it has the warm support of such eminent Soviet scientists as Kapitsa and Landau." To which Khrushchev retorted: "That's not why we admire Kapitsa and Landau." Yevtushenko rose loyally to defend his friends, the abstract painters: "We must have great patience with this abstract trend in our art and not rush to suppress it. I know the artists. I am convinced that formalist tendencies in their work will be straightened out in time." Khrushchev replied, "The grave straightens out the hunchbacked." It was Yevtushenko's turn to deliver an admonition. "Nikita Sergeyevich, we have come a long way since the time when only the grave straightened out hunchbacks. Really, there are other ways." Stunned at first, the audience burst into applause. Even Khrushchev is said to have joined in. These displays of solidarity within the liberal camp, irrespective of medium, help explain why the campaign was so quick to spread from art into literature.

The most sinister episode at the meeting involved the archconservative Galina Serebryakova, widow of two of Stalin's purge victims, Grigory Sokolnikov and L. P. Serebryakov, and herself a veteran of twenty

[25] *Le Monde,* Dec. 28, 1962.
[26] Speech by Leonid Ilyichev, *Pravda,* March 9, 1963.

years in Siberia. In an attempt to discredit Ehrenburg, one of the leading liberals, she accused him of being a favorite of Stalin and an accomplice in his crimes. During the postwar purges of Jews, she declared, he had betrayed his colleagues on the Jewish Anti-Fascist Committee. Serebryakova's charge was not new, but the source she cited was nothing less than sensational — Alexander Poskrebyshev, former private secretary of Stalin. Serebryakova revealed that she had met Poskrebyshev at a sanatorium where he, like so many famous personages before him, was at work on his memoirs and she, whiling away her vacation. It was Poskrebyshev who could confirm her charges against Ehrenburg.[27] Serebryakova's disclosure that Poskrebyshev was alive and not, as nearly everyone supposed, one of the earliest victims of Stalin's successors, created astonishment enough in the hall.[28] More startling still was her open allusion, in the presence of Khrushchev, to Stalin's personal servant who must have been almost as much anathema to Khrushchev as was Stalin himself! [29] Was Serebryakova speaking with Khrushchev's knowledge and approval? If so, strange purposes indeed were at work here. Or were her remarks made at the behest of others as an ominous hint to those members of the leadership, including Khrushchev, who had been no less aware than Ehrenburg of Stalin's crimes in the 1930's?

Another dramatic episode concerned Shostakovich's Thirteenth Symphony, which is said to have been sanctioned by Khrushchev and was scheduled to have its premiere the next night. In an unpublished portion of his speech, Ilyichev sternly demanded that Shostakovich withdraw the symphony.[30]

Yevtushenko's poem "Babi Yar," chosen by Shostakovich as a theme for the opening movement of the symphony, occasioned a stormy intervention by Khrushchev on the subject of anti-Semitism. There is no anti-Semitism in the Soviet Union, Khrushchev declared. Nevertheless, it is better for Jews not to hold high posts in government, for this only stirs popular resentment. Khrushchev added that in his opinion the unrest in Poland and Hungary in 1956 had been caused by the large number of Jews in high places. Such an uneasy stir arose in the hall after these remarks that later Khrushchev went up to Ehrenburg and assured him that his words had not been directed at him personally.

---

[27] *Le Monde,* Dec. 28, 1962, and Benno, *loc. cit.*

[28] Henry Shapiro, Moscow correspondent of UPI, had previously reported in the West that Poskrebyshev was still alive. So far as is known, however, it was the first time such a report had been made before a public gathering in the Soviet Union. Serebryakova's speech has not been published.

[29] In his Secret Speech of Feb. 25, 1956, Khrushchev spoke derisively of Poskrebyshev as Stalin's "loyal shield-bearer."

[30] Benno, *loc. cit.*

"You must understand," Khrushchev told him, "that as a professional politician I have to take things as I find them and warn against dangers." [31] In the aftermath of Khrushchev's statement, Yevtushenko agreed to add several new lines to "Babi Yar." [32]

After the momentous confrontation on Lenin Hills, the premiere of Shostakovich's symphony went forward at the Moscow Conservatory on December 18 in an atmosphere electric with tension. The government box was empty. TV cameras set up to cover the gala event had been dismantled.[33] No one knew whether the performance would go on or not.

Shostakovich is said to have been apprehensive. Shaken by Ilyichev's warning, the choir tried at the last minute to quit. Only after a stirring plea by Yevtushenko[34] did they dare to perform. When Shostakovich and Yevtushenko rose to take their bows at the end, the thunderous applause that greeted them was homage not only to the music but to a signal act of political courage.[35] After a second performance on December 20,[36] further performances were cancelled.[37] The silence of the critics was eloquent.[38]

On the same day the writers of Moscow made their own gesture of defiance. Convening for elections, they threw out the last remaining conservatives and elected a slate of outstanding liberals to the Party

[31] *The Observer* (London), Jan. 13, 1963.

[32] It has been reported that it was Shostakovich who first yielded to demands that new lines be added to the symphonic text of "Babi Yar" and that Yevtushenko complied only after the composer had done so.

[33] According to *Le Monde*, Dec. 28, 1962, the highest official present was a Deputy Minister of Culture.

[34] The symphony is set to five poems by Yevtushenko including "Babi Yar" and "Fears," the poem published in *Komsomolskaya pravda* on Oct. 21, 1962.

[35] Benno, *loc. cit.*

[36] According to *Le Monde,* Dec. 28, 1962, one of those present at this performance was, ironically, Dmitry Shepilov, ousted as a member of the anti-Party group in 1957 for, among other things, too liberal an outlook in the arts. Shepilov had at one time been Minister of Culture.

[37] The symphony was not performed a third time until Feb. 10, when it was played at Moscow Conservatory with the slightly revised text of "Babi Yar" agreed to by Yevtushenko used as choral text for the first time. *The New York Times,* Feb. 12, 1963.

[38] Shostakovich and the symphony were sharply criticized, but not by name, in an editorial in *Sovetskaya kultura,* newspaper of the Ministry of Culture, on Dec. 25, 1962. But the symphony was not formally reviewed until April 2, 1963, and in the newspaper *Sovetskaya Belorussia* (after a performance in Minsk) at that. Yevtushenko was by then a prime target of the anti-intellectual campaign. The reviewer, Ariadna Ladygina, called the music "gripping, absorbing, stunning," but added that Yevtushenko's text seemed "shallow and insignificant alongside the impressive musical background." Concluding that "the poems interfere with reception of the music," she suggested that Shostakovich "revise the text substantially or perhaps even renounce it altogether."

bureau of the Moscow writers' organization.[39] As if this were not enough, they voted formally to reopen the case of Nikolai Lesyuchevsky, a notorious holdover from the Stalin era and an editor of the Sovetsky Pisatel publishing house.[40] A few days later, a special evening of speeches and recitations was held in honor of Marina Tsvetayeva, whose verses, once considered "formalist," have been an inspiration to the younger generation of poets.[41]

Meanwhile, on December 24 and 26, Ilyichev held a meeting at Central Committee headquarters, this time with 140 writers, artists, and cinema workers. In his speech,[42] Ilyichev used the technique of separating sheep from goats, hopeless sinners from those who may yet be redeemed, that was to become a hallmark of the campaign.[43] He praised three speakers at the meeting for their "civic maturity": Neizvestny, Yevtushenko (evidently for agreeing to add new lines to "Babi Yar"), and Vasily Axyonov (for agreeing, after holding out for months, to revise the screen version of his story "Ticket to the Stars"). On the other hand, he was highly critical of the painter N. Andronov (who continued his stubborn resistance and at no time recanted), as well as of the poet-guitarist Bulat Okudzhava, the young twelve-tone composer Andrei Volkonsky, and the writer Yury Nagibin (for an article in *Literaturnaya gazeta* praising Neizvestny). Nagibin's wife, Bella Akhmadulina, was not mentioned at all. Andrei Voznesensky, out of the country on a visit to Paris and Italy, was damned with faint praise. As for the poets Robert Rozhdestvensky, Yegor Isayev, Rimma Kazakova, and Vladimir Firsov, their voices, said the Party leader, "resound more and more strongly." (Firsov and Isayev belong to the conservative-national trend. They were to receive more of a buildup as the campaign wore on.)

Even as Ilyichev was meeting with both artists and writers, a skirmish was clearly under way between moderates, who still hoped to limit the campaign to art, and extremists who wanted to carry it into literature, their target all along because of its role in de-Stalinization. Thus, on December 25, the conservative critic Sergei Baruzdin published a front page article in *Literaturnaya gazeta* urging the paper to stop castigating

[39] *Literaturnaya gazeta,* Dec. 29, 1962.
[40] Benno, *loc. cit.* The question of expelling Lesyuchevsky and Yakov Elsberg from the Writers' Union for informing on other writers during the 1930's had first been raised early in 1962 following the 22nd Party Congress. Elsberg was expelled but the case against Lesyuchevsky — tantamount to a criminal charge — had been dropped.
[41] *Literaturnaya gazeta,* Dec. 29, 1962. Besides Ehrenburg, speakers included Antokolsky, Akhmadulina, Yevgeny Vinokurov, and David Samoilov.
[42] *Literaturnaya gazeta,* Jan. 10, 1963.
[43] See letter by Komsomol members, including Yury Gagarin, in *Komsomolskaya pravda,* Dec. 21, 1962.

the Union of Artists and the Academy of Fine Arts for their liberalism[44] and to concentrate instead on the Union of Writers, "which is much closer to it." Here, warned Baruzdin, "there is something to think and argue about — something even to criticize." In the very next issue of the paper,[45] as though on cue, V. A. Kosolapov was replaced as editor in chief by the more orthodox Alexander Chakovsky.[46] The ostensible occasion for Kosolapov's removal was his publication of "Babi Yar" more than a year before[47] and his more recent refusal to publish an article criticizing abstract art.[48]

Even as Kosolapov was being dismissed, however, signals of an opposite nature were going out — signals that could only mean that moderate forces were fighting to hold the line with support high in the Communist Party. On December 28, for example, *Pravda* published Yury Kazakov's *An Easy Life,* the story of a ne'er-do-well's wanderings in Siberia. The significance of the story's appearance at precisely this moment, and in *Pravda* at that, was striking. For it was well known in Moscow literary circles that Kazakov's tale, written in 1957, had been rejected by publisher after publisher because the morals of the hero were too lackadaisical for a literature that still claimed to abide by the uplifting canons of socialist realism.

On New Year's Day the head of the Writers' Union, Konstantin Fedin, made a public plea that literature be spared. "Extremism," Fedin argued, had been almost nonexistent in literature compared with the fine arts. If there were now to be a "campaign," or "extraordinary measures," writers would be unable "to make a new step forward." Besides, a campaign would only "drive the illness inside." [49] Two days later, *Pravda* ran an astonishingly outspoken letter in praise of the young writers by the venerable Kornei Chukovsky, winner of the Lenin Prize for literature in 1962.[50]

[44] For an example, see "Art and Life" by N. Zhukov, *Literaturnaya gazeta,* Dec. 20, 1962.

[45] *Literaturnaya gazeta,* Dec. 27, 1962.

[46] As of Jan. 22, 1963, six other editors were dropped: V. N. Bolkhovitinov (editor of *Science and Life*), Yury Bondarev (author of "Quietude"), G. M. Korabelnikov, Boris Leontyev, Vladimir Soloukhin, and Yevgeny Surkov. They were replaced by B. Galanov, A. Makarov, Georgy Markov, Yevgeny Osetrov, S. Rostotsky, and Yaroslav Smelyakov.

[47] Benno, *loc. cit.*

[48] *Le Monde,* Feb. 19, 1963, by Michel Tatu.

[49] *Literaturnaya gazeta,* Jan. 1, 1963.

[50] Chukovsky wrote: "A pleiad of prose writers, literary critics, and scholars has arisen which delights me with its bright talent. Everywhere there breathes the creative, innovating spirit of youth. To this new intelligentsia — ardent, humane, loving of the people — belong the future of the '60's, '70's and '80's. I, as its grandfather and great grandfather, send it hearty greetings." (*Pravda,* Jan. 3, 1963.)

January, on the whole, was a time of paradox, of patent indecision at the top. The press saved its fire for "formalism" in the fine arts. Writers were criticized less as writers than as patrons of modern art.[51] Yet on January 17, 1963, an exhibit of three hundred canvasses by the French painter Fernand Léger, an abstractionist who had the grace to be a Communist as well, opened at the Pushkin Museum, where it ran for three months before being shipped back to Paris.[52] The young poets were giving as many public readings as ever and on January 16 the much-criticized Bulat Okudzhava was permitted to perform with his guitar before a crowd of ten thousand at the Sports Palace.[53] Valentin Katayev and the playwright Viktor Rozov left for the United States as planned and Yevtushenko slipped off on a visit to West Germany and France. As he left, he fired a rather defiant poetic parting shot which may reflect inner turmoil over the lines he had been prevailed on to add to "Babi Yar." [54]

In the fine arts there were signs of stubborn resistance even from the public, to say nothing of the artists themselves. At a Komsomol meeting at Moscow University in late December, Yevgeny Katsman, an official of the Union of Artists, was booed when he tried to expound the new line to students. With art officials traveling all over the country on missions similar to Katsman's, some audiences were cool; others, outspokenly hostile. As far away as Irkutsk there were reports of violent debates, with students vehement in their defense of Western abstractionism and Russian avant-garde art of the 1920's. Even art officials showed signs of resistance — members of the Lenin Prize Committee stayed away in a boycott when a painting by Vladimir Serov, "With Lenin," came up for discussion.[55]

Firm as most writers proved to be in their opposition when the campaign later turned full force against them, perhaps it is the artists who were the most silent and stubborn of all. Having had less success than the writers, and having played less of a public role throughout the post-

[51] A. Laktionov in *Pravda*, Jan. 4, 1963, criticized Ehrenburg and Nagibin as art patrons. A. Gerasimov in *Trud*, Jan. 9, bitterly attacked Ehrenburg, Nagibin, and Paustovsky and added the unlikely charge that *Ogonyok*, edited by Anatoly Sofronov, and *Nedelia*, edited by Alexei Adzhubei, had fallen under "leftist" influence. For this act of excessive conservatism he was rebuked in *Izvestia* and, according to *Le Monde*, Jan. 31, 1963, obliged to present a written apology to *Ogonyok*.

[52] For the problems with which the exhibit confronted politically sensitive critics, see Alexander Chakovsky's review in *Literaturnaya gazeta*, Jan. 26, 1963. The scheduled showing in Leningrad was cancelled.

[53] *Le Monde*, Jan. 31, 1963, by Michel Tatu.

[54] *Izvestia*, Jan. 8, 1963, "My Ideology," by Y. Yevtushenko.

[55] *Le Monde*, March 9, 1963, by Michel Tatu.

Stalin era, possibly they have not been so inhibited by a feeling of responsibility. Having had fewer hopes in recent years that by skillful maneuvering they could push the calendar of progress forward, they have been more willing simply to paint "for the drawer" and wait for times to change. Thus, they have had a rather special immunity to blackmail or temptation. The recantations were few and far between.

It was not, in fact, until six weeks after the Party pilgrimage to the Manezh that so much as one of the young painters whom Khrushchev had criticized there could be persuaded to come forward in *Pravda* (January 14) with anything resembling a recantation. This statement,[56] by Andrei Vaznetsov, was scarcely a thing of contrition. Vaznetsov praised three youthful colleagues[57] whom Khrushchev had singled out for criticism. Matisse, Picasso, and Léger he termed "great artists." He called the work of young painters a "natural reaction" against the "pomposity, varnishing, and soullessness" of Stalinist art and declared that "new content does not always fit into old forms." [58] That *Pravda* even printed such a statement is testimony to the difficulty the Party was having — and continued to have — with the artists.

Attack from the Right

Toward the end of January, the campaign took a sharp break. From now on it was aimed first of all at the writers. The turn occurred on January 20, 1963, when *Izvestia* printed a pointed, unsigned attack on the 52-year-old Viktor Nekrasov for his travel notes on Italy and America.[59] Calling his notably fair-minded observations on the West "extremely superficial and profoundly incorrect," *Izvestia* warned that his "fifty-fifty" approach in weighing the merits of the two sides in the cold war is "a very dangerous game."

The charge of pro-Westernism, already a main theme in the campaign, was raised again a few days later in a poem by Nikolai Gribachov in *Pravda,* entitled "No, Boys!" [60] This was a parody of a poem by Yevtushenko that had appeared some months earlier.[61] The fact that the

[56] *Pravda,* Jan. 14, 1963.

[57] N. Andronov, Pavel Nikonov, and A. Pologova.

[58] Vaznetsov points out that even the 19th Century "peredvizhniki," whom socialist realists consider their precursors, had had to break with the academic art of their time. This remark is a curious echo of a statement at a writers' plenum in March 1957, by the young critic Andrei Turkov: "Nihilism is a terrible word, one that frightens us. But what most people forget is that nihilism was a revelation in its day" (*Literaturnaya gazeta,* March 19, 1957).

[59] V. Nekrasov, "On Both Sides of the Ocean," *Novy mir,* Nos. 11 and 12, 1962.

[60] *Pravda,* Jan. 27, 1963.

[61] Y. Yevtushenko, "Let's Go, Boys!," *Novy mir,* No. 7, 1962.

Party newspaper now chose to print so scurrilous a rejoinder was a signal that conservative fortunes were looking up. The formula applied in the poem is something like this: the West equals abstract art, and a liking for either equals treason:

> Devil knows what they slap on their canvasses,
> Or what they shove into their verse. . . .
> They bring us their foreign editions
> Like passports to summits of glory. . . .

The formula continues: Soviet "sons" are ungrateful to their "fathers," who braved war and revolution for their sake. Gribachov then linked up the three, "sons," "abstract art," and the "West," in the person of Yevtushenko. To the latter, he issued a warning that sounds almost like a prophecy of the mishap to come:

> There's that terrible second abroad,
> When you've slipped — and you're already an orphan,
> Under the Red Banner no longer. . . .
> You're alone. . . .
> Condemned to the scorn of your fellows,
> Thus, many have vanished into obscurity,
> Without a trace, the light from their souls
>   extinguished,
> And no lines, no echo of their songs,
> Not even their tears,
>   have reached us.

The deeply nationalistic spirit of Gribachov's poem was henceforth an important feature of the campaign against the writers.

The opening stage of the literary drive reached its climax a few days later when *Izvestia*[62] mounted a blistering attack by Vladimir Yermilov on Ilya Ehrenburg — primarily for the latter's assertion, in his memoirs published in *Novy mir,* that he and other Soviet citizens had been perfectly well aware during the 1930's that millions of Stalin's victims were innocent, but that they had been compelled to live with "clenched teeth" and be silent.[63] Yermilov vehemently denied this. No one, he insisted, unless he enjoyed some special "advantage," was aware at the time that the arrests were largely a frameup. Those rare individuals who happened to know that a particular victim was innocent "fought, and fought not with silence." The point, of course, was that if a journalist

[62] Jan. 30, 1963.
[63] The key quotation used by Yermilov came from an installment of Ehrenburg's *People, Years, Life,* published in *Novy mir,* No. 1, 1961, pp. 105–106. The installment that deals with the purges in greatest detail appears in *Novy mir,* No. 5, 1962. Thus, the storm over Ehrenburg's memoirs was, to say the least, belated.

like Ehrenburg knew, what about high-ranking officials, like Khrushchev, who even then held responsible posts in the party? Were they too cowardly to take steps against the slaughter? Or were they knowingly helping to carry it out?

Ehrenburg lost no time replying.[64] He took issue with Yermilov that people "fought" the arrests of the 1930's: "I was not present at a single meeting at which people took the floor to protest the arbitrary persecution of comrades whose innocence they never doubted. Not once did I read an article of protest."

Izvestia printed Ehrenburg's reply, but only with another attack by Yermilov and a note from the editors supporting the attack. Yermilov's second attack repeated his earlier insinuation: either Ehrenburg was lying, or he enjoyed "special insight" or an "advantage" during the 1930's. Such an "advantage" could mean only the protection of Stalin himself. By attacking Ehrenburg at a point where he was genuinely vulnerable in liberal eyes — he had enjoyed the favor of Stalin — Yermilov hoped to divide the liberal camp and divert its fire from conservative henchmen of Stalin, such as himself and Elsberg and Lesyuchevsky. He wanted to destroy a leading liberal of the older generation, a protector of Western-oriented "sons" like Yevtushenko, as a coward or liar. More ominous still, taken with Serebryakova's unpublished charges of December 17, Yermilov's assault can be seen as a hint that unless Ehrenburg repudiated his remarks, he might one day find himself on trial as an accomplice in the crimes of Stalin.[65]

Immediately after the initial assault on Ehrenburg, *Izvestia* set out to chasten two other members of the older generation who had protected the talented but mettlesome young.[66] The victims were Alexander Tvardovsky, editor of *Novy mir,* and Boris Polevoi, editor of the journal *Yunost.* Mildly, *Izvestia* scolded Tvardovsky for publishing Alexander Yashin's story "Vologda Wedding" — a shocking picture of poverty, brutality, and superstition in a Russian village after 47 years of Soviet rule. Tvardovsky did not reply for three and a half months. Then, in an interview with UPI correspondent Henry Shapiro, he called Yashin's story "excellent" and "full of poetry," [67] He added that the story "was, in my opinion, unjustly attacked in the press." These words were deleted from *Pravda's* account of the interview.[68]

[64] *Izvestia,* Feb. 6, 1963.
[65] This interpretation is suggested also by Michel Tatu in *Le Monde,* Jan. 31, 1963, and by the Moscow correspondent of the *New Statesman,* March 15, 1963.
[66] *Izvestia,* Jan. 31, 1963.
[67] *Pravda,* May 12, 1963.
[68] The words are taken from the UPI text distributed abroad — they constitute the only major discrepancy between the UPI and *Pravda* versions.

In the other half of its double-barreled attack, *Izvestia* took Polevoi to task for "squeezing" into the January issue of *Yunost* "banal little verses about Italy" by the talented Andrei Voznesensky. Contrary to the expectations of many who had known him before the 1959–1962 "thaw" melted all but the most ice-bound reflexes, Polevoi did not apologize. Instead, he denied that the verses were "banal" and suggested that *Izvestia* ought to have taken up its criticisms directly with Voznesensky and not with his editors alone.[69]

After mid-February, there was what one observer has called "a truce, with each camp resting on its positions." For a time, attacks by the extreme conservatives were halted (that is, a violent assault which Yermilov was said to have prepared against Viktor Nekrasov failed to appear),[70] and liberal writers such as Gladilin, Okudzhava, Ehrenburg, Voinovich, Goryshin, Yashin, Nagibin, Yevtushenko, and Kazakov, all appeared in print. An article in *Pravda* even gave cautious praise to Pavel Nikonov — one of the most heavily criticized of the Manezh painters — adding that Soviet art "needs many styles and many intonations of the spirit." [71] Nor were the conservatives silent, going so far as to attack Solzhenitsyn,[72] who had hitherto been virtually above reproach. The Central Committe of the Young Communist League formally censured the journal *Molodaya gvardiya* for publishing "White Flag," a daring and outspoken play by K. Ikramov and Vladimir Tendryakov on the conflict between "fathers and sons"; and *Literaturnaya gazeta,* having printed two sympathetic contributions on Voznesensky,[73] now came out with an editorial rebuttal.[74] From week to week the intellectuals were awaiting a new confrontation with the Party leaders.[75] Yet the meeting was, inexplicably, postponed.

Briefly, the situation in early March was this. Few, if any, of the artists or writers challenged communism as an ideal. Few challenged the right of the Party to direct their work. The more talented, however, hoped the Party would interpret this right more liberally than in the

[69] *Izvestia,* Feb. 14, 1963.

[70] *Le Monde,* Jan. 31 and March 9, 1963, by Michel Tatu.

[71] "On the Living and Dead in Art," by Yury Pimenov, *Pravda,* March 1, 1963.

[72] In *Literaturnaya gazeta,* March 2, 1963, Vadim Kozhevnikov attacked Solzhenitsyn's story, "Matryona's Home," which had appeared in *Novy mir,* No. 1, 1963. Earlier, "One Day" had been criticized by Lidia Fomenko in *Literaturnaya Rossiya,* No. 2, Jan. 11, 1963.

[73] By V. Klimenko, *Literaturnaya gazeta,* Feb. 26, 1963, and B. Sarnov, *Literaturnaya gazeta,* Feb. 28, 1963.

[74] *Literaturnaya gazeta,* March 2, 1963.

[75] Khrushchev announced that such a meeting would take place in a speech in Berlin on Jan. 16, 1963. Ilyichev said in *Pravda,* March 9, 1963, that the meeting originally was scheduled to take place "right after the New Year" but "circumstances prevented this."

past. They sought to experiment with form in poetry and painting, to select themes of their own choosing and develop character in their own ways in fiction. They had been encouraged by the Party's comparatively relaxed cultural stance since 1959. Above all, they were encouraged by its sanctioning of de-Stalinization poetry and fiction. They hoped that de-Stalinization would benefit them in several ways: that it would entail the removal of Stalin's heirs from the cultural bureaucracy and so alter the tenor of Soviet life as to open up to art a whole range of subjects that had formerly been tabu. And they hoped that in reward for the aid they had rendered the Party in de-Stalinization. the slightly wider opportunity they had had for experiment since 1959 would now be granted them as a right.

To a Party headed by Khrushchev, however, even so tentative a hope seemed an intolerable presumption. The Party's right to be arbiter of the intellectual conscience was total. If the intellectuals had recently enjoyed slightly greater freedom — snatched, in the main, while the Party was not looking — that freedom was strictly a privilege subject to withdrawal at any moment, by no means to be construed as a right. If the Party permitted the writers to come to the aid of its de-Stalinization policy now and then, they were not to suppose it was according them any special status. Unable by peasant background and by Communist upbringing alike to comprehend the creative temperament, Khrushchev expected to be able to turn the writers on and off at his pleasure. Even their timid hopes, he viewed as black ingratitude.

On the other hand, unlike its "freezes" of 1954 and 1957, the Party no longer was dealing with a handful of creative artists only. At poetry readings and art exhibitions, the creative few had now come in contact with scores of thousands of intellectuals, many of them young, and sympathy for their work had spread. By the barrage of publicity — the heaviest since the Zhdanov purge of 1946–1948 — which it had given its drive in the arts, the Party had only spread the curiosity and sympathy farther. Thus, after Khrushchev's outburst at the Manezh, the exhibit itself was kept open and the crowds flocked there in far larger numbers than before. Jokingly it was said that the Premier's attack on Neizvestny had brought the sculptor more valuable publicity than any exhibition.[76] Conceivably the hopes of writers and artists contained the kernel of challenge to the Party's demand for total control. But as far as the public went, the Party was dealing more with good-natured curiosity — on the part of a comparative handful of people at that — than with anything in the nature of a revolt. Yet even here, it felt that its authority over the nation's mind and morale was challenged. To deal

[76] *Le Monde,* March 9, 1963, by Michel Tatu.

with this "challenge," extreme conservatives were now demanding that
the Party use "administrative measures," or physical repression, against
the liberal intellectuals.[77] Until March 7, there were reports of persistent
disbelief in Moscow intellectual circles that the Party would consider
anything of the kind. But on the eve of the now famous March 7 meeting, pessimistic rumors were heard. Voznesensky and Yevtushenko, it
was said, were about to become victims of a major offensive.

The Peak of the Campaign

Thus, it was an apprehensive gathering of 600 writers, artists, and
other intellectuals who met in the Kremlin's Sverdlov Hall on March 7
to hear the party leaders speak once again. In Paris, Yevtushenko had
received an urgent cable on February 28 summoning him home for the
meeting. He left on March 4 on the last flight that could deliver him to
Moscow on time. Any doubt as to the mood of the intellectuals is put
to rest by the rows of somber faces pictured in *Pravda,* the rows of
anxious hands scribbling the exact words of the speakers.

Ilyichev was the first major speaker.[78] Acknowledging that the discussion touched off on December 1 was by now "a national debate," he
conceded that the party's drive had been greeted by skepticism, silence,
and open protest. Some people, he admitted, were fearful that there
would now be "creative stagnation" and "suppression of innovational
searches in art." Some "have not merely misunderstood, but continue
stubbornly to defend their mistaken views. Some are even trying to win
others to their point of view, to surround artists who listen to healthy
criticism with a wall of indifference and alienation and to ostracize
them, accusing them of 'apostasy' and 'lack of principle.' " Using his
"divide and conquer" technique, he announced that Yevtushenko, Neizvestny, and Belyutin had "correctly evaluated their errors" (presumably
on December 24–26). So, too, had Vaznetsov in his *Pravda* article.
Several artists and art critics, on the other hand, were "belligerently
taking an incorrect position." [79]

The brunt of Ilyichev's speech fell on Ehrenburg. Like Yermilov and
Serebryakova, he accused the elderly writer of enjoying special protec-

[77] *Ibid.*

[78] *Pravda,* March 9, 1963.

[79] Significantly, Ilyichev singled out officials of the Moscow organization of the
Union of Artists, some of whom, he charged, "have tried to play the role of
buffer between Party criticism and people whose work and views were being
justly criticized ." In a similar vein, A. Gerasimov in *Trud,* Jan. 9, 1963, accused
officials of the same organization of singing "paeans to the 'talented' Falk and
Nikonov."

tion from Stalin. Hadn't Ehrenburg himself, he asked, quoting some of Ehrenburg's flights of prose, praised Stalin in 1951? As if anticipating that this weapon might one day be turned against himself, Ilyichev added: "We all spoke and wrote thus at the time without being hypocritical. We believed and we wrote. And you, it turns out, did not believe, but wrote. These are different positions!"

Ehrenburg chose to make no reply to the vicious attack by Ilyichev, nor, indeed, to any that followed. Immediately after the speech, he retired to his dacha outside Moscow. There he apparently remained in seclusion for several weeks. Before leaving the Kremlin hall, however, he pronounced an epitaph of his hopes to a member of the younger generation: "I shall never see the flowering of the Soviet arts," he said sadly. "But you will see it — in twenty years." Reflecting the dismay of Russians in the hall, one foreign observer concluded that it was difficult to tell whether this prophecy erred on the side of optimism or pessimism.[80]

Ilyichev's assault on Ehrenburg was seconded by others, including Sholokhov, who is said to have declared as he took the floor: "I have wanted to criticize Ehrenburg for a long time." [81] Other speakers included Ernst Neizvestny, who, again (as on December 24–26) engaged in self-criticism, and the director Grigory Chukhrai, who reportedly delivered a courageous speech on behalf of avant-garde film-making. Speakers the next day included Vsevolod Kochetov, Vasily Axyonov, and the critic Elizar Maltsev. Voznesensky is said to have recited two poems and then opened his remarks: "I am not a member of the Communist Party, nor do I intend to become one. I, like my teacher Mayakovsky. . . ." Referring, apparently, to the poet's nonmembership in the Party, Khrushchev broke in: "This is nothing to be proud of." Voznesensky was shouted down as he attempted to go on.[82]

The main speech of the two-day meeting was that of Nikita Khru-

[80] *Le Monde,* March 12, 1963, by Michel Tatu.

[81] *Ibid.,* March 10–11, 1963.

[82] This account is pieced together from Italian Communist sources and *Literaturnaya gazeta,* March 30, 1963, speech by V. Firsov. A year later V. Ozerov, editor of *Voprosy literatury,* added the following details: "There was talk at the meeting of the incorrect conduct of the poet A. Voznesensky. His speech altogether failed to satisfy the participants. When Voznesensky stood at the podium, N. S. Khrushchev spoke to him. The young poet had to listen to a direct, clear, Party appraisal of his speech and his actions alike. For his real talent, there were no demeaning allowances. There was, however, lofty concern for the fate of a talent which can develop fruitfully only on a genuine ideological basis, with any and all prejudices as to the non-Party quality of creative work being rejected. Then N. S. Khrushchev shook hands with the poet, urging him to give serious thought to the criticism and wishing him success in his work" (*Izvestia,* March 8, 1964).

shchev.[83] This was the speech that at last brought home to Moscow intellectuals the full ferocity of the campaign that had been mounted against them. Its crux was the partial rehabilitation not merely of Stalin's tastes in art but of Stalin himself:

> Did the leading cadres of the party know about the arrests of people at the time? Yes, they knew. But did they know that people were being arrested who were in no way guilty? No, they did not know. They believed Stalin and did not admit the thought that repression could be applied against honest people devoted to our cause.[84]

Almost at a single swoop Khrushchev revealed his vulnerability on the question of Stalin's crimes and contradicted his own claims of ignorance. Thanks to a lack of "yes-men," he boasted, major Stalinist purges were averted in Moscow and the Ukraine at precisely the moments when he had been head of the Moscow and Ukrainian party organizations, respectively. Dating the beginning of Stalin's errors as late as 1934 (only a few weeks before, party historians had been dating his errors back to the early years of the 20th century), Khrushchev made his rehabilitation:

> At Stalin's funeral many people, including myself, had tears in their eyes. These were honest tears. Although we knew of some of Stalin's personal shortcomings, still we believed in him.[85]

With these words, Stalin's heirs had gained what they were seeking: they had used what began as a party inquiry into "abstract" art as a lever to halt de-Stalinization.

[83] *Pravda,* March 10, 1963.

[84] Here Khrushchev contradicted his own Secret Speech of Feb. 25, 1956, in which he implied that he and other leaders were aware of Stalin's "serious errors and shortcomings" but failed to take action because of fear and the irregularity of Politburo meetings (see *Current Soviet Policies—II,* New York, Praeger, 1957. p. 187); and the Reply to Communists Abroad of June 30, 1956 (*ibid.,* p. 224), which implied that the Soviet leaders knew of Stalin's abuses, that "it was in no way a lack of personal courage" but that because of popular faith in Stalin any action against him "would not have been supported by the people"; and remarks by himself and other speakers at the 22nd Party Congress in October 1961, charging that the members of the anti-Party group were knowing accomplices in the crimes of Stalin.

Here, for the first time, Khrushchev put the Soviet people and the leaders during the 1930's in the same boat: both trusted Stalin and both were in the dark as to his errors.

[85] Using nearly the same words, Khrushchev partially rehabilitated Stalin following the Hungarian uprising of 1956 [*Kommunist,* No. 12 (August), 1957]. On that occasion, however, his remarks appeared only in the Party theoretical journal, whereas in 1963 they received full press and radio coverage. By 1963, moreover, many more people, especially among the young, were mentally and emotionally committed to de-Stalinization than in 1956–1957. Hence the impact of his words, their capacity to disillusion those who had believed his de-Stalinization to be sincere, must have been considerably greater.

Khrushchev's references to Ehrenburg were venomous. He compared the elderly Jewish author, the alleged beneficiary of Stalin's protection, not only with the writer Galina Serebryakova, Stalin's victim, but also with Mikhail Sholokhov, who in 1933 wrote a letter to Stalin protesting "outrages" and "excesses" in the drive to collectivize peasants in the Don Valley. By explicitly citing archives of the secret police, Khrushchev no doubt hoped to intimidate his audience: he was reminding them that the same archives could be made to yield up material acutely embarrassing to any of them at any moment the party might choose. And he involved himself in a contradiction of the type that seems not to bother him at all: either the collectivization of 1933 was historically distinct from the Great Purges of 1937–1938 of which Ehrenburg had been speaking and the comparison with Sholokhov is irrelevant, or the two purges are to be treated as one and the same. In the latter case, how can Sholokhov have known of the "excesses" and Khrushchev, a high party official at the time, not have known?

Even as Khrushchev was quoting from the archives, he admonished Soviet writers against dipping too freely into their memories. The purges of the 1930's, he warned, are "a very dangerous theme." Revealing that publishing houses were being "flooded with manuscripts about the life of persons in exile, in prisons, in the camps," he added that such material can only "delight" enemies of the Soviet Union abroad.[86]

Khrushchev's somersaults of illogic reflected more than mere vulnerability to the question: Where were you when Stalin was alive? Tacitly or explicitly, who was it who had sanctioned publication of Ehrenburg's memoirs? None other than Khrushchev himself, in pursuit of his anti-Stalin campaign. In the view of this writer, the attack on Ehrenburg had been dynamite from the start precisely because it could be turned against any of the Soviet leaders — there were at least three in the Party Presidium, including Khrushchev — who knew what Stalin was doing during the 1930's and shared responsibility for his crimes. By hinting on December 17 that Ehrenburg had been an accomplice of Stalin, Serebryakova, speaking not for herself alone but for Stalin's heirs[87] high and low in the bureaucracy, may have been reminding these leaders that they, too, could be snared in the trap of complicity were they to push de-Stalinization any farther. By referring openly to Poskrebyshev,

[86] In spite of Khrushchev's warning, de-Stalinization literature did not cease to appear: Solzhenitsyn's novel came out in early 1963 (in an edition of 100,000 copies), Kozhevnikov's *The Fleeting Day* in the second quarter (30,000 copies), and I. Stadnyuk's *Men Are Not Angels* in the third quarter (115,000 copies).

[87] The author uses this term to mean not persons who want to return to the climate of terror prevailing in the 1930's but persons anxious to check further de-Stalinization.

she may have been jogging their memories as to the criminal evidence
that could be brought against them.

Such an interpretation — that in spite of Khrushchev's vast power,
elements desperate to veto further de-Stalinization were capable of veiled
threats even against him — helps explain why Ehrenburg was spared
after March 8 even though he refused to recant. And why in August,
after Kozlov had fallen ill and there had been other changes in the
Party leadership, Khrushchev is said to have spoken personally with
Ehrenburg and encouraged him to finish editing his memoirs! [88]

Elsewhere in his speech, discussing Marlen Khutsiyev's film, *Gate of
Ilyich,* Khrushchev raised what is perhaps the most delicate issue in
Soviet life today: that of "fathers and sons." Perhaps this theme is
particularly close to the Soviet leader's heart because it, too, raises the
question of responsibility during the 1930's. It is the contempt of younger
men, many of whom lost their own fathers in the 1930's, for an entire
generation of "fathers" who allowed the purges to happen. In one
light, it is the special contempt of Soviet young men for old men and
old ideas, for "fathers" who learned hidebound bureaucratic ways under
Stalin and cannot now unlearn them. In another light, it is the eternal
impatience of the young to take over. It is the question of the succession to today's leaders of the Soviet Union in every field — politics, the
economy, the arts. As he spoke of *Gate of Ilyich,* Khrushchev denied,
as he always did, that a "fathers and sons" question exists. Yet the
very vehemence with which he denied it was a measure of his personal
sensitivity to the idea that Soviet "fathers" no longer have anything to
teach their "sons" and that, as he put it, "there's no use turning to them
for advice." [89] Concerned as he was with the "sons," Khrushchev did not
forget their "grandfathers," the handful of brave old men who have
given the young both their protection and a spiritual tie with a world
untouched by Stalinism: the West, 19th-century Russia, and the intensely
experimental Soviet Russia of the 1920's.[90] As we have seen, he had

[88] *Le Monde,* Aug. 14, 1963, by Michel Tatu.

[89] Although Soviet officials insist that the "fathers and sons" question is a Western fabrication, articles on it, mainly by conservatives, appear constantly in the
Soviet literary press. Thus, *Oktyabr,* No. 11, 1962, devoted 20 pages to a discussion of the topic. One of the contributors significantly, was General of the Army
A. A. Yepishev, head of the Central Political Department of the Soviet Armed
Forces. For an unusual admission that the "fathers and sons" problem is a real
one, see *Voprosy literatury,* No. 4, 1963, p. 10.

[90] For an idea of the debt which younger writers feel they owe to such older
men as Pasternak, Ehrenburg, Paustovsky, and Katayev, see "The Young on
Themselves," answers to a questionnaire, published in *Voprosy literatury,* No. 9,
1962. Not only were the series of answers published in *Voprosy literatury* in the
summer and fall of 1962 used as ammunition by conservative against liberal
writers throughout the campaign, they may actually have helped set off the campaign itself.

already dealt with Ehrenburg. He now went out of his way to criticize Valentin Katayev (author of "Squaring the Circle") who, as editor of *Yunost,* had helped nearly all the young writers get their start. Katayev, Khrushchev charged, had been "careless" in his statements in America in January. "They flatter an unstable person abroad," said Khrushchev, "call him 'a symbol of a new era,' and he forgets whence he came, where he has come, and why, and begins to talk nonsense." Finally, he complained that remarks which Konstantin Paustovsky among others, had made on a visit to France in December produced "an unpleasant impression" on him.

Another author whom Khrushchev selected for especially sharp reproof was Viktor Nekrasov. He scolded the Stalin-Prize-winning novelist for remarks he had made while in France, for his travel notes in *Novy mir,* and for his praise of the film *Gate of Ilyich.* For his openmindedness in matters of art and with respect to the West, Khrushchev made clear, Nekrasov was only one doghouse removed from Ilya Ehrenburg himself.

Toward no one was Khrushchev so equivocal as toward Yevtushenko. In one passage he accused Yevtushenko along with Ehrenburg of "a gross ideological error" in liking some contemporary art. Praising him for his speech of December 24–26, however, Khrushchev gave the poet a bit of fatherly advice: "To hold dear the trust of the masses and not to seek cheap sensation, not to bow to the ideas and tastes of the philistines." He made the poet's "Babi Yar" the occasion of the longest published statement he had ever given on Soviet anti-Semitism ("We do not have a Jewish question, and those who dream it up are singing a foreign tune"). At the end of his speech, he again applied carrot and stick in bewildering succession. He contrasted Yevtushenko with Voznesensky, Nekrasov, Paustovsky, and Katayev, on the one hand, as having "conducted himself worthily" on his visit to West Germany and France. On the other hand, in an interview with *Les Lettres Françaises* Yevtushenko "did not withstand the temptation to win the praise of the bourgeois public."

At the moment of Khrushchev's speech, Yevtushenko already was under attack in the press.[91] The attacks did not say so, but it was known in Moscow that the poet had consented to serialization of his five-part autobiography in the French weekly *L'Express,* beginning on February 21. Whether the party would make an issue of the autobiography was a subject of speculation in the Soviet capital.[92] Far from indicating any such intention, Khrushchev's remarks seemed designed to rein in Yevtushenko a little — less than some other writers — on future visits abroad. Even as Khrushchev spoke, he could have been aware of the

[91] *Komsomolskaya pravda,* March 9, 1963.
[92] *Le Monde,* March 10–11, 1963, by Michel Tatu.

content of at least two installments of the autobiography. Khrushchev's speech suggests that he hoped to preserve intact his most famous roving ambassador abroad, the young man who had come to symbolize the new and more liberal image of Russia and who was better known outside the borders of the U.S.S.R. than any Soviet citizen but Khrushchev himself. Apparently the Party leader preferred not to kill the goose that had laid so many golden eggs for Soviet propaganda abroad.

Even before the meeting was over, it was clear that conservatives still were dissatisfied and wanted the drive to go farther.[93] So impatient were they that one of their more moderate members, Alexander Chakovsky, who only a few weeks earlier had been installed as editor of *Literaturnaya gazeta* to restore the conservative line, now warned against carrying the campaign too far.[94] Despite this warning, the newspapers were filled the next few days with numerous articles stridently welcoming the new and stricter Party position on the arts.[95] Yet from those who were under heaviest attack there was at first no sound of contrition. At a meeting of intellectuals in Leningrad on March 14, Nikolai Akimov, 61-year-old director of the Leningrad Comedy Theater, was criticized by the local party secretary Vasily Tolstikov for the "ambiguous ideological message" of several plays staged by Akimov, especially Yevgeny Shvarts' *The Dragon*. (The play's message is that one tyrant is too often toppled only to be succeeded by another unless the struggle against tyranny itself goes on.) In response to Tolstikov's "just criticism," reported the newspaper *Leningradskaya pravda*, "Akimov's speech did not satisfy the audience." [96] Nor did speeches by a painter, Leonid Tkachenko, who defended the artist's "right to unlimited forms" and by an unnamed woman curator of the European art section of the

[93] See speeches by Alexander Prokofyev and Leonid Sobolev. Sobolev sounded the familiar complaint about the "priority of talent over ideological purity." Significantly, both speeches appeared in *Literaturnaya gazeta*, March 9, 1963, and not in *Pravda*. A speech by Vsevolod Kochetov, which evidently went further, was not published at all.

[94] *Pravda*, March 11, 1963, printed on its front page Chakovsky's warning that the achievements of Soviet culture "must be developed, safeguarded, and defended both from anarchist liberals and from dogmatists with the dubious Midas gift of turning everything living that they touch into soulless metal."

[95] In *Pravda*, March 12, 1963, the elderly poet Nikolai Aseyev even criticized—although not by name—Voznesensky, the same poet he had defended from attack only a few months before (*Literaturnaya gazeta*, Aug. 4, 1962). Most of Prokofyev's speech was likewise given over to an attack on Voznesensky.

[96] A statement by Akimov published in *Literaturnaya gazeta*, March 14, 1963, was a masterpiece of reproof mingled with irony. "Good art," he reminded the Party, "is born only in a joyous and cheerful mood." Such works of art must now be created for the "people" [no mention of the Party]. "And" [in spite of everything] "they will be created!"

Hermitage Museum. She, according to the newspaper, described "formalist" art as "joyous creative work." [97]

Of the intellectuals whom Khrushchev personally had criticized, the first to speak out was Neizvestny.[98] His statement, too, was a masterpiece of ambiguity. It concludes: "Again I tell myself: I must work more, better, more ideologically, more expressively — only thus can I be useful to the country and the people." (No mention of the Party.) In a Moscow Radio overseas broadcast on March 19 Neizvestny added: "An artist not only has the right to experiment. He *must* experiment." [99] The only other penitent was the 30-year-old poet Robert Rozhdestvensky. His brief statement was another miracle of ambiguity.[100] It opens: "It is interesting to be alive." Later: "I find it interesting to be alive." He closed with a defense of "quality" (a liberal byword) as well as "ideological purity" (the Party slogan) in art.

So unsatisfactory was the response of young writers that on March 17 *Komsomolskaya pravda* (consistently, now, a mouthpiece of reaction) felt moved to float a proposal by the conservative poet Igor Volgin that was also a threat: "It would be very useful for us to work for a while in local newspapers, journals, and printing combines. The experience would enable us better to understand the 'poet's' place in the working system." This threat, which Volgin, a 20-year-old history student at Moscow University, was clearly putting forward for others, was a sign that conservative forces had interpreted the March 7–8 meeting as a signal to go full steam ahead. So was a militant call by Vsevolod Kochetov for "action" (that is, force), and not "words." [101]

On March 17, *Pravda* contained two new indications that conservatives were on the warpath. The first was a crude, Stalin-style attack on Michel Tatu, Moscow correspondent of the French newspaper *Le Monde*, on whom more than on any other Western source readers outside the Soviet Union had had to rely for information on the cultural offensive. The attack, signed by Yury Zhukov,[102] was an attempt to

[97] Signs of dissent were censored out of accounts of the meeting in *Pravda*, March 15, *Sovietskaya kultura* and *Literaturnaya gazeta*, March 16. A report in *Leningradskaya pravda*, was, however, more revealing. See *Baltimore Sun*, March 19; *The New York Times*, March 20; *Le Monde*, March 20; and *Time*, March 29.

[98] *Pravda*, March 15, 1963.

[99] *The Observer* (London), April 21, 1963.

[100] *Pravda*, March 18, 1963.

[101] *Literaturnaya gazeta*, March 16, 1963.

[102] Once Paris correspondent of *Pravda* and later Chairman of the State Committee for Cultural Relations with Foreign Countries. In the latter capacity he told the Supreme Soviet in the fall of 1959, just before negotiating a new cultural exchange agreement with the United States, that such exchanges are a "Trojan Horse."

force Tatu's recall to Paris and to intimidate his Soviet sources. Clearly, detailed and accurate reporting of the drive in the West was not to the liking of the more intransigent Moscow officials.

On the same day, *Pravda* also announced that Stepan Shchipachov, a nonpolitical poet, who had distinguished himself as head of the Moscow organization by his tolerant attitude toward young writers of talent,[103] had been removed two days earlier as chairman of the Moscow organization of the Union of Writers "at his own request" and been replaced by Georgy Markov, author, ironically, of a new novel with the title *Father and Son*.

Main Target: The Young

Shchipachov's fall was a clue to a sudden shift in direction. With meetings of "art workers" now taking place all over the country, the name of Ilya Ehrenburg began, mysteriously, to vanish. Instead, Western-oriented young writers[104] became prime targets of attack,[105] the most ominous of which took place at a meeting of the Moscow writers' aktiv. Its stated purpose was to discuss "serious defects in the ideological education of writers" while Shchipachov, Elizar Maltsev, and Alexander Borshchagovsky had been guiding spirits of the organization.[106] Pointedly, the ex-leaders were accused of lacking "courage to tell the truth straight out to certain people, for example, to Y. Yevtushenko, for some of his statements in the press." An ominous note was sounded by Yury Zhukov, who revealed that "it fell to me, by the nature of my work [!] to 'go over' the tracks of some of our poets who went abroad, spoke in the press there, and gave interviews." The lone dissenting voice in this increasingly strident chorus was that of Yulian Semyonov,[107] the only young writer to speak at the March meeting, who

[103] Shchipachov is said to have helped Voznesensky and Akhmadulina gain admission to the Writers' Union before they had published the required minimum of two books. For his role in abetting Yevtushenko's travels abroad, see speeches by Anatoly Sofronov (*Literaturnaya gazeta*, March 28, 1963) and Mikhail Sokolov (*ibid.*, April 2, 1963).

[104] See "The Hero Doesn't Want to Grow Up," by Larisa Kryachko (*ibid.*, March 19, 1963) and "From the First Book—Only Ahead!" by Viktor Pankov (*Komsomolskaya pravda*, March 21, 1963).

[105] So, too, did critics who had defended them. See "And Eternal Battle" by Yury Barabash (*Literaturnaya gazeta*, March 16, 1963), an attack on Lev Anninsky, Alla Marchenko, and B. Runin. See also attacks on Runin by Novichenko (*ibid.*, April 2, 1963) and on Vladimir Ognev by Sergei Smirnov (*ibid.*) and by Sergei Baruzdin (*Literaturnaya Rossiya*, April 5, 1963).

[106] *Literaturnaya gazeta*, March 19, 1963.

[107] In a statement in *Yunost*, No. 4 (April), 1963, Semyonov made the interesting revelation that he had been at work for several months in the Revolutionary

called for "creative work and not fruitless discussions on subjects having little to do with literature."

Any doubts as to where Yury Zhukov's dagger pointed were quickly laid to rest as Moscow's two major newspapers appeared bearing devastating satirical verses aimed unmistakably at Yevtushenko.[108] The poems did not mention Yevtushenko by name, nor had the touchy subject of his autobiography as yet been raised in public. Let us take events, one by one, as they unfolded.

On March 26, a plenary meeting of the board of the U.S.S.R. Writers' Union opened in Moscow amid rumors at home and abroad that the moderate liberal Alexander Tvardovsky was to be replaced as editor of *Novy mir* by Yermilov and that the position of Konstantin Fedin as head of the Writers' Union might also be in jeopardy. In its reports of the meeting, significantly, *Literaturnaya gazeta* featured two photos each of Fedin and Tvardovsky, giving the lie to the rumors and showing that both men had powerful moderate support. The meeting opened with a mild plea by Fedin in defense of individuality in art: "We are glad that the importance of artistic individuality has been upheld by Nikita Sergeyevich, too." Fedin was followed to the floor by the aging poet Nikolai Tikhonov who, despite a tone of mild reproof toward the young writers, showed himself, like Fedin, to be a moderate: "Let us so act that we are not dragged from our main work as writers by all kinds of petty matters, by various internal squabbles, so that all our energy may be spent for the good of our socialist society, and not inciting passions, which are not stirred, really, by necessity." [109]

Other speeches at the meeting were less moderate. That of Alexander Prokofyev, Lenin-Prize-winning poet in 1961 and outspoken opponent of Yevtushenko's travels abroad, set the jealous, embittered tone which many were to follow. Complaining that the liberal spirit had now invaded not merely Moscow, but Leningrad and Siberia as well, he asked why Yevtushenko, Voznesensky, and four or five other "neon innovators" were allowed "vast editions" of fifty and a hundred thousand copies, and why a first book of verse by the young Leningrad poet, Viktor Sosnora, got fourteen reviews "while books by those who take a Soviet position receive almost no attention." [110]

archives studying the roles of Bluecher, Postyshev, and Uborevich in the Far East during the last year of the Russian Civil War. So far as this author is aware, the "large tale" by Semyonov based on this research had not, as of June 1, 1964, appeared.

[108] "To a Young Talent" by Sergei Mikhalkov (*Izvestia,* March 22, 1963) and "Pledge of Fidelity" by Vladimir Firsov (*Pravda,* March 24, 1963).

[109] *Pravda,* March 27, 1963.

[110] Prokofyev was quite right in his first charge: in *Kazakhstanskaya pravda* on

Envy and plaintiveness[111] echo through the other speeches. One orator revealed that prior to going abroad some Soviet intellectuals "feverishly leaf through encyclopedias" so as to claim "foreign sculptors, writers, poets," and not Russian ones, as their masters.[112] Bulat Okudzhava, Grigory Baklanov, and Yury Bondarev were repeatedly taken to task for "de-heroization" or what officials view as a pacifist strain in their stories of World War II. Again and again, the speakers cited a questionnaire that had been sent out by *Voprosy literatury* the year before. In their replies, the speakers complained, too many young writers declared that it was Boris Pasternak who had influenced them most (not Mikhail Sholokhov), Hemingway, Salinger, Heinrich Böll, Erich Maria Remarque, and not home-grown Russian authors. One speaker attacked Soviet writers who "have insistently tried, under cover of cybernetics and modern mathematical methods, to resurrect Russian formalism of the 1920's." [113] Another, licking his chops in revenge, revealed that, "inflamed by a thirst for power," Yevtushenko and Voznesensky at one time sought election as officers of the poetry section of the Moscow writers' organization. They were "blackballed," said the speaker, because the voters were "grown-up people and well understood that these comrades were not ripe for leadership." [114]

Yevtushenko, Voznesensky, and to a lesser extent Axyonov were, in-

March 27, for instance, I. Yusupov, First Secretary of the Communist Party of Kazakhstan, accused the young Kazakh poet Olzhas Suleimenov of "formalism" and of being a defender of Voznesensky. Yusupov also indicated that there was support in Kazakhstan for Ehrenburg and Yevtushenko. As for the "vast editions," however, Prokofyev was indulging in hyberbole: even at the height of the liberal tide in 1962, most of the young liberals were appearing in editions of 5 to 30 thousand, far below demand, while the classic Sholokhov and reactionary Kochetov came out in editions as large as 500 thousand.

By contrast, Akhmadulina's first book, *Struna,* is said to have lain at the publisher's for five years before it was published at all (20,000 copies, in 1962) and Voznesensky's second book, *Mozaika,* having been rejected in Moscow, was printed only by a provincial publishing house in Vladimir in 8,000 copies. The only "vast editions" the young poets have received in the post-Stalin era were two volumes by Yevtushenko of 100,000 copies each in 1962 and Voznesensky's *The Triangular Pear* of 50,000 copies the same year.

[111]A good example is this remark by Alexander Korneichuk, which reveals how much provincial and conservative writers envy Yevtushenko and his like their western trips and reputations: "Sometimes a person we criticize is soon afterward sent abroad to 'represent' us and our literature. One comrade told me: 'I have lived my whole life honorably, have fought, written not a few books — I should like to see the West. But evidently you have to make a mistake before they'll send you. So long as you make no mistakes, they take no interest in you.' " (*Literaturnaya gazeta,* March 30, 1963.)

[112] Speech by Sergei Mikhalkov (*Literaturnaya gazeta,* March 28, 1963).

[113] Speech by Ivan Anisimov (*ibid.,* March 30, 1963). See also *Voprosy literatury,* No. 4 (April), 1963, p. 5.

[114] Speech by V. Fyodorov (*Literaturnaya gazeta,* April 2, 1963).

deed, the writers whose names were sounded most often, and in scorn. Yevtushenko especially was subjected to violent attacks, of which the one by Boris Ryurikov, a former editor of *Literaturnaya gazeta* and sometime Central Committee apparatchik with responsibilities in literature, was notable for its virulence.[115] In addition to castigating Yevtushenko, Ryurikov, unlike any speaker so far, pinpointed the error for which Voznesensky and Axyonov now appeared to be under fire: an interview they had given the Polish weekly *Polityka* in which they touched on the twin issues of "fathers and sons" and of responsibility for the purges of the 1930's. Suggesting that it might be a matter of motives, Ryurikov concluded that these young writers fail to take into account "what a sorry role they play — *whether they will it or not*" [italics added] in the cold war.

The speeches reflected the enormous pressure which Yevtushenko and Voznesensky were under — Axyonov was out of town — to make a clean breast of their sins and offer up their hearts to the party. Nor was public pressure by any means the whole story. Privately they were told that in the future they would not be published at all unless they accepted the right of the party to direct their work.[116]

Another kind of threat was in the air as well. The atmosphere in Moscow by now was one of fear. There was a feeling that control had somehow been lost, that anything might happen, including a swing back to Stalinism. It is perfectly possible that Voznesensky and Yevtushenko were led to believe that their confessions were needed to forestall precisely such an eventuality.

It was not too great a surprise, therefore, when the slender, boyish figure of Andrei Voznesensky rose to the podium facing the assembled writers. What followed was concise, only 114 words, and one of the more remarkable statements in the annals of Russian recantations:

It has been said at this plenum that I must not forget the stern and severe words of Nikita Sergeyevich. I shall never forget them. I shall not forget not only these severe words, but also the advice which Nikita Sergeyevich gave me. He said: "Work." I do not justify myself now. I simply wish to say that for me the main thing now is to work, work, work. What my attitude is to my country, to communism, what I myself am, this work will show. (*Pravda*, March 29.)

[115] Ryurikov was the first speaker to mention Yevtushenko's autobiography. Singling out the passage in which the poet describes the crowd waiting to file past Stalin's bier ("The bloody chaos of his funeral—this was Stalin, too"), he launched into a defense of literature, even of life itself, under Stalin. (*Literaturnaya gazeta*, March 30, 1963).

[116] *L'Express*, June 20, 1963, by K.-S. Karol.

To recant at all is, of course, to concede. But here at least was no extra word, no shade of capitulatory meaning that could be sliced off and exploited. If nuances are crucial for what they save or sacrifice of talent for the future, then Voznesensky's gift may have survived relatively intact. In the art of recantation, evidently, he had gone to school to Boris Pasternak, his teacher in life, as in poetry.

Yevtushenko's recantation is a measure of the ambivalence of the man. Alternately defiant and abject, it was published only in part, and hence misrepresented. How grossly, we do not know. According to some sources, the poet defended himself and even counterattacked. Characteristically, he vigorously defended his colleague Neizvestny.[117] In those portions of the statement that appeared in the Soviet press,[118] Yevtushenko confined himself to the autobiography. He did not apologize for writing, or even for publishing it. He did not repudiate what he had actually written. On the contrary, he said that it contained much that is "serious and mature." But he added, "I see now that it has much that is superficial and immodest. My most serious mistake is that I forgot about the morals of the bourgeois press, and for this I was cruelly punished." He had been the victim, he claimed, of distortions and misleading headlines by the editors of *L'Express*. He concluded:

> I have committed an irreparable mistake. I feel heavy guilt on my shoulders. . . . I have lived through and felt a lot in these days. It is a lesson to me for my whole life. I want to assure the writers' collective that I fully understand and realize my error, and will try to correct it by all my future work.

To judge by reports of travelers, so unyielding was the mood of many Moscow young people that they greeted Yevtushenko's and even Voznesensky's statement with anger, disappointment, dismay. The idols were damaged although not, apparently, shattered. The conservative writers at the plenum were dissatisfied, too, albeit in a very different way. Having wrung even a slight admission of fault from the poets, they now were anxious to break them entirely: to destroy symbolically, if they could, the gap in moral stature as well as in talent between the older and younger generations, to make them more and more compliant tools of the party. As Yevtushenko himself might have guessed from one of

---

[117] In a part of his speech that did not appear in the Soviet press, Yevtushenko took Neizvestny's official critics to task. These critics, he said, ought to have aimed "not at destroying a talent but developing it." He was confident, he added, that "new and admirable work by Neizvestny would once again be shown in the U.S.S.R. and abroad." (*Le Monde,* March 29 and March 31, 1963, by Michel Tatu.)

[118] *Pravda,* March 29, 1963, and *Literaturnaya gazeta,* March 30, 1963.

his favorite authors, Kipling: "The bleating of the sheep irritates the tiger."

It was Yevtushenko's fateful combination of rebellion and repentance that seemed to draw him, above all others, irresistibly into the storm. His rebelliousness goaded his enemies on; his repentance led them to hope for more. The howls of the chorus became more strident, with by far the angriest attacks on the poet coming after, not before, he recanted.

Pravda remarked that Yevtushenko's statement "did not satisfy participants at the plenum. The tone of his speech shows that Yevtushenko did not recognize the roots of his mistakes, either in publishing the autobiography or in certain of his poems." Yury Zhukov asked darkly why Yevtushenko had "shifted to a position of capitulation to our ideological enemies." [119] The Ukrainian author Leonid Novichenko called him "an intriguer, a frondeur, a dealer in his own glory." And Vladimir Firsov[120] attacked Yevtushenko for "egocentrism," criticizing him for allowing his autobiography to appear in "one of the most reactionary" French newspapers. What Firsov and his listeners may not have known is that the Soviet government itself bought space in the same reactionary newspaper to publicize a speech by Khrushchev to the Supreme Soviet on December 12, 1962! [121]

Mikhail Sokolov, editor of the journal *Don,* also made a revealing speech. He launched an attack on Alexei Surkov as a signatory of a group letter to Khrushchev the previous December calling for "peaceful coexistence" of differing trends in art. In a speech to the Moscow writers' aktiv that had not been published, evidently because it was not sufficiently self-critical, Surkov disclosed, according to Sokolov, that he withdrew his signature from the letter nine hours after signing it. Sokolov demanded that Surkov now make a fulsome apology. It is "inadmissible to propagandize the coexistence of ideologies for nine seconds, much less nine hours!," he exclaimed. Sokolov demanded also

---

[119] Complaining that "even if we wanted to publish Yevtushenko's memoirs, we would have to go begging to *L'Express* and pay it money, since it is their owner," Zhukov accused Yevtushenko, in effect, of selling republication rights for his own gain. According to K.-S. Karol in *L'Express,* April 11, 1963, this is not true. All republication rights in the U.S.S.R. and other Communist countries were reserved to Yevtushenko. As an ironic consequence, *L'Express* had to refuse sale of the rights to the Czechoslovak magazine *Kulturni zhivot,* which went ahead and published the autobiography anyway.

[120] Interestingly, Firsov charged that the Writers' Union was following a biased admissions policy, filling its ranks with liberals and denying entry to such "militant Party" critics as Arkhipov, Starikov, Bushin, Chalmayev, Idashkin, and Kryachko, most of whom are associated with the journal *Oktyabr.*

[121] *L'Express,* April 4, 1963, by K.-S. Karol.

that Alexander Tvardovsky engage in self-criticism for publishing Ehrenburg, Nekrasov, and two short stories by Solzhenitsyn.[122]

Even now the high point of conservative bitterness had not yet been
reached. This came only with a meeting of the Board of the Writers'
Union of the Russian Republic on April 2–3. It was here that the tide
of reaction came closest to getting out of hand. Four speakers, including
Ivan Kharabarov, once a disciple of Pasternak, demanded that Yevtushenko be thrown out of the Union of Writers itself. One speaker, in
what was described as "an emotionally stirring speech," complained that
the conservative writers had suffered a "feeling of defenselessness"
during the period of liberal successes.[123] As Sergei Baruzdin explained:

> At first we fought, and the literary events of 1956–1957 make it clear
> that we were capable of arguing and attacking; but then — especially in
> the past two or three years — we became either tired or afraid. What did
> we fear? Being voted down by secret ballot? Having labels like "dogmatist,"
> "Stalinist," etc., pinned on us? Or did we fear that our activity might affect
> our artistic fortunes — that we might not get printed, that we might be
> ignored and be bludgeoned with criticism? [124]

Loud complaints were sounded against the Bureau for Propaganda of
Artistic Literature, that had supplied speakers to the poetry readings
at which Yevtushenko, Voznesensky, and others had built their fame
and their following. Viktor Poltoratsky sounded a chauvinistic call:
"Who has even once attempted to arrange an evening of *really Russian*
poetry [at the Polytechnical Museum or Moscow University]? Why not
arrange an evening at which poets would appear from Smolensk, Yaroslavl, Vologda, Rostov, Voronezh (our Russian land has no end of
cities!)? After all, the real poets are there. And listeners would see
where *real Russian* [italics added] Soviet poetry is going and what it
calls for!" [125]

The warhawks, meanwhile, succeeded in collecting one more scalp,
that of Vasily Axyonov, in *Pravda*, April 3. Like his friends Yevtushenko and Voznesensky, Axyonov apologized not for his work itself
— his irreverent and jargon-laden stories "Ticket to the Stars" and
"Oranges from Morocco" had been under heavy fire from the critics
— but for the interview which he and Voznesensky had given to the
Polish weekly *Polityka*.[126] In the course of the interview (which had

[122] *Literaturnaya gazeta*, April 2, 1963.
[123] *Literaturnaya Rossiya*, April 12, 1963.
[124] *Ibid.*, April 5, 1963.
[125] *Ibid.*, April 12, 1963.
[126] *Polityka* (Warsaw), March 2, 1963. The interviewer was PAP correspondent
Adam Perlovsky.

taken place in the fall of 1962)[127] Voznesensky claimed Lorca, Eluard, and Pasternak as his spiritual predecessors in poetry. He disavowed the present generation of literary "fathers" in the Soviet Union and proudly proclaimed that "heredity can sometimes skip a generation." Axyonov put the "fathers and sons" question in a frame more personal than poetic. Pointing out that his own father had been a victim of Stalin, he blamed his father's generation nonetheless: "How could they have allowed the year 1937 to happen?"

In his apology the 30-year-old Axyonov followed the example set by Yevtushenko. He claimed that he had been misquoted. He pointed out, in oblique self-defense, that the interview had, after all, been granted to a Communist, not a capitalist, newspaper. He added that it had taken place under official auspices[128] in Moscow, not abroad under the spell of bourgeois flattery. He promised, all the same, to "work" to correct his errors. Published in its entirety in *Pravda,* his statement seems to have gone farther than those of either Yevtushenko or Voznesensky.

L'Affaire Yevtushenko

No one was under heavier pressure than Yevtushenko. The day after his recantation, *Komsomolskaya pravda* issued a violent broadside comparing him to Gogol's babble-mouthed Inspector General.[129] A week later the paper ran a full page of letters from readers ringing all the changes from the threat of force to the hope of redemption in an effort to wring a new, more self-abasing recantation from him.[130] An editorial in *Yunost* (April 1963) insinuated that unless he improved on his March 29 statement he would be dropped as an editor of the journal.[131]

---

[127] Possibly the Poles delayed publication of the interview in hopes that the campaign would ease off and the damage to Axyonov and Voznesensky be minimal. As it happened, however, the interview appeared at the very moment when it was most likely to strike the eye of zealous guardians of Soviet culture.

[128] The interview was apparently arranged by the Union of Soviet Writers and may have been held on its premises. This makes the stir which it created seem all the more contrived.

[129] "Where Khlestakovshchina Leads," by G. Oganov, B. Pankin, and V. Chikin, *Komsomolskaya pravda,* March 30, 1963.

[130] *Ibid.,* April 7, 1963.

[131] Axyonov as well as Yevtushenko was apparently threatened with loss of his post as editor. In the end, neither was dropped. Other young writers evidently were told that unless they accepted the Party's right to guide their work they could no longer expect to be published. Thus, the April issue of *Yunost* contained statements by seven young writers, carefully worded so as to concede as little as possible. Sure enough, work by three of them — Vitaly Korzhikov, Yulian Semyonov, and Feliks Kuznetsov — appeared in the very next issue of the journal.

Before the middle of April the public pressure, magically, abated.[132] Only the head of the Komsomol, Sergei Pavlov, and the Komsomol newspaper continued to show a tough face in public. At a press conference called on April 19, mainly for foreign newspapermen because of criticism in the West, Pavlov cast new light on the methods being used to break the resistance of recalcitrants. Pavlov praised Voznesensky and Rozhdestvensky for understanding the Party's criticism. (Odd, since Voznesensky had not gone beyond his highly equivocal statement of March 29.)[133] Yevtushenko and Axyonov, on the other hand, still were stubbornly "maintaining silence." (Also odd, since Axyonov had now recanted twice.)[134] Of them all, Yevtushenko was the worst. Molodaya Gvardiya, the Komsomol publishing house, had a new book by Yevtushenko ready for the printer. But the poet, difficult as ever, was claiming that he was "too busy" to discuss it. Pavlov's threat was transparent. Recant again and more satisfactorily this time, he was telling Yevtushenko, or your new book will not be allowed to appear. Pavlov added that the poet's "boastful attitude has destroyed or rather, may destroy, him if he does not stop his shameful behavior." [135] Coming at a moment when Moscow was rife with rumors that the poet had taken his own life in despair, the remark had a particularly brutal ring.[136]

For a time the drive against Yevtushenko was the center and crux of the entire campaign. Moscow critics who had been congratulating themselves on what they called the "flowering of young Soviet literature" whirled on cue and set about destroying the very men and women responsible for it. Soviet officials who basked in the reflected glory of Yevtushenko's verses one week stiffened at the mere mention of his name the next. How did this sudden shift occur?

The unfolding of the drive against a lone poet is so enormously re-

[133] The April issue of Yunost, in which the editors called the "loose and presumptuous talk" of their fellow editor, Yevtushenko, "an insult to the Soviet people," was passed by the censor on April 11, 1963.

[133] Odd, too, since Rozhdestvensky had just published two poems which may have been designed to hearten Yevtushenko: "Work, Comrade River" (Pravda, March 26, 1963) and "Lads with Turned up Collars" [Yunost, No. 3 (March), 1963].

[134] Axyonov's second statement, which he may have felt was the price of keeping his editorial post, was in Yunost, No. 4 (April), 1963. It went further than his earlier statement (Pravda, April 3, 1963) in accepting Party criticism as "correct."

[135] Accounts of this press conference appeared in The Times (London), The New York Times, April 20, 1963; and Le Monde, April 21–22, 1963. According to the first source, Khrushchev had said to the poet: "Be modest. Fame is dangerous. It is a sweet poison you are drinking."

[136] The rumors may have been fed by two poems by Yevtushenko himself, "Tenderness" and "In the Chase after Cheap Popularity," Moskva, No. 1 (Jan.), 1963, in which he dwelled on the idea of dying. The poems were signed for the press on Dec. 21, 1962, before the drive had gone into high gear.

vealing as to the dynamic of the assault on the liberal intellectuals as a whole that it is worth making a digression to examine it in detail. Let us look at the circumstances in which Yevtushenko came to publish his famous *Precocious Autobiography* abroad.[137]

On none of his foreign travels had Yevtushenko appeared more, to the outside eye, to be on an official mission than on the visit to West Germany and France that began in mid-January and ended in early March. In Germany he proposed the creation of a quasi-official society to promote cultural contacts. He lamented the fact that Bonn had no diplomatic ties with the Communist countries of Eastern Europe. Soon the German press began to speculate that he was not so much an "angry young man" as a Soviet diplomat without portfolio. There was similar speculation in France, where the Soviet Ambassador was seen warmly applauding at a poetry reading in the vast Palais de Chaillot.

Yevtushenko arrived in Paris from Germany in mid-February with his autobiography sketched out and partly written. He showed it to K.-S. Karol, a correspondent of the French weekly, *L'Express*. Both agreed that the partial manuscript needed a good deal more work before it would be of suitable quality for publication. Throughout his visit to France, therefore, Yevtushenko was snatching what moments he could away from public appearances to work on his autobiography. The finished product was a work of improbable haste.

As for the editors of *L'Express* they had, at first, reservations. To them as to so many others, Yevtushenko's visit to West Germany and France had the earmarks of an official mission. They simply could not believe that so "official" a poet as Yevtushenko would dare offer a manuscript for publication in the West without the sanction of higher-ups in Moscow. They were wary lest, by printing the autobiography, they would merely be giving currency to propaganda of the Soviet Communist Party. Nevertheless, after some self-scrutiny, they decided to publish. The first installment appeared on February 21, a little over a week after Yevtushenko's arrival in France. The last installment appeared just one month later, on March 21.

Since publication of the autobiography had not been authorized in Moscow, the decision to go ahead entailed enormous risk. Clearly, Yevtushenko knew it. After the Pasternak case in 1958, the Central Committee had issued a new ruling forbidding Soviet writers to publish abroad material, especially books, not already cleared for publication inside the Soviet Union. Yevtushenko had shown that he was keenly aware of this ruling. At poetry readings in Moscow, for example, he

---

[137] Published in English by E. P. Dutton & Co., New York, 1963.

often recited verses that had not yet been printed. After the readings, he had repeatedly refused copies of the poems to any foreigners who happened to be present, presumably on the basis of the "Pasternak ruling."

Nor did Yevtushenko's decision represent merely a break with a rule of the Communist Party. It was a break with his own past custom as well. In Moscow, his unwillingness even to disclose the most everyday facts of his life had given rise to a series of legends about him. Not only had he failed to discourage the legends. By his air of mystery, he gave every sign of encouraging them. How ironic, then, that the major crisis of his career should have been precipitated by, of all things, an autobiography, and the most revealing document to have issued from his pen in years!

Yet Yevtushenko had compelling reasons for wanting to publish and some grounds for thinking he could do so without getting into serious trouble with officials back home. He had published separate articles in the West before without being taken to task.[138] He now felt he had something to say to Western audiences that could not be said in scattered interviews and articles alone.[139] Having been a trailblazer for Soviet writers throughout much of the post-Stalin era, he wanted to expand the limited opportunity he had had to publish abroad into a right others could enjoy as well: to create a precedent so that other Soviet writers, too, might be able to publish on occasion in the West. *L'Express* seemed like a good choice, moreover, because it had been in *L'Express* that officials of the Soviet Embassy in Paris had bought space, less than two months before, for a speech by Nikita Khrushchev. Additionally, Yevtushenko had already contracted with a New York publisher to write an autobiographical introduction of unspecified length for a forthcoming volume of verse. The contract had been signed by Mezhdunarodnaya Kniga, the firm which handles rights of Soviet authors abroad, and thus had official approval. In his contract with *L'Express,* Yevtushenko stipulated that all rights in Communist countries be reserved to himself and in English-speaking countries, to his New York publisher. He thereby identified the articles in *L'Express* as the autobiographical introduction that had been officially sanctioned in Moscow.

[138] He had, for example, written a special article for *The Observer* during a visit to London in April 1962; for the Cuban newspaper *Revolucion* during a visit to Havana in Nov.–Dec. 1962; for *Die Zeit,* Feb. 15, 1963; for an American leftist review; and he had had a short story published in *Die Zeit* and in *Le Figaro Litteraire* (Paris) almost simultaneously with its publication in Moscow.

[139] Françoise Giroud and K.-S. Karol in *L'Express,* April 4, 1963. For a particularly interesting interpretation of Yevtushenko's behavior, see David Rousset in *Le Figaro Litteraire,* April 6, 1963.

Finally, up to the meeting of March 7–8, Yevtushenko underestimated the drive that had been mounted in Moscow. So did his colleagues back home. He had, after all, left home in early January, having been patted on the back by Ilyichev for his "civic maturity." Wolfgang Leonhard, who interviewed him in *Die Zeit,* and friends who talked with him in Paris felt that he was overly optimistic about the attack on writers and artists. If there were trouble over the autobiography he counted on support from Tvardovsky and from Stepan Shchipachov. What he did not foresee was that Tvardovsky would remain silent for a time and that Shchipachov was soon to be toppled from his post as head of the Moscow writers' organization.

True, as Yevtushenko's visit to France wore on, he seems to have developed inklings of doom. He was under close surveillance from Soviet security agents in Paris, and he made no secret of his suspicions. He was aware, moreover, that S. Zykov, correspondent of *Izvestia* who was with him throughout much of the trip, was sending home frequent dispatches about his public triumphs in France. Not one of the stories was published. Moscow seemed to be observing a news blackout about his doings abroad. The poet confided his forebodings to others. His wife, Galina, was openly fearful that publication of the autobiography had been a mistake and that they would not be allowed to leave Russia again. At a press conference in Paris even before the autobiography began to appear, Yevtushenko made a public statement of his apprehensions. Prophetically (albeit in a discussion of formal experiment in poetry), he said of himself and Voznesensky: "Who knows if we may not be, after all, a generation of the sacrificed? We would be, then, like the cavaliers of Napoleon who hurled themselves into the river to make a bridge for others to cross." [140]

What, however, of the motives of Soviet officialdom? From the moment he set foot in Paris, Yevtushenko had cooperation to the point of idolatry from officials of the Soviet Embassy and the French Communist Party. Once the autobiography began to appear, their attitude did not change. No one reproved him. On the contrary, after two installments were out and before Yevtushenko's return to Moscow, Embassy officials and high-ranking French Communists were heard to congratulate him on his "good work for the U.S.S.R." and to joke that Yevtushenko had been paid for his autobiography, while Khrushchev had had to pay to insert his December 12 speech in *L'Express!* [141]

---

[140] *Le Monde,* Feb. 14, 1963. At the same press conference Yevtushenko denied that his decision to alter "Babi Yar" was taken under pressure from the Party leaders: "No one asked me to change 'Babi Yar.'"

[141] *L'Express,* April 4, 1963, by K.-S. Karol.

Yet little more than two weeks later when events had taken a dramatic turn in Moscow and Yevtushenko was rapidly becoming target No. 1, the original copy of his manuscript, sent back to him at 5 p.m. on March 19 by *L'Express* so that he could see the cuts and changes, was lifted in the mails, evidently by Soviet security police.[142] Thus when Yevtushenko rose to defend himself at the writers' plenum a few days later, it was with an incomplete text, translated from Russian to French and back to Russian, knowing that the original was in the hands of the security police!

Was the poet, then, the victim of a giant provocation? Had Soviet officialdom lured him onto the end of a long limb, awaiting only the moment to lop it off? Some Soviet officials, no doubt, wished to do precisely that. Yet the chain of events that led to his becoming the scapegoat for his entire generation—inevitable as such an outcome may have been—seems to have been somewhat more haphazard.

Let us first recall the meeting of March 7–8, at which Ehrenburg and Nekrasov were the main targets. From neither were recantations forthcoming. Nor, short of force apparently, would they be. To sustain the attack without hope of recantation would be not only a defeat for the Party, it could be a dangerous one as well, since the issue raised by Ehrenburg—that of responsibility during the 1930's—could be turned at any moment against several of the Party leaders. A number of older Presidium members and other high-ranking officials, then, must have been only too glad to drop the political hotcake the Ehrenburg case had become. Thus, the attacks on Ehrenburg ceased almost immediately after Khrushchev's March 8 speech appeared in *Pravda*.

Khrushchev's and Ilyichev's speeches, on the other hand, had unleashed the literary right-wingers. And they—the Sobolevs and Kochetovs and Sokolovs—now were howling for blood. To judge by the tone of Khrushchev's speech he was unable or unwilling to put them back on the leash immediately. Another victim, then, had to be found.

To conservatives in literature, the whole group of young liberal writers must have seemed desirable victims because their burgeoning quality was a threat to all mediocrity. To watchdogs in the Party, moreover, the young liberals must also have been logical targets since, with the poetry readings as a forum and their "back to Lenin" idealism as a rallying cry, they had already acquired a sizable following among young people all over the country. Finally, their very success had focused attention on the volatile issue of "fathers and sons."

---

[142] *L'Express*, April 4, 1963, by Françoise Giroud.

Spelled out in political terms, this issue reads: "Let us de-Stalinize the Communist Party. Let us get rid of all those who were in responsible positions during the 1930's and let others who are innocent take their places."

Surely, if the young were to be offered up as victims, then the sacrifice of Yevtushenko could serve as the symbolic sacrifice of all. His jaunty, matinee-idol manner, his privileges, his huge editions, by now had made him the target of innumerable private jealousies. Above all, his was the flaming neo-Leninist spirit, his the incandescent presence at poetry readings. His, then, was the blood the conservatives were after.

Party leaders right up to Khrushchev, however, must have had reservations. Abroad, Yevtushenko was an ambassador extraordinary if not plenipotentiary. His downfall would bring jeers from the imperialists. "What about the new and liberal Russia of Khrushchev?" they would ask. Even more important, Yevtushenko, as he freely admits in his autobiography, had taken on the burden of compromise for his entire generation. Partly by virtue of his compromises, of the split between poet and politician in his personality, the Party had been able to keep the entire youth movement under control. Some may have felt that, grown too big for his breeches, it was time for Yevtushenko to go. Others must have asked: Will the next idol be controlled so easily?

If indeed there were counselors of restraint, timing was not on their side. By mid-March, the next to last installment of the autobiography must have become available in Moscow. In this chapter the poet shows the continuing strength of Stalinist elements within the Party, the struggle the young liberals waged "to fight the mistakes of their fathers," and the persecution Yevtushenko himself suffered as a result. Nothing could have been better calculated to enrage Stalin's heirs on the rampage in Moscow. The pressure to yield up the young poet became irresistible. On March 15 Stepan Shchipachov was ousted as chairman of the Moscow writers' organization partly on grounds that he had championed Yevtushenko's first journeys abroad. Yet Shchipachov may have been merely a "fall guy," taking the rap for others, perhaps even for Khrushchev, who had stood encouragingly by, reaping a windfall of propaganda as the flamboyant Yevtushenko made headlines all over the world.

And so the poet was sacrificed. On March 19 Zhukov announced that he was "going over" Yevtushenko's "tracks" abroad (and possibly those of Voznesensky, Paustovsky, and Nekrasov as well). A day or so later, Yevtushenko's manuscript vanished in the mails. On March 22 and 24 *Izvestia* and *Pravda* printed satirical lampoons against the poet. Any doubts as to high-level strategy were ended by the speech in late March by Alexander Korneichuk, a friend of Khrushchev's in Kiev during his long tenure as Party Secretary of the Ukraine. Khrushchev's tactic, it appeared, was to identify himself with the attack so as to control it and keep it from being turned against him.

Volte Face?

Indeed, in late March and early April the storm showed signs of developing a momentum of its own. Suddenly, nearly as suddenly as it began, the clamor against Yevtushenko and the other young writers subsided. We have only two clues as to the answer: one having to do with protests by Communist Parties abroad; the other with stresses inside the Soviet leadership itself.

In late March or early April, at the height of the campaign against the young writers, all foreign Communist newspapermen stationed in Moscow had been summoned to a meeting. There, the editor of a leading Soviet literary journal showed them a "dossier of the accused." In language reminiscent of the purge era, the "dossier" spoke of an "opportunist faction," from Yury Kazakov ("this descendant of Ivan Bunin") to Yevtushenko, in the tradition of "that dubious political personality, Boris Pasternak." The dossier called Yevtushenko's autobiography (shades of *Dr. Zhivago!*) a "blasphemy on the October Revolution." [143]

This effort to prepare foreign Communist opinion for further draconian action seems to have fallen flat. An elderly Swedish Communist said it sounded like Zhdanovism to him. A Cuban rose to defend Yevtushenko, a national hero in his country.[144] The correspondent of the Italian Communist newspaper, *L'Unita,* Augusto Pancaldi, wrote a critical dispatch. The French were silent. They must, however, have taken the description of Yevtushenko's autobiography as a "blasphemy" as an aspersion on the dialectical competence of Maurice Thorez, Louis Aragon, and other luminaries of the French Communist Party. Not only had they failed to detect the "blasphemy." After sections had ap-

---

[143] *L'Express,* April 11, 1963, by K.-S. Karol.
[144] While Fidel Castro was in Moscow in early May he shook hands publicly with Yevtushenko. Privately he told Khrushchev that, anxious as he and other Cuban leaders were to preserve the purity of Communist ideology, they had no desire to impose aesthetic guidance on creative artists.

peared in print, with the author still in Paris, they had held a reception in his honor! So, too, the Czechoslovaks, who had rushed it into print. The Poles evidently were offended because the *Polityka* interview of March 2 had been used to bully Voznesensky and Axyonov. Finally on the eve of the elections to be held in his country on April 30, Palmiro Togliatti, head of the Italian Communist Party, made a statement disavowing the drive. Nobody, he said, no matter how capable and shrewd he may be, should attempt "to tell an artist how to write a poem, how to create music, or how to paint." [145]

All this at a time when the Soviet comrades, engaged in a quarrel with China, were wooing opinion in the European Communist Parties! By early April, as we have seen, the wave of reaction inside the Soviet Party had gone very far indeed. The adverse response of foreign Communist Parties may well have given a strong argument to moderates among the Soviet comrades who wanted it to go no further.

Still another set of circumstances seems to have played a role. With Khrushchev on vacation in Gagra from about March 20 to April 20, his ceremonial duties were taken over by other senior members of the Party Presidium—Kozlov, Mikoyan, Suslov, Kosygin, and Brezhnev. By the end of March, rumors of high-level dissension began reaching the West via Giuseppe Boffa, correspondent of the Italian Communist newspaper *L'Unita* who was then in Moscow. The disagreement was said to center on Khrushchev's designated successor, Frol Kozlov. Had Khrushchev felt that he was facing a palpable challenge, perhaps he would not have spent nearly five weeks basking in the South. Yet there is, on the other hand, evidence of disagreement among the stay-at-homes, and evidence that it involved Kozlov.

First of all, there were the May Day slogans. On April 8 *Pravda* published the annual May Day greetings of the Communist Party. The people of Yugoslavia were greeted in a manner midway in cordiality between that vouchsafed to Communist peoples and that to countries uncommitted between East and West. Someone very high indeed had taken advantage of Khrushchev's absence, it appeared, to sneak into the slogans a revision of Party policy toward Tito. For on April 11 *Pravda* took the unprecedented step of publishing a correction. The greeting to Yugoslavia now followed the same form as that of other

[145] *Newsweek* (New York), April 29, 1963; *New Statesman* (London), May 24, 1963, interview of K.-S. Karol with Togliatti. In an interview with Italo Pietra, editor of the Italian newspaper *Il Giorno*, Khrushchev tried to allay the apprehensions of left-wing intellectuals in the West. (See *The New York Times*, April 22, 1963, p. 12, for partial text.)

Communist countries in Eastern Europe! On the day the correction appeared, Kozlov fell ill, victim of a second heart attack.[146]

As for the drive in the arts, Kozlov had functional grounds—perhaps more than anyone else—for feeling that Khrushchev had gone too far in sanctioning *One Day in the Life of Ivan Denisovich* and "Stalin's Heirs." As Secretary in charge of the day-to-day running of the Communist Party, it was Kozlov's job to maintain the morale of the Party cadres. His position jeopardized in the face of new de-Stalinization, to whom would the anxious Party functionary turn but to Kozlov? [147]

Lastly, there is the matter of Yevtushenko's poem. "Stalin's Heirs" contains these lines:

Not for nothing, it is clear,
Do Stalin's heirs
Today have their share
Of heart attacks.

It is unlikely that the poet had anyone in the Kremlin in mind. If he was thinking of someone in particular, perhaps it was some elderly crustacean in the literary bureaucracy. Those who decided to publish the poem, however, may have had something more pointed in view. For Kozlov had had a heart attack in 1960, and Molotov in 1962.[148] Asked point-blank about the poem by Wolfgang Leonhard in *Die Zeit* on February 8, 1963, Yevtushenko is reported to have smiled and replied: "I know that a crafty expert in *The New York Times* saw this as an allusion to a certain Soviet leader [here Leonhard interpolated: Kozlov] but I should like my poem to be viewed in a somewhat wider sense." If Kozlov saw the interview—and Kremlin leaders, as a rule, see foreign press clippings about them—he may well have been irritated that Yevtushenko's denial was not a good deal blunter. Be that as it

[146] *Le Monde*, May 26, 1963, gave April 11 as the date Kozlov fell ill. His last recorded public appearance was at a Congress of Artists reception on April 10. He failed to appear at a second reception for the same group on April 13.

[147] Careful reading of the economics vs. politics debate (see footnote 8) can support the idea that Kozlov took the side of "politics," a position associated with a hard line in cultural affairs. According, moreover, to "A Letter from a Soviet Writer" in the Forum Service of the British magazine *Survey*, June 29, 1963, Kozlov and Polikarpov, after the expulsion of Yakov Elsberg from the Writers' Union in early 1962, ordered that the "cases" of Lesyuchevsky and Yermilov, whose complicity in the death of writers in the '30's had already been proved, be immediately terminated.

[148] At the time the poem was written, Kozlov was the highest ranking leader known to have suffered a heart attack. As far as Yevtushenko's subjective intentions are concerned, Molotov appears to be out because the poet stated in *Die Zeit*, Feb. 8, 1963, that he wrote the poem shortly after Stalin's body was removed from the Mausoleum in late October 1961, and that subsequent changes were minimal.

may, the last of a virulent series of attacks on the poet appeared on April 7.[149] Four days later, Kozlov was stricken.[150]

Possibly the easing of the drive that was noticeable by May reflected not only the influence of Communist Parties abroad but also the sudden disappearance of Kozlov from active political life. To contend that Khrushchev did not make the offensive his own following his visit to the Manezh; that it was forced upon him by others; and that he was not genuinely alarmed by unintended repercussions which his policy of de-Stalinization had had in the fields of literature and art is to misconstrue his personal inclinations and the nature of his hegemony alike. Equally, to contend that the removal of any given leader, such as Kozlov, removes opposition to further de-Stalinization of the Party ranks, is to underestimate the depth and extent of Stalinism in Soviet life. One such leader may be cut down, only to be replaced by others.

Perhaps the likeliest explanation of the drive then, is that there was real disagreement in the higher echelons of the Party in the fall and winter of 1962–1963, centering above all on investment priorities and on how open and irrevocable to allow the split with Communist China to become. The controversy which blew up over the intellectuals may have been a function at first of these more portentous disputes. For a Khrushchev embarrassed by the the Cuban fiasco and convinced, as he no doubt was, that writers and artists needed to be taught a thing or two, it must have seemed cheap at the outset to offer up intellectuals to the storm. Aware as the offensive gathered fury, however, that it could eventually be turned even against himself, he could not allow it to go too far. This may have been particularly true of the attacks against Ehrenburg and Yevtushenko, raising as they did the issues of complicity during the 1930's and the wisdom of de-Stalinization. In a sense, Ehrenburg and Yevtushenko served as screens for criticism that as may have had as its ultimate target the First Secretary of the Soviet Communist Party.

On April 20 Khrushchev was back at his desk in the Kremlin. A

[149] Sporadic attacks of the violent type did, however, occur later. See an open letter by two West German workers to Yevtushenko reprinted in *Izvestia*, May 7, 1963; letters in *Komsomolskaya pravda*, May 23, 1963; and Sergei Mikhalkov's poem in *Pravda*, June 3, 1963, "The Titmouse Abroad." While the literary bureaucrats were now restrained, Sergei Pavlov, head of the Komsomol, kept up the attack. Possibly his extravagant praise of Khrushchev at the June plenum of the Central Committee was an attempt to make amends for this excessive zeal. Or perhaps it was simply Pavlov's style.

[150] On the same day, April 11, the *Yunost* editorial hinting that Yevtushenko might be dropped from the editorial board was passed by the censor. In the outcome the poet was retained.

speech which he gave to industrial workers four days later may mark
the turning point not only of the drive against writers and artists, but
of his own political fortunes in the post-Cuba period as well.[151] Behind
Khrushchev's blunt phrases it was apparent that he was rejecting the
demands of reactionaries that the Party use force against progressive
intellectuals. Strongly he asserted the control of the Party over both its
left and its right. And he gave his own explanation of the Party drive
in the arts:

> "Some creative intellectuals have drawn incorrect conclusions from the
> Party's work to overcome harmful consequences of the Stalin cult. They
> failed to grasp that struggle against the cult does not signify a weakening
> of leadership, a denial of authorities. *Some have even begun to maintain
> that the time has come when everyone can determine his own line of
> conduct and the direction of his work* [my italics — P. J.], not reckoning
> with the interests of society and the state. This is nothing but an anarchist
> concept, hostile to Marxism-Leninism."

Thus, in a nutshell, Khrushchev's desire to turn his intellectuals off
and on at will, to let writers, for example, serve de-Stalinization when
and as he chose but never permit them to interpret it according to
some recalcitrant whim of their own. To follow one's own conscience in
artistic matters, he made clear, was not ingratitude only. It was to "slip
away from Marxist-Leninist positions over to those of the bourgeoisie." [152]

A few days after Khrushchev's speech, Alexander Tvardovsky gave
a remarkable interview to Henry Shapiro, chief Moscow correspondent
of the UPI.[153] In the interview the editor of *Novy mir* congratulated the
Central Committee and Khrushchev personally for their "broadminded-
ness" in approving publication of *One Day in the Life of Ivan Denisovich*; chided Yevtushenko and Voznesensky very gently indeed (calling
them "poets who are young not so much in age as in skill" and adding
that "a poet should have a fate, not a career");[154] and stood by all his

[151] *Pravda*, April 26, 1963.

[152] In the same speech Khrushchev remarked: "I am already 69 years old. Everyone understands that I cannot occupy forever the post I now hold in the Party and
state." A month earlier, in a speech to voters of the Kalinin election district reported over Moscow Radio on March 27, 1963, he had also hinted at the possibility of his retirement. Apparently Khrushchev briefly considered relinquishing
the post of Premier and retaining his position as First Secretary of the Communist
Party, but rather quickly gave up the idea.

[153] *Pravda*, May 12, 1963.

[154] Admonitions that were extremely mild after the recent strident attacks. Tvardovsky's criticisms were consistent, too, with his known views (as expressed, say, in
his Pushkin anniversary speech, *Pravda*, Feb. 11, 1962) of their work. Thus Tvardovsky, a conservative poet who is not given to formal experiment, has never pub-

own authors who had been under fire.[155] (His defense of one of them, Valentin Ovechkin, has a special quality, for Ovechkin, an editor of *Novy mir,* is said to have criticized Khrushchev at a public meeting in the fall of 1962. Under heavy pressure, he later attempted suicide and had to be hospitalized.) As for the criticisms of Ehrenburg, Tvardovsky did not admit that they were correct but merely that he took them "seriously, all the more so since the party leaders have described him as a remarkable writer, a talented publicist, and an eminent public figure." [156]

Because of Tvardovsky's oblique support of writers who had been under fire and his restraint on the still apoplectic subject of Yevtushenko and Voznesensky, the interview can be taken as a subtle sign that the peak of the campaign had passed. So can the circumstances in which it appeared in Moscow. The interview originally was requested in late March or early April. From the outset, Tvardovsky agreed only to answer written questions submitted in advance. Once the questions were in his possession, moreover, he again and again put the interviewer off, evidently waiting the proper moment or a signal from higher up. At last, about the end of April, he answered from among the written questions in *written* form, stipulating that UPI print his remarks without deletions or changes. He requested in addition that UPI delay publication abroad until he could arrange for the interview to appear inside the Soviet Union as well. Thus, on May 12, the interview appeared simultaneously in *Pravda* and in newspapers in the West. It was in these unusual circumstances that Tvardovsky chose to break his winter-long silence in the face of calumny and rumor. Publication of his remarks in *Pravda* suggests, furthermore, that persons high in the Party indeed were anxious to send out word inside the U.S.S.R. that the campaign was now to ease off a little.

lished Voznesensky in *Novy mir* and published Yevtushenko only once (*Novy mir,* No. 7, 1962).

[155] He was unable, however, explicitly to defend Viktor Nekrasov. Since Nekrasov's situation was now exceedingly precarious, the best Tvardovsky could do was remain silent. Even this was an improvement over the editorial statement in the *Novy mir* issue for April (see footnote 154). It may reflect an easing of the drive between the date the *Novy mir* editorial was written — the April issue was held in censorship from February 8 to May 3 — and the UPI interview given. Or it may reflect the old and close personal friendship between Tvardovsky and Nekrasov.

[156] In a statement in the April issue, the editorial board of *Novy mir* went further than Tvardovsky's UPI statement, conceding that Khrushchev's and Ilyichev's criticisms of Ehrenburg were "just, and we bear our share of responsibility" and that Khrushchev's remarks about Nekrasov were "correct." This concession was probably the price of continuing to publish Nekrasov: the editors emphasized that Nekrasov and three other writers who were under fire — Yashin, Tendryakov, and Axyonov — were at work on new manuscripts for *Novy mir.*

Uncertainty — and Resistance

A week later, on May 19, an editorial in *Pravda* gave new evidence that extreme militancy had yielded slightly to sober second thoughts. In a statement reminiscent of Khrushchev's speech to Soviet writers of May 1959, *Pravda* proclaimed that the Party saw "no need to watch over every step" by the intellectuals, "to explain in detail how to write a book, stage a play, make a film, compose music. Setting forth the main aim of creative work, the Party urges the masters of literature and art to creative boldness and independence." Although by no means an about-face, the statement represented a real shift in position compared with the angry speeches of March 8.

Meanwhile, an event was to occur that had been postponed three times already and could not be put off much longer. Scheduled originally for December, the greatly heralded conference of young writers had been designed to celebrate the revival of Soviet literature and, above all, the appearance of young writers of talent. As winter wore on, however, nearly all those due to be honored fell victim, instead, of the Party offensive. How could the meeting be held without its intended heroes, all, now, in "disgrace" with the Party, or hovering on the brink: Voznesensky, Yevtushenko, Akhmadulina, Axyonov, Gladilin, Kazakov? There was another irony as well. Since, in its efforts to deny any conflict between the older and younger generations, the Party had been led virtually to deny the existence of differences between them, would it not be a contradiction in terms to hold a meeting of *young* writers at all?

Whatever the difficulties, the meeting convened at last in early May, its proceedings darkened at the outset by an announcement that two of those originally scheduled to appear had been sent instead to the hinterlands to get "closer to life": Axyonov to a construction project in Siberia and Voznesensky to spend part of the time at factory enterprises in Vladimir.[157]

In spite of this shadow, the meeting of young writers went forward as planned. With the bright stars of the literary left absent, the participants proved to be 170 young and untried writers from all over the country, there to redress by their sturdy provincial values what was now called the "shameful behavior" and "ideological breakdowns" of their more luminous elder brothers. Remarkably mild references to Voznesensky, Yevtushenko, Rozhdestvensky, and Sosnora were made by Nikolai Rylenkov, an older poet from Smolensk.[158] By far the sharpest speech

[157] By Georgy Markov, *Izvestia*, May 7, 1963.
[158] *Literaturnaya gazeta*, May 9, 1963.

was delivered, as usual, by the Komsomol head, Sergei Pavlov, who charged that the young poets had "in fact distorted Marxism" while parading as "critics of dogmatic distortions of Marxism."[159] Because of its "dullness," Pavlov revealed, the circulation of *Molodaya gvardiya*, the Komsomol literary journal, had dropped to only 60,000 (compared with *Yunost's* 600,000). To brace up circulation, he admitted, "we resorted to a whole series of measures," such as publication of Tendryakov's and Ikramov's "profoundly discreditable" play "White Flag," for which the editor in chief had now been fired.[160]

By this time the campaign against the intellectuals had received so much attention that it was a subject of concern all over the country. In March and April alone, 10,000 provincial leaders attended 16 regional meetings to discuss the forthcoming Central Committee session which, originally scheduled for May 28, was to be devoted exclusively to ideological matters. The meetings, said the Italian Communist correspondent in Moscow, reflected "reservations and perplexity" over the Party drive in the arts.[161]

In response to an article attacking Yevtushenko, for instance, the newspaper *Komsomolskaya pravda* received 1200 letters, of which some were expressions of support for the poet.[162] Even the conservative Leonid Sobolev had to concede widespread concern over the fate of the intellectuals. "What is striking," he wrote, "is the interest of the most varied layers of Soviet society in events which, it would seem, ought to affect only a narrow circle of people."[163]

Among intellectuals and Party officials in Moscow, two proposals were subjects of heated discussion. One was the suggestion, voiced from the beginning of the campaign, that the present unions of writers, artists, composers, and film workers be abolished and amalgamated into a single union of creative artists. In this way, the conservatives hoped in future to avert liberal breakthroughs such as had occurred in the Moscow writers' organization in April 1962 and in the admissions policies of both writers' and artists' unions. Another serious proposal was designed to tighten control over publishing. Under this proposal, the more liberal cultural newspapers would be weeded out with *Pravda* and *Izvestia* expanded to include more material on the arts. A giant "glavpechat" would be set up to control publishing operations all over

[159] *Komsomolskaya pravda*, May 11, 1963.
[160] For editorial apology, see *Molodaya gvardiya*, No. 3 (March), 1963, pp. 3–10.
[161] *Rinascita*, June 1, 1963, by Giuseppe Boffa.
[162] *Komsomolskaya pravda*, May 23, 1963. In his April 19 press conference, Sergei Pavlov claimed that only 15 of 1000 letters received to date had defended Yevtushenko.
[163] *Literaturnaya gazeta*, May 1, 1963.

the country, possibly with Khrushchev's son in law, Adzhubei, in charge.

With such sweeping proposals in the air, contradictory steps were taken from day to day which indicated that basic policy decisions had not been made. In the wake of the Wynne-Penkovsky spy trial in May, for example, *Pravda* launched a new "vigilance" campaign with an unusually ominous editorial warning Soviet citizens against all contacts with Westerners.[164] Moscow journalists were given similar warnings by Adzhubei.[165] Yet at precisely this period, just as official anti-Western feeling seems to have been at its height, a high-level decision evidently was taken to cease jamming British and American radio broadcasts in Russia! Jamming of Voice of America broadcasts stopped on June 19.

As for the writers, the deeds of the Party were so far at surprising variance with its words. Anxious rumors to the contrary, since the opening of the drive in December, not a single editor had been dropped at any of the major journals in which liberal writers were regularly appearing: *Novy mir, Yunost, Znamya,* or *Moskva.*[166] Surely this was a token of hesitation by the Party as well as extraordinary editorial solidarity.

Liberal authors, moreover, kept turning up on the pages of newspapers and journals.[167] A major publishing house announced plans to go ahead as planned with the largest edition ever, 100,000 copies, of short stories by Yury Kazakov.[168] As for Vladimir Tendryakov, whose work had occasioned an official reprimand by the Komsomol,[169] he had part of a new story in *Literaturnaya gazeta* on May Day, together with an announcement that the rest would soon be appearing in *Nauka i Zhizn.*[170]

[164] *Pravda,* May 26, 1963.

[165] In a revealing article in *Sovetskaya pechat,* No. 5 (May), 1963, Adzhubei wrote: "This or that bourgeois journalist may slap us on the back in friendly fashion in some press bar: All of us journalists are, you see, one big family. But in his newspaper he does not slap us on the back in friendly fashion, he tries to knife us in the back . . . In our world, divided into two antagonistic social systems, there is no single journalism, just as there is no single art. Let no one deceive himself on this score!" For Adzhubei's remarks at a Press Day reception in Moscow on May 4, see *The Economist* (London), June 1, 1963.

[166] Two liberals, Oleg Mikhailov and Alexander Borshchagovsky, were dropped, however, as editors of *Literaturnaya Rossiya* as of April 26, 1963. (Borshchagovsky was also a victim of Zhdanov's purge of theater critics in 1946.) With their departure the weekly fell almost entirely into conservative hands although it had been originally designed, with the abolition of *Literatura i Zhizn,* to be of a liberal orientation.

[167] Among them Slutsky, Yashin, Nagibin, Vinokurov, Goryshin, Samoilov, Borshchagovsky, and Shchipachov.

[168] At the end of 1963, a new edition of Kazakov's *The Blue and the Green* appeared in 100,000 copies.

[169] *Komsomolskaya pravda,* March 2, 1963.

[170] It appeared in *Nauka i Zhizn,* Nos. 9–12 (Sept.–Dec.), 1963. The editor of

On the other hand, the most controversial of the liberal writers had been silenced: Nekrasov, Okudzhava, Voznesensky, Axyonov, and Yevtushenko. Axyonov was briefly in the Soviet Far East. Voznesensky did penance first in Vladimir, where he had lived as a child, then in Riga. Yevtushenko was roaming the country unhappily from Archangel to the Crimea.[171] Trips abroad by the young liberals now were banned.[172] So, too, were the poetry readings.[173]

On the eve of the Central Committee session, *Pravda* began publishing "One Hundred Answers" to a questionnaire it had sent to writers inquiring about their current work.[174] The aim of the exercise, no doubt, was to give the impression that Soviet literature was in a healthy state. It is not known how many writers who received the questionnaire failed to reply, or indeed how much pressure they were under to answer. Certain omissions, nonetheless, are striking. Missing were the names of Surkov, Tvardovsky, and, for that matter, Kochetov. Sholokhov — who, like the Soviet Union's other famed novelist, Leonid Leonov, had refused to publish a word in favor of the Party campaign — was represented by a single, surly sentence. The only liberal to reply was Axyonov. As the Central Committee session drew close, the liberal "conspiracy of silence" continued remarkably firm.

In a sense, the most extraordinary case had been that of Viktor Nekrasov. Surely the main offense of this vastly respected writer must have been his outspoken striving to report only what he saw, and to see nothing through the eyes of prejudice. It is this, above all, which makes the reading of his travel notes such an exhilarating experience.

the journal, V. N. Bolkhovitinov, is one of six editors who were dropped from *Literaturnaya gazeta* on Jan. 22, 1963. The deputy editor is Rada N. Adzhubei, daughter of Khrushchev and wife of Adzhubei.

[171] For a description of Yevtushenko's state of mind during a trip he made to Archangel with Yury Kazakov, see Kazakov's "White Nights: Northern Diary, 1963" in *Literaturnaya Rossiya*, Aug. 2, 1963.

[172] An invitation to Nagibin and Akhmadulina to England was declined because of "illness." Scheduled trips to Italy and the U.S. in April–May by Yevtushenko were cancelled for the same reason. An invitation to Kazakov, Kirsanov, and Voznesensky to visit the U.S. in May was withdrawn at the last minute by the American side. Soviet writers who did go abroad included the conservatives Baruzdin and Kochetov (to India in April), and Tvardovsky, who was sent to Italy in May evidently to mollify the ruffled apprehensions of left-wing Italian intellectuals.

[173] *Komsomolskaya pravda*, May 23, 1963, printed a letter by N. Budyak indicating that even the public recitation of Yevtushenko's poems was forbidden in some provincial towns: "I perform in variety shows. I work in the Lipetsk orchestra where I recite, or rather, used to recite, poems by Yevgeny Yevtushenko. As a result of the articles that have appeared, our director forbade me to recite his verses. I am not a blind worshipper of the poet and I see all his mistakes, am angry and indignant at them. But I cannot agree that it is right to ban recitation of even Yevtushenko's best verses."

[174] *Pravda*, June 16, 18, 23, 25, and 28, 1963.

From the standpoint of the Party, however, this sin might well have been passed over in silence. So, too, might his observations of Italy and America. What could at no cost be allowed to get by were his descriptions of homegrown Soviet follies: the arrest of a well-meaning Italian publisher for taking snapshots of the Kiev marketplace; the walling off of Soviet intellectuals from the writings of Kafka and avant-garde foreign films; above all, the inclusion of secret police watchdogs in Soviet tourist groups traveling abroad. It was for *this* sin that Nekrasov had to be brought low.

After Khrushchev's speech on March 8, in which he was a principal target, Nekrasov was silent. It was not until April 9 that he was compelled to speak up at a meeting of party members and intellectuals in his home town of Kiev. Difficult as it is to piece together his remarks — he has been given no opportunity to speak for himself in the press — Nekrasov apparently refused to recant, declaring that he would write only "the truth, the great truth, the genuine truth." [175] At this point he collided with the ambitions of Nikolai Podgorny, a rising political protégé of Khrushchev. Nekrasov, charged Podgorny,

> . . . has learned nothing and indeed, has no desire to do so. As all of you heard, he considers an admission of errors to be a loss of self-respect as a Communist. For what truth do you, Comrade Nekrasov, stand? Your speech and the ideas you continue to maintain carry a strong flavor of petty-bourgeois anarchy. The party, the people, cannot and will not tolerate this. Comrade Nekrasov, you should ponder this very seriously.[176]

The Long-Awaited Plenum

The attack on Nekrasov was continued by Khrushchev in a speech delivered at the Central Committee Plenum that opened on June 18 — a meeting held in an atmosphere of indecisiveness on the side of the party on the one hand, and silence, even resistance, on the part of the intellectuals on the other. With regard to Nekrasov, to be sure, Khrushchev was far from indecisive, demanding that the writer be expelled from the Communist Party. Incensed both by Nekrasov's views and by his refusal to change them,[177] Khrushchev warned that the

[175] Speech by Podgorny, *Pravda Ukrainy*, April 10, 1963.

[176] *Ibid.* Podgorny disclosed support for Nekrasov among writers of the Ukraine. And a speech by A. D. Skaba, a Party Secretary of the Ukraine, indicated that Nekrasov had support among "certain Moscow writers" (*Pravda*, June 20, 1963).

[177] A speech by A. D. Skaba revealed that Nekrasov — a Party member since 1944 — had, in fact, written to the Ukraine Party Central Committee but the letter was found unsatisfactory. "Recognizing the criticism of his well-known sketches to be on the whole correct," Nekrasov, Skaba charged, "tries to belittle the political significance of his errors" (*Pravda*, June 20, 1963).

"weakening of the class war in the international arena" could drive him to more extreme measures. Gogol's hero, Taras Bulba, recalled Khrushchev darkly, "killed his own son, Andrei, for going over to the side of the enemy. Such is the logic of the struggle."

While there is reason to suppose that Khrushchev's ire was actually caused by Nekrasov's criticism of *Soviet* practices, outwardly the Party concentrated its fire on what it must consider to be Nekrasov's outrageous pro-Westernism — an attitude related to the one-world, Christian outlook expressed by Yevtushenko in Germany:

> The basis of all fruitful discussion is trust. When is a new Messiah going to appear on earth who simply tells men to "trust one another," and we not crucify him? How can we facilitate such trust? I can criticize the West in many things and with justice. And the West can, with equal justice, criticize the East.[178]

What all these attitudes — pacificism, pro-Westernism, a one-world, Christian outlook — spell is a "peace at any price" sentiment among the Soviet people, which the party itself has fed by its own peace propaganda. The strength of this sentiment helped make Nekrasov a scapegoat as it had helped make scapegoats of Ehrenburg and Yevtushenko before him. It is the strength of this sentiment as well that has caused party critics in recent months to step up their attacks on Okudzhava, Bondarev, and Baklanov for "deheroization," or pacifism, in their stories of World War II.[179] Hence, a key point stressed by the plenum in its final decree is the need to inculcate "Soviet patriotism."

Although Khrushchev's allusion to Taras Bulba was strong stuff indeed, raising as it did the specter of physical violence, his speech once again threw into high relief his real dilemma: how to make intellectuals conform *without* a resort to force. Covering up the rejection of coercion — the alternative demanded by the reactionaries — by brutal phrases, he came up with what in fact was a much milder alternative, the threat of expulsion from the Party. In other respects too, his speech was gentler than that of March 8. He was at pains to avoid a frontal assault on the intellectual milieu as a whole or on those individuals who might prove to be rallying points, singling out, besides Nekrasov, only the film director Mikhail Romm for criticism. And he gave pointed praise to

[178] *Die Zeit*, Feb. 15, 1963: "Let's Break the Ice. Thoughts on My Departure from Germany," by Ye. Yevtushenko. For violent criticism, see *Komsomolskaya pravda*, March 30 and May 23, and *Nedelia*, No. 16, 1963. Yevtushenko's article may well have been as crucial to his becoming a victim as his more widely criticized autobiography.
[179] See article by V. Novikov, *Znamya*, No. 9, 1963, pp. 184–187 and report of speeches by Alexander Chakovsky and Generals A. A. Yepishev and Rodion Malinovsky, *Krasnaya zvezda*, Feb. 9, 1964.

Fedin, Sholokhov, and, significantly, Tvardovsky. Here, tangibly, was the hint of conciliation.

Khrushchev was at his most revealing as, somersaulting back over his speech of March 8, he now again defended de-Stalinization. Read alongside the speech of Adzhubei — who was in a position to be more outspoken — his remarks are more revealing still. Thus, one of the major charges raised against him by critics of de-Stalinization was that the drive destroyed respect for authority and was responsible for the crisis between "fathers and sons." He took credit for the decision to attack Stalin's crimes, thereby simultaneously defending himself against the suggestion — implicit in Ehrenburg's memoirs — that he had had a share in those crimes. In 1956, he declared, when the decision was taken to speak out at the 20th CPSU Congress, there was a "very strong struggle." Some people, "feeling very great guilt for the crimes they had committed with Stalin, were afraid." "Stalin is dead," they reasoned, "so are many of his victims. The state is growing, we have leaders, why stir everything up?" Khrushchev, on the other hand, told them: "We ought to tell the truth at the 20th Congress because it is the first congress after Stalin's death. If we tell it only at the 21st Congress or later, the people might fail to understand. Not to bring into the open and condemn is to approve, to make legitimate in the future." There were "long arguments," Khrushchev continued. But at length even those with anguished consciences "agreed to raise this question at the congress." Thus, Khrushchev's claim: whatever Ehrenburg might say, *his* conscience was clear on the score of the purges.

Had he himself been afraid of Stalin (another implication of Ehrenburg's memoirs)? Not at all. Khrushchev describes an occasion when he spoke up to Stalin. The peasants of the Ukraine are dissatisfied, he told the dictator. The 19th Party Congress (October 1952) has declared that the grain problem is solved, and still the peasants have no white bread to eat. With all the unknowing majesty of a Marie Antoinette came Stalin's reply: "The Ukrainians must be given white bread."

Adzhubei was more explicit. Let Ehrenburg and the other doubters, he declared, look at a resolution passed by the Moscow Party aktiv headed by Khrushchev on March 17, 1937, condemning the cult of the individual. The truth is not, as Adzhubei suggested, that Khrushchev at the height of the purges took his life in his hands to oppose the Stalin cult. The Moscow Party organization did adopt a resolution condemning the cult and Khrushchev did speak in favor. Far from being aimed *against* Stalin, however, the resolution was passed *at his instigation* to support the expulsion from the Party of Bukharin and Rykov.[180]

[180] Speech by N. S. Khrushchev, *Pravda*, March 17, 1937.

Adzhubei evidently put forward his claim free of worry that ordinary Soviet readers would be able to check newspapers of the purge period in their libraries!

Elsewhere in his speech Khrushchev addressed himself to the proposals to tighten organizational control over the arts. He was lukewarm to the idea of setting up a single union in place of the present unions of artists, writers, and so on. He had no objection to the continued existence of separate unions, he indicated, so long as their work did not collide with the Party line. On the other hand, he was favorably disposed to the creation of a single publishing enterprise for reasons which he illustrated in his usual graphic manner:

> A writer writes a bad book. He goes to one publisher; nothing comes of it, so he goes to another. If he lives in Moscow or Leningrad and they don't take his manuscript, then he sometimes goes to some far-off region. There, in some city or other, they'll publish him because it flatters them to put out a book by a writer from the capital.[181]

Tighter controls over publishing, Khrushchev concluded, are needed but are not by themselves enough. New and more vigilant people will have to be drawn into the work of editing and censoring books, plays, symphonies, films, and radio broadcasts. Significantly, Khrushchev had harsh words for literary and art critics. Too often, he scolded, they had approached their work "not from principled positions but from group positions. We must rearrange this work and organize it differently." Critics and even censors, apparently, had been going over to the side of the liberals! [182]

Nothing so clearly illustrates the improvised quality of the plenum, the lack of the old, Stalin-style coordination, than Khrushchev's remarks on the suggested changes in publishing and on the single union of creative artists. With Khrushchev one of the last to speak, the others, apparently unaware that he was going to give it his blessing, scarcely mentioned the proposed publishing reform at all.[183] Several, on the other hand, spoke up for the single union, to which he was to indicate indifference. Those in favor included Ilyichev; the Secretary of the Leningrad

---

[181] Khrushchev was right as to the practice, and some of the books which have appeared by this method would seem good to us, bad to him: an edition of Sologub's *Petty Demon* in Kemerovo in 1958; Voznesensky's *Mozaika* in Vladimir in 1960; *Tarusskiye Stranitsy* in Kaluga in 1961 (released for sale by Khrushchev himself); and a small edition of poetry by Gumilev in Leningrad in the spring of 1962.

[182] In "Letter from a Soviet Writer," *The New Leader* (New York), Dec. 9, 1963, p. 18, a Soviet author using the pseudonym Nikolai Gavrilov gave one reason for the reimposition of tight controls over publishing: "It was discovered that several Glavlit inspectors had become friends and abettors of the new authors."

[183] Except Ilyichev, who spoke in favor.

City Party Committee, G. I. Popov; and the head of the Composers' Union, Tikhon Khrennikov. The final decree adopted by the session made no reference to either proposal.

Some of the speeches provide a clue not only to the air of irresolution at the plenum, but also to the erratic course of the cultural drive from the outset. With Khrushchev preoccupied with more pressing matters, such as the dispute with China or the visit of Fidel Castro, lower-ranking officials had been left to luxuriate in rivalry among themselves. Not a few, therefore, had been using the campaign not only to promote "Party spirit" in the arts, but also to advance their own careers.

Thus, Adzhubei, whose newspaper, *Izvestia,* had been notable for its downplaying of the cultural offensive, cited several examples of the "low coefficient of useful effect of our ideological work" as carried out by "workers of the Ideological Section of the Central Committee." Adzhubei did not bother, then, to disguise his jibes at Ilyichev. The latter, on the other hand, was critical of the Ministers of Secondary and Higher Education for "shortcomings in rearing the younger generation" and added that "more energetic leadership might have been expected from the Ministry of Culture." To this, the Minister of Culture, Yekaterina Furtseva, obligingly responded that Ilyichev's criticisms were "just" and her ministry "guilty." [184]

In eloquent contrast to his earlier role as a zealot, Sergei Pavlov, the head of the Komsomol, almost failed to refer to the cultural drive and did not mention the young writers and artists at all. Sensing, perhaps, that he may have carried zealotry too far, he now paid more flowery praise to Khrushchev than any speaker at the meeting. The plenum was notable for other things as well. Summoned to discuss ideology and the arts, much of the session seems actually to have been given over to the developing split with China. Three major speeches[185] were not published. Even a section of Khrushchev's speech dealing with the break seems to have been suppressed.

Still more remarkable for a Central Committee meeting devoted to art and literature, not one of the writers who belong to the Central Committee or any of its related bodies took the floor! [186] Vsevolod Kochetov did not speak. Neither did Yury Zhukov or Alexander Prokofyev, who had also been identified with the harshest stages of the

---

[184] *Pravda,* June 21, 1963.

[185] By Mikhail Suslov, Boris Ponomarev, and Yury Andropov, all of whom are Central Committee Secretaries concerned with Communist bloc affairs.

[186] Nonspeakers included Mikhail Sholokhov and Alexander Korneichuk, full members of the Central Committee; Nikolai Gribachov and Alexander Tvardovsky, candidate members; and Zhukov, Prokofyev, and Kochetov, who belong to the mandate commission.

campaign. Their silence, like the tone of Pavlov's speech, was a sign that the more hardnosed protagonists of the drive were now under wraps. Extremes, then, were avoided. So, too, were decisions. Furtseva's vigorous defense of the success of Soviet cultural contacts with the West was another sign, a more positive one, of the softening of the drive. Derisive toward those who gave, and are still giving, moral support to the modern artists, she took a jab also at critics of modern art. One painter-critic who had attacked Neizvestny violently at the December 17 meeting, she revealed, had earlier paid him 12,000 (old) rubles for a statue! And the choice of the outspoken film director Grigory Chukhrai as a speaker may even have been a gesture of conciliation to the liberals.[187]

Ilyichev's three-hour speech, while scarcely conciliatory, refrained nevertheless from naming names or giving gratuitous offense. Careful to strike a balance in nearly everything he said, he was at pains not to challenge the entire intellectual milieu as the speeches of March 7–8 had done. Thus, in speaking of those who yearn to be free of Party intervention, he added:

> But let us all remember that we are speaking of Soviet artists, people who are politically close to us. Our task is not to excommunicate them but to help them understand their artistic and ideological mistakes. It would not be in the spirit of our party to relegate creative workers who have made mistakes to the ranks of the hopeless and incorrigible.

In harsher passages, he called upon the editors of *Yunost, Novy mir,* and *Neva* to explain their publishing errors. Finally, he warned his audience against thinking that it had all been a " 'temporary' campaign, destined soon to pass, that 'all will be forgotten' and that it is possible in the meantime to sit it out and be silent. It won't do! The Party is waging not a campaign but a consistent struggle."

How the Party was to wage the "struggle," however, neither Ilyichev nor any speaker at the plenum could say. The resolution adopted at the session contained not a single concrete proposal. If the events of recent years prove anything, it is that maintenance of "ideological purity" in the arts — whatever that means — is rarely at the center of Party attention for long. Occasionally, owing to a juncture of political circumstances, it can briefly become so. As soon as the leaders turn away to a more pressing crisis or a more practical dilemma, officials of the second and third rank are left to cultivate political pastures of their own in the at-

[187] Chukhrai stressed the liberal slogan of "quality" and criticized "formalist-reinsurers" who, robbing art of form, would deprive it of content as well. At a meeting of Soviet and Italian film directors in Moscow in early April, Chukhrai boldly conceded that the struggle of Soviet artists against "dogmatism" and "reactionary tendencies" is "not simple or easy."

mosphere the leaders have established. It was in this fashion, in the interstices of the leaders' attention, so to speak, that literature and art made some of their gains in the 1959–1962 period. That the regime may be distracted from its more intangible goals in the future as well is all the more probable in view of the continued ascendancy of economic over ideological tasks.[188]

After the Plenary Session

Since the plenum, however, the Party has made a sustained effort to keep its attention to the arts from lapsing. Through all of June and July of 1963 there was intense and bitter discussion of the proposal for a single creative union, a proposal which, since it would have meant the disbanding of all the existing unions of composers, writers, and artists and required each member to apply separately for admission to the new union, could effectively have barred liberals in all the arts from having their work played, published, or exhibited.[189] Making official art an exclusive preserve of right-wing orthodoxy and driving most of the country's creative talent underground, this proposal might well have required a resort to coercion.[190] Although it was strongly backed by the more extreme conservatives,[191] the proposal had evidently been rejected by the Party before July was out[192] in favor of devices more typical of the Khrushchev era: tighter administrative control and a shakeup of personnel. First to be overhauled was the Moscow writers' organization, stronghold of liberal strength and far and away the largest, most influential writers' group in the U.S.S.R.[193] In the revamping of that organization, liberals were shaken out of virtually all the positions they

---

[188] See *Kommunist,* No. 17 (November), 1963, pp. 3–11.

[189] See speech by G. I. Popov, *Leningradskaya pravda,* June 19, 1963, and article by Michel Tatu, *Le Monde,* July 3, 1963.

[190] "The Party and the Writers," by David Burg, *Grany* (Frankfurt), No. 54 (November), 1963, see especially pp. 128–131.

[191] While there can be little doubt that the extreme right wing wanted the Party to resort to force, some conservative writers appear to have been weakened in their effort for a single union by the fact that writers — the conservatives, with their vast editions, are the richest — would have had to share their dachas, rest homes, and travel funds with the more indigent artists' and composers' unions. See "Wave of the Future," by Nikolai Gribachov, *Literaturnaya gazeta,* June 27, 1963, and Michel Tatu in *Le Monde,* July 3, 1963.

[192] *Literaturnaya gazeta,* July 30, 1963, and *Literaturnaya Rossiya,* Aug. 2, 1963. Anticipating Party approval, however, officials in some republics, such as Uzbekistan, are said to have jumped the gun and gone ahead with fusion of arts organizations (*Le Monde,* Aug. 13, 1963).

[193] According to *Literaturnaya Rossiya,* Aug. 2, 1963, the Moscow organization comprises one half the membership of the Writers' Union of the Russian Republic and one quarter that of the entire U.S.S.R.

had won the year before. A tight, eleven-man Secretariat replaced the old looser, more liberal Presidium. In an effort to dissipate the easygoing, clublike, rather specialized literary atmosphere in which liberalism had taken root in Moscow, moreover, writers were attached to Party cells at factories and institutes and urged to expend fewer of their energies on lyric themes and more on the rhythm of work in the Moscow area.[194]

Finally, in the most Khrushchevian gesture of all, with existing creative organizations left intact, a new State Committee for the Press was set up to supervise book publishing throughout the land.[195] Pavel Romanov was appointed to head it. He had been head of Glavlit and the man mainly responsible for preventing "state and military secrets" from finding their way into the printed word. From the negative task of chief censor, in other words, Romanov now took over the positive role of policy-maker, deciding what books should appear and in editions of what dimension. The reform, it is clear, was aimed at the editorial polycentrism that had come into being since 1959, whereby an author whose book was rejected by one publishing house found himself increasingly able to appeal to another.[196] According to one complaint, publishing houses had come to "live like appanage princes: one does not know what the others are doing." [197] Or, as a frustrated official phrased it, it was high time to "plug up the chinks" in the edifice of publishing control.[198] To date, the most visible step taken by the new committee has been one of consolidation: from 62 central publishing houses, the total has been reduced to 44.[199] The slow seepage of work from "the drawer" onto the printed page has been curtailed. And the inadvertent appearance of unorthodox volumes has, for the time being, been stopped. In the long run, however, even Khrushchev could not have expected new State Committees to solve his problems with the writers. For of all types of human activity the creative process, quicksilver thing that it is, is the most elusive of bureaucratic control. In the atmosphere of Soviet society today, how are mere censors to mold it?

Much as Khrushchev may have yearned for the old simplicities of

[194] *Literaturnaya gazeta,* July 11, 1963; *Literaturnaya Rossiya,* Aug. 2, 1963; *Sovetskaya Rossiya,* Aug. 31, 1963.

[195] *Pravda,* Aug. 11, 1963. Parallel State Committees were also set up in each of the union republics. For the list of those appointed to head them and description of their work see *Sovetskaya pechat,* No. 12 (Dec.), 1963, pp. 24–25.

[196] "Letter from a Soviet Writer," by Nikolai Gavrilov, *The New Leader,* Dec. 9, 1963, and "On Militant Positions," by Yury Barabash, *Kommunist,* No. 17 (Nov.), 1963.

[197] Speech by M. Sivolobov, *Sovetskaya Kirgizia,* July 11, 1963.

[198] *Sovetskaya kultura,* April 6, 1963, by A. Rybin.

[199] "The Book — Mighty Weapon of Socialist Culture," by P. Romanov, *Kommunist,* No. 4 (March), 1964, p. 75.

1959, when the Party could fairly simply hold a balance between liberal and conservative camps among the intellectuals; much as he may, in times of crisis, have aspired to have his intellectuals react like flawlessly conditioned Agitprop puppets, he must have been aware throughout the campaign that he could not accede to conservative demands that he expunge the liberals from literature. For the differences of outlook among creative artists are tolerated only by virtue of differences inside the Communist Party itself.

In the spring of 1963, the balance of forces within the Party was no longer what it had been in the aftermath of the Cuban crisis. In April, Kozlov fell ill. In early June, an opening date was set for test-ban talks with Britain and the United States that could not fail to overlap with the ideological talks with China scheduled to begin in July. In the latter half of June, the Central Committee meeting that had been called to discuss ideology and the arts was given over in large part instead to the developing differences with China.

As is often the case, the young writers were an early barometer of the altered political conditions. Thus, the existence of counterpoint tendencies even toward those who had been under heaviest fire was already apparent before the Central Committee plenum. In early June, *Literaturnaya gazeta* printed a reference to Voznesensky[200] and, a month later, to Yevtushenko,[201] that were so neutral, or so mildly unfavorable, as to seem almost propitious compared with the vicious attacks that had gone before.[202]

Then, in mid-July, a storm blew up at Moscow's Third International Film Festival. Sudden as it was, the storm was not wholly uncontrived. Arriving for the festival, several Italian film directors who are usually at odds in all but their left-wing views joined forces for once to badger Moscow officialdom with questions about their beleaguered brethren Romm, Chukhrai, and, above all, the youthful Marlen Khutsiyev.[203] By naming Federico Fellini's introspective, somewhat surrealistic film *8½* as the Italian entry, moreover, they were making a choice that could not fail to confound their hosts in the Kremlin. Predictably, the Italian entry outclassed all others in the two-week competition. It made the Soviet entry, an exercise in socialist realism called *Meet Baluyev,* seem painfully banal by comparison. Thus, when the 15-man jury — nine from Communist countries, one each from France, India, Japan,

---

[200] By B. Tomashevsky, *Literaturnaya gazeta,* June 1, 1963.

[201] By V. Pankina, *Literaturnaya gazeta,* July 9, 1963.

[202] In addition, Tvardovsky's poem, "Tyorkin in the Other World," was sent to press on June 14, four days before the opening of the plenum (although passed by the censor only on Aug. 21).

[203] *New Statesman,* Aug. 16, 1963.

the United States, Italy, and the United Arab Republic — sat down to its deliberations, it faced a thorny dilemma: to award the prize to an inferior entry and damage the festival's reputation abroad, or give it to Fellini and outrage its sponsors in Moscow.

Sure enough, the jury was deadlocked. As late as July 21, the day the festival was to end, no way out had been found. Liberals in the Soviet film world are said to have privately urged that the award go to *8½*. Stanley Kramer, the American judge, is reported to have felt that even Communist-bloc members of the jury wanted him to force the issue. The last morning, the six jurors from non-Communist countries voted to give the prize to Fellini, with the nine from bloc countries casting their ballots against. At this point Sergio Amidei, the Italian judge and himself a Communist, stalked out, shouting angrily, "What kind of festival is this, when the juror from Czechoslovakia tells me Fellini's film is best but he can't vote for it?" He was followed by Kramer and the other non-Communist judges. Staying behind, a Communist from Brazil sought vainly to persuade the bloc judges to vote for *8½*, accompanying the vote with a disclaimer of some kind. Stanley Kramer left for a showing of one of his own films. Less than an hour after the walkout he received a tap on the shoulder: the jury wanted to see him. As the non-Communists filed into the room Chukhrai, one of the Soviet judges, asked: "If we vote for the film, will you come back?" Unanimously, the verdict went to Fellini. During the hour that had elapsed, so went speculation in Moscow, the issue had gone straight to Khrushchev and a decision was reached to give the award to Fellini rather than compromise the festival's standing abroad.[204]

Soviet officials wasted no time throwing cold water on the hopes of Moscow intellectuals who might take the decision as a sign of relaxation on the cultural front. Even before the award, an article appeared blasting *8½* over the always meaningful signature of Yury Zhukov.[205] *Pravda* downplayed its announcement of the prize and a few days later a second violent attack was published.[206] Behind the scenes Yekaterina Furtseva, the Soviet Minister of Culture, is said to have scolded Stanley Kramer for being "the bad boy on the jury."

His curiosity stirred, meanwhile, by talk of the film among younger Russian intellectuals, Khrushchev is said to have asked for a private showing of *8½*. In a rage, he walked out after half an hour, calling

---

[204] *The New York Times,* July 26 and 30, 1963.

[205] "Eight and a Half Circles of Cinematographic Hell," by Yury Zhukov, *Literaturnaya gazeta,* July 20, 1963.

[206] "The Moscow Festival and Foreign Maligners," by Literator [writer], *Literaturnaya gazeta,* July 27, 1963.

upon Alexei Romanov, chairman of the newly formed State Cinematography Committee, to do something about it. At the press conference that ensued, Romanov sought to dissociate Soviet officialdom from the award, stressing the "international" character of the jury. Emphatically he denied that the award to Fellini meant "a rejection by the leaders of Soviet art of the basic principles of Soviet art" or any "concession by us in the ideological struggle." [207] He indicated that *8½* would not be shown inside the Soviet Union. Significantly absent at the press conference was the liberal Grigory Chukhrai who, as one of the Soviet judges, was evidently under a cloud for failing to fend off the award. No doubt Moscow officials were especially wary lest, coming at a moment when ideological talks with China had been broken off and test-ban talks with Britain and the United States were under way, the award would seem at home and abroad to signify an ideological rapprochement with the West.

What shows better than the furor over *8½* the dilemma in which the quest for prestige abroad, expressed in participation in festivals of this kind, can embroil the Soviet leaders? What better illustrates their vulnerability to pressure from Westerners whose good opinion they covet, especially when those Westerners happen, like the Italian directors at the festival, to be bona fide Communists as well?

As he flew off, Stanley Kramer expressed the serene hope that the award to *8½* would give a much-needed boost to liberals among the Moscow film-makers. For awhile Kramer's hopes were confounded. Right after the festival, work on 13 movies then in production is said to have been halted temporarily by officials fearful of runaway liberalization. Thus the festival, and its aftermath, illustrates how fretful and erratic are the vagaries of the Soviet cultural scene. To every action, there is an equal and opposite reaction.

Just how troubled the course of "cultural coexistence" can be was demonstrated once again when a hundred writers from East and West came together in Leningrad on August 5–8, under the auspices of UNESCO and the left-wing Community of European Writers, to discuss the modern novel. Opening, auspiciously enough, on the day the nuclear negotiators were signing the test-ban agreement in Moscow, the meeting got off to a turbulent start nonetheless when Ivan Anisimov and Konstantin Fedin contemptuously dismissed Proust, Joyce, Kafka, Musil, and Beckett as bearers of the deadly virus of "decadence." [208]

[207] *Pravda,* July 30, 1963, p. 6.

[208] Western accounts of Fedin's speech have ignored this crucial sentence, which seems to explain the ban on the European modernists in the U.S.S.R.: "If Soviet novelists were to follow the intuitivism of Proust, it would then be logical to res-

Leonid Leonov made matters worse by ridiculing a short-wave radio broadcast he had recently heard of "Ave Maria" in syncopated time, adding that he did not know whether "the broadcast emanated straight from hell or from one of its branches here on earth." The foreigners in the hall were unamused, both by Leonov's suggestion that the West is a hell and by his holding them responsible for Western culture in its every manifestation.[209] For a while the meeting, as the French novelist Natalie Sarraute described it, resembled nothing so much as "a dialogue of the deaf." With the Soviet writers and their guests unable even to agree on a definition of "realism," "humanism," or "moral values," matters had come to a dead end, a failure of common conversation. An especially low ebb was reached when Konstantin Simonov compared the responsibility of the writer with that of the airplane pilot, solemnly admonishing his audience that neither has the right "to be himself at the expense of others." At this point Alain Robbe-Grillet had had enough. Literature, he burst out, "is not a means of transport." Attacks on the "new" French novelists, moreover, he termed "a scandal for a country that calls itself the cradle of revolution." [210]

The conferees had cause at this moment to be grateful to Ilya Ehrenburg, who had arrived a day late, trailing clouds of rumors that he had come straight from the presence of Khrushchev. Whether the writer and Khrushchev had talked face to face or only, as some sources say, over the telephone,[211] Ehrenburg's belated appearance at the conference betokened a dramatic return from Achillean exile. According to one observer, the excitement it evoked among the younger Soviet writers immediately infected the Western conferees as well.[212]

Ehrenburg lost no time applying his skills as a mediator. The writer may indeed be a pilot, he soothed, but if so, then the test pilot is as im-

urrect some of our homegrown modernists as well." (*Literaturnaya gazeta,* Aug. 6, 1963.)

[209] Again, Western commentators seem to have overlooked Leonov's last paragraph which, to this observer, raises a question as to whether he meant his speech to be taken at face value at all: "I ask you, in conclusion, not to judge me either for the wearisome didacticism of this speech or for the extraordinary insistence of my conclusions inasmuch as it has required much more of me to convince myself than to convince you of the primacy of the citizen over the artist." (*Literaturnaya gazeta,* Aug. 8, 1963.)

[210] For a fuller account of this exchange, see "Khrushchev and Letters" by Bernard Pingaud in *L'Express,* Aug. 22, 1963.

[211] According to Michel Tatu in *Le Monde,* Aug. 14, 1963, Khrushchev received Ehrenburg in person. Others have suggested that only a telephone call passed between them.

[212] From an account of the conference by the German writer Hans Werner Richter originally published in *Süddeutsche Zeitung,* Aug. 28, 1963, and reprinted in *Novoye Russkoye Slovo* (New York), Sept. 22, 1963.

portant as any other. Ehrenburg's speech, his first public utterance since Khrushchev's and Ilyichev's violent attacks on him in March, was at once subtle and supple, testimony to the daring and the sense of immunity which old age can confer on a public personality in the Soviet Union. Westerners in the audience must have silently whispered "amen" as Ehrenburg alone of the Soviet speakers remarked of Kafka and Joyce: "To me, this is the past. I do not make banners, but neither do I make targets of them." He chided his Soviet colleagues for their attacks on foreign authors they have not read. And he advanced the un-socialist realist notion that there are writers for the few and writers for the many ("Joyce is a writer for writers"), adding: "We need have no fear of experiment."

Ehrenburg's remarks so altered the atmosphere that, according to a West German who was present, "it was as if the ears of the deaf had been opened." [213] The speeches by Tvardovsky, by the Leningrad novelist Daniil Granin,[214] and by Vasily Axyonov[215] likewise encouraged the Westerners to hope that dialogue with the Russians might, after all, be possible despite seemingly irreconcilable conceptions of the role of art and the unfamiliarity of each side with the work of the other. Axyonov, whose speech was distinguished from that of any other Soviet speaker by its straightforward, personal tone, figured also in a moving exchange with the young West German poet-critic Hans Magnus Enzenberger. In his speech Enzenberger remarked that, unable to deal with fascism by realistic tools alone, such post-World War II German writers as Gunter Grass and Uwe Johnson had had to resort to new methods of portraying reality. As an eyewitness put it, Enzenberger's comment elicited "noisy approval" among the younger Soviet writers, who discussed it excitedly late into the night. At one point Axyonov went up to the table where several of the foreigners were sitting and personally thanked Enzenberger for what he had said.[216] Whether it was the feeling of the younger Soviet writers that extra-realistic methods might be well suited to a portrayal of the Stalin era, too, the observer did not say. From private conversations he concluded, however, that two problems overshadowed all others for Soviet participants at the meeting: de-Stalinization and the unfolding conflict with Communist China.

From Leningrad the writers journeyed briefly to Moscow and thence to Khrushchev's Black Sea villa at Gagra. Nothing better illustrates the

[213] *Ibid.*

[214] *Literaturnaya gazeta,* Aug. 15, 1963.

[215] Axyonov's speech was not published until Aug. 27, 1963, *Literaturnaya gazeta.* Significantly, it was printed simply as an article, without the customary note that it was the transcript of a speech delivered at the Leningrad conference.

[216] Hans Werner Richter, *loc. cit.*

former Party leader's erratic personality or the vagaries of the Soviet cultural scene than the audience they had with him there. That Khrushchev would receive such a group at all — 16 from Eastern and Western Europe and 12 from the Soviet Union — was a token of the significance he attached at that moment to East-West exchange. All the more so, as one of those present pointed out, since Khrushchev availed himself of the occasion to make the kind of political observations he delighted in rather than a routine denunciation of bourgeois culture.[217]

The meeting was rife with contradictions, beginning with the makeup of the two delegations. Absent from the Soviet midst were the three liberals who had redeemed the Soviet performance at Leningrad — Ehrenburg, Axyonov, and Granin. Conspicuously present were such standard-bearers of the literary right as Georgy Markov, Leonid Sobolev, and Alexander Prokofyev. The Westerners, on the other hand, included several whose work had been considered too experimental, too pessimistic, too obscure, or too preoccupied with sex to be translated into Russian: Angus Wilson and William Golding of England, and France's Alain Robbe-Grillet and Natalie Sarraute.

These minor ironies were as nothing, however, compared with the major anomalies of Khrushchev's impromptu remarks. Having received the writers at all, he opened by declaring that peace is one thing, writing quite another. There can be compromises for peace, but none in the war of words and ideas. Cuba, he went on, had given the Americans a valuable fright: the British and Americans had come to negotiate the test ban only out of fear.

Unsolicited, he gave an oblique defense of his actions during the Hungarian uprising. Tsar Nicholas I, he remarked, had been quite right from his class point of view to send troops to suppress the popular rising in Austria in 1848. A worker who helped build a prison for other workers cannot escape responsibility. The same holds for writers who write for capitalists — "Those writers are you." Reminded at this point by a Pole that the Western writers present were not of that political complexion, Khrushchev paused, undaunted, and went off on another tangent: the folly of the Chinese in measuring the sincerity of Communists by their willingness to go around in rags.

What struck the English observer Angus Wilson most of all was not so much the contradictions of Khrushchev's speech itself, but the glaring contrast between his willingness — itself a symbol of coexistence — to receive the writers on the one hand, and the tone of his remarks on the other. The tone, as Wilson described it, seemed set against cultural co-

[217] This account draws heavily on Angus Wilson's "What Khrushchev Told the Writers" in *The Observer*, Aug. 18, 1963.

existence, intended, even, to convey a shock. And then there were the ever astonishing flip-flops on the subject of Stalin. At first Khrushchev was critical of Stalin's isolation from the people. Later, however, he added that for all his faults Stalin had laid the groundwork for the present atomic detente. Finally, in the most baffling gesture of all, he called upon Alexander Tvardovsky to recite his long poem "Tyorkin in the Other World," a devastating satire on the Stalinist bureaucracy.

In the poem Tvardovsky takes Vasily Tyorkin, an ordinary Russian soldier, hero of his famous epic published in 1946, into the world of the dead. Only, the "other world" turns out to be a parody of Stalin's Russia, with its callousness to human beings, its mindless pursuit of bureaucratic directives, its network of secret police informers, its finger printing, even its tobacco that does not smoke. All this, and a Supreme One too, erecting monuments to himself.

Why Khrushchev chose first to praise Stalin to the writers assembled and then to unleash Tvardovsky and "Tyorkin" is anybody's guess. The episode illustrates why writers and artists were hard put to decipher their enigmatic, if garrulous, leader! The afternoon was a paradoxical one for Tvardovsky, too. Surely it is extraordinary for the editor of a major literary journal, alternate member of the Party Central Committee at that, to be author of a politically unpublishable poem that had been circulating in the semiunderground world of Moscow manuscript readers for, some say, as long as six years! [218] At the Party plenum in June, moreover, Ilyichev had made clear that Tvardovsky was by no means restored to full grace. Suddenly, when he returned to favor and his manuscript was admitted to this world, it was at the imperial bidding, in the sunny light of a Gagra afternoon! [219]

Khrushchev's extraordinary gesture made sense — as has often been the case — as part of a larger design. At this period he was trying to rally sentiment for a conclave to read China out of the world Communist movement. With anti-Stalin and anti-China gestures closely twined together, he evidently felt the time ripe to legitimize Tvardovsky's brainchild. By the same token, it was an opportune moment for a coexistential flourish toward the West. By the garden party at Gagra, he was able to serve both objectives.

Soon afterward, moreover, Ehrenburg had a long article in *Pravda*,[220]

[218] A version of the poem had, moreover, appeared in the Russian-language emigre journal *Mosty* (Munich), No. 10, 1963.

[219] *Novy mir,* No. 8 (Aug.), 1963, which contained Tvardovsky's poem, was delivered to the printer on June 14, four days before the opening of the June plenum, and passed by the censor on August 21, three days after the poem had appeared in *Izvestia.*

[220] Ehrenburg's article, "A Good Beginning" (*Pravda,* Sept. 6, 1963), celebrates the test-ban agreement and brands the Chinese as warmongers.

Yevtushenko a poem in *Yunost*,[221] and Voznesensky part of a poem in *Pravda*[222] — it was, significantly, the first time the latter two had appeared in print since the attacks on them in the spring — that contained unequivocal thrusts against the Chinese leaders. The exigencies of the Sino-Soviet quarrel appear, then, to have had a good deal to do with the easing of the drive in the arts and the return of the writers to respectability.

Nor did Khrushchev have to worry that the appearance of "Tyorkin in the Other World" would set off too great an anti-Stalin ferment at home. Stunning as the poem was in its content and implications, it appears to have been partially defused by the fact that it had long been circulating in manuscript and many readers were familiar with it already. As Alexei Adzhubei put it, with lively understatement, in his *Izvestia* foreword, the poem "is in no need of a special introduction." [223] Thus as it turned out, publication of the poem was not a political event of nearly the same magnitude as the appearance of *One Day in the Life of Ivan Denisovich* less than a year before. Where *Ivan Denisovich* had been a high-energy explosive detonating subterranean rumblings all over the Soviet Union, "Tyorkin" was more like a rocket flare in the night, signaling that the worst of the intellectual drive was over and de-Stalinization on the agenda once again.

All this was cold comfort to the spiritual bureaucrats of the literary right. With that faction amply represented at Gagra, the sound of teeth gnashing must have been nearly audible, even in Khrushchev's own garden. In view of the poem's lofty patronage, wrath repressed and under wraps was as much as the critics dared venture in the few reviews that appeared. Even so, the sternest accused Tvardovsky of "providing grist for the enemy's mill" and "collecting in one heap all the bad there is in Russia." [224] Another conceded that some people felt frustrated that "after so much has been said about the positive spirit of our litera-

---

[221] Yevtushenko's "Again at Stantsiya Zima," in *Yunost,* No. 9 (Sept.), 1963 (passed by the censor Sept. 13), contains these lines:

> You of the ultra-left phrase
> And unsobered heart,
> You who want to light a fire,
> Don't cherish illusions.

[222] Voznesensky's "Longjumeau" (*Pravda,* Oct. 13, 1963) contains these lines:

> The school of Lenin is a school of peace.
> Do not pin his name to him
> Who plots his progress on a pile of bones,
> Turning half a planet to scorched earth.

[223] *Izvestia,* Aug. 18, 1963.

[224] "Tyorkin vs. Tyorkin," by D. Starikov, *Oktyabr,* No. 10 (October), 1963, pp. 193–207.

ture [i.e., after March 7–8] they go and print Tvardovsky's poem." [225] To such critics, publication of the poem must have seemed an about-face in the cultural policy of the Party. Soon, however, they were faced by a new danger, the possibility that Alexander Solzhenitsyn might receive a Lenin Prize for *One Day in the Life of Ivan Denisovich,* with all that that would imply for a renewed, far-reaching round of de-Staliniziation of the Party and the ranks of the literary bureaucracy.

L'Affaire Solzhenitsyn

In spite of the blessing of Khrushchev, *One Day in the Life of Ivan Denisovich* had begun to draw fire from the critics as soon as the campaign against intellectuals moved into high gear. Early in 1963 Lidia Fomenko leveled the criticism that has since become a leitmotif: the author failed "to rise to a philosophical perception" of the Stalin era or to realize that despite all Stalin could do, the Party had gone on, building socialism.[226] A few weeks later, a similar criticism was raised again, this time against "Matryona's Home": "Without a vision of historical truth, there can be no full truth, no matter what the talent." [227]

At the end of the summer, controversy over Solzhenitsyn flared up again. A new story, "For the Good of the Cause," [228] was the starting point. Taking up the cudgels, Yury Barabash, deputy editor of *Literaturnaya gazeta,* called the story — from an artistic standpoint, Solzhenitsyn's weakest so far — "a failure." [229] In a reply a few weeks later,[230] Daniil Granin made a strong moral plea for the humanization and democratization of Soviet life and praised Solzhenitsyn for his "faith in the people who are forging the cause and who have the right to judge what is in the interests of the cause and what is not." Granin added: "There are people who find that democratization gets in their way. Why does it get in their way? How do they work, what are their methods, what their philosophy? This is what Solzhenitsyn is investigating."

Almost immediately, *Literaturnaya gazeta* printed a new article criticizing Solzhenitsyn's story and Granin's defense alike. In a special note, the editors of the newspaper made it clear that they, too, were critical of Solzhenitsyn's "creative mistakes." They hinted that Solzhenitsyn

[225] "Alive for the Living," by Yu. Surovtsev, *Literaturnaya Rossiya,* Sept. 27, 1963.
[226] "Great Expectations," by Lidia Fomenko, *Literaturnaya Rossiya,* No. 2, Jan. 11, 1963.
[227] *Literaturnaya gazeta,* March 2, 1963, by Vadim Kozhevnikov.
[228] *Novy mir,* No. 7 (July), 1963.
[229] "What is Justice?" by Yury Barabash, *Literaturnaya gazeta,* Aug. 31, 1963.
[230] "Is the Critic Right?" by Daniil Granin, Oct. 15, 1963.

had violated the canons of socialist realism by "mechanically transplant-
ing" the 19th century "tradition of critical realism to socialist soil."
This, they concluded, "represents a great danger." [231] In light of the
Lenin Prize discussion which developed later, it may be helpful to recall that as early as October 19, the editors of *Literaturnaya gazeta* were
on record as critical of Solzhenitsyn's work.

By this time, to judge by the increase of polemics, word may already have leaked out that Solzhenitsyn would be up for the prize, although the names of candidates were not to be announced until the
first of the year. Thus, in October, *Oktyabr* magazine printed what
was perhaps a sharper attack on Solzhenitsyn than any that had yet appeared.[232] V. Chalmayev concentrated on "Matryona's Home" and "For
the Good of the Cause." In the first of these stories, Chalmayev charged,
Solzhenitsyn celebrated two principles: "righteousness as a form of
moral feat" and the "elevation of man through suffering and tears."
Neither, the critic made clear, was acceptable in today's "angry, heroic
world."

As for "For the Good of the Cause," here, said Chalmayev, Solzhenitsyn had revealed "his utter inability to interpret modern, living material. Everything in it is toylike, stage setting, borrowed. The naive counterposing of 'bureaucratic' designs to the dictates of personal kindness,
of the official to the human, all these contrived constructions crumble to
dust in comparison with modern life." Even these words do not convey the sharp, ironic tone of Chalmayev's assault.

As if this were not enough, the same issue of *Oktyabr* delivered an
oblique blow against *One Day in the Life of Ivan Denisovich* by reviewing, in ecstatic terms, a rival description of prison life. [233] Suggesting
that Solzhenitsyn's work had "simplified the actual state of things" in
the camps, the review praised a novel by Boris Dyakov called *Endured*
for showing the prisoners' "unbending faith in Communist ideals, in the
durability of Soviet power, in the triumph of justice and warm love of
the homeland."

The burgeoning controversy over Solzhenitsyn had reverberations as
far away as Alma-ata, where on October 6 *Kazakhstanskaya pravda*
published a major attack on *Ivan Denisovich* by a former camp inmate.
Dubbing Solzhenitsyn's hero "a lackey, ready to toady to anybody for

---

[231] See " 'Today's' is More Like 'Yesterday's,' " by N. Seliverstov, *Literaturnaya
gazeta*, Oct. 19, 1963, and "Note from the Editors," *ibid.*

[232] " 'Saints' and 'Devils,' " by V. Chalmayev, *Oktyabr*, No. 10. (October), 1963,
pp. 215–217.

[233] "Unbending Spirit," by N. Sergovantsev, *ibid.*, pp. 212–215. Sergovantsev was
also the author of one of the earliest and most violent criticisms of Solzhenitsyn
ever published. It appeared in *Oktyabr*, No. 4 (April), 1963, pp. 198–207.

a piece of sausage or a pinch of makhorka tobacco," the author, one Alexander Afanasyevich Gudzenko, accused Solzhenitsyn of distorting prison life. "There were some Ivan Denisoviches who smoked secretly under the covers, but they were exceptions and not the rule." Gudzenko's attack, which was in the form of a letter to the newspaper, struck several notes that had already been sounded earlier by conservative writers, such as Lidia Fomenko and Galina Serebryakova. They were gratitude to the Party and Khrushchev for "smashing the Stalin cult" and releasing so many inmates, and gratitude even to the camp guards. "There were fierce ones among them, but very many, at risk to themselves, showed a humaneness forbidden by the rules." (The frequency and insistence with which this matter of "humaneness" on the part of prison guards is raised suggests that there may be considerable hue and cry behind the scenes that not only informers but former personnel at the camps be brought to trial for crimes of the Stalin era.)[234]

The next development was a surprising polemic between two Moscow publications that showed how heated passions had become. In its October issue, *Novy mir* had published three letters from readers defending "For the Good of the Cause" against the attack by Yury Barabash.[235] In December, *Literaturnaya gazeta* printed a long editors' note affirming earlier criticism of Solzhenitsyn's story and accusing *Novy mir,* in effect, of publishing only letters favorable to the story and suppressing those that were against.[236] In an unusual reply, the editorial board of *Novy mir* dropped its usual stance of silence in the face of criticism, or even of turning the other cheek. The *Novy mir* editors delved into their mailbag in detail. They had received 58 letters on "For the Good of the Cause," they conceded. Of these, 55 were unequivocally in favor. Two letters contained stylistic criticism. Only one expressed disapproval of the story itself. This letter, the editors went on, was so "intolerably abusive" that they considered its publication inappropriate. The real surprise of the *Novy mir* reply was yet to come. Of the 55 favorable letters, the editors remarked, 12 were carbon copies. The originals had gone to *Literaturnaya gazeta*. It was *Literaturnaya gazeta,* they charged, that had suppressed letters favoring Solzhenitsyn and "abused

---

[234] An illustration of how a former prisoner still feels about his chief torturer at Moscow Lefortovo prison during the late '30's is this passage from Gen. A. V. Gorbatov's memoirs, "Years and Wars," which appeared in *Novy mir,* Nos. 3–5, (March–May 1964): "I have no idea where is now. If he is alive, I wish he could read these lines and feel not only the hatred I bear him today but that which I bore him then, when I was in his hands."

[235] Letters by Y. Yampolskaya, L. Reznikov, and V. Sheinis in *Novy mir,* No. 10 (October), 1963, pp. 193–198.

[236] *Literaturnaya gazeta,* Dec. 12, 1963.

a claim to represent its readers' opinions." Perhaps from some Trojan horse on the paper, the editors of *Novy mir* had an accurate count of letters received by *Literaturnaya gazeta*. For the newspaper's reply to the charge by *Novy mir* was conspicuously lame.[237] In fact, *Literaturnaya gazeta* mended its ways at the start of the New Year by printing at least one letter backing Solzhenitsyn unequivocally for the prize.[238]

Although bitter polemics were already occurring, the Lenin Prize debate was formally open only after announcement of the nominations on December 28. As for the candidates with the most formidable backing, they appeared to be Oles Gonchar, head of the Ukrainian Writers' Union; Daniil Granin for his novel *I Go into Thunder*; Yegor Isayev for his poem "Court of Memory"; Galina Serebryakova for "Prometheus," a trilogy on the life of Karl Marx; and Alexander Chakovsky, editor of *Literaturnaya gazeta,* for "Light of a Far-Off Star." A serious candidate with comparatively insubstantial backing was Leonid Pervomaisky's "Wild Honey." Another was Solzhenitsyn's masterpiece — from a literary standpoint, probably the finest prose work to have appeared in the Soviet Union in decades. From the outset it was the gossip in Moscow literary circles that Solzhenitsyn had very little chance since his support came only from Tvardovsky and the group of writers clustered around *Novy mir*. (Had the decision been left to the Prize Committee alone, a glance at the names of its literary representatives could have borne out such a forecast. The only out-and-out liberal was Tvardovsky. Those difficult to classify included Sholokhov and Korneichuk. Among the conservatives were Ivan Anisimov, Nikolai Gribachov, Georgy Markov, Leonid Novichenko, Alexander Prokofyev, and Leonid Sobolev. Nearly all the other judges were past prizewinners from minority language groups. Two judges were candidates for the prize as well: Chakovsky and Isayev. Another candidate, Gonchar, was an ex-officio Vice-Chairman of the Prize Committee.)

In spite of its apparently flimsy prospects, Solzhenitsyn's candidacy dominated the public debate. At meetings of Moscow writers called to discuss the nominations, speakers seem to have been loath to talk about any other subject. The press and the prize committee received four

---

[237] For the *Novy mir* rebuttal and *Literaturnaya gazeta* reply, see *Literaturnaya gazeta,* Dec. 26, 1963.

[238] This letter, by M. Lezinsky, appeared in *Literaturnaya gazeta,* Jan. 11, 1964, p. 3. For other contributions on Solzhenitsyn's candidacy, see articles by V. Pankov, *Literaturnaya gazeta,* Jan. 18, 1964; by L. Zhukhovitsky and Gr. Brovman, *Literaturnaya Rossiya,* Jan. 1, 1964; by V. Bushin, *Literaturnaya Rossiya,* Jan. 10, 1964; and by V. Trufanova and Ravil Gazizov, *Literaturnaya Rossiya,* Jan. 31, 1964. These letters were translated in *Current Digest of the Soviet Press,* Vol. 16, Nos. 5–6.

times as many letters as they had the previous year.[239] In January, moreover, *Ivan Denisovich* received significant support, notably a piece of
enthusiastic advocacy in *Pravda* by Samuil Marshak, winner of the
prize in 1963.[240] At about this time, too, two of Solzhenitsyn's own
characters stepped forth from the pages of the book to support the
candidacy of their creator. The first was Boris Burkovsky, chief of the
naval museum on the cruiser Aurora, in Leningrad harbor. Importuned
by an enterprising correspondent of *Izvestia*, Burkovsky turned out to
be none other than Commander Buinovsky, the unreconciled naval
officer who, in Solzhenitsyn's story, was serving 25 years for receiving an
inscribed souvenir from a British admiral he had met in the line of
duty during the war.[241]

Burkovsky scored several points that were crucial to the controversy
— all the more so, since conservative critics had been suggesting that
he, Burkovsky-Buinovsky, as the one really "positive" character, ought
to have been the hero of the book instead of Ivan Denisovich Shukhov.
With an air of perfect innocence Burkovsky declared first that life in the
camps was "exactly the same" as Solzhenitsyn described it. This was
a pointed rebuttal of the conservative charge that camp life had not been
so bad after all. Secondly, Burkovsky made it clear that Solzhenitsyn,
the author, and Shukhov, the hero, were by no means one and the same.
By identifying author and hero, critics of the book had suggested that
Solzhenitsyn was endorsing what they called his hero's "passivity." Next,
Burkovsky went on, he couldn't remember who had been the prototype
of Ivan Denisovich "because there were many such people." This was
a direct refutation of the Alma-ata letter, which maintained that Ivan
had been an "exception," that most prisoners thought beyond the next
crust of bread. Burkovsky made it plain that they did nothing of the
kind. "Many," he declared, "fell out of the habit of speculating on the
future, probably because they didn't expect anything good. They
thought only of the next day — what kind of work there would be,
how to get some tobacco, how to mend torn mittens." Burkovsky
ended with the strongest pitch of all: the characters in the novel, like

---

[239] *Le Monde,* April 23, 1964, by Michel Tatu.
[240] *Pravda,* Jan. 30, 1964.
[241] "Greetings, Commander," by V. Pallon, *Izvestia,* Jan. 15, 1964. Publication
of this article does not mean, however, that *Izvestia* took a clear stand in favor
of the Solzhenitsyn candidacy. On Dec. 29, 1963, *Izvestia* ran a letter from a
reader named Viktor Ivanov, the ambiguous tone of which evidently reflected the
attitude of the editors. The letter refusd to accept Ivan Denisovich as the embodiment of a positive hero: "Thank you, A. Solzhenitsyn, for the artistic truth about
the past. But as for the comrade critics who strain to make Shukhov into a positive hero, spare us. We prefer the path of struggle for our ideals, for a communist society!"

the men in the camps, had in their hearts "never broken with the Party. They never identified the evil done to them with the Party, with our system. I and thousands like me were physically torn away from the Party and people, but our hearts and thoughts were still with both."

A few days later, still another character in the book came to life, this time at a meeting of Moscow writers called to debate the nominations.[242] The character in question was the unforgettable Tsezar Markovich, said in real life to be a charming and colorful poet by the name of Lev Kopelev. Kopelev took the floor to defend Solzhenitsyn once more against the charge that *Ivan Denisovich* ought to be denied the prize on grounds that it exalts a "Tolstoyan philosophy" of "passivity."

The meeting was notable, too, for the additional support it revealed for the Solzhenitsyn candidacy — letters were read from Kornei Chukovsky and Ilya Ehrenburg urging that the prize go to *Ivan Denisovich* — and for the emergence of at least two figures prominent in the literary debates of March–May 1957. Thus, one of the speakers for Solzhenitsyn was Veniamin Kaverin, who himself had been under heavy fire in 1957. And a principal foe was Dmitry Eremin, 1957 attacker of another famous novel, Vladimir Dudintsev's *Not by Bread Alone*.

Eremin, a Secretary of the Moscow writers' organization, repeated his attack on *One Day in the Life of Ivan Denisovich* at a combined meeting in late February of the Secretariats of the Moscow writers' organization and the Russian Republic Writers' Union.[243] He was joined by many standard-bearers of the conservative camp, including two, Boris Dyakov and a General A. Todorsky, who were apparently brought in to refute again the accuracy of Solzhenitsyn's portrayal of life in the prisons. At this meeting, as in a final, editorial comment in *Literaturnaya gazeta*,[244] criticism of Solzhenitsyn's work took the shape of a violent assault on a youthful literary critic and deputy editor of *Novy mir*, V. Lakshin, author of a remarkably strong and open defense of Solzhenitsyn at the beginning of the year.[245] Publication of Lakshin's article in *Novy mir* had, in fact, pointed up a remarkable feature of the debate over Solzhenitsyn: abandonment by the liberals, or at least by those around Tvardovsky, of the restraint that had characterized their strategy

[242] "Exactingness: Moscow Writers Discuss Works Put Forward for Lenin Prize," *Literaturnaya gazeta*, Feb. 8, 1964.

[243] "Responsibility!" *Literaturnaya Rossiya*, March 6, 1964, pp. 2–3, 10.

[244] "Editor's Diary: The General Work of Criticism," *Literaturnaya gazeta*, Feb. 20, 1964. Here, as in its editorial statements throughout the controversy, *Literaturnaya gazeta* neglected to mention that its chief, Alexander Chakovsky, was himself a candidate for the Lenin Prize.

[245] "Ivan Denisovich, His Friends and Foes," by V. Lakshin, *Novy mir*, No. 1 (Jan.), 1964, pp. 223–245.

in the past few years and appeared to be an appreciable factor in their pre-Manezh successes. The principal reason, no doubt, was dedication to literary quality of a kind that had not been seen in Russia in many a long year. And anger felt not in literary circles alone but by very many ordinary Russians for whom reading Solzhenitsyn's novel had been an experience of rage relived and remembered. Finally, perhaps Tvardovsky — who is endowed with a superb sense of timing and whose own anti-Stalin poem had so recently been sanctioned by Khrushchev — suspected that with the Sino-Soviet polemic in a virulent new stage, Khrushchev might at the last moment find it opportune to award the prize to Solzhenitsyn, win or lose. Tvardovsky may have concluded, by waging a fight the liberals might recover some of their losses since the Manezh. By the violence of their reaction the conservatives showed that they are alert, as always, to the threat posed to them by work of genuine literary quality on the one hand, and by the promise of deeper de-Stalinization of Soviet life on the other.

Whatever the cause — had there been an order from above to halt a debate that had become too heated, pending a decision by the Party? — the argument over Solzhenitsyn simmered down in March. Then, in April, came an editorial intervention in *Pravda* indicating that a decision had been taken at a high level of the Party against making the award to Solzhenitsyn.[246] The reasons given by the editors were the story's lack of militant spirit, its "kind-hearted, compassionate, leveling humanism" and the fact that by failing to observe the "best traditions of the Russian literary language," the author had forgotten "his highly important role in educating aesthetic taste." *Pravda* even went so far as to make a veiled criticism of Tvardovsky for suggesting that Solzhenitsyn's story become the "measuring stick" by which Soviet literature should be judged.

After this, announcement of the award on April 22 as something of an anticlimax. The choice, *Tronka,* a tale of life on the Ukraine steppes by Oles Gonchar, was no doubt designed as a tribute to the non-Russian nationalities in Soviet literature and to the now favored theme of heroism, to which much of Gonchar's earlier work is devoted. It was a tribute, above all, to the theme of harmony between the older and younger generations. Overshadowing the award itself, however, was denial of the prize to anyone extreme or controversial: above all, of course, to Solzhenitsyn: but also to the liberal Daniil Granin; the extreme conservative Galina Serebryakova; to Isayev and Pervomaisky, the two candidates put forward by *Oktyabr*; and last but not least, to

[246] "From the Editor's Mail: Lofty Exactingness," *Pravda,* April 11, 1964.

Alexander Chakovsky, whose newspaper had taken so strong a stand in the debate. Behind the scenes, it may well be the liberals were assured that Solzhenitsyn would not be cheated of his Lenin Prize: that he would receive it not next year, perhaps, but in a few years' time; not for *Ivan Denisovich,* perhaps, but for some subsequent story or for the entire body of his work.[247]

It is unlikely that the rough edges of controversy can be smoothed over for long. For the issues that rose to the surface during the debate are issues that divide liberals from conservatives in every sphere of politics and art. There is the question, how bad was the Stalin era, with the more extreme conservatives being compelled to uphold not merely art but virtually to defend life itself as it was lived in the Stalin years. And another question: What should be the role of art? Should it depict life as it truthfully is, or should it aim above all to uplift and educate? It was odd, in a country so haunted by its classics, to see Solzhenitsyn accused of being at once too Tolstoyan and too Dostoyevskian; told that Ivan Denisovich and Matryona are two sides of a single character, Platon Karatayev and Sonya Marmeladova, alike a celebration of "holy" passivity. At one level the question was: Should literature dedicate itself to the "positive" hero who will show man how he ought to live, or should art be democratized, should it describe "little," broken men as well as big, not merely leaders but the led? To those Soviet liberals who felt, and felt fervently, that *One Day in the Life of Ivan Denisovich* was an invaluable contribution to the Russian, and Soviet, tradition of realist art, denial of the prize to Solzhenitsyn must have signified that, indeed, a prophet is not without honor, except in his own country.

Why, since it was he who had authorized publication of the book in the first place, did Khrushchev not step in and command that the Lenin Prize go to *One Day in the Life of Ivan Denisovich?* Possibly at some moment between January and April he dallied with the idea of doing precisely that. In the end he did not or could not because the symbolic significance of such an award would have been virtually as great as the original appearance of the book in the autumn of 1962. It would be

[247] In the account of the meeting of Moscow writers reported in *Literaturnaya gazeta,* Feb. 8, 1964, the following passage appears:

"Much was said in the course of discussion about the manner of awarding Lenin Prizes. D. Eremin noted that in making the awards for literature and art it might be better to establish a different time period, not an annual one, so as more fully to determine the value of a work of art. It is essential to let a work 'settle' in the consciousness of readers so that a work honored by the people's highest award should be truly a milestone on the creative path of Soviet art. And another consideration: if the statute decrees that an artist may receive the Lenin Prize only once in a lifetime, then it would be better to award it not for a single work, but for his work as a whole."

taken to mean that a sweeping new round of de-Stalinization had now been ordained from above. The spring of 1964, with the Sino-Soviet quarrel flaring out into the open, was no time to send out a signal so disruptive of Soviet domestic tranquility. What does seem likely, however, is that a final decision to withhold the prize from Solzhenitsyn was taken only in early April, at a very high level indeed.

Who Publishes Whom?

During the long months of the Solzhenitsyn controversy, how were other writers and artists faring, especially those who came in for heaviest criticism during the winter of 1962–1963? Those who were symbolic targets, it appears, all have now returned, symbolically at least, to print. The same is true of the sculptor Ernst Neizvestny, object of numerous anxious inquiries by Western visitors during the summer of 1963. After Madam Furtseva had assured a group of foreign film directors in July that no Soviet intellectual, no matter how much he might have been criticized, would be subject to administrative or financial sanctions, Neizvestny, who had been expelled from the Union of Artists and thereby cut off from orders, was officially commissioned to do a series of bas reliefs for the Pioneer Palace[248] and statues for the Ministry of Culture.[249] In addition, the artists whose work had been criticized by Khrushchev at the Manezh and then impounded under lock and key were miraculously given their statues and their canvasses back nearly a year later.[250] Indeed, the law of the Party appeared to be that if a writer or painter had been severely enough attacked, then he was to be enabled to make a "comeback." By an ironic corollary, some who were younger or less renowned and hence spared at the height of the drive,[251] have had a comparatively difficult time since. Not being at once protected and treacherously exposed in the mantle of fame, it has been of less symbolic urgency that they be restored to grace.

The signal, apparently, was publication of Tvardovsky's "Tyorkin in the Other World" in August of 1963. From that moment on, the more prominent of the errant poets had only to give the Party some pretext for claiming that its "criticism had not been without effect" [252] to be rushed into print. The first, not surprisingly, was Yevtushenko, with a clutch of

[248] *New Statesman,* Aug. 16, 1963, by Ralph Parker.

[249] *The New York Times,* Nov. 29, 1963. The statues were of the scientists Lev Landau, Mystislav Keldysh, and Mikhail Lavrentyev.

[250] *Christian Science Monitor,* March 10, 1964, by Paul Wohl.

[251] For the surprising case of Viktor Sosnora, see account of Leningrad plenum, *Pravda,* July 5, 1963, and "The Party and the Writers" by David Burg, *Grany,* No. 54, 1963, p. 125.

[252] "Editor's Diary," *Literaturnaya gazeta,* Nov. 30, 1963.

verses in *Yunost* in September. His performance in "Again at Stantsiya Zima," the longest and most subjective of these poems, failed to reveal "an humble and a contrite heart," as the Party no doubt was hoping. It did, however, display a perfectly poised ambiguity: renunciation of his "Die Zeit" one-worldism balanced against almost pacifist repetition of the peace theme; restatement of a neo-Leninist "all men are equal" and a passage aimed against China; braggadocio self-assertiveness matched against a breastbeating renunciation of the egotism for which critics so often had blamed him, especially since the autobiography.

The symbolic meaning of Voznesensky's return to print was equally great, for here was a poet who had tangled face to face on March 8 with Khrushchev. Voznesensky's "Post with Verses" appeared in *Znamya* in November with an introductory note by the author: "It is idiotic to be occupied with formalism, with ornamentation. Poetry, like modern architecture, should be all transparent, full of light and depth." The poems within, however, were as full of formal innovation as ever, as irreverent, as filled with images incongruously juxtaposed. "Longjumeau," a section dedicated with deceptive iconolatry to a Party school founded by Lenin, was published by *Pravda*[253] and pounced upon by critics as a token that Voznesensky had benefited by a poetic sea-change. Others, however, quickly woke up to the fact that "in places, an artificiality of form is still noticeable." [254]

If Voznesensky, who had suffered a spell of depression after the Party attacks, had impishly turned the tables, Bella Akhmadulina went further still. Exhorted by the critics to turn from private to public themes, she now addressed herself to the idea of harmony of generations that was being urged upon young writers as a vehicle of rehabilitation. "My Family Tree," [255] the long poem that resulted, is a tour de force of irreverence. In another poem, "Rain," which appeared by some miracle in a Georgian literary journal,[256] she heaped contempt on the political "Boss" who tries to tell poets how to write.[257] Here, Akhmadulina's scorn is matched only by her virtuosity.

[253] *Pravda,* Oct. 13, 1963.
[254] "The Poet Turns to Lenin," by V. Grigoryev, *Komsomolskaya pravda,* Dec. 7, 1963.
[255] *Yunost,* No. 1, 1964.
[256] *Literaturnaya gruzia,* No. 12, 1963.
[257] *Zarya vostoka,* Feb. 2, 1964, contains the following passage from a speech by D. G. Sturua, a Secretary of the Georgian Communist Party:

"The journal *Literaturnaya gruzia,* No. 12, 1963, published a fragment of Bella Akhmadulina's poem 'Rain.' While we must welcome the editors' effort to acquaint the readers of our republic with examples of Russian Soviet poetry, it is essential to know how to select the best in both an ideological and artistic sense. Resorting to allegory in this fragment, the author patently belittles the significance of the meetings between leaders of the Party and government and figures of litera-

Indeed, of the poets who had been criticized, the only one who appears to have consented to write "to the Party's order" is Robert Rozhdestvensky, who obediently sat down to the unity of generations theme and, after a visit to the United States in November 1963, to a rather crude anti-American cycle.[258] Since Rozhdestvensky had suffered only pale criticism, his "comeback" had a rather contrived quality, as if he had worked hard simply to stay in the same spot.

At the opposite end of the spectrum is Bulat Okudzhava, who never recanted, has been published only once,[259] is no longer permitted to perform publicly with his guitar, and is said to be suffering financially. There is Alexander Yashin, who was personally hard hit when Khrushchev criticized him behind the scenes, but who replied only by silence and continued to be published, largely, it appears, through the efforts of well-placed friends. There is Viktor Nekrasov who, according to a Ukraine Party Secretary, "continues to defend his ideological errors," [260] whose expulsion from the Party is said to be still under consideration,[261] but who appeared once in *Novy mir*[262] and is scheduled to appear again in 1964. There is Vasily Axyonov who, despite his recantation, has so far written nothing "to order" for the Party, and Yulian Semyonov, who answered an attack in *Izvestia*[263] with a blistering counterattack.[264] There are, finally, such writers as Vladimir Tendryakov, Yury Nagibin, Vladimir Voinovich, Yury Kazakov, Anatoly Gladilin, Viktor Konetsky, and Viktor Sosnora, Shchipachov, Paustovsky, and Ehrenburg, who confronted criticism by silence and, in some cases, by long sojourns away from the capital.

As for the policy of the Party, it is aimed first of all at routing the "star system": at breaking the ties between a handful of glamorous young poets — talented but unpredictable — and their once adoring public. Poetry readings go on as before, but they have lost a good deal of the old spontaneity. Poets of the second and third rank may recite, but rarely the heroes of yesteryear, Yevtushenko, Voznesensky, and Akhmadulina. Robert Rozhdestvensky is being offered instead, as a safer,

ture and art. Akhmadulina is grieved by the 'drought' which is said to have beset creative life. We would like to remind Comrade Mrevlishvili, editor of the journal, and the entire editorial board, of Mayakovsky's wonderful dictum about how 'we must answer non-Party sorrow with Party alarm.' "

[258] *Yunost*, No. 10 (Oct.), 1963; *Pravda*, Dec. 25, 1963, and Jan. 12, 1964; and *Komsomolskaya pravda*, Feb. 8, 1964.

[259] *Yunost*, No. 2 (Feb.), 1964.

[260] Speech by Yury Zbanatsky, *Radyanska Ukraina*, July 6, 1963.

[261] *Christian Science Monitor*, March 10, 1964, by Paul Wohl.

[262] *Novy mir*, No. 11 (Nov.), 1963.

[263] "I Go to the Movies," by L. Ivanova, *Izvestia*, Feb. 19, 1964.

[264] *Izvestia*, Feb. 26, 1964.

easier-to-control substitute — Rozhdestvensky, who self-consciously apes Mayakovsky and tosses out eagerly snapped-up tidbits of news to the crowds about the once ubiquitous Yevtushenko. Rozhdestvensky, indeed, to borrow a phrase from Boris Pasternak, is being "propagated like potatoes in the reign of Catherine the Great." To keep temperamental new idols from arising, the Party is following a policy of limited concessions: encouraging the critics, for example, to promote a pleiad of gifted but hitherto somewhat overlooked writers, of whom several belong to the so-called wartime generation now in its late '30's and '40's and some to the category of liberals. Such writers include Boris Slutsky, Alexander Mezhirov, David Samoilov, Mikhail Lukonin, Vladimir Sokolov, and, above all, Yevgeny Vinokurov and Vladimir Soloukhin.[265]

As for Yevtushenko, Party officials seem moved by two emotions, contempt that he recanted as far as he did, and outrage that one whom they trusted to serve as lightning rod for the volatile emotions of the young betrayed them by publishing his autobiography abroad. Hence their policy has been harsh — a news blackout coupled with occasional vilification[266] — yet not so harsh as to make him a martyr. He has been published occasionally and, very occasionally, has recited his verses in Moscow.[267] His poems were turned down, however, for the 1963 almanac *Poetry Day*.[268] Currently he is at work on a long poem on a strictly Party theme, the responsibility of the younger generation to the builders of the Bratsk dam. One may guess that he will continue to be under great pressure to write as the Party wishes or not be published at all.

Nor does a vindictive attitude toward Yevtushenko and an effort to keep new Yevtushenkos — and Okudzhavas — from arising exhaust the Party's stock of resources. It tries to anticipate tactical breakthroughs by the liberals so as to keep them from acquiring new strongholds. Thus, the editorial board of *Poetry Day* has been overhauled from top to bottom with the chief editor, Mikhail Lukonin, replaced by the conservative Viktor Poltoratsky.[269] And the Party has greatly extended its use of "social criticism," usually in the form of signed letters to an errant writer from a group of readers urging him to get back in line.[270]

---

[265] See articles by Sergei Narovchatov, *Izvestia*, Dec. 5, 1963, and Vladimir Yermilov, *Literaturnaya gazeta*, Dec. 17, 1963.

[266] Letter of Tatyana Tess in *Izvestia*, Oct. 17, 1963.

[267] *Yunost*, No. 9, 1963; Moskva, No. 2, 1964; *Literaturnaya gazeta*, March 3, 1964.

[268] *Daily Worker* (London), Dec. 23, 1963.

[269] *Literaturnaya gazeta*, March 5, 1964.

[270] The first example was a letter from a group of Komsomol members to young writers at the beginning of the campaign (*Komsomolskaya pravda*, Dec. 21, 1962); next, from the citizens of Vologda Province to Alexander Yashin (*Komsomolskaya pravda*, Jan. 31, 1963); the series addressed to Yevtushenko

Finally, despite Furtseva's assurances, financial pressures are a reality for many, although not in a blatant way. Some liberal poets are cut off from the fifteen rubles each poetry reading used to bring them, others, being published less, from book royalties and fees from journals and newspapers. The same is true of a number of liberal critics. Hence, tried and true methods of mutual succor are resorted to: "protection" of less secure writers by the more secure; translation of work in foreign or Soviet minority languages into Russian; the writing of reviews or critical articles by liberals not under their own, semi-indexed names but under pseudonyms. Even these time-honored practices have only to be exposed to view for someone to attack them.[271]

Of all the balancing acts of recent months, perhaps the most intriguing has been that of the literary journals, torn as they are between uncertainty which way the Party will jump next and a desire to maintain circulation. None has been so cynically successful as *Yunost,* edited by Boris Polevoi. Under his management, *Yunost* no longer brings out work in depth by young and experimental authors. It has, however, made a point of publishing each of the writers who was most violently criticized by the Party at least once, except for Viktor Nekrasov. Thus, it has enabled the Party to deny that these writers were being discriminated against, and at the same time has exploited their names for circulation purposes. Capitalizing at once on the Party's trust and on the reputation the magazine acquired under its first editor, Valentin Katayev, Polevoi was able to boost the magazine's circulation as of January 1964 from 650,000 to one million.

Oktyabr, too, has pursued a rather surprising policy of reinsurance for several years now, apparently on the premise that to keep up its political influence it cannot afford to fall behind *Novy mir* in circulation. Thus, in recent months it has published, besides Pervomaisky, Vladimir Maximov, Pavel Antokolsky, and Svetlana Kuznetsova, as well as work by the ex-liberals Pankratov and Kharabarov. More recently it printed a de-Stalinization novel, Nikolai Sizov's *The Difficult Years,* which shows Malenkov preparing a purge of the countryside in the early '50's with Khrushchev above all as its main target and Beria whispering sinister advice into the ear of Stalin, but which ultimately bolsters the con-

(*Komsomolskaya pravda,* March 30, April 7, and May 23, 1963); from a group of farm workers near Leningrad to Fyodor Abramov (*Izvestia,* July 2, 1963); to Konstantin Simonov (Izvestia, Oct. 25, 1963); from a group of Leningrad workers to writers (*Pravda,* Jan. 10, 1964).

[271] The following remark by Nikolai Gribachov may be aimed at cutting off translation as a form of mutual help: "Translation, which is important to the state, must be put on a state scale so as to eliminate the personal handicraft principle: 'I'll translate you, you translate me, and we'll be in contact with each other'" (*Literaturnaya gazeta,* March 3, 1964).

servative claim that all through the Stalin years there were good people, ready to do battle for the right even at the price of their lives.

As for *Novy mir,* it continues to concentrate on social criticism, above all on work that patiently probes the Stalin theme, first from one angle, then from another. It is notable, too, that with Alexander Tvardovsky as editor, the journal never missed a chance to link Khrushchev with this theme and frequently thanked him in public for making it possible at last "to tell the truth" about the Stalin era. As for *Moskva, Voprosy literatury,* and *Molodaya gvardiya,* a conservative name on the masthead appears occasionally to provide protective coloration that enables the journals to print good poetry, prose, or criticism. A remarkable case is that of *Molodaya gvardiya,* which was thoroughly reorganized in early 1963 after the scandalous publication of "White Flag." Today, *Molodaya gvardiya* is publishing a monthly column by Vladimir Turbin, whose book, *Comrade Time and Comrade Art,* was one of the high-water marks of liberal success in 1961–1962. Of all the publishing anomalies of Moscow, none evoked more mystification abroad than the appearance of Franz Kafka's *In the Penal Colony* and *The Metamorphosis* in *Inostrannaya literatura.*[272] Choice of the former story seemed particularly surprising, since it is a parable of dictatorship, portraying the difficulties of a comparatively mild ruler in dismantling the torture machine of an utterly ruthless predecessor. Like all such events, publication of Kafka has a history which explains much, if it does not explain quite all. This history goes back to 1956, when work by Kafka began to appear in Poland. Later, he had a vast impact on intellectuals in Hungary, Czechoslovakia, and Yugoslavia. In July 1962, at the World Peace Congress in Moscow, Jean-Paul Sartre brought the Kafka "question" into the open, deploring the fact that the "East's" refusal to publish or even read Kafka had made it all the easier for the West to use him as a weapon in the cold war.[273] Later that year, Viktor Nekrasov's memoirs appeared, including a passage describing his discomfiture and that of several other Soviet writers in 1956, when they had to admit to Alberto Moravia that not only had they not read Kafka, they had never even heard of him. Then, in May 1963, Professor Eduard Goldstücker of Charles University in Prague organized a conference in Liblice, Czechoslovakia, on how to fit Kafka into the framework of a socialist society. Ernst Fischer, a Communist writer and critic from Austria, hit home with the question: "Are you going to give Kafka an entry visa?" Fischer

---

[272] *Inostrannaya literatura,* No. 1 (Jan.), 1964.
[273] See "The Struggle for Kafka and Joyce," by Hans Mayer and François Bondy in *Encounter,* May 1964, and "Kafka's Nightmare Comes True," by George Bailey in *The Reporter* (New York), May 7, 1964.

and Roger Garaudy, a philosophy professor and leading member of the French Communist Party, helped matters further by attributing the condition of "alienation" which Kafka describes to modern industrial society, rather than to any political system. The Kafka question came up again at the East-West conclave on the novel in July 1963 at Leningrad, where two writers from Czechoslovakia, Jiri Hajek and Ladislav Mnachko, made strikingly effective interventions. Thus, when Kafka was published at last in Moscow, it appeared that Soviet officials had in part been embarrassed into it because *socialist,* and not bourgeois, writers had made an issue of his work, claiming that Kafka was, after all, the "realist" who foresaw fascism and pointing out the inconsistency of accepting Berthold Brecht, yet behaving as though Kafka had never existed.[274]

All this, however, fails to explain the choice of *In the Penal Colony,* or of *Inostrannaya literatura* as vehicle, since the editor, Boris Ryurikov, is surely the most unreconstructed of Soviet Stalinist bureaucrats! About the best guess is that the story can be fitted, after all, into the framework of de-Stalinization, and that the editors may have counted on an attention-getting story of this kind to help their journal rival *Novy mir* in popularity. One can rarely overrate the cynicism of Soviet editors or their unceasing quest for political reinsurance!

What of the Future?

Now that the tumult and shouting have died, what is the long-term impact of the drive of 1962–1963 on relations between the regime and the intellectuals likely to be? First of all, as we have seen, the offensive in the arts was anything but a carefully thought-out attempt to deal with the public opinion that has gradually come into being since the death of Stalin, or to deal with the possibility that a public conscience may develop that is independent of the conscience of the Party. Rather, the drive was closely bound up with such disputes within the Party as investment policy and its future policy toward China. Used in the end by Party reactionaries to bolster their positions on these issues, it appears originally to have been conceived by them as a weapon to defend personal positions that had been imperiled by de-Stalinization and to weaken the power of Khrushchev, who was publicly known as the architect of de-Stalinization.

[274] This explanation is based in part on the editorial note accompanying the stories, in Y. Knipovich's article in *Inostrannaya literatura,* No. 1 (Jan.), 1964, pp. 195–204, and on "Realism and the 'Algebra' of Schematism," by D. Zatonsky, *Literaturnaya gazeta,* Feb. 18, 1964.

Carried out clumsily, with enormous publicity, the drive provided invaluable advertising for the practitioners of abstract art and experimental rhyme. Hundreds of thousands of Soviet citizens who were innocent of these phenomena before are aware of them today. More important, perhaps, the drive must have spread the mood of opposition. For the writers and artists whom we call "liberal" have no political program, no common set of political or aesthetic ideas to unite them. They are united, instead, by the law that unites creative artists everywhere: by a common desire to have their work published, performed, exhibited. So long as men are not frozen by terror, the tighter the controls that are forced upon them from above, the larger the group that is united in this kind of "opposition."

Even more important than the spreading of opposition has been its hardening, a loss of illusions, a deeper drawing of the lines between the Party and the more perceptive of the people. For many men and women, Khrushchev's partial rehabilitation of Stalin on March 8, 1963, must have brought a crisis of the spirit, an awareness that de-Stalinization, for them a painful deeply felt commitment, was for Khrushchev at one instant an authentic outpouring of hate, at another a tactic to be used or shelved as the political exigencies of the moment might require. Coupled with this loss of illusions there must have been frustration on the part of many intellectuals at their continuing lack of access to Khrushchev: *they* could explain their positions to him only at ritual public meetings, whereas *conservative* writers and bureaucrats, being more trusted, appeared to have more or less continuing access to him in private. Greatly as the accessibility of Soviet leaders has increased since Stalin's day, the harsh limits that remain and the brutal phrases which Khrushchev directed toward creative intellectuals drove home a discomfiting lesson: the Party neither trusts nor respects the more independent and honest among them. Rather, it tries to make use of them for its political needs of the moment. So doing, the Party defies them to make use of it in return.

Moreover, its failure to unleash total terror upon them, plus the decline in public respect for those poets and artists who recanted during the spring of 1963 must have rammed home still another lesson: that it is possible to resist the demands of the Party with impunity, that to capitulate is not only unnecessary, but a political mistake as well, since it entails a loss of one's public following — one's only real source of strength vis-à-vis the Party. Already there is evidence that this lesson has not been lost. Twice at least since the peak of the drive writers and artists have flocked to append their names to petitions protesting arbitrary action by the police. The most recent instance was a petition protesting the arrest and exile to Siberia of 24-year-old Iosif Brodsky, an unpublished Leningrad poet whose gifts already are legend.[275]

Thus, we have a situation in which the Party, having set itself at odds with the intellectuals, having unburdened them of many of their illusions and taught them the value of resistance, now is bidding for their help in eliciting popular support for its new attitude of official hostility toward the leaders of Communist China.[276] This help the intellectuals can render without a twinge of conscience, since to most of them the quarrel with China spells better relations with the West, and better relations with the West mean an easing of internal controls. As a result of the 1962–1963 offensive, however, they may be more inclined than ever to exact the highest possible price for aiding the Party on any issue whatever.

Disillusioned as many of them became in the myth of Khrushchev's liberalism and the sincerity of his de-Stalinization; aware, as most of them were that he was truly a mental product of the Stalin era, perhaps some of them were less than fairly inclined to give his erratic and unpredictable personality its due. By one of the ironies of history, this personality, that seems so strangely to have resisted the conditioning of the Stalin years, that blew hot and cold and that honest men found to their chagrin they could never wholly count upon, probably did more for them than any of his policies could have done. For it loosed the genie of spontaneity on a land gone totally rigid.

Just where Party policy will lead now is anybody's guess. The question is a crucial one, especially in the realm of de-Stalinization. If the furor over *One Day in the Life of Ivan Denisovich,* over "Stalin's Heirs" and Ehrenburg's memoirs means anything, it would appear to be that de-Stalinization cannot for the moment go deeper, that more profound de-Stalinization will have to await a generation of leaders who have nothing to fear from confronting the facts about the past. It would appear to doom Russia for the time being to the lie and the half-lie, for admission of what everyone knows to be the truth — that among the leaders of the Party several, still, were accomplices in the crimes of Stalin — would be a devastating blow to the Party's authority. In domestic terms the Stalin issue is, and will continue to be, an enormously disruptive one, disruptive of the authority of the Party in the eyes of the people, and disruptive of the morale of the Party bureaucracy.

Yet in tactical terms the Party has need of the issue, greater need than before the dispute with the leaders of China blew into the open. It

---

[275] *The Guardian* (London), May 13, 1964, by Victor Zorza and *The New York Times Book Review,* June 21, 1964, by Patricia Blake.
[276] *The New York Times,* May 24, 1964.

needs the Stalin issue and its corollary, the issue of the "anti-Party group," as a stick with which to flay China abroad, and hidebound officials and secret sympathizers with China at home. Aware of the uses of de-Stalinization and aware likewise of its dangers, the Party leaders have shown a preference for raking over the same old coals on the fire of de-Stalinization, rather than adding any single large log.[277] Yet on this most volatile of issues it is difficult to display either perfect foresight or perfect control. Some event could well come along to confound them. The new leaders of the Party might again, for the sake of tactical advantage, authorize some act of de-Stalinization, such as the publication of *One Day in the Life of Ivan Denisovich,* whose impact exceeds their expectations. Thus, they may again be tugged farther and faster than they intend. The Party may again, as it has so often in the recent past, have to turn handsprings to deal with the unintended consequences of its own acts.

The situation confronting the Party leaders has, moreover, a new and perverse dimension: the break with Communist China. Conceivably this break could unbalance the inner equilibrium of the Soviet political mechanism, as already it has destroyed the cohesion of the Communist bloc. Here, the crucial element is not the existence of differences with the Chinese leaders — these differences have, after all, existed below the surface of Soviet politics for several years now — but the fact that at last they are out in the *open.* Throughout the post-Stalin era, one of the checks on the pace of change has been a curious overmatching of liberal forces by conservative. Essential to this overmatching, and to the Soviet political balance, has been the fact that the forces that wanted change or resisted authority could always be branded, and frequently were, as

[277] Among the de-Stalinizing moves made during the winter of 1963–1964 were: the rehabilitations of Nikolai Krestinsky (*Izvestia,* Oct. 27, 1963) and Alexander Kosarev (*Pravda* and *Izvestia,* Nov. 14, 1963); observance of the 60th birthday of Nikolai Voznesensky (*Pravda* and *Izvestia,* Dec. 1, 1963); rehabilitation of Pavel Dybenko (*Pravda,* Feb. 17, and *Izvestia,* Feb. 18, 1964); revelation by L. Shaumyan that as early as the 17th Party Congress of 1934, delegates considered removing Stalin from his post as General Secretary of the Party (*Pravda,* Feb. 7, 1964); portrayal of Zinoviev alongside Lenin in the film version of Emmanuil Kazakevich's "Blue Notebook" (*The New York Times,* Feb. 14, 1964); revelation that a book by Konstantin Paustovsky on Marshal Bluecher had been suppressed on the eve of the purge of the generals (*Literaturnaya gazeta,* Feb. 22, 1964); the large amount of publicity that attended the film premieres of Yury Bonderev's *Quietude* and Konstantin Simonov's *The Living and Dead* in January and February; publication of two articles on the economy by A. Arzumanyan (*Pravda,* Feb. 24–25, 1964); speech by N. S. Khrushchev (*Pravda,* March 7, 1964); publications of a section of Nikolai Sizov's novel, *The Difficult Years,* in *Nedelia,* No. 8 (Feb. 16–22, 1964), and of the entire novel in *Oktyabr.* Nos. 3–4 (March–April 1964); publication of the memoirs of Gen. A. V. Gorbatov, *Novy mir,* Nos. 3–5 (March–May 1964).

traitors, as "hirelings of the Western imperialists." Now at last the liberal forces have a weapon of equal value. For the first time, they, too, can call their opponents traitors, lackeys of China's "Trotskyite warmongers." Contingent on any future political accommodation with the United States this weapon could come, with unstabilizing speed, to outweigh that of the conservatives. Aware that a new element has been added to the inner dynamics of the Soviet political scene, the Party leaders themselves may be in a mood for testing, for cautious tinkering rather than for bold new moves.

Another factor making for caution as a result of the dispute with China is the Party's heightened reliance on its ideologists to give its actions against China an aura of Leninist legitimacy. For it is the full-time ideologists who are the most conservative element in the Soviet Union today, the most suspicious of the challenge posed by the creative intellect to the authority of the Party, the most threatened by de-Staliniza-tion. It is they whose role was crucial in unleashing the offensive in the arts. As far as the anti-Stalin campaign goes, and with it, any effort to cleanse Soviet life from within, the Party may be more like a convoy than ever, forced to move at the pace of its slowest ship. That ship is the ideological bureaucracy.

In spite of all these elements that militate toward caution, the forces of change within the Soviet Union today are very great indeed. For the leaders, it will be a greater and greater challenge to keep the reins, to maintain the exquisite equilibrium of control. Since the Party's drive in the arts seems to have made relations between it and the intellectuals more and more of a standoff, how far does it seem likely that the intellectuals would go in exploiting any opening, either now or years hence, under the impact of some future crisis of succession, in which the Party seemed in danger of losing control over the population? How hard a bargain are they prepared to drive now, when the regime has need of their support? The answer is not a dramatic one. Just as many writers and artists were blackmailed in the past, prior to the events of 1962–1963, by the myth of Khrushchev's liberalism, so today they are haunted by the specter of the repression that could come were the Party to lose control. Disappointed as they were in Khrushchev, they were fearful of a new crisis of succession, and of what a successor to Khrushchev might bring. Tormented still by the memory of Stalin, the more constructive among them apparently prefer to abide with the "evil" they know than "fly to others that they know not of." In spite of all their disappointments, they seem more likely to cooperate with the regime, to abide by its rules and work within those rules for change, than to attempt bold new moves that could threaten the edifice of Party control.

Since, however, a desire to lead more open and truthful lives, to have done with the lies of the Stalin era and the half-lies of the Khrushchev era, is a law of the Soviet artistic conscience, as it would be of the artistic conscience anywhere, it is likely that the writers and artists of Russia will keep pressing for more and more truth about the past, for more thoroughgoing and consistent de-Stalinization. In the Soviet split with China, they have now been presented with their biggest opening since Khrushchev's attack on Stalin in 1956 — with what may in fact be their biggest opening in the entire post-Stalin period.

As for the repression in the arts of 1962–1963, it bids fair, like the crackdowns that preceded it in the 1950's, to pave the way to future, more climactic encounters between the regime and the intellectuals. Unless control itself comes to be interpreted in a radically new light — unless the forces that are coming into being are given a far greater role than in the past in determining what Soviet society is to be — the events of 1962–1963 may well be remembered by history as merely another, noisy stage in the erosion of Party control over the minds of the Soviet people.

Documents

1

STALIN'S HEIRS

YEVGENY YEVTUSHENKO

Mute was the marble.
                    Mutely glimmered the glass.
Mute stood the sentries,
                    bronzed by the breeze.
Thin wisps of smoke curled over the coffin.
                    And breath seeped through the chinks
as they bore him out the mausoleum doors.
Slowly the coffin floated,
                    grazing the fixed bayonets.
He also was mute —
                    he also! —
                              mute and dread.
Grimly clenching
                    his embalmed fists,
just pretending to be dead,
                    he watched from inside.
He wished to fix in his memory
                    each pallbearer:
young recruits from Ryazan and Kursk,
so that he might later on
                    gather enough strength for a sortie,
rise from the grave,
                    and reach out to these unreflecting youths.
He was scheming.
                    Had merely dozed off.
And I, appealing to our government, petition them
to double,
          and treble,
                    the sentries guarding this slab,
and stop Stalin from ever rising again
                    and, with Stalin,
                                      the past.

I refer not to the past, so holy and glorious,
of Turksib,
             and Magnitka,
                          and the flag raised over Berlin.
By the past, in this case,
                     I mean the neglect
of the people's good,
                false charges,
                             the jailing of innocent men.
We sowed our crops honestly.
Honestly we smelted metal,
and honestly we marched,
                      joining the ranks.
But he feared us.
                Believing in the great goal,
he judged all means justified
                         to that great end.
He was far-sighted.
                 Adept in the art of political warfare,
he left many heirs
                behind on this globe.
I fancy
       there's a telephone in that coffin:
Stalin instructs
              Enver Hoxha.
From that coffin where else does the cable go!
No, Stalin has not given up.
                        He thinks he can
                                      outsmart death.
We carried him from the mausoleum.
But how carry Stalin's heirs
                         away from Stalin!
Some of his retired heirs tend roses,
thinking in secret
                their enforced leisure will not last.
Others,
       from platforms, even heap abuse on Stalin
but,
    at night,
            yearn for the good old days.
No wonder Stalin's heirs seem to suffer
these days from heart trouble.
                          They, the former henchmen,
hate this era
            of emptied prison camps

and auditoriums full of people listening
                                        to poets.
The Party discourages me
                            from being smug.
"Why care?"
                some say, but I can't remain inactive.
While Stalin's heirs walk this earth,
Stalin,
        I fancy, still lurks in the mausoleum.

Translated by George Reavey
Copyright by George Reavey
1963, 1964

2

A FILM DIRECTOR SPEAKS OUT

Yevtushenko's poem, "Stalin's Heirs," and Solzhenitsyn's short novel, One Day in the Life of Ivan Denisovich, *were high points of the literary ferment following the 22nd Congress of the Soviet Communist Party in October 1961. Several utterances by writers and artists that were not published, however, were even more explicit in condemning the past under Stalin. A speech given at a meeting of film and theatrical workers in the fall of 1962 by the film director Mikhail Romm is an example.*

TRADITIONS AND INNOVATIONS. A speech *by* Mikhail Romm.

The subject of the report "Traditions and Innovations" offers an occasion to talk about such serious things. The Voronezh theater director, Comrade Dobrotin, spoke before me very well and with much passion. He vehemently protested against the remnants of Stalinism in the field of consciousness.

He told us the story of those leaders in a province who — after a drunken party — started a fire on the terrace of a sanitarium and imposed disciplinary measures against the person responsible for cultural affairs at the sanitarium because he tried to protest. This is a significant example!

At the same time, however, Comrade Dobrotin advised that Comrade Leonov[1] should be called before the CC [Central Committee] and told

---

[1] Leonid Leonov, with Sholokhov the premier novelist of the U.S.S.R. Born 1899, author of numerous novels, stories, and plays. His best work was perhaps done in the 1920's.

to write a comedy. And if Comrade Leonov has other wishes? If at the moment he doesn't feel like working for the theater? In accordance with Dobrotin, if the Party's CC asks it, Leonov will start writing, obediently, and turn out a good comedy. Are there no other means? You don't seem to understand, Comrade Dobrotin, that this way of thinking also stems from the old methods, that it resembles a bit starting a fire on a terrace. [Applause.]

During your speech you let yourself go about the modern ballet. You expressed regret that on New Year's Eve your actor Popov did a Western dance. I have never danced in my life; simply because I can't dance, be it the waltz, the mazurka or the *pas de patineur*. But it seems to me that in a small hall it is preferable to do a Western dance rather than the mazurka because for that the hall would be too small.

For many years we tried to invent a real Soviet dance. Finally it was invented. It is called the "Promenade" and requires a lot of room. On putting it on television, the explanations concerning certain steps of this dance took four sessions, but no spectator understood all its finesse. On the other hand Popov learned how to do this dance at once. Evidently it was a simple dance. I should like to know if, performing this on New Year's Eve, Popov did much harm and what the harm was exactly.

Comrade Dobrotin also let himself go on singers without voices. For myself, contrary to him, I like singers without voices. I prefer Bernes and, in general, those who talk instead of sing, their mouths wide open, emitting trills. Of course, the aria *Perdona, Celeste Creatura* must be sung by a well-trained voice. On the other hand the song *The Little Girl Goes toward the Fields* needs other qualities. In the field of art, I like everything that is expressive. [Applause.]

In our country, however, certain methods were imposed against which it is necessary to fight. I'm ready to fight against my own shortcomings still remaining from the past.[2] Precisely because of that, before we take up traditions and innovations I should like to clarify the problem of certain traditions which were imposed in our country. There are good ones and there are very bad ones: for example, the one of playing the Overture of Tchaikovsky's *Symphony 1812* twice a year.

Comrades, as I understand it, this Overture expresses a very clear political idea — the idea of the triumph of orthodox religion and autocracy over revolution. It's a bad piece of music written by Tchaikovsky on command. It's a thing Peter Ilyich was himself ashamed of at the end of his life. I'm not a specialist in the history of music, but I am convinced that this Overture was composed for transitory reasons, with the very clear aim of pleasing the church and the monarchy.

Why should the Soviet power humiliate the *Marseillaise,* the marvelous

---

[2] Here Romm seems to be referring to the fact that he was a dutiful and well-rewarded director during the 30's and 40's, producing some of the most effective adulatory films for Stalin.

hymn of the French Revolution, by drowning it out with the noise of church bells? Why should it celebrate the triumph of Czarist ideology, the ideology of the "Black Hundreds"?

Stalinism Still Pervades Art World

But to play this Overture has become a tradition. After the October Revolution, this Overture was played the first time during those years when the expression "cosmopolite without a fatherland" was invented to replace that other expression "dirty Jew."

Among other things, and in certain instances, the latter expression was even printed. On the cover of the [satirical] magazine *Crocodile* a cartoon appeared during those years presenting a "cosmopolite without a fatherland" of clearly Jewish type, holding a book in his hands on which one could read in big characters the word "GID." Not "André Gide" but simply "Gid." [3]

Neither the cartoonist nor any of those responsible for this scoundrel's joke has been condemned by us. We have preferred to keep quiet, to forget all this, as one could forget that dozens of our best theater and movie people were declared "cosmopolites without a fatherland": for instance, comrades Yutkevich,[4] Leonid Trauberg,[5] Sutyrin,[6] Kovarsky,[7] Bleiman,[8] and others present here. They have been authorized to work again, some in the Party, some in their particular union. But is it really possible to heal the wounds, to forget what one has suffered for many years, when you were trampled on and covered with mud? [9]

[3] In Russian the words "Gide" — and *"Zhid,"* dirty Jew, are pronounced exactly alike.

[4] Sergei Yutkevich, born 1904, originally a painter, became one of a group of experimental artistic designers and directors of films in the 1920's. Until the late 1940's, he had achieved enormous success with a long series of films. A 1947 movie, *Light Over Russia*, was banned because of "serious errors." By 1949, when the cultural purge presided over by Andrei A. Zhdanov was in full swing, he was under attack and his career threatened because he had contributed favorable articles to volumes in honor of D. W. Griffith and Charlie Chaplin.

[5] Born 1902, another of that galaxy of silent screen experimenters of the 1920's and an established director in subsequent decades. Like Romm, Yutkevich, and all the others to be mentioned below — except for Kalatozov — he is a Jew, and came under vicious attack in the late 40's for, among other things, "spreading and elaborating the false and un-Soviet myth that the American film director D. W. Griffith was the father of world film art."

[6] Vladimir A. Sutyrin, born 1902, a distinguished film critic and theoretician of the cinema.

[7] Nikolai Kovarsky. Also a distinguished film critic.

[8] Mikhail Bleiman. Born 1904. Highly successful screen writer until the late 40's.

[9] All the above were attacked at that time as a "group of aestheticizing cosmopolitans in the film industry, . . . miserable tramps of humanity, . . . homeless and nameless cosmopolitans of the cinema . . . base spokesmen of reactionary aestheticism . . . who conducted an organized slander campaign against its [the Soviet film's] lofty ideology, its truthfulness and its patriotic content."

And those who directed this shameful campaign with joy and pleasure, who racked their brains to invent other things and to drag other people into the mire, have they been made to pay for what they did? People don't even reproach them, holding that this would show lack of tact!

The magazine *Oktyabr*,[10] edited by Kochetov,[11] has recently become interested in motion pictures. From January to November it published articles smearing all the progress achieved by Soviet films, expressing suspicion toward the critics of the great artists of the older generation and even the new one. These articles were inspired by the same persons who led the campaign of denunciation of "cosmopolites without a fatherland." It seems to me, however, that we should not forget all that happened.

Today many writers are starting to do scripts for the theater or motion pictures denouncing the Stalinist epoch and the cult of the personality. This is because it has become possible and necessary, while three or four years ago it was still thought that Nikita Sergeyevich's speech at the 20th Congress was sufficient. A more or less leading official told me this clearly: "Listen, the Party has shown infinite courage. Study Comrade Khrushchev's speech, and that's enough. Why stick your nose into this business?"

Today it has become definitely clear that it was not sufficient, that it is necessary for us to think for ourselves, to speak and write for ourselves.

It is very important to unmask Stalin and Stalinism, but the heritage left by Stalinism is not less important. And it is not less important to look around at what surrounds us and to formulate a judgment on events that occur in the social life of art.

Our meetings are conducted in a calm, tranquil, academic tone. In the meantime a very energetic group of rather bad writers hits out viciously in the magazine *Oktyabr* against the new literature and nobody answers them in this arena. On the other hand, the very moment Yevtushenko published his poem "Babi Yar," this group printed a reply in the journal *Literatura i Zhizn*.[12]

Not long ago I happened to be in Italy and America, and I should like to say that what was considered to be a scandal in the West was not Yevtushenko's poem, but the response to it. The local journalists asked me, "What do you think of the new wave of anti-Semitism in the U.S.S.R.?"

I asked with perplexity what they were talking about. They mentioned Starikov's article[13] and Markov's poem.[14]

---

[10] A major literary monthly, the stronghold of the literary Stalinists.

[11] Vsevolod Kochetov. Born 1911.

[12] Now defunct organ of the Writers' Union of the Russian Republic, a consistent Stalinist paper.

[13] Dmitry Starikov, a well-known Soviet literary critic, who, on September 27, 1962, eight days after the publication of "Babi Yar," published a violent attack on Yevtushenko. He accused him of provocation and of a "monstrous" insult to the Soviet people, and of nurturing chauvinism and fanning the "dying flames of nationalist attitudes."

[14] Alexei Markov, author of a poem which attacked Yevtushenko for defiling the Russian people with "pygmy's spittle."

That issue of journal *Literatura i Zhizn* was shameful, as are the latest issues of the magazine *Oktyabr*.

Oktyabr Attacks Romm

Since the articles in *Oktyabr* are aimed at me, it is difficult and embarrassing for me to reply. Difficult but necessary.

The attacks against films carried in *Oktyabr* began in the January issue with an article on the picture *Peace to Him Who Enters,* an article written in an absolutely inadmissible tone of political denunciation. The only error in calculation made by the editorial board was that they failed to name anyone specifically in their denunciation. Ten years ago, after such an article somebody would be put in chains, forbidden to work, sent to faraway regions. But it is a fact that times have changed and that this denunciation probably wasn't even read. But the denunciation remains!

Then came the attack on the films *The Unmailed Letter, If This Is Love,* and *Nine Days in a Year.*[15] The themes of the accusations were not new. For *Nine Days* the hero wasn't "positive." The same thing applied to *The Cranes Are Flying.* In *The Unmailed Letter* a decadent pessimism is to be found. Reisman's[16] heroes show moral deficiencies and amorality is decadent.

In the past, one was severely punished for such shortcomings. Today denunciations like these haven't had any consequences, simply because the authorities in charge don't read them or don't even exist any more. That is why neither Kalatozov[17] nor Reisman nor myself were hunted out of the movies, and the magazine became very angry. In the first and second issues of that magazine some terrible articles were published, containing general accusations against everything and everyone. Only the word "cosmopolitan" wasn't used. For the rest there was a surprising resemblance to articles published fifteen years ago.

The author of the article that appeared in number two of the magazine *Oktyabr* writes among other things: "Whereas the Italians themselves recognize that neorealism is dead, Romm continues to praise it." (I quote from memory.) In fact neorealism is dead. It died with the help of the Vatican and the capitalist censorship. The artist of Italian neorealism created films like Germi's *The Railwaymen,* De Sica's *The Bicycle Thief, Two Coins in the Fountain, Rome 11 O'clock in the Morning,* and other really great and unforgettable masterpieces.

Never has the film industry under a bourgeois regime created such work

[15] The most recent film, 1961, directed by Romm.

[16] Yuly Reisman. Born 1903. Active as a leading screen director since the early 1920's. Won a Stalin Prize for his 1945 documentary, *Berlin*. Now again experimenting.

[17] Mikhail Kalatozov. Born 1903, a Georgian. Major film director and administrator. Surrealistic in early 1920's and up to 1930, then became orthodox. In post-Stalin period, director of *The Cranes Are Flying* and *The Unmailed Letter,* the latter of which was considerably revised by censors.

before, in any case not as a group and with such unity. All forces were mobilized against Italian neorealism — the censorship, bribery, threats, sabotage of distribution, violence of all kinds. All this in order to destroy, to break, to crush this group of artists. World reaction as a whole went into action against Italian neorealism. At that time a single article was published in our country, unfortunately signed by Polevoi,[18] a man I respect. In that article, Polevoi also attacked Italian neorealism. I was ashamed of that article, a reaction common to all of us. That happened six years ago. We didn't encourage this current, which was very close to the Italian CP. They were strangling neorealism and we attacked it! And it was only recently that Solovyeva[19] finally wrote a book on neorealism. She wrote it when it was necessary to treat the subject on a historical plane.

Three years ago I ventured to intervene in favor of Italian neorealism. And even today people who insist on the importance of remaining loyal to tradition recall this sin. How did I dare intervene in favor of neorealism? But in my opinion, neorealism has had an influence on the youth. It must be admitted. If this influence existed, it did exist! You have to decide then whether this influence was positive or negative. I know our youth. I know the impression created by the Italian films. I can underline that this influence was real!

Something Also Exists in the West

Why should we bow in all fields to what is called "the first" as we had to do in the past? I am not at all certain that this "first" is always a good thing. Let's suppose that a lone American genius invented the phonograph and that we developed the invention. Who then should be proud of it? In my opinion we should, because genius wasn't recognized in America while we developed the phonograph. We, to the contrary, make it appear that we invented everything, the cinema, the phonograph, the electric light, and the telephone while in fact it was the Americans who developed all these good things. There is no reason why we should be proud of this!

We are combing history hunting for someone who invented the locomotive before Stevenson although we know very well that we didn't build one at that time. We should give ourselves airs because of our lack of efficiency, our backwardness! Those who built the first locomotives, who made the first flight, they were right. We should be proud of being the first to fly into outer space, of having the biggest power stations in the world, and not about what occurred two hundred years ago, about the man who said "E" for the first time, whether it was Dobchinsky or Bobchinsky!

By defending and sometimes inventing this claim to be "the first" at all costs, it's impossible to say how far you can go. Only ten years ago, we

[18] Boris Polevoi, famous novelist, also editor of *Yunost* ("Youth"), a literary journal.

[19] Inna Solovyeva, film historian, published the volume, *Neo-Realism in Italian Movies* in 1961 (Moscow).

tried to cut ourselves off completely from Western culture — and this, too, was covered by the word "tradition."

I was very happy today to hear Yutkevich speak about innovations and about spending much time in the West. We have lost the habit of considering that something also exists in the West. And this in Russia, the country in the world where more foreign literature is translated than anywhere else. One of the strong points of the Russian intellectuals was precisely the fact that they read all of world literature, that they stood at the top in knowledge of world culure. This, too, is one of our traditions. An excellent tradition which we needn't be reminded of today.

The translation of this speech, with minor word changes, has been reprinted from Commentary *(New York), December 1963. The footnotes are from* Commentary.

3

KHRUSHCHEV ON MODERN ART

On December 1, 1962, Nikita Khrushchev, then First Secretary of the Communist Party and Prime Minister of the Soviet Union, paid a visit to a display of "Thirty Years of Moscow Art" at the Manezh, a reconverted Tsarist riding stable close by the Kremlin. The exhibition included a small selection of nonrepresentational painting and sculpture, none of which was avant-garde by Western standards. Khrushchev's remarks proved to be the signal for the most far-reaching crackdown on the creative arts in the Soviet Union since the Zhdanov purge of 1946–1948. Khrushchev was not alone. He was accompanied by four other members of the Communist Party Presidium and four members of the Party Secretariat, and flanked by Vladimir Serov and Sergei Gerasimov, painterofficials known for their reactionary views on art.

THE FIRST ASSAULT: MODERN ART

The first extended pause is in front of one of Falk's paintings.

N. S. KHRUSHCHEV: "I would say that this is just a mess. It's hard to understand what this still-life is supposed to represent. I will probably be told that I have not reached the point where I can understand such works — the usual argument of our opponents in culture. Dimitry Stepanovich Polyansky told me a couple of days ago that when his daughter got married, she was given a picture of what was supposed to be a lemon. It consisted of some messy yellow lines which looked, if you will excuse me, as though some child had done his business on the canvas when his mother was away and then spread it around with his hands."

Then, further along: "I don't like jazz. When I hear jazz, it's as if I had gas on the stomach. I used to think it was static when I heard it on the radio. I like music a lot and often listen to it on the radio. I even went so far as to carry a little Japanese radio around in my pocket. They make them very well there. . . .

"Even Shostakovich surprised us once in this connection. At the final concert of the plenary meeting of the Composers' Union we were regaled with a trio which wasn't entirely pleasurable listening. . . .

"Or take these new dances which are so fashionable now. Some of them are completely improper. You wiggle a certain section of the anatomy, if you'll pardon the expression. It's indecent. As Kogan once said to me when she was looking at a fox-trot, 'I've been married 20 years and never knew that this kind of activity is called the fox-trot!' . . .

"Jazz comes from the Negroes. They've had it for a long time, and here it's treated as a novelty. I understand our own Russian dances a lot better— Georgian and Armenian ones too. They are wonderful dances. . . .

"People tell me that I am behind the times and don't realize it, that our contemporary artists will be appreciated in 100 years. Well, I don't know what will happen in 100 years, but now we have to adopt a definite policy in art, emphasizing it in the press and encouraging it materially. We won't spare a kopeck of government money for any artistic daubing. . . .

"As long as I am president of the Council of Ministers, we are going to support a genuine art. We aren't going to give a kopeck for pictures painted by jackasses. History can be our judge. For the time being history has put us at the head of this state, and we have to answer for everything that goes on in it. Therefore we are going to maintain a strict policy in art. I could mention that when I was in England I reached an understanding with Eden. He showed me a picture by a contemporary abstractionist and asked me how I liked it. I said I didn't understand it. He said he didn't understand it either, and asked me what I thought of Picasso. I said I didn't understand Picasso, and Eden said he couldn't understand Picasso either."

When passing by the satirical drawings of Reshetnikov and Kukriniksy, N. S. Khrushchev indicated his approval, laughing in particular at Reshetnikov's satire on abstractionist painters.

In front of paintings by Andronov, Mikhail and Pavel Nikonov, Vasnetsov, and Yegorshina:

V. A. SEROV (pointing to these paintings, and especially to "The Raftsmen" by Andronov and "The Geologists" by Nikonov): "Some connoisseurs claim that these pictures are programmatic. We dispute that."

N. S. KHRUSHCHEV: "You are entirely correct." Then, in front of "The Geologists": "He can paint and sell these if he wants, but we don't need them. We are going to take these blotches with us into communism, are we? If government funds have been paid for this picture, the person who authorised it will have the sum deducted from his salary. Write out a certificate that this picture has not been acquired by the government. . . .

"But who ordered it? And why? This painting shouldn't have been hung in the exhibition. Pictures should arouse us to perform great deeds. They should inspire a person. But what kind of picture is this? One jackass is riding on another. . . .

"No, we don't need pictures like these. As long as the people support us and have confidence in us we will carry out our own policy in art. And if pictures like these appear, it means that we are not doing our work properly. This includes the Ministry of Culture and the Central Committee's Commission on Ideology.

S. V. GERASIMOV (or V. A. SEROV): "People say, by the way, that pictures like these are supported in the press. For instance, Konenkov's article in *Izvestia* praises the sculptor Neizvestny and some of the other formalists."

In passing by paintings of Korzhevsky and Zhevadronova, N. S. Khrushchev says: "These are good pictures, especially that one over there. You can feel the essence of youth in it. But why these bad pictures — a spoonful of pitch in a barrel of honey."

A propos a painting by Kugach: "It looks like a real winter scene!"

After a quick look at the upper halls, where the formalist paintings are hung, N. S. Khrushchev says: "What is this anyway? You think we old fellows don't understand you. And we think we are just wasting money on you. Are you pederasts or normal people? I'll be perfectly straightforward with you; we won't spend a kopeck on your art. Just give me a list of those of you who want to go abroad, to the so-called 'free world.' We'll give you foreign passports tomorrow, and you can get out. Your prospects here are nil. What is hung here is simply anti-Soviet. It's amoral. Art should ennoble the individual and arouse him to action. And what have you set out here? Who painted this picture? I want to talk to him. What's the good of a picture like this? To cover urinals with?"

The painter, Zheltovsky, comes forward.

N. S. KHRUSHCHEV: "You're a nice-looking lad, but how could you paint something like this? We should take down your pants and set you down in a clump of nettles until you understand your mistakes. You should be ashamed. Are you a pederast or a normal man? Do you want to go abroad? Go on, then; we'll take you free as far as the border. Live out there in the 'free world.' Study in the school of capitalism, and then you'll know what's what. But we aren't going to spend a kopeck on this dog shit. We have the right to send you out to cut trees until you've paid back the money the state has spent on you. The people and government have taken a lot of trouble with you, and you pay them back with this shit. They say you like to associate with foreigners. A lot of them are our enemies, don't forget. "

Then, in front of a painting by Gribkov: "What's this?"

GRIBKOV: "It's the year 1917."

N. S. KHRUSHCHEV: "Phooey. How much the state has spent on you, and this is how you repay it. My opinion is that you can all go to hell abroad. This is an art for donkeys. . . .

"Comrade Ilyichev, I am even more upset by the way your section is doing its work. And how about the Ministry of Culture? Do you accept this? Are you afraid to criticize? . . .

"They say that some of our writers praise these pictures and buy them. That's because our honoraria are high. Our writers are too prosperous and have money to throw away."

BELYUTIN, one of the ideologists of the formalists, comes up.

N. S. KHRUSHCHEV: "Who are you? Who are your parents?"

Belyutin answers.

N. S. KHRUSHCHEV: "Do you want to go abroad? Who supports you?"

BELYUTIN: "I am a teacher."

N. S. KHRUSHCHEV: "How can such a person teach? People like him should be cleared out of the teaching profession. They shouldn't be allowed to teach in the universities. Go abroad if you want; and if you don't want to, we'll send you anyway. I can't even talk about this without getting angry. I'm a patriot."

In front of a painting by Shorts: "Why aren't you ashamed of this mess? Who are your parents?"

Shorts gives information about his parents, mentioning that his mother is dead.

N. S. KHRUSHCHEV: "It's a pity, of course, that your mother is dead, but maybe it's lucky for her that she can't see how her son is spending his time. What master are you serving anyway? Our paths are different. You've either got to get out or paint differently. As you are, there's no future for you on our soil."

One of the bystanders says, "These are graphic artists. They do these pictures in their spare time to improve their skill" (general laughter).

N. S. KHRUSHCHEV: "I remember the Ukrainian satirist, Ostap Vishnya. In one article he gives the following conversation: 'Do you believe in God?' and the answer, 'At work I don't, and at home I do.' That's what these scratchings of yours are like. . . .

"I used to be on friendly terms with the sculptor, Merkuryev. He was a great man, a real man. Once, in the Dresden Gallery, he pointed to some paintings of the Dutch masters and told me that our artists maintain that to appreciate a painting you have to stand back from it. The Dutch masters painted differently. You can look at their pictures through a magnifying glass and still admire them. But your paintings just give a person constipation, if you'll excuse the expression. They don't arouse any other feelings at all."

Turning to Zhutovzky, "Do you want to help us build communism? No, what you want is for people to consider you a misunderstood genius — a painter whom the future will appreciate. You are a hypocrite!"

In front of Zhutovsky's self-portrait: "Externally there is no resemblance. The picture is unnatural. But there is certainly a spiritual resemblance between the portrait and the original. You are stealing from society. You are a parasite. We have to organize our society so that it will be clear who is useful and who is useless. What right do you have to live in an apartment built by genuine people, one made of real materials?"

ZHUTOVSKY: "But these are just experiments. They help us develop."

N. S. KHRUSHCHEV: "Judging by these experiments, I am entitled to think that you are pederasts, and for that you can get 10 years. You're gone out of your minds, and now you want to deflect us from the proper course. No, you won't get away with it. . . .

"Gentlemen, we are declaring war on you."

Reprinted from *Encounter* (London), April 1963.

4

PROVIDING AN IDEOLOGICAL FRAMEWORK

On December 17, 1962, the first of several meetings took place between creative artists and leaders of the Communist Party. The only speech that has been published is that of Leonid Ilyichev, Chairman of the recently formed Ideological Commission of the Central Committee. The text that follows is by no means complete: Ilyichev is said to have spoken for ten hours.

CREATE FOR THE PEOPLE, FOR THE SAKE OF COMMUNISM. Speech by Party Central Committee Secretary L. F. Ilyichev at the meeting of Party and government leaders with representatives of literature and the arts, December 17, 1962.

Some two and a half years have gone by since last meeting of representatives of literature and the arts with the leaders of the Party and government.

Much water has passed under the bridge since then and many important events have taken place in our country and in the international arena. The 22nd Party Congress has been held. The new Party Program has been adopted. Our Party and the Soviet people are following the Leninist course to the victory of communism. The international prestige of the Soviet Union has risen still higher.

Today we are gathered again to exchange opinions on the problems of most concern to all of us in the development of socialist culture. Nothing exceptional or extraordinary has happened, of course. Our Party's Central Committee is satisfied with the state of affairs in the sphere of culture — its development is proceeding on a healthy basis, in the correct direction, in step with the times. Our art is striking accurately at the right target.

Meetings, both confidential and open talks by the leaders of the Party and government with the men and women of Soviet culture have already become a tradition, one that everyone approves of.

To judge by everything, the previous talks were useful. They played a favorable role in the consolidation of all the creative forces of Soviet culture. Today's meeting, which, it is hoped, will also be useful, carries on this good tradition. Undoubtedly it will encourage the further solidarity of writers and people in the arts on the basis of service to the noble cause of building communism.

Both the Party Central Committee and the writers and people in the arts have recognized the timely need for such a talk. Many acute ideological questions have arisen on which it is necessary to ponder together, to clarify points of view, to clarify positions, so as to move forward more successfully.

To the arsenal of ideas of our intelligentsia of the arts there have recently been added such remarkable documents of creative Marxism-Leninism as the materials of the 22nd Congress, the Party Program, and N. S. Khrushchev's statements on questions of literature and the arts.

Each Soviet artist can now appreciate even more deeply the great function of literature and the arts, his place in the people's struggle for communism. Now, when we have entered the epoch of the full-scale construction of communism, the responsibility of the intelligentsia of the arts for the development of Soviet society's ideological, spiritual life has increased immeasurably.

We cannot fail to give thought to the purity and firmness of our ideological positions, to the chief direction, the chief line in the development of Soviet literature and art.

Abstractionist Pretensions

N. S. Khrushchev and other leaders of the Party and the government recently visited the Exhibition of Moscow Artists and also acquainted themselves with works by abstractionists and by the sculptor E. Neizvestny. Right there at the exhibition these works, as well as formalist works by several other artists, were sharply but justly criticized. The abstractionist daubs on canvas, lacking any common sense, represent nothing but pathological eccentricities, miserable imitations of the depraved formalist art of the bourgeois West.

"Such 'creative work' is alien to our people; they reject it," N. S. Khrushchev said at the exhibition. "This must be pondered by people who call themselves artists but who create 'pictures' that make you wonder whether they were painted by the hand of man or daubed by a donkey's tail. They must understand their mistakes and work for the people."

Thus N. S. Khrushchev and other comrades expressed a negative attitude to formalism and abstractionism and gave a businesslike and very convincing criticism of formalist art, primarily for its divorce from the life of the people, for the deliberately ugly depiction of reality. *The Leninist principles of the Party and folk nature of art are and will continue to be the foundation of our Party's policy in the sphere of the development of socialist culture.*

The meeting of Party and government leaders with Moscow artists at the exhibition devoted to the 30th anniversary of the Moscow branch of the Artists' Union did not, of course, happen by accident.

The Party Central Committee and the U.S.S.R. Council of Ministers, and Nikita Sergeyevich Khrushchev personally, have lately begun receiving letters whose authors, representatives of various groups among the creative intelligentsia, bring up acute questions, probably the most basic questions, relating to the development of our arts.

What, briefly stated, is the gist of these letters? Their authors protest in emphatic terms against instances of the flouting of the realist traditions that are the glory of Russian classical and Soviet art. Some artists, for instance, are evincing an ever clearer attraction to abstract painting, which is disturbing. The abstractionists have turned to vigorous action — they have been arranging exhibitions of their "works," publicizing them obtrusively within the country and outside it, making themselves out to be the sole representatives of genuine art and disparaging all who are committed to socialist realism as "conservatives."

There are some who even challenge the demand that art be intelligible, comprehensible. Voices are actually heard claiming that truly innovative art is always incomprehensible, since the masses supposedly cannot understand the language of contemporary art, and that along with artists for the masses there can and should be artists for the few, the elect.

A large group of artists addressed a letter to the presidium of the recent plenary session of the Party Central Committee. They wrote:

V. I. Lenin's dicta and the Party decisions on realist art are at present being challenged by the formalists as outdated. The formalists are directing their statements and actions at resurrecting the formalist trends condemned in the Party's decisions.

We request the Party Central Committee to state what in these decisions has become outdated. If they are not outdated, the statements against these decisions in the press and over the radio and television must be regarded as revisionist and conducive to the infiltration of an ideology alien to us.

The authors of the letter go on to say that the group of advocates of formalism, capitalizing on the fact that in the past an erroneous attitude prevailed toward the work of such artists as D. Shterenberg, A. Shevchenko, R. Falk, A. Drevin, and others, have now taken up these formalist works as their banner. Under this banner some artists are endeavoring to insinuate into our representational arts an ideology alien to us.

And the fact is that at the Exhibition of Moscow Artists many lively and at times quite sharp discussions have been arising in front of such paintings as R. Falk's "Nude" and "Still Life," D. Shterenberg's "Aniska" and "Still Life: Herring," A. Vasnetsov's "Breakfast" and P. Nikonov's "The Geologists," A. Pologova's sculpture "Motherhood," and other works.

One cannot but agree with the visitors to the exhibition, the overwhelming majority of whom denounce these pictures and are indignant at the grotesque portrayal of Soviet people and of our life as a whole.

The "works" of the abstractionists — for instance B. Zhutovsky's "Self-Portrait" and "Tolka," V. Shorts' "Cosmonauts" and "Stretch of Water," L. Gribkov's "1917" and others — leave an impression that is even more painful and simply repelling. E. Neizvestny's works "Classics Demolished," "The Crab," and several others also evoke a feeling of protest.

While there is still some room for argument about the merits and de-merits of the works of P. Nikonov, R. Falk, and A. Vasnetsov, there is nothing at all to argue about when it comes to the so-called "canvases" of the young abstractionists who have grouped themselves around E. Belyutin and who dignify themselves with the name of "seekers" — they are outside of art. In November these formalists arranged an "exhibition" of their "works." And, of course, the foreign journalists were quick to put in their appearance. Their cameras clicked, the motion-picture cameras whirred (so we must expect yet another film of a familiar variety to "come out" abroad before long), they interviewed people and then played the whole story up widely in the bourgeois papers. In a word, they made it seem that a major "event" had occurred in the cultural life of the Soviet capital. And with what object? With the sole object, clearly, of insulting and depreciating our genuinely Soviet art: "Just look, the realist traditions of Repin are coming to an end."

The point, however, is not only, and not even so much, that formalist pictures portraying hopelessly glum, morose, and grotesque people, pictures painted in patent imitation of bourgeois art of the period of its decadence, are represented at the Exhibition of Moscow Artists. What matters most is that the pictures of the formalists are being extolled by some undiscriminat-ing Soviet critics as innovational, as alone entitled to exist, and are being set up against all the best, the life-affirming, that has been produced by realist art. They would thereby pass off formalism and even its extreme expression, abstractionism, as the high road of Soviet art.

When you read the articles by "theorists" of this kind, you realize that under the pretense of working for *diversity* in art they are trying to establish *formalistic uniformity,* in the name of eliminating *alleged dictation* they are trying to impose actual dictation, the *dictation of the subjective tastes* of people who have lost touch with life, tastes alien to any normal, healthy person.

It is to this end that even grubby daubing is proclaimed the last word in "artistic insight."

We have certain art specialists who are prepared to contend that the main trouble with our art is the insufficient popularization of abstractionism, which in their opinion is capable of breathing some sort of new life into socialist art. Yet — and herein lies the full irony of the situation — even in the West the abstractionist craze is now passing, the exhibitions of the ab-stractionists are fiascoes and their pictures are ridiculed. For good reason the people are little by little coming to see the light.

Some artists have taken offense at the Soviet public's just criticism of abstractionism and formalism.

But what, really, is there to take offense at? After all, *abstractionist and modernist "innovations"* represent a trend that has never epitomized healthy art; they represent *a deviation from the basic line of development of Soviet literature and art* and repudiation of the ties between art and the life of the people, the practical building of communism.

How contemptuous of their people must they have become to declare that the people were "not mature enough" to understand the revelations of the abstractionists!

But to what point is it necessary to mature? To the point of losing common sense and normal human tastes? And how is it possible to go so far as to repudiate the wonderful socialist traditions of our art, traditions reinforced in struggle and tested by life? Why should worship of bourgeois art, which, to quote V. I. Lenin, tries to "stupefy" man, to paralyze his will and energy in the struggle for a bright future, be considered an advanced, innovational position?

Let there be no reservations here. Our homegrown abstractionists, so to speak, and idolaters of bourgeois fashions have come into direct conflict with the Party Program approved by the entire Soviet people.

We quite often see efforts made to present not only A. V. Lunacharsky but even V. I. Lenin as all but partisans of abstractionist "innovation." This view is erroneous in the case of A. V. Lunacharsky, and in the case of V. I. Lenin it is nothing short of blasphemy.

Recall the devastating sarcasm with which V. I. Lenin, in a talk with C. Zetkin, spoke of the abstractionists' pretentions to innovation:

> Yes, dear Clara, we're both old and that's that. It's enough for us that we at least remain young and in the front ranks when it comes to the revolution. For us there's no keeping up with the new art; we'll hobble along behind.

Who will fail to sense here the bitter irony of Lenin's words! It is not V. I. Lenin and the Party but the sorry excuses for innovators representing the modernist trend who have always lagged behind the transforming revolutionary activity of the masses, and consequently behind genuinely revolutionary art as well. A. V. Lunacharsky, as we know, compared modernists of every sort with kids who run whooping ahead of the first platoon and impishly mimic real soldiers.

A Passion for Grubbing in Backyards

Formalist tendencies have unfortunately begun to spread not only in the representational arts but in music, literature and the cinema as well.

In music, for example, despite general progress we observe an infatuation with the outlandish yowlings of various foreign — and not only foreign —

jazz bands. This refers not to jazz music in general but to the cacophony of sounds with which listeners are sometimes assailed and which is dignified with the name of music only through a misconception.

In the cinema, too, where we can see a general advance that has been stimulated by beneficial reforms in all spheres of our life, ideologically immature works appear, films that suffer from a studied cleverness and complexity of form and that are therefore rejected by the moviegoer.

Poems and prose works are often published in which, in the pursuit of originality of form and in the name of being "different" from others, not only is the vital content emasculated but often all sense is lost and the Russian language is mutilated and cluttered up.

Some writers and artists are simply possessed with a passion for grubbing in backyards and will not see what is happening on the main highways of our development.

It is a known fact that foreign "tourists" on special assignments and some correspondents for bourgeois newspapers hunt around in our country for people who are dissatisfied with one thing or another and who know how to hold a pencil in their hands. They try to get from scribblers of this kind all sorts of lampoons maligning our way of life.

A comparatively short time ago a book by a certain Alexander Yesenin-Volpin, *Spring Serf,* was brought out in New York and widely publicized. The book contains a pretentious and illiterate "philosophical treatise" as well as misanthropic anti-Soviet doggerel, the ravings of a mental case.

The "philosophical treatise" makes plain the author's "credo": "My political ideal is anarchy." This ideal is expressed in his poems as follows:

"I know not what I live for
 And what I want of the beasts
 That inhabit wicked Moscow!"

Al. Yesenin-Volpin writes with scorn about our young people, exhorting them to the blackest deeds. Nourishing his thoughts with "the juices of the gall bladder" and hating everything under the sun, he promises nothing good even to those who may follow him. "Kill everyone," he urges.

These boys can understand
That to love or to trust is ridiculous,
That their tyrants are their mothers and fathers,
And it is high time to kill them!
These boys will end up with their heads in the noose,
But no one will condemn me —
And these verses will be read
By lunatics a hundred years hence!

What is this? How can a sane man write, and how can anyone publish, verses of this kind? But precisely this vicious concoction, sickening to any healthy person, is being lauded to the skies by our enemies. Naturally! After all, it is imbued with savage hatred of Soviet society and the Soviet people. Al. Yesenin-Volpin's book is being palmed off abroad as a "manifesto" of the new generation of "rebellious" Soviet youth.

This, of course, is nonsense. This rogue represents no one. He is nothing more than a poisonous mushroom that is rotten to the root.

But the fuss made over his utterly worthless scribbling is highly characteristic and symptomatic. It shows that the propaganda hostile to us will go to any length in its effort to spread the poison of skepticism, to disorient inexperienced people, to foment unwholesome developments and tendencies in our art, especially in the creative efforts of young people, and to set the generations at loggerheads, range "fathers and sons" against each other. Our ideological adversaries are yelling their heads off about a "new wave," about "dissonant voices," about a "crisis" in Soviet art.

The young Soviet cultural figures who are proudly taking over the baton from the older generations deny these vicious fabrications and insinuations. We must, however, be vigilant and intolerant of any wrong tendencies and ideological waverings and remember that formalist hocus-pocus represents not innocuous pranks but surrender to an alien ideology in art. We must go on holding high the banner of socialist realism.

Our literature and art as a whole are developing in the right direction, and our artistic intelligentsia are the Party's reliable helpers in the Communist remaking of the world, in educating the working people. But for this very reason any deviations from the main line of development of our literature and art are intolerable. They have met and will continue to meet with protest from our people, who are able to distinguish works of genuine spiritual value from ideological counterfeits and artistic surrogates.

But why is it that in our representational arts (and is it in these arts only?) there are some people who have begun to depart from the fundamental premises of socialist realism and to imitate currents that were characterized by V. I. Lenin as the most absurd affectations?

Obviously, developments of this kind are not accidental. They bear witness that some comrades misunderstand the nature of the struggle against bourgeois ideology and sometimes lose sight of the irreconcilability of our ideological positions and the impossibility of compromise on them.

We should remember as an immutable truth that art always has an ideological-political bent, that in one way or another it expresses and defends the interests of definite classes and social strata. And when we encounter this or that trend in art, the first question that naturally arises is: Whose interests does it serve, what does it call for, what social ideals does it affirm?

If we consider the nature of abstract art there can be no two opinions: It does not serve the interests of the working people, it does not express the mentality of the working people, it is designed to cater to the perverted tastes of the satiated.

IN THE ABSTRACTIONIST'S STUDIO. Cartoon by D. Oboznenko,
verse by M. Romanov; reprinted from *Boyevoi karandash*
[*The Fighting Pencil*], Leningrad.

> They say
>   there was
>   this artist's Mrs.
> Who for her husband's style
>   saved her kisses,
> But once, in the studio, she
>   her own portrait spied,
> And that is how her hubby died,

                     (*Pravda,* December 23, 1962, page 6)

Indeed, can abstractionism and decadent art generally be the banner of progressive classes, especially the banner of the Soviet people building communism? There can be only one answer here: An art cut off from life is incapable of serving the transformation of life; the spiritual weapon of a dying class cannot raise the militancy of a class advancing toward victory; the culture of communism cannot be created out of the products of the disintegration of the old society.

Sometimes it is asked: Can a man devoted to the Soviet system be reproached for serving the interests of classes hostile to socialism solely on the basis that, let us say, his creative method and the methods of art alien to us are as alike as two drops of water? After all, the artist himself does not want to inflict harm upon our country, for which he may even have shed blood during the war; he is guided by the best intentions!

The complexity of the problem lies in the fact that the artist's subjective intentions are by no means the same as the objective significance of his work. The artist's good intentions by no means prevent his works from actually and objectively serving the interests of hostile forces.

Recall what V. I. Lenin wrote to A. M. Gorky in the period of the great proletarian writer's ideological vacillation. "Your good intention remains your private affair, a subjective 'innocent desire,'" wrote Vladimir Ilyich. "Once you have written [a work], it goes to the *masses* and its significance is determined not by your good intention but by the *balance of social forces,* the objective correlation of classes."

Whatever good intentions may guide our formalists in art, they are obliged to remember firmly Lenin's wise warning. It must always be borne in mind that ideological adversaries of communism may seize upon and are already seizing upon their mistakes for purposes hostile to the Soviet people.

No Peaceful Coexistence in the Arts

After the Party and government leaders viewed the art exhibition at the Manezh and voiced critical comments about the abstractionists and formalists, rumors spread among a certain part of the creative intelligentsia that, if you please, a campaign against persons seeking new forms and new paths in art had again begun.

N. S. Khrushchev received several letters expressing this thought: Do everything to prevent a repetition of what took place in the period of the Stalin cult.

I shall quote several excerpts from a letter sent to the Party Central Committee by a group of persons engaged in literature and the arts. They write:

Dear Nikita Sergeyevich: We appeal to you as the person who has done most to eradicate Stalinist arbitrariness from the life of our country.

We are persons of different generations, we work in various spheres of art, each of us has his own tastes and artistic beliefs. We are united in this appeal to you by concern for the future of Soviet art and Soviet culture.

The letter continues:

We have rejoiced at seeing the party restoring the spirit of Lenin: freedom and justice. The architects rejoice at the opportunity to erect modern buildings, the writers at the possibility of writing truthful books; composers and theater workers find it easier to breathe; our cinematography is now making films of diverse artistic trends, pictures that meet with understanding and recognition both among our people and abroad.

After expressing satisfaction over the opening of the Moscow artists' show at which the works of artists of different trends were displayed, the writers of the letter point out:

Such an exhibition became possible only after the 20th and 22nd Party Congresses. We can have various judgments of one or another work exhibited at the show. If we all appeal to you through this letter, it is only because we wish to say in all sincerity that without the possibility of existence of various art trends, art is doomed.

We are now seeing how artists of the very trend that alone flourished under Stalin, giving others no possibility of working or even living, are beginning to interpret the words you uttered at the art exhibition.

We deeply believe that you did not desire this and that you are against it. We appeal to you to stop the swing in representational arts to past methods that are repugnant to the whole spirit of our times.

Shortly afterwards a somewhat similar letter, with several variations, signed by another group of comrades, was received. This letter contained, inter alia, even a plea for "peaceful coexistence" of *all* trends in art, which objectively sounds like an appeal for peaceful coexistence in the sphere of ideology.

But the comrades who signed this latter letter decided, no doubt after careful reconsideration, to retract the letter, and they recalled it. Evidently they had not thought through all the points in their letter too thoroughly, and it is to be regarded presumably not as a document but as a draft, a rough outline of a document.

But what gave rise to these appeals to the Party Central Committee by persons engaged in literature and the arts?

There need be no doubt — they were called forth by profound concern for the state of affairs in literature and the arts, by a sincere desire to promote their successful development and flourishing. But the writers of the letters evidently are confusing two different questions: creative community among workers of literature and the arts and the attitude toward various alien ideological trends in art.

Creative community among workers of literature and the arts who, possessing diverse styles and creative ways, follow in the channel of socialist realism and truthfully reflect life: This is one thing. The Party is for such community, for the most comradely, genuinely brotherly mutual relations among the various detachments of our creative intelligentsia.

Socialist realism affords wide opportunity for community, for creative competition of the most diverse artists — the adherents of the generalizing-romantic, the strictly analytical and other stylistic currents in our art. Without this community there cannot be development of our Soviet literature, of our Soviet art.

But does this mean that we are for community, for "peaceful coexistence," among such opposite ideological trends in art as socialist realism and abstractionism, which in the final analysis reflect not only opposed positions in esthetics and ideas but also opposed political, class positions?

We must make this utterly clear:

There has not been and cannot be peaceful coexistence between socialist ideology and the ideology of the bourgeoisie. The Party has opposed and will continue to oppose bourgeois ideology and all of its manifestations. Following Vladimir Ilyich Lenin's directives, it has always defended and will go on defending the Party nature of literature and art.

The Party has stood and stands resolutely and unshakably for the Leninist course in the development of literature and art.

In ideology the battle with the bourgeois world goes on and does not cease for a moment, a struggle for the souls and hearts of people, particularly young people, a struggle to shape them, these young people, a struggle over what they will take from the past and carry into the future. We have no right to underestimate the danger of subversion by bourgeois ideology in the sphere of literature and art, just as in other spheres.

The idea of coexistence in the sphere of ideology is in actuality nothing but betrayal of the interests of Marxism-Leninism, of the interests of socialism.

And in art we sometimes encounter a retreat from class and Party positions, we sometimes encounter instances of reconciliation with bourgeois ideology. This finds expression, in particular, in a false interpretation of "human nature," in the propaganda of abstract humanism, a kind of evangelical all-forgiveness, as though there were not hostile classes, no capitalism in the world, and no struggle for communism!

We Communists inherit and are multiplying all the genuine human values that have been distorted and perverted in private-property society. But we are resolutely against a classless treatment of human nature, against the replacement of Communist Party spirit and militant socialist humanism by the false preachment of class peace and all-forgiveness.

In our era what is genuinely humanist is what is Communist, since it is in Communist society that the fullest development of the individual takes place and all the best human traits and qualities are manifested. One cannot therefore dissolve our Communist ideals in some abstract, classless concepts, for this inevitably leads to surrendering our ideological positions.

In a letter to the Party Central Committee a group of young abstract artists assure us that they are seeking a path in socialist art and claim that there cannot be any advance without such searches. They claim that they are seeking to glorify "the purity of Russian woman," to express "the beauty of Soviet man conquering outer space."

As to the purity and beauty of Russian woman, it must be said that it is sufficient to look at the works of the abstractionists in order to be convinced of the absurdities to which a person can go when he has been pursuing a fashion alien to us. And as for the "searches," I should like to tell the abstract artists: You are not seeking, you have been sought out and pulled along, it is precisely in your formalist "works" that our enemies are trying to obtain a bridgehead for attacks on the Communist ideology.

Such are things that not only young formalists but also their defenders and inspirers should be pondering.

Artists as Anarchists

The Party is carrying out a policy of further development and deepening of democracy in Soviet society.

Who can deny how much more free and creative the whole atmosphere of our life has become, what favorable conditions have been established in our country for the work of the intelligentsia of the arts? But among those who work in arts, or more accurately, among those who inhabit the fringes of the art world, are there not persons who want to make it appear that a time has come when anarchist-minded elements may run amok with impunity?

It is just such people who, babbling about freedom of creation, oppose Party guidance of the arts.

There should be complete clarity in the question of freedom of creation. Remember how V. I. Lenin, speaking for genuine freedom, freedom for the people, exposed demagogic attempts to assert the anarchist concept of freedom as *freedom from society, from duty to the people.*

We have complete freedom to struggle for communism. We do not have and cannot have freedom to struggle against communism.

M. Gorky was profoundly right when he passionately assailed anarchistic indulgence. "I am against the freedom that begins at the line beyond which freedom turns into unbridled behavior, and we know that this change begins where a man, losing consciousness of his genuine social-cultural values, gives free rein to the age-old individualism of the philistine that lies concealed within him and cries: 'I am so wonderful, original, unique, yet they do not let me live as I choose.' It is even good if he only shouts about it, because when he begins to act as he chooses, he becomes a counterrevolutionary on one hand or a hooligan on the other, and these are almost equally vile and harmful," wrote Alexei Maximovich.

World reaction and its ideologists would like very much to restore the "freedom" of exploitation in the Soviet Union, the "freedom" to deceive the working people, and for a beginning at least to bring about the anarchist variety of bourgeois conceptions of "freedom of creation."

There are persons who conceive the matter thus: Since an end has been put to arbitrariness in our country and people are not arrested for political dissent, this means that everything is allowed and there are no restrictions on what one wishes. One may not only paint ugly pictures, one may laud them to the skies as original searchings. One may slander the progressive traditions of our art, but it appears that one may not defend them, because this, you see, would be "restriction" of freedom, "pressure" or "administrative bossing."

Such persons would like no one to dare contradict them when they try to defame everything created by our people in the difficult, deprivation-filled but great struggle for the victory of the socialist system.

It is reported that sometimes in the discussion of creative questions at one or another meeting a situation arises in which it is considered inconvenient and unfashionable to defend correct Party positions; one might gain the reputation of being, so to say, a reactionary and a conservative, one might be accused of dogmatism, sectarianism, narrowness, backwardness, Stalinism, etc.

At a recent conference of motion picture workers, the famous director Sergei Gerasimov declared in alarm that courage is now required to defend the positions of socialist realism, that the revolutionary barricades in our country are sometimes turned into a barrier full of holes through which one can easily crawl back and forth.

Can one take a tolerant view of such phenomena, however rare they may be, can one trail along in the wake of backward attitudes?

Condemning formalist distortions in representational arts in the early years of the revolution, V. I. Lenin emphasized that they are alien to the healthy taste of the normal person. It is significant that Vladimir Ilyich considered it very important for the realist artists themselves, with all their professional knowledge and experience, to oppose the alien, hostile ways and trends in contemporary art. This was in the early years of Soviet rule, when the forces of the young socialist art were still very weak.

How could those who have created the art, who have earned the love and respect of millions of people in our country and abroad, tolerate the revival of formalist trickery?!

Sometimes it is said: "Let us create as we ourselves wish, do not force any prescriptions upon us, do not restrict us." Hence the demand — exhibitions without juries, books without editors, the right of the artist to display without an intermediary anything he wishes. We have before us essentially nothing but an attempt to obtain an utterly unrestrained opportunity to force upon the people a swollen, subjectivist willfulness. This means placing one's own interests above the interests of the people, the interests of society as a whole.

True freedom of creation and anarchy are incompatible. V. I. Lenin called anarchism "bourgeoisness turned upside down."

It is the great happiness of our art that the Party, expressing the fundamental interests of the people and basing its entire activity on the most progressive world outlook, defines the tasks and direction of artistic creation.

Indeed, if it is not the people who are to judge works of literature and art, who then should act as their highest judges? And why is such a lordly, scornful attitude sometimes displayed toward public judgment of works? Why is public opinion often treated as "common," while the judgment of a small group of esthetes is regarded as the expression of indisputable truth?

Our artistic intelligentsia firmly opposes those who, currying favor with any foreign fashion, are ready to cross off the great achievements of Soviet culture. One cannot support persons who take the positions of Shchedrin's "Scorn-Trough." Such persons are ready to ridicule everything, to hoot it down, to reject everything.

The Soviet people carefully preserve and develop the best traditions of socialist art, the traditions of living truth, of Communist Party spirit and closeness to the people, of high revolutionary spirit and civic ardor.

Solzhenitsyn Endorsed

Wherein lie the chief line and the chief inspiration in the development of our art, and what is the attitude toward the so-called "critical trend"?

The chief line in the development of literature and art was laid down in the Program of our Party. It consists in strengthening ties with the life of the people, in the truthful and highly artistic depiction of the richness and diversity of socialist reality, the inspired and vivid portrayal of all that is new and genuinely Communist, and the exposure of all that hinders the progress of society.

The Party is creating all the prerequisites for the successful development of literature and the arts.

Some comrades would have us believe, however, that efforts are being made to obstruct criticism of the negative features of our life, that the Party does not endorse or encourage works that have a critical orientation. Such assertions are untrue, as are the allegations that socialist realism demands the prettifying of reality, the smoothing over of contradictions, rosy complacency, philistine smugness, etc.

No, the highest criterion, the core of socialist realism is artistic and social truth, however harsh it may be.

Who else but our party and its Leninist Central Committee courageously told the people the truth about the cult of Stalin, exposed his crimes against the Party and people and are determinedly eradicating the effects of the cult of the individual in all spheres of life?

Our party endorses the healthy, life-affirming critical trend in the art of socialist realism. Artistically and politically powerful works that truthfully and boldly expose the arbitrariness that prevailed in the period of the cult of the individual have been published lately with the approval of the Party Central Committee. It is enough to mention A. Solzhenitsyn's tale *One Day in the Life of Ivan Denisovich.*

So it is not a question of skirting negative features in our life; they exist, and the Party is taking the lead and setting an example in eradicating them.

The point is that while boldly exposing everything that stands in our way, we must not strike at Soviet society itself. We must differentiate between life-asserting works of sharp critical orientation, which rouse and inspire people to combat shortcomings, and works that are decadent, alarmist, and slanderous, that sow lack of faith in Soviet society and weaken the force and energy of the people in the struggle to achieve communism.

The authors of the letters to the Party Central Committee saw in the critical remarks about false and harmful tendencies in art the danger of a reversion to the earlier methods of guiding artistic creation. What a misapprehension! On what grounds were such conclusions drawn? It appears that criticism had but to be leveled at formalistic monstrosities for us to hear an "SOS" — talk of reversion to the old methods, the methods that prevailed in the period of the cult of the individual.

This matter is of fundamental importance and needs to be examined.

In the period of the cult there were substantial morbid accretions and distortions in the sphere of spiritual culture. The Party exposed and did away with them and removed the obstacles that had been blocking the development, the further advance of the art of socialist realism. Having rectified and eliminated the errors and perversions of the past, our Party set down in its new Program that it would unfailingly see to the development of literature and the arts in the right direction and to ensuring their high ideological and artistic level, and would unswervingly carry out Lenin's behests on the guidance of art.

V. I. Lenin ridiculed and rejected the position of noninterference by the Party in the development of socialist culture.

Some comrades seem to be placing an incorrect and highly arbitrary interpretation on the Party's policy of decisively overcoming the effects of the cult of the individual and promoting broad democracy in all spheres of our life.

The Party has indeed been actively and consistently pursuing a Leninist policy, and it will continue to do so. It is removing all the hurdles and obstacles that have kept the people from displaying their creative powers. Only under such conditions will the vigor, initiative, and talents of the Soviet people show themselves to the full and ensure our country's accelerated advance along the path of Communist construction.

Need one say how important all this is for the progress of literature and art, how warmly the Party's Leninist policy was welcomed among our cultural workers?

Here too, as everywhere else, creative initiative and vigor are surging, new young creative forces are emerging. Artists are striving for the worthy portrayal of the difficult and heroic Leninist road, the only true road, which our country has traversed as it moves toward a new life.

But it would be wrong to close our eyes to the negative features and incorrect tendencies in art.

In exposing the Stalin cult the Party is getting rid of everything that impedes us in our course. But we must not permit socialist society, socialist ideology, and socialist culture to be shaken and weakened under pretext of the struggle against the cult of the individual. The exposure of the cult and the overcoming of its consequences should not weaken but rather should strengthen our forces. If under pretext of criticizing the effects of the cult of the individual we belabor our society and our ideology, we shall not create the great art of communism but shall forfeit all that we have gained.

The Soviet people are aware of and can see the great achievements of Soviet art, the salutary influence that the new atmosphere in our country has had on it. They have high regard for the work being done by their creative intelligentsia and appreciate the enormous importance of this work in the whole spiritual life of the country.

The sharp critical comments voiced by Party and government leaders during their visit to the Exhibition of Moscow Artists were received by the Soviet people as a new display of the Party's concern for our socialist art and evoked a feeling of deep satisfaction.

When N. S. Khrushchev's remarks about the abstractionists were made public, the Soviet people received them as an important step in the Party's efforts to usher in the culture of communism, as the start of a new stage in the improvement of Party guidance of the development of artistic creation. Some comrades are said to have summed up the Party's criticism in the well-known words: "There *is* such a Party!" [1]

Yes, there is such a Party. It has guided and will guide, has shaped — to quote V. I. Lenin — and will continue to shape the results of the artistic process in our country. It is the Communist Party of the Soviet Union.

(*Pravda,* December 22, 1962. In full.)

5

THE POET AND THE COMMISSAR

The December 17 meeting, at which 400 artists, writers, film workers, and composers were present, produced some extraordinary exchanges. The dialogue between Khrushchev and Yevtushenko was one of the more remarkable.

Yevtushenko vs. Khrushchev

YEVTUSHENKO: First of all I want to thank the leaders of the Party and the government for kindly making it possible for me to speak here. Permit me to begin my speech with a verse which I wrote not so long ago which I consider very timely. [Recites the two last lines of the poem, "Babi Yar."]

COMRADE KHRUSHCHEV: Comrade Yevtushenko, this poem has no place here.

YEVTUSHENKO: Respected Nikita Sergeyevich, I especially selected this poem and with the following purpose in mind. We all know that no one has done more than you in the liquidation of the negative consequences of the Stalin cult of personality and we are all very grateful to you for this. However, one problem yet remains which is also a negative consequence of those times, but which today has not yet been resolved. This is the problem of anti-Semitism.

[1] V. I. Lenin at the First All-Russian Congress of Soviets, 1917.—Trans.

COMRADE KHRUSHCHEV: That is not a problem.

YEVTUSHENKO: It is a problem, Nikita Sergeyevich. It cannot be denied and it cannot be suppressed. It is necessary to come to grips with it time and again. It has a place. I myself was a witness to such things. Moreover, it came from people who occupy official posts, and thus it assumed an official character. We cannot go forward to communism with such a heavy load as Judophobia. And here there can be neither silence nor denial. The problem must be resolved and we hope that it will be resolved. The whole progressive world is watching us and the resolution of this problem will even more greatly enhance the authority of our country. By resolution of the problem I mean the cessation of anti-Semitism — [not clear], along with instituting criminal proceedings against the anti-Semites. This positive measure will give many people of Jewish nationality the opportunity to take heart and will lead us to even greater success in all areas of Communist construction.

I would like to say a few words about abstract painting and our artists. I think that our young artists have acted incorrectly in organizing the "underground exhibition" and inviting foreign correspondents to it.[1] This was done without forethought and deserves widespread censure. We also cannot permit our artists to sell their works abroad. This can only be a blow to our prestige and to our art. But I want to say that we must have great patience with this abstract trend in our art and not rush to suppress it, for the result may be the opposite. I know the artists in question, I know their work, and I can emphasize that side by side with the abstract aspect, they are attracted to the realistic manner of expression. I am convinced that several formalistic tendencies in their work will be straightened out in time.

COMRADE KHRUSHCHEV: The grave straightens out the hump-backed.

YEVTUSHENKO: Nikita Sergeyevich, we have come a long way since the time when only the grave straightened out hump-backs. Really, there are other ways. I think that the best way is to display patience and tact and give examples of how to work at our art. I think that we should permit the existence of various schools in painting and let art, our Soviet art, progress in the arguments among them. Artists, like writers and musicians, are most sensitive to any pressure. Therefore, it is best not to resort to it. Everything will remain in its place.

COMRADE KHRUSHCHEV: I don't believe that you personally like abstract art.

YEVTUSHENKO: Nikita Sergeyevich, there are all kinds of abstractionism. What is important is that it should not be charlatanism. I submit that a situation can occur when it would not be possible to convey the newest

[1] Yevtushenko refers to a semi-private exhibit of young artists organized on November 26, 1962, at the studio of Eli Belyutin, an art teacher. A number of Western correspondents were invited to view it, as well as some Soviet cultural officials and a couple of hundred of Soviet citizens. This exhibit was closed after a few hours and then summoned to be hung at the Manezh.

trends of our epoch in the old manner of writing. I must openly admit that I do not like our portrait painting although it is realistic. I very much respect those comrades who are depicted in these portraits, but the portraits themselves seem to me to be ordinary color photographs incapable of stirring the viewer. I cannot permit the idea, Nikolai [sic] Sergeyevich, that you can like the tastelessly drawn picture, "N. S. Khrushchev among the Workers." The latest period of my life has been closely linked up with Cuba. I like Cuban abstract art very much. It would be good if we would organize an exhibition of Cuban art. Cuban abstract art is very popular among the Cuban people and their leaders. Fidel Castro is attracted to it. Cuban abstract art is helping the Cuban revolution and is walking in step with it. I think that our art, including the abstractionists, is also going in one straight line of fighters for communism. I appeal not for appeasement, but I call for self-restraint, for the deepened study of the theory and practice of modern art, and in the final analysis, a consolidation of the forces of literary and artistic workers for the good of our country.

Thank you for your attention.

Reprinted from Commentary (New York), December 1963.

6

THE CASE AGAINST ILYA EHRENBURG

Soon after the accusations against Ilya Ehrenburg at the closed meeting of December 17, attacks on him began to appear in the press. The first, by the old-line realist painter Alexander Laktionov in Pravda *on January 4, 1963, declared: "Had we listened to the voice of I. Ehrenburg, we would long ago have had to stand under the banner of formalism, to deny our love of our Russian realist art and to espouse various 'isms,' mostly of French origin." The second appeared in* Trud *on January 9 by Alexander Gerasimov, who was said to be Stalin's favorite painter.*

It was an attack by the literary critic Vladimir Yermilov, however, that pointed to Ehrenburg's worst offense. The choice of Yermilov as hatchetman was significant: during the purge era, he was known and feared for denouncing fellow writers to the police.

Ehrenburg's reply to Yermilov elicited a rejoinder that was even more vehement than the original attack. The editors of Izvestia, *moreover, gave their support to Yermilov's rejoinder. But the attack on Ehrenburg had not yet reached its culminating point. That was to come only in the major policy speeches of Khrushchev and Ilyichev in March.*

THE NEED FOR ARGUMENT. On Reading I. Ehrenburg's Memoirs *People, Years, Life*. By V. Yermilov.

If a poll were taken on the question "What are the chief shortcomings of literary criticism?" one would have to say that our criticism is far from always esthetic criticism. The fact is often lost sight of, for example, that in appraising works of art, genuinely esthetic criticism considers their always distinctive inner laws, their uniqueness, their own artistic logic. It contemplates a work from within, makes no demands of it that are not relevant to its nature, its purpose, its genre, to the work as a concrete whole, but determines its main underlying artistic principle and investigates to see whether or not the writer is faithful to this principle, whether he consistently adheres to his principle or departs from it.

The weekly *Literaturnaya Rossiya* [Literary Russia] (No. 2, 1963) carried an article by L. Fomenko entitled "Great Expectations." The article does contain accurate observations and comments, and it is written with vitality and feeling. But it also contains departures from the demands of esthetic criticism, and for that matter of esthetic justice. The charge is leveled against A. Solzhenitsyn's story *One Day in the Life of Ivan Denisovich*, which portrays the flagrant iniquities of the period of the Stalin cult, that it "fails to bring out the total dialectics of the time," that it "has not attained to . . . broad generalization capable of embracing the contending phenomena of the epoch." But the artistic principle underlying the story relates specifically to local phenomena. The generalizations, the character portrayals, etc., are presented here within an artistically limited field of action defined by the given, particular circumstances, by the given realities. As for the "contending forces," they are, needless to say, represented here: the brutality of camp life is countered by the characters of Soviet people, by the whole nature of the narration, by the whole artistic assessment of what is described. On the other hand, in censuring the story for not giving us a broad, generalized treatment of the epoch, the critic is in effect asking the writer to transcend the inner logic, the inner laws of the work, to broaden the sphere of depiction to include other aspects of life. This is quantitative criticism, not qualitative: describe not only this, but that! The entire structure of A. Solzhenitsyn's story is based on a clearly expressed artistic principle; no inner contradictions impair the unity of this work, a work wedded to the traditions of Russian literature.

The article "Great Expectations" also discusses other works, including I. Ehrenburg's memoirs *People, Years, Life*.

This is in many respects a valuable and fascinating work, and it discloses a number of new facets of the author's talent. The writer's artistry as a portraitist has been much enriched. The reader is introduced in the memoirs to a large and varied procession of individuals who played prominent roles in the artistic, cultural, ideological, and political life of the time. Naturally, they are for the most part artists: writers, painters, musicians, directors, actors. The author writes of them with unfeigned love, sometimes with reverential respect; he is passionately enamored of some and venerates others, while at the same time noting what seem to him to be their weaknesses and short-comings. The writer conveys their total absorption in their difficult work, in their impassioned, solicitous reflections on art and the times, their obsession with the desire to understand *people,* the *years,* and *life.* For all the distinctive personal characteristics of each of the artists whose portraits appear before us, we see traits that link them together: above all, the keen sensibility in-trinsic to the very nature of the artist; the incessancy of their restless and often agonizing searchings for answers to the question of the relationship between art and life, the position of art, the artist, humaneness, and human-ism in a complicated, contradictory, in many respects tragic epoch that is at the same time passionately seeking the one and only human truth.

Among the portraits lovingly drawn by I. Ehrenburg are those of persons the mere mention of whose names arouses in the reader a special feeling of poignant grief and bitterness over their fates, mixed with love for them. We are referring to artists who perished innocently in the period of the Stalin cult — I. Babel, V. Meyerhold, T. Tabidze, P. Yashvili, P. Markishe, O. Man-delshtam. The times we are living in, symbolized by the 20th and 22nd Party Congresses and the struggle to restore Leninist norms, have afforded us a chance to tell the painful truth about the fate of these wonderful people and the proud truth about their selfless labors, about their humanism.

The author of the article "Great Expectations," though he dwells in detail on A. Solzhenitsyn's story and, as we have seen, makes demands of it that are incompatible with the nature of the work, has no critical remarks to make about I. Ehrenburg's work, confining himself to a general favorable reference: "This is a significant work of art by Ehrenburg. His memoirs are highly lyrical." Strange as it may seem, this is all that is said of I. Ehren-burg's memoirs as a whole. There follow a few lines referring to the part of the memoirs that was published in 1962. But I. Ehrenburg's memoirs, for all their merits, suffer from inner contradictions that to a certain extent impair their artistic unity and oneness, and the actual artistic principle underlying them lacks sufficient clarity.

Censures Ehrenburg on Modernism

People, Years, Life is constructed according to the laws of memoirs. But the memoir genre is "imperceptibly" joined by another genre — the genre of the treatise on art, on what the art of the age is like and what it ought to be. The decreeing of particular esthetic views is altogether incompatible with art. Yet when the author's esthetic views are stated incidentally, "in passing," in the general flow of the memoirs, the inevitable result is just that — decreeing, since analysis, argumentation, and substantiation are lacking.

As for the actual views that I. Ehrenburg states on the art of this epoch, they prompt the need for argument.

The author of *People, Years, Life* spotlights the art of modernism in its various forms, as if the epoch, its searchings, and its doubts were primarily represented by modernism. For instance, cubism is presented for the most part from the positive side. It was cubism, in the author's opinion, that made it possible to convey the paramount features of the epoch, to show the "face of war." "Different artists," writes I. Ehrenburg, "came to cubism by diverse paths. For Picasso it was not an outer garment but his skin, even body, not a painting style but a way of seeing and a philosophy of life; from 1910 up to the present I think there has not been a year in which, along with other works, Picasso has not painted several canvases that represent a continuation of his cubist period. . . . For Léger, cubism was bound up with his love of modern architecture, the city, work, the machine. Braque said that cubism enabled him 'to achieve my fullest self-expression in painting.' . . . Cubism . . . taught much to" Diego Rivera, etc.

As we see, the author gives us a favorable assessment not only of the work of artists in one way or another connected with cubism but of cubism itself, as an extraordinarily fruitful movement in art. But the relationships of great artists with any "isms" are always immeasurably more complicated and contradictory than I. Ehrenburg represents them to be. Quite often it is the violation of a particular "ism," the exploding of its canons from within, that yields the artist a triumph. Since he is talking not just about particular works of art now but about definite theoretical esthetic programs, the author ought unquestionably to have examined the modernist theoretical conceptions in their substance.

We encounter the same kind of decreeing in connection with another modernist movement, surrealism. "Despite its name," writes I. Ehrenburg, "surrealism was not a take-off but a good launching pad, and notwithstanding the boisterous naivete of its first declarations it gave us such poets as Eluard and Aragon." A good launching pad must at least be stable. Did surrealism meet this requirement if, as I. Ehrenburg himself says, the dogma of this movement was "automatism" of the creative process and the exaltation of dreams? A launching pad is not too good a place for dreams, nor are dreams always or only naive. Can surrealism be said to have *given* us such poets as Eluard and Aragon? Is it not more accurate to say that socialist realism *took* these poets away from surrealism? But of realism and its fruitfulness Ehrenburg says nothing. While he delightedly states that modernism "taught much" to particular artists, realism seems to have taught no one anything. And again and again, unfortunately, we continue to encounter unsubstantiated declarations in I. Ehrenburg's work. A number of artists in the West complain of the "abstractionist terror," which seeks despotically and monopolistically to suppress all other artistic trends. N. S. Khrushchev stated at the meeting on Dec. 17 that if the leaders of the modernist trends had absolute material power they would ride roughshod over artists of opposing schools and aspirations. This penetrating and accurate opinion was greeted with fervent applause. Incidentally, there is an interesting little detail cited in the memoirs *People, Years, Life*. I. Ehrenburg recalls the artistic life of the years just after the revolution:

The futurists decided that people's tastes could be changed just as swiftly as the economic structure of society. The magazine *Iskusstvo kommuny* [Art of the Commune] said: "We do indeed claim that we should be allowed to use the power of the state to carry out our artistic ideas and probably would not hesitate to do so."

No, for all its otherworldliness, its absorption in naive dreams abstracted from mundane reality, modernism has no objection at all to decreeing in the arts so long as the decrees are oriented in its favor.

Describing the artistic life of the years just after the revolution, the author of *People, Years, Life* here again has eyes for and places primary emphasis on the activities of representatives of various modernist movements: cubists, futurists, suprematists, and Jacks of Diamonds. I. Ehrenburg says about the activity of the modernists in the years just after the revolution that something in it *troubled* him. "What was it that troubled me in the triumph of these artists and poets, who reminded me (if only outwardly) of the best friends of my early youth?

"First of all — the attitude toward art of the past." I. Ehrenburg was troubled, too, by the "artistic reaction which followed the brief appearance of 'left art' on the streets."

Reaction is that which succeeds progressive phenomena. But unfortunately, I. Ehrenburg has eyes for the futurists, cubists, and suprematists and not for the new art, the art of the revolution, which was emerging and trying to find itself. It is impossible to understand how, describing the artistic life of the years just after the revolution, one can have eyes for the modernist currents and take no notice of A. Blok's "The Twelve," of that poem's influence on the entire development of Soviet art! I. Ehrenburg speaks of his ideological doubts of 1921, "of the intelligentsia that accepted the October Revolution and was withal filled with doubts. When you reread the early stories of Vsevolod Ivanov, Malyshkin, Pilnyak, and N. Ognev, the early poems of Tikhonov, it becomes clear that these doubts grew out of a craving to bring a critical approach to bear on the facts, as Lenin said." I. Ehrenburg contends that the doubts felt by those writers whose names he mentions here and the doubts that he, I. Ehrenburg, felt were of the same order. Dealing with the activities of writers who played the historic role of pioneers of the new literature, he puts the accent on the doubts and loses sight of what was most important: their passionate poetic endorsement of the new world, their laying of foundations for the new literature. Perhaps this assessment is partly attributable to the simple fact that I. Ehrenburg was not an active participant in a number of events in the development of our literature.

Realist Traditions and Modernist Schemes

No, not doubts primarily, but the joy of the difficult task — the road lay through virgin country! — of establishing the new world, the new man, the new attitude to life characterized the works of writers like Vsevolod Ivanov, Alexander Malyshkin, Nikolai Tikhonov, and Nikolai Ognev, as well as of

Konstantin Fedin, Leonid Leonov, and Lidia Seifullina, writers who represented the intelligentsia I. Ehrenburg is speaking about.

The author of *People, Years, Life* is enthusiastic when interpreting Western modernist movements in their interconnection with Western reality (we pass over the question of whether these attempted interpretations are or are not successful). But the memoirs reveal no enthusiasm in the interpretation of the new Russian art on its own soil, in its interconnection with the new historical reality and with the entire preceding ideological and artistic development of Russian literature. The modernist movements were unable to hold their own in the soil of revolutionary reality and quickly passed from the picture, primarily because a new world was emerging, ideals of singular breadth and complexity were emerging, to confront the new art, a new hero was appearing who mentally and emotionally aspired to take in everything under the sun, to entrench the ideal of achieving justice and freedom in reality and not in dreams and modernist abstractions. The ideals toward which the age was oriented had been evolved, through much suffering, by Russian thought and Russian literature over their entire antecedent development. Russian literature was realistic precisely because it aspired to establish real human happiness in this, the real world. No literature did as much to pave the way for and establish the man free from the pettiness, narrow-mindedness, and egoism of the old world as Russian realistic literature, the literature of Tolstoy, Dostoyevsky, Chekhov, and Gorky; it cleansed the soul of mankind. And now coming into the world was a man of a great romantic dream and great realistic deeds, and to such a man the great Russian literature of the past was near and dear. Could this dream, these deeds, these ideals, and these traditions be accommodated in modernist schemes? It was precisely because the new, revolutionary literature reflected the birth of this man, this dream, and these deeds that it was able to exert a major influence on the whole body of world literature of the epoch. Historical accuracy and internationalism call for appreciating the influence exerted by the literature born of the October Revolution on the development of world literature. The memoirs *People, Years, Life* have no room even for Mikhail Sholokhov's "The Silent Don," which was such an event in the development of Russian and world literature. A certain tendency to lay down the law in the sphere of art shows itself in Ehrenburg's work — in details, for example, such as the flat statement that Tolstoy's sentence structure *cannot* be employed for depicting the present day. But, after all, can't it? Tolstoy's complex and yet simple sentence expressed the artist's desire to embrace as many aspects as possible in every twinkling of the eye, as many relationships and environmental details as possible. I think that just as it is ridiculous to impose Tolstoy's sentence structure on writers, it is wrong to proscribe that structure.

In I. Ehrenburg's work we unfortunately encounter oversimplification of some important problems, some controversies, as well as several questions concerning the ethical, social conduct of the artist (how should the artist order his life?). I. Ehrenburg writes, for example, about obsequious deference

to things foreign and says in this connection: "There can, of course, be
various attitudes to Europe — 'open a window,' seal up the doors; or one
can remember that our entire culture — from Kievan Rus to Lenin — is inseparably linked with the culture of Europe." This, of course, is correct, but
it is not too interesting in view of its obvious incontestability. "To seal up
the doors" against Europe is a rather senseless pursuit, if only because our
country has not been excluded from Europe by anybody and cannot be,
which circumstance is well known to any lower-grade schoolboy. It would
have been more accurate to speak not of Europe but of the West, would it
not? As for "remembering" the link between Russian culture and the culture
of the West, is that the point at issue? The point at issue is not whether to
remember but *how* to remember. One can remember the mutually enriching influence of one culture on another, with each retaining its national
independence, its national originality. And one can "remember" in such a
way that nothing is left of the national independence of a particular culture.
Needless to say, we do not and cannot have any disagreements with the
author of *People, Years, Life* on the necessity for Soviet writers, who uphold ideals of internationalism and national dignity, to combat views that
deny the national independence of one or another culture. But it seems to
me that the question of the interrelations between our culture and the culture
of the West ought not to be oversimplified and reduced merely to a willingness or a refusal to acknowledge ties.

Ehrenburg and the Stalinist Cult

There is a motif running like a refrain through I. Ehrenburg's memoirs that
is not fully comprehensible. It is the necessity for silence on the writer's
part in certain difficult and painful historical circumstances, for a kind of
inner submission to these circumstances. I. Ehrenburg says that in 1917–1918
he

> . . . grieved for neither estates, factories, nor securities: I was poor
> and had despised wealth since I was a child. It was something else that
> disturbed me. I had grown up with a conception of freedom that had
> come down to us from the 19th century; from my school days I had
> respected disrespect, listened to the counsel of the disobedient. I failed
> to understand that not only usages but concepts were changing; the new
> age brought much, and it took away much. . . .
> Later I, like all my contemporaries, was forced to undergo more than
> a few trials; I proved to be prepared for them: At 46 the line of life was
> far clearer to me than at 26. . . . I knew that one had to be able to
> live with clenched teeth, that one could not approach events as one did
> a dictation exercise, doing nothing but underlining mistakes, that the
> road to the future was not a smooth highway. As the poet Tvardovsky
> has said, "One cannot take away a single word" — in history, as in the
> life of the individual, there are many bitter pages, not everything works
> out as we would like it to.

It is not clear what conception of freedom inherited from the 19th century is referred to. The concept of true freedom was evolved in the 19th century by Marx and Engels — in Russia by Belinsky, Herzen, Dobrolyubov, and, indeed, the whole of Russian democratic literature. No, the new age did not call for repudiation of the concept of freedom. Quite the reverse. The freedom for which Russian literature had been striving had now been made the express goal of the day in the revolutionary remaking of life — the greatest freedom of the individual, achievable only in conjunction with the freedom of the people as a whole. This became the content of the new art. And, of course, only the revolutionary, innovative remolding of the great earlier realistic traditions bound up with the ideals of real freedom and with broad and profound social thought could create the new forms for the new content.

There is something else that is hard to understand. I. Ehrenburg says that twenty years after 1917–1918 — that is, in 1937–1938 — he realized that one had to be able to live with clenched teeth, that is, be silent, that one should not underline the "mistakes," since history does not always work out as we would like it to and "one cannot take away a single word." The Soviet people, and Soviet writers among them, were grievously affected by the tragic events of 1937–1938 associated with the Stalin cult. But the tragedy lay, among other things, in the prevailing certainty that Stalin was right, that everything done under the shield of his name was unimpeachable. The Party and its Central Committee for good reason named this period the period of the *cult!* It could not be put more accurately! The doubts that arose in people were repressed by an inner voice. But these doubts were building up, and the Party responded to them with the historic 20th Congress. If there had been a prevailing conscious decision to "clench teeth," silently turning the "bitter pages" of history, it would have meant, in particular, that as early as 1937–1938 the groundlessness of such phenomena as mass repressions was entirely clear. But if that were the case, the ethical principle of being "able to live with clenched teeth" could not bear ethical criticism. Ehrenburg oversimplifies the tragedy.

The motif of silence is also developed in connection with Ehrenburg's decision in 1931, as he puts it, "to take my place in the battle formation," exchanging the life of the dreamer for the life of the soldier, the result of which decision was the appearance in 1934 of *The Second Day,* a book that signalized the writer's shift of attention to Soviet life. Here again he says: "I was not repudiating what I held dear, was not renouncing anything, but I knew that I should have to live with clenched teeth, to learn one of the most difficult sciences — silence." It is very hard to understand, however, why the decision to take his place in the battle formation was accompanied by a decision to learn the science of silence. The ethical principle of silence is simply incomprehensible for a writer. But Ehrenburg is firm on the point. For instance, he reminisces: "I said of my devotion to the new era: 'We love it with no less "strange a love" than the love our forebears had for the "fatherland." ' " But further on it turns out that "this feeling likewise calls for 'leaving things unsaid.' " We never do learn, however, when our forebears spoke about "leaving things unsaid" or what kind of things, or what kind I. Ehrenburg has in mind. Equally enigmatic is the following proposition: "Now" (in 1936–1937 — V. Ye.) "I knew for a certainty: No matter what happened, however agonizing might be the doubts (not as to the propriety of the idea, but about the intelligence of the people in command), one had to be silent, to fight, to win." Evidently, I. Ehrenburg had a great advantage over the overwhelming majority of ordinary Soviet people, who in those years had no doubts about the propriety of the actions of the "people in command." Ordinary Soviet people at that time felt bitter and shocked that there should prove to be so many enemies of the people. However, there were many who, doubting the propriety of some particular action, championed justice for a particular individual who they were certain was not an enemy; they fought, and fought not with silence. There were quite a few statements, too, at meetings and in the press, which, even though they were concerned with protest against a particular case, a particular occurrence, in reality related to the essence of the Stalin cult. There was criticism, for example, of "cultist" literary works. In I. Ehrenburg's memoirs the whole body of Soviet literary critics figure merely as a collective, zealous "hatchet man," the most insidious and industrious possible. To be sure, a posture of this kind looks "liberal." However, this is a highly superficial liberalism. The theme of silence preoccupies Ehrenburg to such an extent that he even cites a 1938 poem of his celebrating his suspension of thought and his silence: "Do not let me complete the thoughts in my mind; break off my voice, I beg you; that the memory may dissolve and this sadness lift; that people may jest, and laughter resound; so that, remembering, I may jump up, stop myself, not complete the thoughts in my mind; that I may live without stirring from sleep — drink at a gulp like a drunkard, and fall to the floor; so that the clock may tick at night and this faucet may drip, drop by drop; bring statistics, rhythms, something — some appearance of urgent rush work; to fight the enemy, with bayonet, under bombs, under fire, to endure death, and to look others in the eye. Do not let me look, do this kindness, I pray: Do not let me see or remember what has happened to us in our life." The poem, as we can see, is unfortunately a poor one — poor in both form and content. The wish not to think things through, not to see or remember what "has happened to us in our life," cannot be considered typical of the experiences and feelings of the overwhelming majority of Soviet people in that period. On the contrary, what was typical was their anxiety to think things through at all costs, to understand everything, however painful it might be. The Party was thinking, the whole country was thinking. Had it been otherwise, could there have been such maturity and clarity in the great ideas and decisions of the 20th Party Congress? N. S. Khrushchev made a wonderful statement: "It is our duty to make a thorough and comprehensive study of all such cases rising out of the abuse of power. Time will pass, we shall die, we are all mortal, but as long as we continue to work we can and must find out many things and tell the truth to the

Party and the people. We are obliged to do everything possible to establish the truth now. . . . This must be done so that phenomena of this sort can never be repeated in the future." [1] There is the truth, which cannot be and must not be forgotten, the truth, which looks us straight in the eye. No, we must not "let memory dissolve." The author ends the chapter in which this poem is quoted by saying: "I think this chapter will help the reader to understand the author better. The French proverb claims that a door must either be open or shut. No, the curtain of the confessional may be both lowered and raised at the same time." The reference, presumably, is to the Catholic confessional. I do not know what the situation is where Catholics are concerned, but the French proverb is all the same right: A door must, in fact, be either open or shut. Dialectics is not relativism. Hence one cannot agree with another of I. Ehrenburg's ethical postulates: "Life is more complicated than elementary logic, many crimes can lead to good deeds and there are good deeds fraught with crimes." That is so, but all the same crimes remain crimes and good deeds remain good deeds. Yes, the French proverb is right.

Of course, I. Ehrenburg's thoughts on the utility of the "science of silence" do not and cannot have anything in common with, for example, the entries in the diary of André Gide that are quoted in *People, Years, Life*. This ancient butterfly, as I. Ehrenburg characterizes him, wrote: "If tomorrow what I dread happens and we are deprived of freedom of thought, or at least of freedom to express thought, I shall endeavor to convince myself that art and thought will lose less from that than from excessive freedom of thought. Oppression cannot debase the best; as for the rest, it doesn't matter. Long live suppressed thought!" In his reasoning about silence, I. Ehrenburg is, to be sure, a long way from an apologist for suppressed thought. Still his reasoning on the advantage of silence for a writer makes no sense; it is not clarified.

I. Ehrenburg asks the reader some questions relating to the assessment of his work.

"Am I really a skeptic, cynic, nihilist?" He says that in his works he has noted both the good and the bad in life and that people need both "exposure of society's vices, spiritual defects, and ulcers" and "affirmation of nobility, beauty, and harmony." This is undoubtedly true. As for whether the wonderful writer I. Ehrenburg is a "skeptic, cynic, nihilist," that, of course is a question that cannot occur to anyone, save perhaps in an improbable surrealist dream. "Though I am not a cynic or a skeptic" says the hero of a Chekhov story. I. Ehrenburg, a lover of Chekhov, will surely not take offense at this joke. But speaking seriously, it is a long time since anyone considered I. Ehrenburg a skeptic, cynic, nihilist, or a kind of specialist in exposing the vices, spiritual defects, and ulcers of society. I. Ehrenburg is a highly talented, kindly writer (even now and then with a tinge of sentimentality, which can-

---

[1] The quotation is from Khrushchev's concluding remarks at the 22nd Party Congress. — Trans.

not, of course, be called a virtue), eager to affirm the heartfelt and joyful. And his memoirs are an interesting, pithy, and frequently gripping work. If there are some things in them that are erroneous and that prompt an objection or doubt in the reader, I. Ehrenburg is doubtless well aware that the desire to argue with him is prompted by respect for his work.

(*Izvestia,* January 30, 1963)

EHRENBURG'S REPLY:

THE HEART OF THE DISPUTE MUST NOT BE IGNORED. — Letter to the Editor of Izvestia.

Dear Comrade Editor! In issue No. 25 of Jan. 29 [sic], 1963, *Izvestia* carried an article by V. Yermilov, "The Need for Argument," devoted to my book *People, Years, Life*. I believe that an author should not intervene in an argument about the merits or shortcomings of his work: What he wanted to say he said in his book. For this reason, I am not going to take issue with those parts of V. Yermilov's article in which he speaks as a literary critic. However, a considerable part of the article has nothing to do with my work: V. Yermilov endeavors by insinuations to insult me as a man and a Soviet citizen. To this I am forced to reply.

While harking back repeatedly to my statements on the necessity of living, working, and battling with clenched teeth in the years of the cult of the individual, V. Yermilov never once mentions that at that time I found myself for the most part among the enemies of my country or at the front (in the prewar years I was Paris correspondent and war correspondent in Spain for the same paper that carried V. Yermilov's article). What I wrote was: ". . . I concluded that I should be constrained to silence for a long time: in Spain people were fighting, and I should be unable to share my experiences with anyone."

Let me move on now to the heart of the matter. Yermilov writes of the events of 1937–1938: "Evidently, I. Ehrenburg had a great advantage over the overwhelming majority of ordinary Soviet people, who in those years had no doubts about the propriety of the actions of 'the people in command.' Ordinary Soviet people at that time felt bitter and shocked that there should prove to be so many enemies of the people. However, there were many who, doubting the propriety of some particular action, championed justice for a particular individual who they were certain was not an enemy; they fought, and fought not with silence. There were quite a few statements, too, at meetings and in the press, which, even though they were concernd with protest against a particular case, a particular occurrence, in reality related to the essence of the Stalin cult." In my book I tell of how our military people fighting in Spain and our writers and journalists in Moscow learned with anguish of the arrest of one or another individual who they were sure was innocent. Often we would talk about it among ourselves, but it was not possible for us to protest publicly. I was not present at a single meeting at which people took the floor to protest the arbitrary persecution of comrades whose innocence they never doubted; not once did I read an article protesting against a "case" or "occurrence," protests that, to quote V. Yermilov, in reality related to "the essence of the Stalin cult." Unfortunately, I possessed no special insight, and in the book *People, Years, Life* I wrote: "We thought (probably because we wanted to think it) that Stalin did not know about the senseless persecution of Communists and the Soviet intelligentsia. . . . Not only I but very many others thought the evil came from the small man they called 'the Stalinist Commissar.' We had, after all, seen people arrested who had never belonged to any opposition, who were loyal supporters of Stalin or honest non-Party specialists. The people christened those years the 'Yezhovshchina' [the Yezhov times]."

After the 20th and 22nd Congresses I learned of the letters sent to Stalin by Postyshev and Eikhe, who evidently shared the delusions of many and paid with their lives for their courageous behavior. Among ordinary Soviet people, too, there were surely heroes who tried to make Stalin see that crimes were being committed in the country and who shared the fate of Postyshev and Eikhe.

Izvestia's circulation is many, many times greater than that of the magazine that is publishing *People, Years, Life,* and this obliges me to present a lengthy quotation from my book as a reminder of my attitude to the past and present:

I knew a misfortune had happened. I also knew that neither I nor my friends nor our whole people would ever take the step back from October, that neither the crimes of individual persons nor much that had maimed our life could turn us from the difficult and great path. There were days when I did not want to go on living, but even on such days I knew that I had taken the right path.

After the 20th Party Congress I met friends and acquaintances abroad. Some of them asked me and, indeed, asked themselves whether a fatal blow had not been struck at the very idea of communism. Some things they do not understand. I, an old non-Party writer, know: the idea proved so powerful that Communists appeared who told our people and the whole world too about the crimes of the past, about the distortions of both the philosophy of communism and its principles of justice, solidarity, and humanism. In spite of everything, our people continued to build their house, and several years later they beat off the fascist invasion and completed the house, in which boys and girls who have not known the cruel mistakes of the past now live, study, kick up a noise, and argue.

In his desire to malign me, V. Yermilov, probably unthinkingly, casts aspersions on the people of my generation, and I want my letter, like my book, to show the young people who have started out in life in a far easier and cleaner time the kind of circumstances in which we were called upon to live, to work, and to fight. — Ilya Ehrenburg. Feb. 1, 1963.

(*Izvestia,* February 6, 1963)

YERMILOV'S REJOINDER
REPLY TO THE AUTHOR OF THE LETTER. By V. Yermilov.

In the article "The Need for Argument," I made bold to voice not only favorable but also critical comments on Ehrenburg's memoirs *People, Years, Life*. The article dealt with aspects of the development of the art of our age, the role of Russian literature of the 19th century and of the literature engendered by the October Revolution, modernism and realism, and with the artist's relationship to reality. Finally, it dealt with the concept of silence on the writer's part in the face of specific events covered by the memoirs.

The editors of *Izvestia* have been good enough to let me see I. Ehrenburg's letter. To my astonishment, I perceived that I. Ehrenburg has reduced the whole issue to personal accusations against me: no less than accusations that I have been guilty of insinuations.

In his letter to the editor, I. Ehrenburg tries to make it look as though there is no such thing as a concept of silence in his memoirs, that there are merely everyday, practical considerations with regard to silence: For a long time he found himself mainly "among the enemies" of his country and at the front in Spain and could not "share my experience with anyone."

Let us look at the facts. Do I. Ehrenburg's memoirs present the concept of silence as a kind of ethical principle of the writer's, or do they merely enlarge upon considerations regarding silence that were bound up with the author's being at the front in Spain and "among the enemies" of his country?

Ehrenburg writes in the memoirs: "I said of my devotion to the new era: 'We love it with no less "strange a love" than the love our forebears had for the "fatherland." ' " And further on he explains that "this feeling" (devotion to the new era. — V. Ye.), "likewise calls for 'leaving things unsaid.' "

The kind of love for the revolutionary era and the fatherland that calls for leaving certain things unsaid certainly is a "strange love." But it has nothing in common either with Lermontov's "I love the fatherland . . ." or with the love others among our forebears had for the fatherland or with love for the revolutionary era.

Thus in I. Ehrenburg's opinion the very emotion of love for the new era calls for "leaving things unsaid." What do the front in Spain and being "among the enemies" of his country have to do with it?

The author of the memoirs writes that in 1931 he resolved "to take my place in the battle formation," the result of which decision was the appearance in 1934 of *The Second Day*, a book that signalized the author's shift of attention to Soviet life. "I was not repudiating what I held dear, was not renouncing anything, but I knew that I should have to live with clenched teeth, to learn one of the most difficult sciences — silence." In the article "The Need for Argument" I expressed my bewilderment as to why the writer's decision to take his place in the battle formation should have been accompanied by a decision to live with clenched teeth, to learn the science of silence. Silence about what? About what the writer held dear? About things he was not inwardly renouncing? As we know, a different moral, and at the same time esthetic, postulate has been put forward in literature: *I cannot be silent!* And a popular proverb states ironically about the postulate of silence: "Save your breath to cool the porridge."

I. Ehrenburg also endorses the concept of silence in connection with other historic periods. He writes that in 1937–1938 he realized that one had to be able to live with clenched teeth, that is, be silent, and must not underline the "mistakes," because history does not always work as we would like it to, "bitter pages" are inevitable in it and "one cannot take away a single word." This is very close to what is called objectivism. Lenin pointed out that an objectivist is always in danger of turning into an apologist for the facts.

I. Ehrenburg consistently propounds the ethical principle: I can be silent!

As we see, there is no connection between the concept of silence propounded by I. Ehrenburg and his being "among enemies" of his country or at the front in Spain. But just where, in that case, does I. Ehrenburg perceive an insinuation about him in the article "The Need for Argument"?

Let us examine a second argument that he advanced in support of his claim that insinuations have been made. In my article I cited an excerpt from the memoirs: "Now" (in 1936–1937. — V. Ye.) "I knew for a certainty: No matter what happened, however agonizing might be the doubts (not as to the propriety of the idea, but about the intelligence of the people in command), one had to be silent, to fight, to win." It is in what I wrote about this excerpt that I. Ehrenburg perceives the "essence" of the insinuation. And what I wrote was the following: "Evidently, I. Ehrenburg had a great advantage over the overwhelming majority of [ordinary] Soviet people, who in those years had no doubts about the propriety of the actions of 'the people in command.' "

Could I have kept from making an ironic comment about I. Ehrenburg's "advantage"? After all, he says that he had agonizing doubts about "the intelligence of the people in command." Yet at the same time he felt: "I must be silent." I. Ehrenburg characterizes my bewilderment in this regard as an attempt to insult him as a man and a citizen. I. Ehrenburg took umbrage at my remark about his "advantage." In his letter to the editor he writes: "Unfortunately, I possessed no special insight, and in the book *People, Years, Life* I wrote: 'We thought (probably because we wanted to think it) that Stalin did not know about the senseless persecution of Communists and the Soviet intelligentsia. . . . Not only I but very many others thought the evil came from the small man they called "the Stalinist Commissar." We had, after all, seen people arrested who had never belonged to any opposition, who were loyal supporters of Stalin or honest non-Party specialists.' "

I. Ehrenburg again and again puts himself in the position of a man who was well aware that senseless persecution was taking place, that evil was being done, and who decided to "keep silent" about it. He had no faith in Yezhov, who arrests innocent people. Yet people at the time called Yezhov "the Stalinist Commissar." This means that in those times people still trusted Yezhov. They felt bitter and shocked that there should prove to be so many enemies of the people. They resented this or that action of Yezhov's. But they did not yet know that at the bottom of his actions lay evil. Yet I. Ehrenburg, it appears, knew it as early as that?

I must say that, all the same, I do not think that I. Ehrenburg's position was as it appears to be from his memoirs and his letter to the editor. In actual fact, I. Ehrenburg was probably in just the same position as the rest of society, and it is doubtful indeed whether he possessed such "special insight" as his interpretation might lead one to believe. It would seem that I. Ehrenburg has been so carried away by his postulate of silence that without noticing it he makes false accusations against himself. It cannot be denied that I. Ehrenburg does this with remarkable persistence and without mercy for himself. A close reading of what he has written cannot possibly lead one to any other conclusion than that I. Ehrenburg has "a special insight," or, as I put it, "an advantage." Where is the insinuation? Who is making insinuations against whom? Who is insulting and maligning whom? Why, it is mainly I. Ehrenburg who is insulting and maligning himself.

In his letter to the editor he declares: "In his desire to malign me, V. Yermilov, probably unthinkingly, casts aspersions on the people of my generation. . . ." This, of course, is nonsense. I. Ehrenburg goes on: "I want my letter, like my book, to show the young people who have started out in life in a far easier and cleaner time the kind of circumstances in which we were called upon to live, to work, and to fight."

But in I. Ehrenburg's letter just what kind of figure do the Soviet people who lived, worked, and fought in the time I. Ehrenburg is telling us about cut in the eyes of youth? After all, according to both his memoirs and his letter, it turns out that everybody, or at least the majority of people, knew even by that time that evil was being done in the name of Stalin, that the mass repressions were unjustified — knew and were silent. And that means insulting a whole generation of Soviet people in an effort to give oneself a clean bill of health.

The great purifying role of the 20th Congress for the whole people lay precisely in the fact that the Party established and disclosed the truth about the perversions and iniquities perpetrated in the period of the Stalin cult. But the establishment and disclosure of that truth constituted a whole historical process; by virtue of historical circumstances, that truth could not yet have been clear in the years referred to in I. Ehrenburg's memoirs.

I. Ehrenburg, by sensationally accusing me of making insinuations, seeks to escape the necessity for argument on the substance of the issue on which public attention is currently focused: the effort toward a fresh upsurge in our arts, toward the truthful and artistically diversified portrayal of life, toward true innovation, etc.

I. Ehrenburg explains the stand he has taken of stifling the argument by saying that "an author should not intervene in an argument about the merits or shortcomings of his work: what he wanted to say he said in his book." There might perhaps be some sense in this if a literary work of a different genre, a novel or poem, were involved; we shall not undertake to settle that question. But the author of *People, Years, Life* speaks as a publicist and as a critic of literature and art, espouses definite esthetic concepts and develops his own esthetic views. Can he really be disinterested in argument on the substance of the problems he has raised? Does he really feel it unimportant to defend his esthetic and ethical views and convictions? Can this be regarded as being in the tradition of work and Russian social thought, literature, publicism, and ideological life in general? Or is that same principle of "the science of silence," of being able to "live with clenched teeth," at work here? To set up a clamor that some sort of disservice has been done to him as a man and a citizen on the ground that critical remarks were made with regard to his book, and at the same time to remain silent on the substance of the issues that have arisen in connection with the book — this position of I. Ehrenburg's cannot be called a position of integrity.

From the Editors. — We are publishing today two letters: one from the writer I. Ehrenburg and the other from the critic V. V. Yermilov. Unfortunately, the writer I. Ehrenburg has avoided talking to the point, and his letter boils down to groundless accusations against the critic V. Yermilov.

We should have derived far more satisfaction from having started this conversation had I. Ehrenburg not evaded the most agitating and burning issues: Party spirit and identification with the people in literature; the paths of genuine innovation; the bold quest for new images, characters, and forms; the effort to combat varnishing; the truth of life and the truth of art.

Unfortunately, I. Ehrenburg's letter indicates that the author is more concerned about the accusations that he himself has invented than about the essentials of these big, fundamental issues.

I. Ehrenburg says with his letter: "My thinking will be the same in the future as it has been in the past." Well, that is his right. But in that case it is the right of the critic to write in no uncertain terms about a number of incorrect tendencies in I. Ehrenburg's position.

(*Izvestia*, February 6, 1963)

7

THE STORM BREAKS

The confrontation between Party leaders and the intellectuals, interrupted after December 17 by pressing matters of state, such as the debate behind the scenes with China, was resumed in the Kremlin on March 7 and 8. A large part of Ilyichev's speech was given over to an attack on Ilya Ehrenburg. Ilyichev was at his most revealing when he acknowledged that the campaign of the Party had met widespread resistance among in-

tellectuals. In the face of Party demands that they apologize for "errors"
they had committed, too many writers and artists, he warned, "have
maintained a stance of silence."

ON THE ARTIST'S RESPONSIBILITY TO THE PEOPLE. Speech by L. F. Ilyichev,
Secretary of the Party Central Committee, on March 7, 1963, at the
meeting of Party and government leaders with workers in literature and
the arts.

Comrades! We have gathered once again in order to continue the exchange
of opinions on questions of literature and the arts. The talk held on December 17, 1962, proved to be so interesting and trenchant that N. S. Khrushchev
proposed that it be continued. We had hoped to meet again right after the
New Year. Circumstances prevented this, however, and the interval lasted
longer than was contemplated.

But, as the saying goes, it's an ill wind that blows no good.

Events have developed in such a way during this time that it seems as
though there has been no interruption. During the almost three months that
have intervened we have had a lively discussion on the most acute questions
of the development of Soviet art. The discussion, begun in connection with
the visit of Party and government leaders to the art exhibition in the Manezh
and the exchange of opinions on December 17, has transcended the bounds
of the creative unions, has expanded its audience, and to all intents and purposes has been transformed into a national debate.

There is nothing astonishing in this. After all, the questions under discussion — on ways for developing creative art, whose interests it should serve
and what ideals it should affirm — are very close to the people and of deep
concern to Soviet man.

In a word, what is being discussed is *the artist's responsibility to the*
people.

Pseudo Innovators and Lounge Lizards

We all live and work for the people. Thus the important thing for us is
how Soviet people have interpreted the Party's concern for the further development of Soviet art, of our literature.

Their opinion, as should have been expected, has proved to be just about
unanimous. A great many letters, telegrams, articles, responses, and messages
have been received by the Party Central Committee and the U.S.S.R. Council of Ministers and by the newspapers and magazines. Their authors — workers, collective farmers, scientists, engineers, artists, writers, students — express approval and warm support for the Party's struggle for the vital truth
of Soviet art and literature, for their Communist ideology and high artistic
value.

It would be interesting, of course, to read you letter after letter here. You
would obtain a very impressive picture. But this would take too long.

Still and all, some of them must be mentioned.

I will remind you of the letter signed by F. Bogdanovsky, Yu. Gagarin, G. Lamochkin, V. Petrishcheva, and others that was published in *Komsomolskaya pravda*. These comrades clearly express their negative attitude toward the formalist enthusiasm of certain artists, poets, and composers. They write of those who in pursuit of cheap sensations, masked in some cases by empty declarations, drag to exhibitions or load the airwaves with nonsensical combinations of colors or sounds, and moreover attempt to palm off their wares as "innovations." The authors of the letter — deriding the pseudo innovators who, alluding to a handful of lounge lizards, say "The young people are for us" — declare:

> No, Soviet youth has always been and always will be against the counterfeiting of innovation, against the preaching of nonsense and individualism, against everything that hinders young people from understanding life, from working out firm convictions to live by, and from correctly evaluating the facts and phenomena of the past.

The agitated words of the young builders of communism cannot fail to touch the hearts of those who are prepared to sacrifice the interests of great art to formalist tricks and abstractionist daubing, to decadent doggerel accompanied by the hysterical twanging of guitars.

In spite of the contemptuous attitude of some artists to the "nonprofessional" opinion of "simple people," the working people express extremely mature judgments on the state of affairs in art. They emphasize with absolute truth that formalist enthusiasms are far from being as harmless as some people try to make them appear, that they represent a loss of all principles, ideological and artistic, and political.

I shall quote excerpts from the letter by V. Koval, a teacher in Lugansk Province.

"One can only be struck by how much sharper class feeling is among bourgeois ideologists than in some of our artists and writers." Bourgeois artists have always known very well whom they were serving, and they have not armed themselves with the ideologies of other classes. But we have people who do this and, what is more, do it under the guise of "innovation." If this is innovation, then what is one to call apostasy from socialist realism? "Socialist realism is not a fabrication and it is not an invention," Comrade Koval writes further. "It is a method called to life by life itself, *by the life of ideas embodied in life*. It could have another name, but it could not be anything other than an instrument in the creation of the new society."

A very apt and intelligent observation!

The Soviet reader and viewer turns out not to be as "simple" as some workers in literature and art think. He favors not some faceless "general truth" that is outside of time and class, but our Soviet, *Communist truth*. He does not understand and does not accept the dubious opinions about "realism sans prefixes"; his world outlook and his high civicmindedness can be expressed only in the art of *socialist realism*.

The Soviet man loves and knows art; he clearly distinguishes true artistic values from pretentious substitutes, no matter how noisily they are advertised.

And when formalists and abstractionists attempt to glorify themselves as "lovers of truth," "seekers after the truth," "innovators," "the only defenders of the beautiful," their declarations are interpreted simply as completely unfounded claims, as an attempt to grab something that does not belong to them.

"Enough," the Soviet people say to them, "your claims are beyond your means, beyond your resources; you are encroaching on what is not yours. Only the art of socialist realism, the art of the renewal of life, is by right, by its very essence, innovational; it is the genuinely true artistic perception of the world, the expression of the beautiful in art."

The discussion that has spread within the creative organizations and outside their confines has shown on the whole the ideological maturity of our artistic intelligentsia. What is particularly important, under the influence of the salutary ideas of the Party the very atmosphere of the creative discussion changed; a number of creative workers began to lose their feeling of "defenselessness," people have been speaking out about Party spirit [partiinost] and folk ties [narodnost] in art, about socialist realism, without fear of being considered reactionaries and conservatives.

Everything is returning to its place.

The participants in an expanded session of the Secretariat of the U.S.S.R. Artists' Union, held under the chairmanship of that great master of Soviet painting S. V. Gerasimov, interpreted the instructions of the Party with complete understanding and approval and sharply condemned those who are attempting to implant individualistic anarchy in our art. The secretariat's resolution discusses the serious errors committed in the selection of the paintings at the Exhibition of Moscow Artists; many remarkable realist painters — A. Ye. Arkhipov, N. A. Kasatkin, M. V. Nesterov, K. F. Yuon, I. E. Grabar, V. K. Byalynitsky-Birulya, and many others — were represented either inadequately or not at all in the exhibition's halls, while formalist works of the 1920's and the works of a certain group of young contemporary artists were given generous space.

Many artists came out in complete support of the Party's Leninist line on questions of art at an open Party meeting in the U.S.S.R. Academy of Arts and a conference held by the Russian Republic Artists' Union, as well as in articles published in the press.

A great and creative discussion took place at a session of the Secretariat of the U.S.S.R. Writers' Union.

Well-known and respected figures of Soviet literature saw in the Party's struggle against alien tendencies in artistic creative work an expression of the demands of millions of Soviet people. They spoke with deep concern about cases of formalism and of imitation of the "fashions" of bourgeois literature in the creative work of some Soviet writers and poets. K. A. Fedin, one of our most prominent writers, very rightly said that "it is as though the Party is revealing the enemy to us." "For me, a veteran writer," Konstantin Alexandrovich declared, "this enemy is not new. We have already encountered him in the struggle for the new, socialist art and literature."

Creative and ideological-artistic questions were especially examined at a session of the Ideological Commission under the Party Central Committee with the participation of young writers, artists, composers, cinema and theater workers, and critics.

The exchange of opinions here was useful in all respects and was very frank. First of all, the fact that the majority of our creative youth, knowing the true value of formalism and abstractionism, expressed their negative attitude toward them unequivocally was reason for joy. Having quietly thought over the critical remarks and having felt the loving concern of the Party, the young poets, artists, and sculptors who had committed mistakes correctly evaluated their errors. In the first place E. Neizvestny, E. Belyutin, and Y. Yevtushenko must be mentioned.

The article by the young artist A. Vaznetsov in *Pravda* is worthy of attention. His seriousness and sincerity and his striving to comprehend the sources of his creative mistakes are touching. It is good that A. Vaznetsov and other comrades are attempting to respond to the criticism not by speeches alone but by deeds as well, and have already set about realizing new creative conceptions. We will hope that they will yet speak their own, truly new word in art.

The correct attitude of progressive people in foreign countries to the ideas of our party cannot but delight us. Here, for example, is what Juan Marinello, one of the most important figures of Cuban culture, writes: "Abstract art can in the end be traced back to frankly reactionary ideas and interests. They must be struggled against, as is being done in the Soviet Union." The Italian newspaper *Il Paese Sera,* touching on the remarks made by N. S. Khrushchev at the art exhibition, wrote that "this was a kind of quintessence, a theoretical expression of the protest" of Soviet people against ugliness in art. The newspaper remarked that the abstractionists in the West are now evoking "bewilderment, to say the least," and that their Soviet followers are in error if they think that people in the West "understand" them.

As we see, our homegrown formalists and abstractionists enjoy no "credit" whatever not only with us but even among their confreres in the West.

Talentless Cast-Iron Windpipes

But other voices are also heard. In particular, a fear is expressed that criticism of formalism and abstractionism will lead to creative stagnation, and to the stifling of innovational searchings in art and to the justification and encouragement of naturalism, photographism, and the like.

It is hardly necessary to dwell on the fact that such apprehensions are completely groundless.

People's Artist A. A. Plastov, in an article in *Literaturnaya gazeta,* wrote very graphically and truly:

> At present one can hear talk to the effect that now that the locusts have been driven from the fields, rooks of some kind will turn up to take the locusts' place. The sort that prospered under Stalin and have now come out of the torpor in which they have been living in recent years and have begun to sniff around suspiciously. What can one answer to such warnings? Only one thing: These warnings have no real ground beneath them. It must be known and believed that we have forever asserted the Leninist course in life, and the Party Central Committee headed by N. S. Khrushchev is the guarantee of this. [Applause.]

Every unprejudiced person understands that criticism of formalism and abstractionism does not represent an amnesty for naturalism. No, the attitude toward flat, uninspired naturalism remains unchanged. One must only warn against attempts to fight against realist artists under the guise of struggling against naturalism, as well as accusing of formalism people engaged in searching for new forms in realist art. After all, *the very nature of socialist realism lies in the quest for the new, the artistically beautiful, the true to life, interpreted from the position of the Communist world view.*

It was to be anticipated that the blow against formalism, abstractionism, and other incorrect tendencies in Soviet art would provoke the usual storm of animosity in reactionary bourgeois circles. So it has turned out.

What are our ideological opponents not writing about us!

Here are the inevitable discussions about the "crisis" and "deadlock" in which Soviet art allegedly finds itself, and the assertions about the "bankruptcy" of socialist realism. Here also are the cock-and-bull stories about the "rebellion" of creative youth against the "fathers" who allegedly "compromised themselves" during the years of the cult of the individual; and the fables to the effect that the Marxist-Leninist ideology is in general incompatible with freedom of creativity. Thus — so our enemies preach at us — if you wish to preserve socialist realism in art, then you cannot escape a "return" to the methods of "the Stalin epoch." In a word, they propose that we throw the art of socialist realism overboard.

What rank stupidity and class blindness!

Our opponents have put a new term into circulation: "the freeze." It has been introduced in contrast to "the thaw" — an ambiguous term and one that for that very reason has long had currency in the pages of the bourgeois press.

They are attempting to subsume under the newly coined term literally everything in our creative life that in one way or another opposes bourgeois notions of art. One has only to criticize the fallacious idea of coexistence in the field of ideology and it is a "freeze." One has only to speak of revolutionary traditions, of the great achievements of Soviet culture, and again, "freeze." One has only to upbraid someone for ideological immaturity, for neglecting the feeling of Soviet national pride and for copying bourgeois fashion, and there are cries of "freeze!" It is sufficient even simply to recall the holy of holies of Soviet art: the necessity for close ties with the life of the people, with the struggle for communism, and again it is "a freeze"!

Unfortunately (this must be spoken of also) the sharp and just criticisms of incorrect tendencies in artistic creative work have been incorrectly understood by some figures in Soviet art and literature. And they have not simply misunderstood but continue stubbornly to defend their erroneous views. Some people are even attempting to win others to their point of view, to surround with a wall of estrangement those artists who heed the wholesome voice of criticism, to subject them to ostracism, reproaching them for "lack of principle" and "apostasy." But they pass off their own demagogic statements as models of "principledness" and "firmness."

The incorrect views are expressed in different ways. Some still wish to create the impression that nothing essentially has happened, simply that someone incorrectly informed the Party Central Committee, someone secretly plotted to bring off the visit to the exhibition, someone "palmed off" his point of view, etc. Others say that generally speaking we have neither formalism nor abstractionism and never have had. It is all a myth, an invention.

Both these and the others are dissatisfied with what has taken place, and they are not dissatisfied merely passively but are trying to exacerbate both their own and others' nerves. They may lack talent, but they have cast-iron windpipes; they scream, dance around, "fight" against this person, "expose" that one. But they have to their name neither ideas nor thoughts nor a sincere aspiration to serve the people. [Applause.] How well Rasul Gamzatov put it: There are masters of the word (*slovo*), specifically of the artistic word, and they must not be confused with the masters of glory (*slava*), i.e., the experts at self-glorification.

Such individuals sow distrust in the minds of young people toward the completely clear and precise statements of the Party against tendencies alien to Soviet art, and they try to pass themselves off as spiritual "mentors," spiritual "leaders" of our young people.

But *we have had, have, and shall continue to have only one spiritual leader of the people, of Soviet youth — our great Communist Party!* [Applause.]

The line taken by individual members of the Moscow artists' executive bodies cannot be accepted as clear. Some of them have been evasive, have attempted to play the role of buffer between Party criticism and the people whose creative work and views have been justly reprehended.

It may be said of some members of the Moscow Branch of the Soviet Artists' Union who are bellicosely occupying an incorrect position, such as the artists and critics N. Andronov, M. Nefedov, I. Vilkovir, and A. Gastev, that they have so far understood nothing and learned nothing. Generally speaking, the capital's organization of artists, from which one would expect an example of adherence to ideological and artistic principle, at times allows itself to be carried away by individual irresponsible demagogues.

In the serious conversation about serious matters the voices of some artists and writers are not heard. But whom, strictly speaking, do they hope to embarrass by their "stance of silence"? The Party, the people? Among creative workers are there not a definite number who show no inclination to write, to compose, to create for a time?

But this is a middle position, unworthy of a Soviet man. One can understand, let us say, the writer who works for a long time over a piece, who puts his mind and heart into it, who works, as one writer graphically put it, until his palms sweat. But it is impossible to understand a writer if he keeps silent for a long time.

After all, silence also means something, also expresses some point of view.

Attack on Ehrenburg

So far it has been chiefly the young people who have been under discussion.

But sometimes extremely prominent figures of Soviet culture defend positions with which it is very difficult to agree. You all remember, of course, the speech delivered here the last time by I. Ehrenburg. He expressed a few propositions that in essence sounded like generalizations. And this is not the first time he has expressed them. His main idea was that, strictly speaking, there is no need for us to quarrel over tastes in art. One person may like R. Falk's paintings and another may not; well, so be it. The creative work of every artist has the same right to exist. A truly innovational work, according to I. Ehrenburg, is always disliked by someone.

The esteemed speaker referred to Vladimir Ilyich Lenin; according to Ehrenburg, while Lenin did not care for the verses of Mayakovsky, he did not impose his opinion or his tastes on anyone. The speaker's thought was not completed; it was left hanging, so to speak, but each person can carry it "to its logical conclusion." It is as though we are invited to conclude that V. I. Lenin did not wish to interfere in questions of artistic creative work, that in general his views on art were distinguished by great tolerance, by an "intellectual liberalism" that it wouldn't hurt us to follow today.

It is impossible to accept such an interpretation as authentic. It is a departure from historical truth, a distortion of Lenin's positions.

Although I. Ehrenburg constantly appeals for tolerance in art, his own position is not marked by it.

For example, he lauds formalist artists to the skies, as workers in the graphic arts have correctly pointed out in *Pravda*, but he finds nothing of value in the great realist artists, in the Peredvizhniki [wandering artists], in Repin. Nor does I. Ehrenburg accept the living, direct ties of Soviet art with realist traditions. He describes the development of Soviet painting after the 1920's as a counterattack by naturalism, the school of the mundane, academic forms, decorousness, simplification, and photographic conventionality, and he ironically hints at its adherence to the canons of the Bologna Academy School of the 16th and 17th centuries.

For a long time nothing appeared in our press about I. Ehrenburg's memoirs *People, Years, Life*. So long as the narrative concerned days long passed, many readers were prepared to accept the memoirs as the vivid, objective testimony of an eyewitness. But now that the memoirs are dealing with recent events, the author's subjectivism puts people on guard. Readers are sending letters to newspapers and magazines in which they express disagreement with I. Ehrenburg; they believe that the author describes Soviet reality onesidedly, defends narrow group interests, and in a number of instances simply distorts events, changes their faces to suit himself.

The authors of the letters are right in many respects.

In describing the years of the cult of the individual, I. Ehrenburg has put forward the so-called "theory of silence," which allegedly was the norm of conduct for Soviet people at that time, including, of course, the author of the memoirs himself. At that time Stalin's abuses of power were allegedly known to many, but they saw no way out other than to live "with clenched teeth." Everyone was trying to survive, believing that with time everything would change. The "theory of silence" was subjected to criticism in V. V. Yermilov's article in *Izvestia*.

It is impossible, comrades, to agree with such a false, incorrect "theory."

First of all, it casts a shadow on the Soviet people who were enthusiastically building socialism and who believed in the correctness of Stalin's actions. Yet according to I. Ehrenburg, one might think that they all, knowing about the deviations from Leninism, were merely saving their own skins and thereby helping the evil to grow stronger.

The reasons why the Party and the people did not at that time come out against Stalin are to be found in the well-known Party Central Committee resolution "On Overcoming the Cult of the Individual and Its Consequences." Thus there is no necessity for repeating them here. It is necessary only to state clearly: *The Communists, our Party, never made silence a principle.*

Incidentally, the "theory of silence" is not true even in regard to I. Ehrenburg himself. After all, you were not silent then, Ilya Grigoryevich, but eulogized, and eulogized with all your talent as a publicist.

Does what you said about Stalin in 1951 really look like silence? You said literally the following: He "helped me, as all of us, to write much of what I have written, and he will help me to write what I am dreaming about." And after Stalin's death you — expressing your personal sentiments, and not somebody's will — wrote of him as a person who "loved people, knew their weaknesses and strength, understood the tears of the mother who had lost her son in the war, understood the labor of the miner and the stonemason," one who "knew the thoughts and feelings of hundreds of millions of people, expressed their hopes, their will to happiness, their thirst for peace."

If I quote your words, it is not in order to single you out from among the many and blame you for the words quoted. We all spoke and wrote thus at the time, without being hypocritical. We believed and wrote. And you, it turns out, did not believe but wrote! These are different positions! [Applause.]

It must be said that I. Ehrenburg experienced no restrictions in stating his views. He was, for example, free in the novel *The Life and Death of Nikolai Kurbov* to put into Kurbov's mouth words that denigrated our revolution and its heroes. In the short story "The Stormy Life of Lazik Roitshvants," published in Berlin in 1928, he was free to describe the Soviet reality of that time in a biased manner. The story depicts the sufferings and afflictions of a poor tailor from Gomel, and the Soviet regime is presented as hostile to the simple man, as a state where only swindlers flourish, where every living thought is crushed, where the "authorities," who consisted of hypocrites and scoundrels, strangle the honest man, do not give him a chance to live.

I. Ehrenburg's story was written a long time ago, but it is still being widely used in anti-Communist propaganda. Somehow, though, we have not heard that the author has expressed his attitude towards this.

The problem, consequently, is not that certain links in the chain of command limit the writer's freedom, the problem is how the artist himself thinks, what he loves and what he rejects. Does he come forward before the face of history with "a prayer for Russia," does he doubt, dream, sigh, and moan, or does he dedicate all his talent, all his aspirations, and, if you wish, his blood and life to the one sacred cause, the great cause of rebuilding human society on Communist principles?

In the first case he will always be subject to cyclones blowing from the depths of the old world. In the second case, he is bound to the people, ideologically armed, and thus free in his creative work.

The readers of the memoirs *People, Years, Life* cannot agree with many of the author's other assertions. And how can one agree, for example, with the appraisal the author gives of the literary works on the Great Patriotic War? I. Ehrenburg writes that V. Nekrasov, E. Kazakevich, V. Grossman, V. Panova, A. Bek, and others devoted excellent novels to the war years. Some of the authors named unquestionably did create good works, worthy of the events they describe. But still, the selection here is patently tendentious. I. Ehrenburg has "absentmindedly" included the works of M. Sholokhov, A. Tvardovsky, A. Fadeyev, L. Leonov, K. Simonov, and the writers of the Ukraine, Belorussian, and other republics among the "others."

I will point out one more case of silence. I. Ehrenburg wrote in great detail about V. Meyerhold, for example. But while lauding the very weakest and most formalistic aspects of his creative work, he is silent about the other aspects.

I will take the liberty of reading a document, a letter from V. Meyerhold to I. Ehrenburg, that was published in the magazine *Novy zritel* [The New Audience] (No. 18, 1924). A part of this letter, but only a part, is quoted in *People, Years, Life*. "I don't understand," V. Meyerhold writes to I. Ehrenburg, "on what grounds you appealed to me to 'refuse to produce' Comrade Podgoretsky's play?

"On the basis of our talk in Berlin? But after all, that conversation made clear that even if you were to set about reworking your novel *The History of the Fall of Europe,* you would write the play in such a way that it could be presented in any city of the Entente." Here I. Ehrenburg breaks off the quotation. "But," V. Meyerhold continued, and this is the most important thing in the letter, "in my theater, which serves and will serve the cause of the Revolution" — it is precisely because of this that V. Meyerhold was rehabilitated (*applause*) — "tendentious plays are needed, plays that have only one goal in mind: to serve the cause of the Revolution. I recall that you resolutely refused to pursue the Communist trends, pointing out your lack of belief in the socialist revolution and your natural pessimism."

One can hardly come out forcibly and convincingly against the coloring of the truth if one colors the history of one's own life.

Comrades! In these remarks an attempt has been made to give concise information on the discussion of the questions of literature and the arts during the time that has passed since the visit by the Party and government leaders to the Manezh and the Dec. 17 meeting with creative workers.

At the last meeting I. Ehrenburg's speech drew particular attention. For this reason I had to speak in more detail on his position. We all know Ilya Grigoryevich as a major writer and publicist, a prominent public figure and an active fighter for peace. We remember and value highly many of his statements, especially during the period of the Patriotic War. But it was impossible not to address critical remarks to him when such serious matters as ideological-creative questions are under discussion. Talk about ideological-artistic questions can and must be only principled, deeply Party in spirit.

I would like to repeat that the existing situation in Soviet art and literature is on the whole healthy. The fact that the truthful and solicitous voice of the Party has reached the heart of the creative intelligentsia, has compelled it to ponder the most important tasks of artistic work and has given it new strength in the struggle for communism, is cause for joy. [Applause.]

(*Pravda,* March 9, 1963. In full.)

8

KHRUSHCHEV SPEAKS AGAIN

Khrushchev's speech of March 8 was the most sweeping statement on literature and the arts by a Soviet leader since Andrei Zhdanov's pronouncement of August 21, 1946, attacking the poet Anna Akhmatova and the satirist Mikhail Zoshchenko. His remarks, like those of Zhdanov seventeen years earlier, bristled with military metaphors. If words were deeds, surely Khrushchev would have succeeded, as Zhdanov did, in putting Soviet artists back in uniform!

Behind its harsh language, however, the speech had an oddly defensive ring. Khrushchev seemed apprehensive, first of all, at the questions being voiced in private as well as publicly by Ehrenburg, as to whether he and the other Soviet leaders were not, after all, accomplices in the crimes of Stalin. Clearly he was aware of the threat which these questions posed to his own authority. And he appeared fearful as to where any weakening of the Party's authority might lead, especially among young people and intellectuals.

Lofty Ideology and Artistic Craftsmanship Are the Great Forces of Soviet Literature and Art

Dear comrades, this is the second time we have met in recent months. And if one takes into account the meeting of the central committee of the party with young writers and artists arranged by the Ideological Commission, then today's meeting is the third.

The materials of these meetings were published in the press and aroused keen interest. We note with pleasure that the position of the central committee of the party on problems of art has met with warm support among the creative workers, the party, and the people, and our foreign friends.

In his speech Comrade Ilyichev has already told you how much lively comment the statement of the central committee of the C.P.S.U. on problems of literature and art aroused among the Soviet and foreign public. He justly noted how the activity of the creative workers had grown in the country in the struggle against unhealthy tendencies in literature and art.

Many comrades who spoke at this conference voiced interesting views and advanced a number of valuable proposals. All this clearly shows that the questions we are discussing have fundamental importance for the development of socialist culture and of Soviet literature and art in the direction determined in the Program of the Communist Party.

Communism and Creative Art

The activities of the writers, painters, composers, sculptors, film and theatrical workers, and of all intellectuals constantly have the attention of the party and the people. And this is perfectly understandable. We are living at a time when literature and art, as Lenin predicted, have become an integral part of the cause of the whole people.

The Soviet people, under the leadership of their Leninist Party, are building a Communist society. Our chief aim in building communism, and I stress this, is to create all the conditions for a better life for working people. And Communist society will be precisely a society of working people.

The need to work is organically natural to people. Only capitalism, by placing working people in inhuman conditions, corrupts them and has a demoralising effect upon the attitude of many people to work. Those people who do not reconcile themselves to oppression of man by man develop their class consciousness in the process of work and become active fighters for the interest of the working people, against the exploiters.

Others, who are guided only by their own personal interests, are passive in public life and do not participate in the class struggle for the overthrow of the bourgeoisie and the building of a new society. Still others live at the expense of the labor of others. These are the exploiters and the oppressors of the working people.

Communism is being built by the labor of millions and only by that. That is why the party exerts every effort to see that all the Soviet people, in one monolithic* working collective — workers, collective farmers, engineers, designers, technicians, teachers, doctors, agronomists, scientists, cultural workers, and people engaged in literature and art — take an active part in building communism.

Now everybody can see that the party's efforts are yielding wonderful results; our people have achieved important successes on the way to communism. But we cannot shut our eyes to the difficulties that have to be overcome in building a new society. To these difficulties belong the survivals of the past in the consciousness of some people in all sections of society. This is seen primarily in their negligent attitude to work, to the fulfillment of their public duty and their duty to the people.

Of great importance in the battle for communism we are waging is the education of all the people in a spirit of Communist ideals. And this is the main task of the ideological work of our party at the present time. We must bring all the party's ideological weapons, including such powerful means of Communist education as literature and art, into combat order.

Our meetings, which have become a good custom, are actually a kind of review of the forces of literature and art, of their creative activity and revolutionary fighting spirit.

The party and its central committee are of the opinion that Soviet literature and art are developing successfully and in the main fulfill their task well.

It would be very harmful, however, to overestimate the successes in literature and art and not to see the serious shortcomings in the work of writers, painters, composers, film and theatrical workers. There have been no ideological-creative failures of an extreme nature, but nevertheless there have been important shortcomings, and in a number of cases also errors, which cannot be tolerated.

Life has shown, and this has been confirmed in the speeches of some comrades at the last meeting and today, that not all creative workers correctly understand the tasks in the field of literature and art outlined in the Party Program. The need therefore exists to explain once again our party's

* "Monolithic" appeared in the original text; it was omitted from the official translation [P. J.].

attitude to vital questions of creative art in the period of the all-round building of communism.

Which works of art do the Soviet people want? Which ones do they appreciate? And which do they reject?

The literature and art of socialist realism have reached great artistic heights, have rich revolutionary traditions, and enjoy world renown. Remarkable works of art and great spiritual values, of which the peoples of our country are justly proud, have been created in all the Soviet republics.

The creative work of leading representatives of Soviet literature and art is a great service by them to the people, and an inspiring example of a worker in art serving his country.

What greater satisfaction can a worker in art gain than the knowledge that his talent is fully devoted to the struggle of the people for the construction of communism and that his works are accepted and highly appreciated by the people?

Demyan Bedny

Remember how the poetry of Demyan Bedny[1] was adopted as a weapon* at the time by our people. In the years of the Civil War, when the Soviet people were defending the world's first socialist state of workers and peasants in fierce fighting against the world imperialism, the Red Guardsmen and the Red Army men and the guerrillas went into battle singing Demyan Bedny's songs. These songs stirred everyone, were understandable to everyone, even illiterate peasants, in the Red Army.

The thoughts of the people are imprinted in "My Mother Saw Me Off to the War," a very popular song at the time. The poet was in the militant ranks of fighters for the revolution and devoted the whole of his enormous talent to the great cause of liberation of the working people from the yoke of the exploiters.

Demyan Bedny possessed the amazing gift of probing the soul of the toiling peasant. With what understanding and artistic skill he exposed the duality of the soul of the peasant! In his works of the Civil War period, the poet convincingly revealed the psychology of the peasant with all his peculiar features at the time. On the one hand, the peasant was pleased that the new Bolshevik government had given him land, of which he had dreamed, and for which an armed struggle went on at the time. On the other hand, some peasants, having received land from the Soviet government, did not show that they understood that the people's power, and the gains of the revolution, had to be defended with arms in hand.

[1] Demyan Bedny (Efim Alekseevich Pridvorov, 1883–1945), one of the few Russian writers who belonged to the Bolshevik party before the revolution, is best known as the producer of "applied lyrics", political slogans for newspapers, conferences, etc. During the last years of his life he was under a cloud for having "besmirched the heroic past of the Russian people. . . ."

* The phrase "as a weapon" was omitted from the official translation [P. J.].

The tremendous educational importance of Demyan Bedny's works consisted in the fact that the poet angrily condemned from revolutionary positions the hesitation and instability of the peasant, and, at the same time, explained to him the disastrous effects of this unsteadiness and vacillation for the interests of the peasantry itself. The poet helped the peasant to realize that it was in his interest to be in an unbreakable union with the working class under the leadership of the Bolshevik Party.

And now when people of my generation get together on festive occasions, they recall with pleasure their past life and their experiences in the Civil War, and they sing Demyan Bedny's songs, because these songs ring out fresh and timely today. Their charm is that they remind us of times which, though hard, were wonderful. They swell our hearts with pride for those who, in most difficult conditions, heroically fought for Soviet power, for the liberation of working people, for the people, for socialism, and triumphed in this struggle.

Monumental Sculpture

Let us take another example which convincingly shows what strong and noble sentiments are evoked among the people by genuine works of art. Most of you must know the memorial to Soviet soldiers in Berlin, the creator of which is the noted sculptor, Yevgeny Vuchetich.[2] The delegations of the fraternal parties, which attended the recent Sixth Congress of the Socialist Unity Party of Germany, participated in laying wreaths on the graves of Rosa Luxemburg, Karl Liebknecht, and other champions who gave their lives for the cause of the working class.

Later, wreaths were laid at the foot of the monument to Soviet soldiers in Berlin. Those were moving minutes. Hundreds of people came, the music rang out solemnly, everyone approached the memorial silently, no one could talk loudly, the atmosphere itself affected the people. The grand sculpture evokes feelings of profound respect for and gratitude to the heroic Soviet soldiers, feelings of reverence for those who fell in the struggle against the evil forces of fascism.

A short time ago members of the Presidium and secretaries of the central committee of the party examined the sketches for a Victory over Fascism Memorial, to be erected in Moscow in accordance with Comrade Vuchetich's plan. This design gives us grounds for believing that a work of realistic art of great power will be created, glorifying the victorious people and supporting the struggle to build up the strength and invulnerability of our great socialist motherland.

The monument to Karl Marx in Moscow, created by Comrade Lev Kerbel, is a splendid work of art. The sculptor has succeeded in catching the great-

[2] Yevgeny Viktorovich Vuchetich (b. 1908). The Berlin Soldiers' Monument apart, his best-known work is (or was) the enormous Stalin statue at the Volga-Don canal. Vuchetich received no less than five Stalin prizes (1946–1950).

ness of the brilliant founder of scientific communism. One cannot help but stop at this wonderful monument.

Only outstanding works of a great revolutionary and creative character reach a man's heart and mind, arouse high civic feelings in him and the resolution to devote himself to the struggle for the people's happiness. The authors of such works properly and deservedly enjoy the recognition of the people. It is to create works of such high ideological content and artistic impact on the minds and feelings of people that the Communist Party urges writers, artists, composers, cinematographers, and theatrical workers.

Our people need a militant revolutionary art. Soviet literature and art are called to reproduce in bright artistic imagery the great and heroic epoch of Communist construction and to depict truthfully the assertion and victory of new Communist relations in our life. The artist must be able to see the positive things and to rejoice at them since they comprise the essence of our reality; he must support these things but meanwhile, of course, he must not overlook the negative aspects and all that interferes with the rise of what is new in life.

Everything, even of the finest kind, has its dark side. Even the most beautiful of human beings can have faults. The great thing is how to approach the aspects of life, from what angle to assess them. What you look for, you find, as they say. A person without prejudice, who takes an active part in the constructive labor of the people, objectively sees both the good and the bad in life; he correctly understands and rightly assesses these aspects and energetically supports the assertion of the advanced, the important, and all that is decisive for social progress.

All those who look at our reality from the sidelines, however, will fail to see and to reproduce a truthful picture of life. It unfortunately happens that some representatives of the world of art judge reality only by the smells coming from the latrines, portray people in a deliberately ugly way, and lay gloomy colors on thick in their paintings, colors which can only plunge people into a state of despondency, hopelessness, and ennui. They depict reality according to their own biased and distorted subjective impression, through anemic stereotypes of their own invention.

The last time we saw the nauseating concoctions of Ernst Neizvestny, we were disgusted to notice that this man, who is evidently not devoid of talent and who has graduated from a Soviet institution of higher learning, is repaying the people with such black ingratitude. It is a good thing that we have few artists of this sort, but, unfortunately, he nevertheless is not alone in the world of art. You have also seen some other products of the abstractionist artists. We denounce such ugliness openly, giving no quarter, and will continue to do so.

Cinema

Comrades, our party regards the Soviet cinema as one of the most important artistic vehicles for educating the people in the spirit of communism.

There is nothing to compare with the cinema in its power of impact on human minds and hearts and in the breadth of audience it reaches among the people. The cinema is accessible to all walks of society, to all ages, one may say, from schoolboy to old. It penetrates into the remotest of districts and villages.

This explains why the central committee approaches all that has to do with the development of the Soviet cinema with such attention and such exacting demands.

We see and greatly appreciate the achievements scored in the making of feature films. At the same time we maintain that what has been achieved is not equal to our tasks or the possibilities before film-makers. We cannot remain indifferent to the ideological trend of cinema art or to the artistic merits of pictures shown on the screen. In this respect the state of affairs in the cinema is far from being as good as many film-makers imagine.

The fact that many very mediocre pictures of poor content and weak form, which either annoy or bore the cinema-goer, are shown is a matter for great anxiety.

We have been given a preview of the material for a picture bearing the responsible title of *Ilyich Zastava*.[3]

The film is being made by Comrade Khutsiev at the Gorky Film Studios under the art direction of the well-known film director, Comrade Sergei Gerasimov. One must say quite frankly that there are some moving sequences. But, in fact, they serve to cover up the real meaning of the film which is to assert ideas and standards of public and private life which Soviet people find unacceptable and alien. That is why we categorically reject such an interpretation of a great and important theme.

We need not have spoken about this, since work on the film is still in progress. But since the "qualities" of this picture are being praised high and low in our press and in certain public statements issued by writers and film-makers, we feel we must state our point of view.

The name of the picture *Ilyich Zastava* is allegorical. After all the very word "Zastava" meant a watch-post before. Even now, we call our frontier posts on the country's borders by this word. We are apparently to believe that the picture's main characters represent precisely those advanced sections of the Soviet youth who staunchly stand watch over the gains of the socialist revolution, the behests of Lenin.

But anyone who sees this picture will say that this is not true. Even the most positive characters in the picture, the three working lads, by no means personify our wonderful youth. They are portrayed in a way which shows that they do not know how they should live and what they should aspire to. And this, mind you, takes place in our period of the all-round building of communism, a time illuminated by the ideas of the Communist Party Program!

Is it, indeed, young people of this sort who today, with their fathers, are

[3] The name of an area in Moscow called after Lenin's patronymic name Ilyich, by which he was widely known.

building communism under the party's leadership? Is it, indeed, on young people of this sort that our people can pin their hopes for the future, or believe that they will inherit the great gains won by the older generations, who carried through the socialist revolution, built socialism, defended it arms-in-hand in bitter battles against the fascist hordes, and created the material and cultural requisites for the all-round building of a Communist society?

No! These are not the sort of people society can rely upon. They are not fighters, not remakers of the world. They are morally sick people, who have grown old while still young, who have no high aims or vocation in life.

The intention was to give a negative picture and criticize trenchantly the idlers and semidegenerate characters who love and respect no one, who are still to be encountered among our young people; they not only have no faith in their elders, they hate them. They are displeased with everything, grumble at everything, mock and despise everything, spend their days in idleness and their nights in disreputable carousals. They speak of work with snobbish scorn. Moreover, while gobbling their daily bread, these good-for-nothings jeer at those who make this bread by the sweat of their brow.

The makers of the film were not able to realize their intention of castigating the idlers and parasites. They lacked the civic courage and anger to stigmatize and pillory such degenerates and scum; they made do with just a weak slap in the face for the wretches. But a slap in the face will never reform such riff-raff.

The film-makers do not show the audience those strata of youth which they ought to. In their life, their work and struggle, our Soviet youth carry on and multiply the heroic traditions of the generations who went before, the generations who demonstrated their great loyalty to the ideals of Marxism-Leninism both in peacetime construction and at the front in the Patriotic War. Our youth are depicted well in Alexander Fadeyev's novel, *The Young Guard*. It is a great pity that Gerasimov, who filmed this novel, did not advise his pupil Khutsiev to show in his picture how our youth keep alive and develop the wonderful traditions of the Young Guards.

I remarked yesterday that the sequence in which the hero meets the shade of his father who was killed in the war provokes grave objections on points of principle. When the son asks the ghost how he ought to live, it in turn asks the son how old he is. Hearing the son say 23, the father says he is 21 . . . and vanishes. Do you really want us to believe that such a thing could be true? No one will ever believe that! It is common knowledge that even animals don't abandon their offspring. If you take a puppy from its mother and throw it into the water, she will at once dash in at the risk of her own life to save it.

Can one indeed believe a father would not answer his son's question and help him by advising him how to find the correct and proper road in life?

There is more to this than meets the eye. There is a definite meaning to this. The idea is to impress upon the sons that their fathers cannot teach them in life, that there is no point in asking them for advice. In the opinion of the film-makers, young people ought to decide by themselves how they should live, without asking their elders for advice and help.

Well, we can say that the point of view of the film-makers is stated quite clearly. But haven't you overdone it? Do you really want to set youth against the older generations, to make them quarrel, and to introduce discord in the great friendly Soviet family which welds both young and old together in the joint effort for communism?

With full responsibility, we declare to them: Nothing will come of your efforts!

In our time, the father-and-son problem is not what it was in Turgenev's day, because we live in a historical epoch which is quite different, one which is characterized by a different type of relations between human beings. In Soviet socialist society there are no contradictions between generations. There is no "father-and-son" problem in its old sense. It has been invented by the makers of the film and artificially inflated with not the best of intentions.

This is the way in which we understand the relations between people in our society and we want these relations to be truthfully portrayed in works of literature, plays, films, music and painting, in every kind of art. Let those who still do not understand this stop to think about it. We shall help them to adopt the correct position.

May we take the liberty of asking Comrade Khutsiev, the director of the picture, and Comrade Gerasimov, his teacher, how they could have thought up such a picture?

The film's grave errors are self-evident. One would have thought that the film-makers who saw it would have told its director so quite frankly and bluntly. However, some incredible things have started around it. Although no one had seen the picture, a great campaign to boost it as the most outstanding and "extraordinary event in our art" was started on an international scale. Why was that necessary? You can't do such things, comrades, you simply can't!

Perhaps some people will say that Khrushchev is calling for photography, for naturalism in art. No, comrades! We are calling for striking artistic effort, for a truthful reflection of the real world in all the diversity of its colors. Only such art can bring joy and delight to people. Man will never lose his artistic gift and will not allow dirty daubs to be presented as works of art, dirty daubs which can be made by any donkey with its tail.

There is no doubt that the people are strong enough to rebuff such "innovators." And those of them who have not lost their faculties will think matters over, take the road of serving the people, and will create canvases full of joy, inspiring people to work.

Partisanship and Art

In their creative work in recent years, writers and artists have been paying great attention to that chapter in the life of Soviet society which is bound up with the Stalin personality cult. All this is quite logical and there is every reason for it. Works in which Soviet reality during those years is truthfully reflected from party positions have appeared. One could give as illustrations among other works Alexander Tvardovsky's *Distant Horizons,* Alexander Solzhenitsyn's *One Day in the Life of Ivan Denisovich,* some of Yevgeny Yevtushenko's poems, and Grigory Chukhrai's picture *Clear Skies.*

The party gives its backing to artistic creations which are really truthful, whatever negative aspects of life they may deal with, so long as they help the people in their effort to build a new society, and so long as they strengthen and weld together the people's forces.

Everyone knows what an important role satire, in particular fables, plays. Comrade Mikhalkov, for example, often produces things in this genre. Satire is like a sharp razor-blade. It points to man's extraneous growths and at once cuts them out like a good surgeon. However, one must know how to wield the weapon of satire, just as skillfully as the surgeon uses his knife, so as to cut out the dangerous growth without endangering or harming the organism. Mastery is necessary in this case. If you haven't got this mastery, don't undertake this job, because you will do others harm and cut your own hands into the bargain. Those mothers who don't give children sharp things until they learn how to use them are doing the right thing.

At the same time, we consider it necessary to draw the attention of all creative workers to certain mistaken motives and tendencies in the works of individual authors. These wrong tendencies consist mainly in concentrating attention one-sidedly on instances of lawlessness, arbitrary reprisals, and abuse of power.

The years of the personality cult indeed had grievous consequences. Our party told the people the whole truth about that. At the same time one must bear in mind and remember that those years were not a period of stagnation in the development of Soviet society, as our foes imagine. Under the leadership of the Communist Party, under the banner of the great Lenin's ideas and behests, our people worked to build and did successfully build socialism. By their efforts, the party and the people turned the Soviet Union into a powerful socialist state, which withstood the grimmest ordeals of the war with flying colors and victoriously came through battles unprecedented in history, and utterly routed the fascist hordes.

That is why we say that writers who assess that particular stage in the life of our country from an extreme and one-sided angle, trying to make out that nearly everything was gloomy, and to paint everything in dark colors, are wrong. We still have writers who prefer to poke about in refuse heaps for material and who want to present such works as being truthful portrayals of the life of the people. The supporters of this point of view maintain that all works which speak of our people's achievements and of the positive things in life, are "white-washing." One cannot agree with such assertions. It is common knowledge that we had prettifying in some works and that the party has expressed its condemnation of this. However, after all is said and done, not everything in that particular period was bad; in that period of socialist construction too, the people showed heroism and for that reason we cannot blacken everything.

We must rebuff the kind of people who are fond of sticking the label "whitewasher" on writers and artists who bring out the positive side of life. What name then should we give to those who ferret out only the bad in life and depict everything in black? Evidently we should call them the "smearers." The good sides of life should be suitably reflected in literature and art.

Writers and artists must make a deeper study of what is taking place in life and depict it more correctly in their work. Everyone must serve the people and our common cause with the tools he knows how to use. I mean every writer, sculptor, composer, film-maker, and man of the theater. And the tool of every kind of art must be used to benefit our people, to crush our enemies, and to pave the way for the bright future of a Communist society.

We must always keep that in mind. It is unnecessary to boast. People judge every creative worker by what he has created. There are some who censure everyone who wrote at that time and saw what was positive in our life. We must not denigrate wholesale everything that was created at that time. They may call this a departure from the line of the 20th and 22nd Congresses. Not at all. It is an assertion of the line of the 20th and 22nd Congresses!

Reading Ehrenburg's memoirs one cannot help noticing that he presents everything in gloomy colors. Comrade Ehrenburg himself was not persecuted or subjected to restrictions in the period of the personality cult. The fate of a writer like, let us say, Galina Serebryakova, who spent many years in imprisonment, was quite different. But, despite that, she did not lose heart, remained loyal to the cause of the party, and upon her rehabilitation immediately resumed creative life, took up her pen and has been creating works which are needed by the people and the party.

Great productive forces were created and a cultural revolution carried out in the country. Now the whole world sees the remarkable fruit of those outstanding victories of the Soviet people in the powerful step of our country marching towards communism, in the great discoveries of science and engineering, and in the conquest of space. Our present victories cannot be regarded in isolation from the economic and cultural achievements of those years.

Stalinism

A question often asked now is why the violations of the law and abuses of power were not exposed and cut short when Stalin was alive and whether it was possible then. Our point of view on this has been more than once stated fully and with the utmost clarity in party documents. Unfortunately, some people, including certain workers in art, still try to present events in a false light. This is why we have to dwell on the question of the Stalin personality cult again today.

The question arises whether the leading cadres of the party knew about, let us say, the arrests of people in that period. Yes, they did. But did they know that absolutely innocent people were arrested? No, they did not. They believed in Stalin and could not even imagine that repression could be used against honest people devoted to our cause.

From the very first days of the October Revolution until the complete elimination of the exploiter classes in the country, Soviet society lived in an atmosphere of most acute class struggle. The class enemies were defeated in the open battle of the Civil War, but they were not destroyed physically and did not give up their perfidious schemes to harm the Soviet system. They changed the form of struggle and started using such methods as sabotage, subversion, assassinations, terroristic acts, and revolts.

Was it necessary for the revolution to defend its achievements? Yes, it was; and the revolution started to do so with the utmost resolution from the beginning. It is generally known that such a formidable organ against the enemies of the revolution as the All-Russian Extraordinary Commission for combating the counterrevolution was set up at Lenin's decree in the first months of Soviet power. When conspiracies against the Revolution were uncovered, Stalin, in his capacity as secretary of the central committee, conducted the struggle to purge the country of the plotters and carried it out under the slogan of combating the enemies of the people. He was believed and supported in this. And it could not have been otherwise, for, in the past, there was more than one case of treachery and betrayal of the cause of the revolution in the history of our party, as, for example, the provocative activity of Malinovsky, a member of the Bolshevik faction in the State Duma.

At that time Stalin headed the struggle of the party against the enemies of the revolution and of socialist construction. This raised his prestige. Everybody knew also about the contribution made by Stalin during the revolutionary struggle before the October Revolution, during its course and in the subsequent years of the construction of socialism. Stalin's prestige became particularly high in the period of the struggle against anti-Leninist trends and oppositional groupings within the party, the struggle for strengthening the ranks of the party and Soviet power, against such anti-Leninist tendencies and oppositional groupings within the party as the Trotskyites, Zinovievites, the right-wing opportunists, and bourgeois nationalists.

After Lenin's death, the party conducted a discussion with the Trotskyites and Zinovievites on the radical problems of the construction of socialism and the situation within the party. That discussion revealed and exposed the anti-Leninist and antisocialist views and activities of Trotsky, Zinoviev, and their henchmen, aimed at frustrating the Leninist policy of the construction of socialism in our country in the conditions of capitalist encirclement.

Following the Trotskyites, the right-wing opportunists headed by Bukharin, Rykov, and Tomsky came out against the Leninist course of the party. Their views, if asserted in practice, would inevitably have made the Soviet economy dependent on the capitalist countries, which, in its turn, could have led to the restoration of capitalism in our country. The line of the right-wing opportunists could have disarmed our country militarily in the face of the hostile, aggressive, capitalist encirclement.

Our party's policy of industrializing the country and collectivizing agriculture was a Leninist policy, which was supported by the entire party and by all the working people of our country. In ten years we had to cover an historical stage in economic development which had been covered by Western Europe in a hundred years. In the first years after Lenin's death, Stalin upheld the Leninist positions in the struggle against the Trotskyites, Zinovievites, Bukharinites, and bourgeois nationalists, and played a considerable role in the struggle. Therefore, the party and the masses believed in him and supported him.

But grave faults and mistakes, to which Lenin drew the attention of the party at the time, were characteristic of Stalin.

The great Lenin pointed out the danger that Stalin, having gathered great power into his hands, would not be able to use it correctly, owing to his great personal shortcomings. Advising that Stalin be removed from the post of General Secretary of the central committee of the party, Lenin at the same time considered that a leader should be placed in this post "who above all would differ from Comrade Stalin in these respects, namely, greater tolerance, greater loyalty, greater politeness, and a more considerate attitude towards the comrades, a less capricious temper, etc."

Lenin considered Stalin to be a Marxist, a leading worker of our party, loyal to the revolution. Lenin put forward his views in a letter to the pending party congress which was discussed by the delegations to the 13th Party Congress. When deciding this question, the party proceeded from the real correlation of forces within the central committee at that time, and taking into account Stalin's positive aspects as a leader, believed his assurances that he would be able to overcome the shortcomings pointed out by Lenin. Afterwards, Stalin violated his promise and abused the party's confidence, and this led to those grave consequences which were current in the period of the personality cult.

The Purges

The party has most uncompromisingly denounced and denounces the gross violations of the Leninist standards of party life, the arbitrary acts and abuse of power committed by Stalin which seriously damaged the cause of communism. But, nevertheless, the party pays credit to Stalin's services to the party and to the communist movement. We continue to maintain that Stalin was devoted to communism. He was a Marxist, and this cannot and should not be denied. His fault was that he committed gross mistakes of a theoretical and political nature, violated the Leninist principles of state and party leadership, and abused the power entrusted to him by the party and the people.

At Stalin's funeral many, including myself, were in tears. These were sincere tears. Although we knew about some of Stalin's personal shortcomings, we believed in him.

To have a clearer picture of how great was the belief in Stalin and his authority, I shall cite the following example. Many remember Comrade Yakir. He was an important military leader and a bolshevik of crystal purity who perished tragically and without guilt in those years. Sentenced to death, he believed that Stalin had nothing to do with it, and his last words before being shot were "Long live Stalin!" During the investigation Comrade Yakir told the interrogators that his arrest and accusation were a provocation, that the party and Stalin were being deceived, and that they would look into the whole matter and would see that people such as he were losing their lives as a result of provocations. Not only Comrade Yakir, but many other outstanding party leaders and statesmen who suffered without guilt were of the same opinion.

In the last years of his life Stalin was a seriously sick man, suffering from suspiciousness and persecution mania. The party has widely informed the people how Stalin hatched such "cases" as the "Leningrad case," the "doctors' case," and others. However, comrades, there would have been considerably more of such "cases" if all who worked close to Stalin during that period had agreed with him in all matters. In one of my speeches I mentioned how Stalin intended to whip up the so-called case of "the Moscow counterrevolutionary center." However, as is generally known, he was not supported in this and the cadres of the Moscow party organization were not subjected to new mass repressions.

It is also known that Stalin intended to destroy a considerable part of the artistic intelligentsia of Soviet Ukraine. Evidently, on the instigation of Beria and Kaganovich, he suspected that some kind of nationalist tendencies and sentiments were developing among the artistic intelligentsia in post-war Soviet Ukraine, and he started to push matters in a direction which would enable him to do away with the most prominent writers and art workers of the Ukraine. If the Ukrainian bolsheviks at that time had given in to Stalin's wishes then the Ukrainian intelligentsia evidently would have suffered greater losses and probably a "case of Ukrainian nationalists" would have been hatched.

Knowing Stalin's morbid distrust and suspicion, the intelligence services of the imperialist countries "planted" such cases and such "documents" which looked quite authentic and fully convinced him that groups of military specialists were operating in our country against Soviet power and against the Soviet state and that plots of various criminal groups were being engineered.

Sholokhov and Stalin

But we also have comrades and very well-known writers and workers in art who, one might say, felt the effects of Stalin's arbitrary rule on their own backs and who, even during those extremely difficult times, did not resign themselves to such events, but protested and addressed frank statements to Stalin personally.

In the spring of 1933, our esteemed Mikhail Sholokhov raised his voice in protest against the arbitrary rule that reigned on the Don at that time. Not long ago two letters to Stalin and Stalin's replies were found in the archives. One cannot remain calm reading Sholokhov's truthful words, written with a bleeding heart, about the shocking deeds of people who engaged in criminal activities in the Veshenskaya and other districts of the Don.

Sholokhov, in his letter of April 16, 1933, wrote to Stalin:

> Countless such examples could be cited. *These are not legalized cases of going it too strong, but a legalized "method," on a district scale,* of conducting grain procurement. I have heard about these facts either from communists or from collective farmers themselves, who came to me asking "to have this printed in the papers" after having been subjected to all these "methods."
>
> Joseph Vissarionovich, do you remember Korolenko's article *In a Pacified Village?* The same kind of "disappearance" has been the fate of tens of thousands of collective farmers — not three peasants suspected of having stolen grain from a kulak — and, as you see, with a wider use of technical means and in a more refined way.

Further on, Sholokhov asked Stalin to have a closer look at what was happening in the districts.

> The cases not only of those who have committed outrages against collective farmers and Soviet power, but also those whose hand directed them should be investigated. . . .
>
> If everything I have described merits the attention of the central committee, send to the Veshenskaya district real Communists who will have enough courage to expose, irrespective of the person concerned, all those responsible for the mortal blow delivered to the collective farm economy of the district, who will investigate properly and show up not only all those who have applied loathsome "methods" of torture, beating up, and humiliation to collective farmers, but also those who inspired them.

Other extracts could be cited from Comrade Sholokhov's letter — a direct, frank, and courageous letter which incidentally has never been printed in his works or reminiscences. . . .

But I want to dwell on another thing, on what Stalin replied to Sholokhov's letters. He wrote to him: "your letters create a somewhat one-sided impression." And Stalin said:

> I thank you for the letters, for they reveal a sore in our party-Soviet work and show how our workers, wishing to curb the enemy, sometimes unwittingly hit friends and descend to sadism. But this does not mean that I agree with you *on all points.* You see only *one* side, though you see it quite well. But this is only *one* side of the matter. In order not

to go adrift in politics (your letters are not *belles-lettres* but 100 per
cent politics), one has to observe and to be able to see the other side
as well. And the *other* side is that the esteemed grain-growers of your
district (and not only of your district alone) carried on an "Italian
strike" (sabotage!) and were not loath to leave the workers and the
Red Army without bread. That the sabotage was quiet and outwardly
harmless (without bloodshed) does not change the fact that the esteemed grain-growers waged what was virtually a "quiet" war against
Soviet power. A war of starvation, dear Comrade Sholokhov. . . .

This, of course, can in no way justify the outrages which, as you
assure me, have been committed by our workers.

Stalin wrote further on.

And those guilty of these outrages must be duly punished. Nevertheless, it is clear as day that the esteemed grain-growers are not so
harmless as they could appear to be from afar.

Here you are: it turns out that author Sholokhov, who wrote to Stalin
about atrocious lawlessness, saw events "as they could appear to be from
afar," and this was said to a writer who was in the very midst of the people
and created the best, truthful, Communist-spirited book about collectivization, *Virgin Soil Upturned.*

As a real bolshevik writer, Sholokhov refused to accept crying injustice;
he rose against the lawlessness which was rampant at the time, but Stalin
remained deaf to these warnings from Sholokhov, just as he did to many
similar warnings from other courageous Communists.

Beria, the Real Culprit

Stalin's abuse of power and the facts of his arbitrary rule became known
to us only after his death and the exposure of Beria, that sworn enemy of
the party and the people, that spy and infamous *provocateur.*

It should be borne in mind that Beria, this loathsome person, who did
not even deem it necessary to conceal his joy at Stalin's coffin, was frantically
reaching out for power, for leadership in the party. Such a danger was real
at that time; it constituted a grave danger to the gains of the October Revolution, to the cause of Communist construction in our country, and to the
successes of the international Communist movement.

Even in the first days after Stalin's death Beria began to take steps to
disorganize the work of the party and to undermine the Soviet Union's
friendly relations with fraternal countries of the socialist camp. For instance,
he and Malenkov came out with the provocative proposal to eliminate the
German Democratic Republic as a socialist state, to recommend the Socialist
Unity Party of Germany to abandon the slogan of the struggle to build
socialism. The central committee promptly and indignantly rejected these
treacherous proposals, and gave a crushing rebuff to the *provocateurs.*

The measures taken by the central committee guarded the party and the country from the foul purposes of Beria, that inveterate agent of the imperialists.

Comrades, everyone who creates works about the life of Soviet society, about its present and past, should remember all this well, and be able to gain a deep understanding of historical events. The Soviet people have traversed a great and glorious path from the destruction of the old bourgeois world to the building of the new socialist society which has won a final victory in our country.

It has not been an easy path. In the struggle for the victory of socialism our people have heroically overcome all the difficulties and hardships which confronted them. It is in the overcoming of difficulties that the spiritual composition of the Soviet man has been formed, the man of the new society, the fighter for the revolutionary remaking of the world. A noble, Leninist loyalty to principle, unbending will, readiness to sacrifice oneself for the sake of the triumph of the Communist ideals, these are the outstanding traits of the generations of Soviet people educated by the Communist Party. Scepticism, weak will and slackness, pessimism, and a nihilistic attitude to reality are foreign to Soviet people.

Against Despondency

It is surprising to see some literary works, films, and plays depict in every way people's gloomy, despondent feelings, caused by the difficulties in their life. Such a portrayal of life can be given only by individuals who have no share in the constructive effort of the people, who are not carried away by the poetry of their labor and look at everything from a distance. I can say from my own experience, as a participant in the events in those years, which are sometimes painted in gloomy colors and dull shades, that those were bright, happy years, years of struggle and victories, of the triumph of Communist ideas.

Not long ago Comrade Walter Ulbricht showed us the documentary film *The Russian Miracle* made by the German film-makers Annelie and Andrew Thorndike. It is a remarkable film. When we saw it we saw truthful pictures of the life of our country. Looking at it, at the masses of those who took part in the Civil War, I saw, as it were, myself; such were the Red Army fighters of those days. The film is based on our documentary materials. We hope that our own film workers will create more such good, truthful films as this. *The Russian Miracle** contrasts our yesterday with our today. Seeing this film you realize what a colossal stride forward our country has made!

And we would like to give a piece of advice to our young people: learn from the lessons of the revolution, from the history of the struggle in which your fathers and mothers took part, and sacredly revere the memory of those who are not with us any longer, treat respectfully those who live on, take

* The Thorndikes made other "good and truthful" films before they got into trouble in wartime Germany: documentaries then glorifying the Wehrmacht and the Navy fighting for Hitler's Thousand-Year Reich [P. J.].

from them everything they have to arm yourselves, so as to be worthy people, worthy inheritors of the cause of your fathers. If you fail to preserve your dignity, you will cover yourselves with shame.

We have a profound faith in our people, in their strength, in their creative revolutionary spirit. We believe that our young creative workers will carry on the cause of their fathers, that they will always march in step with the people.

A fighter, inspired by the noble desire for victory, does not notice the difficulties of the marches and battles, no matter how great they may be. He gives his life for the sake of the principle, because at the moment of the keenest struggle that principle becomes for him greater than any difficulties, and soars above everything else.

A man's assessment of the incidents of life and the events of history depends on what ideological positions he has held and holds in his attitude to these incidents and events. Books exist about our revolution and socialist construction, written by people who watched the revolution and the work of the people remaking life "as if from garret windows."

Books about the revolution, about the life and deeds of the Soviet people, have also been written by people whom the revolution had driven out of long-occupied warm nests, who had not understood and refused to accept the revolution. The wave of events had tossed them about — from Moscow to the Crimea, from the Crimea to Tbilisi, from there to all parts of the world. In their stories, novels, and memoirs they make a great fuss about their experiences due to the difficulties encountered over having had to eat rotten fish and other such things. At that time our Soviet people were scoring victories over their enemies while half-dressed and half-starved and sometimes even without rotten fish; but they did not whine or complain but fought staunchly and unselfishly to defend the gains of the revolution.

Our party has always been for partisanship in literature and art. It salutes all workers in literature and art, both old and young, both party members and nonparty people, provided they adhere firmly to communist ideology in questions of creative work. They are the party's support, the party's faithful soldiers.

We support them and will continue to do so. We show concern and will continue to do so in order that our creative forces will grow bigger and stronger, in order to rally them into a single fighting family of revolutionary artists, consistently defending Marxism-Leninism in their creative work, artists irreconcilably opposed to all that is rotten, alien, and hostile, no matter from what source.

We have heard the poet R. Rozhdestvensky speaking here and arguing against Gribachov's poem "No, Boys!" Comrade Rozhdestvensky's speech was imbued with the thought that the sentiments of our youth are expressed solely by a group of young authors, and that these authors are the tutors of our youth. That is certainly not so. Our Soviet youth has been brought up by our party, it follows the party and sees in it its educator and leader.

Models for the Young

I would like to offer as a model to the young poet Rozhdestvensky the poet-soldier and poet-communist Nikolai Gribachov, who has a good eye and never misses when striking at the enemies of our ideology.[4] We live in a period of acute ideological struggle, in the period of the struggle for the minds and the re-education of people. This is a complicated process, much more difficult than the reconstruction of machine tools and industrial plants. Figuratively speaking, you writers and artists are the smiths who reforge human psychology. You have strong tools in your possession, tools which should always be used in the interests of the people.

To be more precise, there is actually no such thing as nonpartisanship in society. Those who advertise their nonpartisanship do so with the purpose of concealing their disagreement with the views and ideas of the party in order to recruit supporters. There were cases in history when the most inveterate reactionaries and counterrevolutionaries employed the slogan of nonpartisanship, and it was only later that their bourgeois partisanship became manifest.

One can quote quite a few such examples from the history of the struggle of the working class and working peasants of our country to strengthen Soviet power. At different stages and at different periods, the enemies of the workers and peasants used different means for fighting against the communists and against the construction of socialism, camouflaging their actions by nonpartisanship.

In the first years of Soviet power, the Social Revolutionaries, Anarchists, Mensheviks, Constitutional Democrats, and other riff-raff, expressing the will of the exploiters and interventionists for whom they acted as agents and servants, came out openly and directly against the revolution, against Lenin, and against the power of the workers and peasants.

In the last years of the Civil War the camp of the enemies of the working class and peasants had capitalists and landlords acting in alliance with the foreign interventionists. All the Menshevik, Social Revolutionary, and Anarchist scum began to serve the counterrevolutionaries.

In the heat of the fierce battles against the counterrevolutionaries and interventionists, the working people of our country went through a school of political education; they learned the political ABC from their own experience and decided whom they were to follow, with whom they were to side; they became bolsheviks.

This is depicted in a very fine and convincing way in Furmanov's book and the film *Chapayev*, in Serafimovich's novel *Iron Flood*, in Fadeyev's novel *The Nineteen*, in Ostrovsky's novel *How the Steel Was Tempered*, and in other works by our Soviet revolutionary writers. Imbued with ideas of

[4] Nikolai Gribachov (b. 1910), poet and pamphleteer, one of the pillars of the "conservative" faction in Soviet literature, Stalin prize-winner in 1948 and 1949.

partisanship, their works are still very important and are the tools of our party in its ideological struggle. No wonder the book *How the Steel Was Tempered* enjoys great popularity in Cuba and in some of the other countries fighting for freedom and independence!

As Lenin's ideas gripped more and more the minds of the workers and peasants, and the influence of the Communists increased among the people and the prestige of Soviet power kept growing, the enemies of the revolution made an attempt to oust the Bolsheviks and to seize the Soviets, and with this purpose they launched the slogan: "Soviets without Communists."

What are Soviets without Communists? They represent an empty form devoid of revolutionary content. The counterrevolutionaries realized this very well, and by launching the slogan "Soviets without Communists" they counted on transforming them from organs of revolutionary power into a medium for their own influence on the masses. They wanted to use the prestige of the Soviets to implement their designs against the people.

The point is that what matters is not what an organization is called, but what policy it pursues and the interests of which class it defends.

For instance, communes have existed for quite a long time in France. As you see, these organs of administration have a revolutionary name but a capitalist essence, and they defend the interests of the monopolists. The French bourgeoisie is not at all afraid of the revolutionary word "commune" because that is what it calls its organs of administration.

There are a great many bourgeois leaders now in various countries who disguise their bourgeois policy with socialist phrases. They talk about the construction of socialism and at the same time imprison and execute communists. They proscribe Communist Parties and say that they are fighting for socialism. They do this because the ideas of socialism are becoming ever more popular with the masses in all countries and are winning their minds.

The example offered by the peoples of the Soviet Union is a revolutionary beacon for the nations. That is precisely why bourgeois leaders, particularly the representatives of the left-wing bourgeoisie, make extensive use of the slogan of the construction of communism to deceive the working people.

Peaceful Coexistence and Ideology

Historical experience shows that in the political and ideological struggle one cannot trust words and declarations. One must be capable of telling who has advanced them, and for what purpose. For this it is necessary first of all to be a Marxist-Leninist, a convinced Communist who has devoted his whole life and talent to the struggle for the happiness of all the working people on earth.

One cannot regard oneself as a champion of the interests of the working people and stand at the cross-roads between the struggling parties, "equally indifferent to good and to evil."

Every level of society is drawn into the class struggle. It can even break up families. It sometimes happens that the members of one and the same family stand opposed to one another on different sides of the barricade.

There is a category of people who explain their nonparticipation in the revolution from "humane" considerations; they dare not, so to speak, raise their hands against their kind. But who kills men, if it isn't their own kind?

Revolutions are carried out by social classes. A revolution of workers and peasants to overthrow the capitalist class is the supreme manifestation of humanity. Participation in the revolution on the side of workers and peasants is the highest manifestation of humanity. Without the overthrow of the system of exploiters there can be no liberation of the working people and no creation for them of a happy life. Is it so hard to understand that those who fail to take part in the struggle on the side of the working people are virtually assisting the bourgeoisie? He who is not with the workers and peasants is inevitably against them. That should be well understood, comrades!

There have been, and still are, people who declare that they accept the idea of communism and sometimes even champion it, but do not take an active part in the struggle. They get under the feet of the fighters themselves, tripping them and themselves up.

A revolution is not just pious wishes. It is a grim and sharp struggle. The revolution must be fought for not only during the course of its accomplishment, but also in the period of the consolidation of its gains, right up to the building of communism. Essays, lectures, reports, and the like are not enough here. It is necessary to join in the shooting, too, when the circumstances demand it.

In the complex conditions of the struggle between the classes, vacillating people sometimes fall, against their wish, into an unenviable position. Let me remind you of the case of Anatole Lunacharsky. Fearing that armed workers shooting at the enemy might hit some of the historical monuments and ruin them, he went to Lenin with a protest and even threatened to resign his post in the Soviet government. Lenin derided this philistine idea of revolution. Lunacharsky himself realized this later.

Ehrenburg

In this connection I should like to say a few words about Comrade Ehrenburg. There was a time when Comrade Ehrenburg visited Lenin in Paris and was welcomed by him with sympathy, as Ehrenburg writes himself. Comrade Ehrenburg even joined the party and then left it. He evidently took no direct part in the socialist revolution, but assumed the attitude of an onlooker. I think we shall not be distorting the truth if we say that it is from that same position that Comrade Ehrenburg appraises our revolution and the entire subsequent period of socialist construction in his memoirs, *People, Years, Life*.

It is the highest duty of the Soviet writer, artist, and composer, of every creative worker, to be in the ranks of the builders of communism, to put his talent at the service of the great cause of our party, to fight for the triumph of the ideas of Marxism-Leninism. We must remember that a sharp struggle is going on in the world between two irreconcilable ideologies—the socialist and the capitalist.

It is the task of the artist actively to contribute by his works to the assertion of Communist ideas, to deal crushing blows at the enemies of socialism and communism, and to fight against the imperialists and colonialists.

A vivid example of patriotic, party understanding of the artist's mission is the works of our outstanding writer Mikhail Sholokhov. Take his novels, *And Quiet Flows the Don* and *Virgin Soil Upturned,* his story, *The Fate of a Man,* and the chapters from his novel, *They Fought for Their Country.* These are real works of art of great force and revolutionary spirit, works imbued with the spirit of Communist partisanship and the spirit of the class struggle of the workers and peasants of our country for the victory of the revolution and socialism. Comrade Sholokhov himself took an active part in the struggle during the Civil War, during the elimination of the kulaks as the last class of exploiters, and during the years of the Patriotic War against the fascist invaders. He took part in those battles not as an observer but as a soldier, and in time of peace he remains the same fighter for the happiness of the working people.

Sholokhov possesses the wonderful gift of deep understanding of the substance of social phenomena and events, of clearly seeing his friends and discerning his enemies, of depicting, with talent and from a party position, impressive scenes of real life. It is with great love that he reproduces in his works the image of Communists and working men.

It is with irreconcilable class hatred that he exposes and strikes the enemies of our social system. How vividly and convincingly does he draw his battle scenes! If his cavalrymen clash, they cross their sabers with such frenzy that the sparks fly. They wield their sabers for the sake of the people's truth, and that truth wins out.

From the example offered by Sholokhov's work, everybody can see that, far from cramping his artistic individuality, the writer's Communist partisanship actively aids his talent and raises his work to the level of paramount social significance.

We adhere to class positions in art and resolutely oppose peaceful coexistence between the socialist and capitalist ideologies. Art belongs to the sphere of ideology. Those who think that both socialist realism and formalist and abstractionist trends can peacefully live together in Soviet art inevitably backslide into positions of peaceful coexistence in the sphere of ideology, which are alien to us. We have recently encountered such sentiments. This bait has unfortunately been taken by some Communists — writers and artists — and even by some of the leading workers in the creative organizations. It should be noted at the same time that such nonparty men as Comrade

Leonid Sobolev, for instance, have been staunchly defending the party line in literature and art.

On the last occasion, Comrade Ehrenburg said that the idea of coexistence had been expressed in his letter as a joke. Let us assume that it was so. If so, it was a malicious joke. One cannot be allowed to make such jokes in the sphere of ideology. Let us see what would indeed happen in Soviet art if the advocates of peaceful coexistence of various ideological trends in literature and art got the upper hand. As a first step, a blow would be dealt at our revolutionary gains in the sphere of socialist art. By the logic of struggle, things would hardly end there. It is not impossible that these people, on gathering strength, would make an attempt to come out in opposition to the revolutionary gains.

I have already had occasion to say that peaceful coexistence in the field of ideology is treason to Marxism-Leninism, betrayal of the cause of the workers and peasants. Soviet society has reached the stage now when complete, monolithic unity of all the socialist nations of the country, of all sections of the people — workers, collective farmers, intellectuals — successfully building communism under the leadership of the Leninist party, has been achieved.

Our people and party will not tolerate any infringement of this monolithic unity. One of the manifestations of such infringement is the attempt to impose upon us peaceful coexistence of ideologies. That is why we come out both against these pernicious ideas and against their propagators. In this, I hope we are all agreed.

We call upon those who are still mistaken to reflect, to analyze their errors, to understand their nature and sources, to overcome their mistakes, and together with the party, in the same ranks, under the red banner of Marxism-Leninism, actively to participate in the building of communism and to multiply the successes of socialist culture, literature, and art.

Abstractionism and formalism, whose right to a place in socialist art is advocated by some of their champions, are forms of capitalist ideology. It is to be regretted that this is not understood by some people, including some of the creative workers with extensive experience of life.

Comrade Ehrenburg's memoirs include the following paragraph which I shall quote:

> There was a multiplicity of literary schools: comfutists (communist futurists), imaginists, proletcultists, expressionists, futurists, nonsubjectists, presentists, accidentists, and even nothingists. Of course, some of the theoreticians talked a lot of nonsense. . . . But I feel like defending those remote times.

It appears that the author of the memoirs has great sympathy for the representatives of the so-called "left" art, and asumes the task of defending this art. The question arises: defending it against whom? Apparently, against our Marxist-Leninist criticism. Why do this? Apparently, in order to support the opportunity for the existence of such or similar phenomena in our modern art. This would mean recognition of coexistence between socialist realism and formalism. Comrade Ehrenburg is making a gross ideological mistake, and it is our duty to help him to realize this.

Yevtushenko

At our last meeting Comrade Yevtushenko came out in defence of abstractionism. He attempted to justify his position by alleging that there are good people both among realists and formalists, and he referred to the example of two Cuban artists who had sharply differed in their views on art and then died in the same trench fighting for the revolution. Such an instance could occur in life as a private case.

An example of a totally different nature could be cited. After the Civil War, an ugly formalistic monument was erected in the city of Artymovsk, Ukraine, the author of which was the cubist sculptor Kavaleridze. It was an awful sight, but the cubists were rapturous over it (the monument was destroyed during the war). The author of this formalistic monument, who remained on the territory occupied by the fascists, behaved in an unworthy manner. So that the example cited by Comrade Yevtushenko cannot serve as a serious argument in favor of his views.

Comrade Yevtushenko's stand on abstractionism in essence coincides with the views supported by Comrade Ehrenburg. This poet, who is still a young man, apparently fails to understand much in our party's policy, wavers, and displays instability in his views on the questions of art. But his speech at the meeting of the Ideological Commission gives us confidence that he will succeed in overcoming his waverings. I should like to advise Comrade Yevtushenko and other young writers to prize the confidence of the masses, not to seek cheap sensations and not to play up to the sentiments and tastes of the philistines. Don't be ashamed, Comrade Yevtushenko, to admit your mistakes. Don't be afraid of what enemies will say about you. It should be clear to you that when we criticize you for departing from positions of principle, our opponents begin to praise you. If the enemies of our cause start to praise you for works which please them, the people will justly criticize you. So choose what suits you best.

The Communist Party is combating and will continue to fight against abstractionism and all other formalistic distortions in art. We cannot be neutral regarding formalism. When I was in America some artists, I do not know if they are prominent or not, presented me with a painting. Yesterday I showed you this daub. Apparently these people are not my enemies. Otherwise they would not have presented me with the fruit of their labor. But even under these conditions I cannot consider the gift a great masterpiece or, in general, a *chef d'œuvre* of fine art.

What does it portray? It is said that the painting gives a view of a city from a bridge. But no matter how hard you look at it you make out nothing but varicolored strips, and this daub is called a painting!

And here is another such "masterpiece." One sees four eyes, perhaps there are even more. It is said that the picture conveys the idea of horror, of fear. What limit is there to the artistic absurdity of the abstractionists? These are specimens of American painting.

Here are several instances from the realm of our architectural art. In Moscow, in Sokolniki, there is the Rusakov Club which was built to the design of the architect Comrade Melnikov. This is an ugly and uncomfortable building, as ugly as sin. But in its time it was presented as a progressive innovation.

The Soviet Army Theater in Moscow, built to the design of architects Alabyan and Simbirtsev, is an example of unreasonable passion for form in architecture. Kaganovich foisted the ridiculous idea of building a theater in the form of a five-pointed star upon the architects. The five-pointed star as a symbol, as an emblem, is one thing; it is another thing to erect a building for practical purposes in the form of a star. In practice, it has many useless corners and much wasted space!

The Soviet Army Theater probably is the most unwise building erected. It was this way: Kaganovich submitted his idea to Stalin, who liked it and it was decided to erect the building in the form of a five-pointed star. No one sees nor will see the star: it has to be seen from the sky. A silly idea, a tribute to an immature notion of beauty and reason in art and in life.

It is inconceivable why, and for what purpose sensible, educated people play the fool, give themselves airs, and present the most absurd products as works of art, while life around them is full of natural and thrilling beauty.

Winter in the Forest

On New Year's Eve I was returning to Moscow from the suburbs. I spent the whole of December 31st, from early morning, in the woods. It was a poetic day, a most beautiful Russian winter's day, and it could only have been a Russian winter's day, because not everywhere are there such winters as we have in Russia. Of course, this is not something national but a phenomenon of the climate and of nature — I would not like you to misunderstand me. [Laughter.]

That day the forest was especially beautiful. Its beauty was in the trees covered by powdery hoar-frost. I remember, in my youth, reading a story in the *Ogonyok* magazine. I don't remember the author of the story, which contained such words as "dear silvery shadows." The author described an orchard in its winter dress. The story was probably well written, but perhaps at that time I was less fastidious in literature. However, I liked the story and today I still remember the impression it made upon me. I especially like the description of trees in their winter apparel.

The winter forest on New Year's Eve was so beautiful that it impressed me strongly. Perhaps the shadows were not silvery, but words fail to express the deep impression the forest made on me. I observed the sunrise and the forest, covered by hoar-frost. Only those who have been in the forest and have seen such living pictures can understand this charm. It is precisely the advantage of the artist that he can reproduce thrilling pictures; however, not everyone possesses this gift.

I said to my companions: "Just look at these firs, at their apparel, at the snowflakes which are glistening and sparkling in the rays of the sun! How wonderfully beautiful all this is!" And now the modernists, the abstractionists, want to paint these fir trees upside down, and claim it as the new and progressive in art.

It is impossible that such art will ever be recognized by normal people, that people will be deprived of the opportunity to enjoy paintings of nature, reproduced by artists and beautifying the halls of our clubs, houses of culture, and homes.[5]

---

[5] Some Western observers of the Russian scene have been paying more Marxian attention to "the mode of production" and its effect on the cultural "superstructure" than the dialecticians in Moscow. As Alain Besançon writes (*Survey,* Jan. 1963):

"Since about 1958, Soviet architects, who previously devoted their best efforts to exceptional buildings, have suddenly had to adapt themselves to mass construction. They have had to assimilate a series of new techniques (prefabrication, standardisation of materials, construction by means of large units, certain kinds of utilisation of preset concrete, and the creation of large urban buildings) — techniques which, in the West, have progressed hand-in-hand with an architectural æsthetic that owed a great deal to the new painting. It has been found difficult to borrow some elements of this modern complex without adopting all the others. And although a fresco of Gerasimov may harmonise with an architecture like that of the Hotel Ukraine, it clashes irremediably with that of a construction of glass and steel like the great exhibition pavilion at Sokolniki — which is derived, if distantly, from Mondrian. The problem is acute, and is a frequent subject of discussion, especially among architects. . . ."

As for the decorative artists:

"Here again, the requirements of mass-production are getting the better of the heavy, curvilinear, last-century style that answered to the limited demand of a small minority which was in love — as Power in Russia traditionally is—with pomp and solemnity. But you cannot supply millions of people with carved armchairs, bronze electroliers in the Victorian style, or with huge sofas upholstered with red velvet. So these arts had to look over the frontiers where they found not only techniques of furnishing and of production in series, but also an international style fully elaborated. Armchairs and chairs in moulded plastics, book-cases and cupboards in sections, geometrical shapes and vividly contrasted colours—all these are to be found today in the new Soviet flats, clubs, and restaurants. . . .

Thus the architects and decorators are creating a new setting for the daily life of the Russian people and giving them an artistic education in opposition to that of the last hundred years. Unlike the effort of the intrepid *avant-garde* of the 'twenties, this is a mass education corresponding to the cultural level of the country. It is particularly well received among the young, who associate technical progress with a certain modernism of forms. Even if this does not amount to a real introduction to modern art, it is preparing the public to accept its major products later on. . . ."

Against Formalism

I don't understand why the adherents of formalism and abstractionism call those art workers who adhere to the position of socialist realism conservatives, while abstractionists are considered representatives of what is progressive in art. Are there any grounds for this? I think there are no grounds, nor can there be any grounds for this, as formalist and abstractionist vagaries are alien to and not understood by the people. And anything alien to the people does not get their support, and certainly cannot be progressive.

The artist A. I. Laktionov has recently written an article in *Pravda* expressing his irreconcilable attitude to abstractionist art. The abstractionists and their patrons have castigated his article for allegedly supporting the conservative trend in art. And the paintings of Comrade Laktionov are condemned by these people as naturalist.[6]

Let us compare two paintings — the self-portrait of A. Laktionov and the self-portrait of B. Zhutovsky. No matter what some people may think or say on the subject, it is clear to any sensible person with unspoiled taste that the painting by Laktionov holds one's attention through its humanity, that it arouses respect for man. You look at it with admiration and rejoice for man.

But whom has B. Zhutovsky portrayed? A freak. Looking at his self-portrait, you could be frightened. Shouldn't anyone be ashamed of wasting his efforts on such a disgraceful object! How can it be that he has studied at a secondary school and a higher educational institution, that the people's money has been spent on him, and he eats the bread provided by the people? And how has he repaid the people, the workers and peasants for the money they have spent on his education, for the benefits they are giving him now? With this self-portrait — this abomination and monstrosity. It makes you sick to look at such a filthy mess and to listen to those who defend it.

No matter what abuse is hurled against artists who adhere to positions of realism, and no matter how much glory is heaped on the abstractionists and all the other formalists, all reasonable people understand clearly that in the first case we are dealing with real artists and genuine art, and in the second, with people with perverted tastes whose brains are, so to speak, topsy-turvy, with ignoble hack work that insults people's feelings.

Soviet society discards everything in art that is stillborn, just as every living organism discards dead cells.

Soviet Music

Music has a big and important place in the spiritual life of our people, in ideological work. In this connection it is necessary to make some remarks

[6] Alexander Ivanovich Laktionov (b. 1910), one of the best known painters in the traditional style, a pupil of Brodsky (the official portraitist of Lenin and Stalin). Laktionov's best known picture is "A Letter from the Front" (Stalin Prize 1947) which was shown at the famous exhibition at the Manezh last December.

about the trend in the development of music. We do not want to act as judges, or to stand on the podium and conduct composers.

In music, as in the other arts, there are many different *genres,* styles, and forms. No one has banned any one of these styles or *genres.* But all the same, we want to present our attitude to music, to its tasks and the trend in its development.

To put it briefly, we stand for melodious music with content, music that stirs people and gives rise to strong feelings, and we are against cacophony.

Who is there who doesn't know the song about Budyenny's army! The Pokrass brothers have composed many good songs. I very much like the song about Moscow, written, I must confess, at our request, when I was secretary of the Moscow party committee. I remember that at a meeting of the Moscow committee, one of them sang this song for the first time. He was not much of a singer, but the Pokrass brothers wrote good music.[7]

How stirring the old revolutionary songs are — songs such as "Whirlwinds of Danger," for instance, and others! Who is there who doesn't know the "Internationale"? How many years we have been singing that song! It has become the international anthem of the working class. What revolutionary thoughts and feelings it awakens! It inspires men and women to greater heights and mobilises them against the enemies of the working people!

When I listen to Glinka's music, tears of joy always come into my eyes.

Perhaps I'm old-fashioned, getting on in years, but I like to listen to David Oistrakh playing the violin; I also like to listen to the violinists' group of the Bolshoi Theatre — I don't know what that group is called in professional language. I have listened to it many times and have always enjoyed it immensely.

I do not, of course, claim that my knowledge of music should become some kind of standard for everybody. But we can't humor those who palm off cacophonous sounds as genuine music, whereas music which the people like is treated scornfully by some persons as being out-of-date.

Every nation has its own traditions in music and loves its own national folk melodies and songs. I was born in a Russian village and was brought up on Russian and Ukrainian folk music, on its melodies and folk songs. It gives me great pleasure to listen to the songs of Soloviev-Sedoy, to Kolmanovsky's song, with words by Yevtushenko, "Do the Russian People Stand for War?" I also like Ukrainian songs; I'm fond of the song "Rushnichok," with music by P. Maiboroda and words by Andrei Malyshko. One could listen to that song forever. We have many good composers and they have written many good songs, but, as you will realize, it is impossible to enumerate all of them in my speech.

[7] Daniil Yakovlevich Pokrass (1905–1954) and Dmitrii Yakovlevich Pokrass (b. 1899). Authors and composers of famous marching songs, among them the Budyenny March, "Moscow on a May Morning", "If War Breaks Out To-morrow" (Stalin Prize, 1941).

Jazz

Musical works also have certain serious shortcomings. The enthusiasm for jazz music and jazz bands which has developed cannot be regarded as normal. It should not be thought that we are against all jazz music; there are different kind of jazz bands and different music for them. Dunayevsky has managed to produce fine music for jazz bands, too. I also like some of the songs performed by Leonid Utesov's jazz band. However, there is a kind of music that gives you a feeling of nausea and a pain in the stomach.

After the plenary meeting of the Composers' Union of the Russian Federation, Comrade Shostakovich invited us to a concert in the Kremlin Theater. We were very busy but we went to hear the music because we were told that the concert would be an interesting one. And, indeed, we realized that there were some interesting items in the program. But then, for some reason, a jazz band appeared, then a second one, then a third, and then all three at once. You feel unhappy when there is too much of a good thing. It was very hard to stand that salvo of jazz music and you couldn't hide, even if you wanted to.

Music without melody gives rise to nothing but irritation. They say this happens because you don't understand it. And, indeed, there is some jazz music that you can't understand and hate to hear.

A feeling of distaste is also aroused by some of the so-called modern dances, brought into our country from the West. I have had the opportunity to travel round the country a lot. I have seen Russian, Ukrainian, Kazakh, Uzbek, Armenian, Georgian, and other dances. They are beautiful dances and it is a pleasure to watch them. But the so-called fashionable modern dances are simply something unseemly, mad, and the devil knows what! They say that one can see such unseemly things only in the religious sect of the *Triasuny* (Shakers). I don't know whether that is actually so, because I have never attended any of their meetings.

It transpires that among workers in the field of art you can meet young people who try in vain to prove that melody in music has lost the right to exist and that its place is now being taken by "new" music — "dodecaphony," the music of noises. It is hard for a normal person to understand what the word "dodecaphony" means, but apparently it means the same as the word "cacophony." Well, we flatly reject this cacophonous music. Our people can't use this rubbish as a tool of their ideology. [Shouts in the hall: *That's right*]

We are for music that provides inspiration, that summons people to exploits on the field of battle and in their work. When a soldier goes into battle, he takes what he needs, and a band is always with him. The band is a source of inspiration on the march. The music for such bands can be produced and is produced by composers who stick to the principles of socialist realism, who are not divorced from life and the people's struggle, and are supported by the people.

Our policy in art, a policy of rejecting abstractionism, formalism, and any other bourgeois distortions, is a Leninist policy which we have been pursuing unswervingly and shall continue to pursue in the future.

Vladimir Ilyich Lenin maintained that literature and art should serve the interests of the workers and peasants, the interests of the people.

The so-called left-wing art which is being extolled by some people, was described by Vladimir Ilyich as the strangest of antics and grimaces, unnatural and incongruous. At the present time, the myth is being spread around that Lenin was tolerant and even sympathetic towards formalistic exercises in art. Unfortunately, one of those guilty of circulating the lie about Lenin's views on art is Comrade Ehrenburg. He writes in his memoirs: "Anatoly Lunacharsky told me that when he asked Lenin whether 'left-wing' artists could be allowed to decorate the Red Square for May Day, Vladimir Ilyich replied: 'I am not a specialist in this, and I don't want to impose my tastes on others.' "

In this case, Comrade Ehrenburg tries to convey to his readers the idea that Lenin admitted the possibility of different ideological trends coexisting in Soviet art.

That is wrong, Comrade Ehrenburg. You know very well that it was actually Lenin who put forward the principle of introducing party ideology and partisanship in literature and art. Later this view was ardently supported by Gorky and other writers, who firmly took the stand of Soviet power, the stand of the struggle for the cause of the working class, the stand of the struggle for the victory of communism.

It was for its partisanship, its high ideological level, and its artistic skill that Vladimir Ilyich Lenin praised so highly Maxim Gorky's book *Mother*.

The strength of works of art lies in their artistic skill and the clarity and accuracy of the ideological views expressed. However, this does not seem to be to everyone's liking. Sometimes the ideological clarity of works of literature and art is attacked under the guise of a struggle against rhetorical and didactic tones. Such sentiments have been expressed in a most candid form in Nekrasov's[8] notes "On Both Sides of the Ocean," published in the magazine *Novy mir*. In an assessment of the film *Ilyich Zastava* he writes:

> I am infinitely grateful to Khutsiev and Shpalikov for not dragging in by his greying whiskers some old worker who understands everything and always has a clear and ready explanation for everything. Had such a character appeared with his didactic words, the film would have been sunk.

[Shouts in the hall: *Shame!*]

[8] Viktor Nekrasov (b. 1911), a leading Soviet writer of the "middle generation." Author of *In the Trenches of Stalingrad* (Stalin Prize 1947), *Kyra Georgievna* (recently translated, *Kyra,* The Cresset Press, London, 1963). Nekrasov has come under heavy attack for his travel reports from Italy, France, and the United States in which he suggested closer cultural relations between these countries and the Soviet Union, and generally speaking for revealing too much interest in various aspects of Western culture. In *Novy mir* (Nov. 19, '62), he wrote: "We used to write that Stalin was great, wise and infallible, and they believed us, many people believed us. Now, we are no longer writing about his infallibility, rather about his sins, and people are asking us, 'What were you thinking about before?' . . ."

And that was written by a Soviet author in a Soviet magazine! It is impossible to read without indignation such things, written in a haughty and contemptuous tone, about an old worker. I believe that it is absolutely impermissible for a Soviet writer to adopt such a tone.

Furthermore, the notes which I have mentioned not only express a definite attitude to a particular example in art; they also proclaim a principle which is absolutely unacceptable for our art. This cannot but arouse our most determined protest.

On Absolute Freedom

Some people can be heard talking about some kind of absolute freedom for the individual. I don't know what they mean, but I consider that never — not even under complete communism — will there be absolute freedom for the individual. "We don't believe in 'absolutes.' " — That was how Vladimir Ilyich Lenin answered the advocates of "absolute freedom" in his day. [*Collected Works, Russian edition, vol. 32, p. 479.*] Under communism, too, the will of one person will have to submit to the will of the whole collective. Unless that is so, anarchic self-will will sow dissension and disorganize the life of society. Not only socialist society, but society in general, any social system, even the smallest collective of people, is unable to exist without the organizing and guiding principle.

There is no need to prove that at all stages of social development, beginning with the primitive state, people united in collectives in order to obtain the means of existence. And in our time, the time of the atom, electronics, cybernetics, automation, and production lines, it is all the more necessary to have harmony, ideal coordination, and organization in all the links of the social system, both in the field of material production and in the sphere of spiritual life. Only in such conditions can use be made of all the benefits of science created by man and only in such conditions can they be made to serve man.

Can there be, under communism, breaches of public order and deviations from the will of the collective? There can. But evidently they will be individual cases. It cannot be supposed that cases of psychological disorders will be ruled out and that the rules of the community will be safe from being violated by persons who are mentally deranged. I can't say exactly how, but there will obviously be some means of curbing the outbursts of lunatics. Today, too, there is the straitjacket which they put on lunatics and thereby restrain them in their wildness and stop them doing harm to themselves and others.

In present-day conditions we have to wage a stubborn struggle against the survivals of the past within the country and to repel the attacks of the organized class enemy in the international arena. We have no right to forget this for a single moment. And some persons are trying to push us on to the road of peaceful ideological coexistence and to palm off the rotten idea of "absolute freedom." If everyone tries to foist his own subjective views on society as a rule to be followed by all and seeks to secure the acceptance of those views, contrary to the generally-accepted standards of socialist society, this will inevitably lead to disorganization of the normal life of the people and of the activity of society. Society cannot permit anarchy and self-will on the part of anyone.

The guiding force of socialist society is the Communist Party of the Soviet Union. It expresses the will of the entire Soviet people, and the struggle for the vital interests of the people is the aim of its activity. The party enjoys the people's confidence, which it has won and is winning by its struggle, by its blood. The party will remove from the road of Communist construction everything that is against the people's interests.

We must introduce clarity into the question of humanism, into the question of what is good for whom and what is bad for whom. We approach this question, as we do all other questions, from the class standpoint, from the standpoint of defending the interests of the working people. So long as classes exist on the earth, there will be no such thing in life as something good in the absolute sense. What is good for the bourgeoisie, for the imperialists, is disastrous for the working class, and, on the contrary, what is good for the working people is not admitted by the imperialists, by the bourgeoisie.

We should like our principles to be well understood by everyone, and especially by those who are trying to foist upon us peaceful coexistence in the sphere of ideology. There can be no joking in matters of political policy. Anyone who advocates the idea of political coexistence in the sphere of ideology is, objectively speaking, sliding down to positions of anticommunism. The enemies of communism would like to see us ideologically disarmed. And they are trying to achieve this perfidious aim of theirs by propaganda for the peaceful coexistence of ideologies, with the help of this "Trojan horse," which they would gladly smuggle in among us.

We are confident that all the attacks made by the enemies of socialism and communism against our Marxist-Leninist ideology will be smashed against the monolithic ideological and political unity of the working class, the collective-farm peasantry, and the people's intelligentsia of our country.

The press, radio, literature, painting, music, the cinema, and the theatre are a sharp ideological weapon of our party. And it sees to it that this weapon is always in fighting trim and hits the enemy without fail. The party will not allow anyone to blunt this weapon or weaken its effect.

Guidance of the Party

Soviet literature and the Soviet arts are developing under the direct guidance of the Communist Party and its central committee. The party has brought up remarkable and talented forces of writers, artists, composers, and film and theatrical workers who have inseparably linked their lives and their work with the Leninist party and the people.

The party, the people, and Lenin are inseparable. The cause of Lenin is the cause of the party and the people. This was well expressed by that fine poet, Vladimir Mayakovsky:

> *The party and Lenin*
> *Are twin brothers.*
> *Who is more valuable*
> *to Mother History?*
> *We say: "Lenin,"*
> *And mean: "The party."*
> *We say: "The party,"*
> *And mean: "Lenin!"*

The Leninist party is the foremost section, the militant, tested vanguard of the people.

No citizen of our country, no matter who he is, whether a worker or a member of a collective farm, a scientist or a writer, an artist or a composer — no sons and daughters of its people can imagine themselves outside the life of the people, outside their creative endeavor. Partisanship and kinship with the people in art are not in contradiction with one another; they make up a single whole!

Those workers in the field of art who still do not understand their place in society need to be helped to comprehend it well.

Just as a conductor sees to it that all the instruments in his orchestra sound in harmonious accord, so the party directs the efforts of all people in social and political life towards the attainment of a single goal.

Through the party, as the guiding force, socialist society is removing everything that hinders and interferes with the normal life of the people, and is creating the necessary material, cultural and ideological prerequisites for building communism.

The party's criticism of formalistic perversions is in the interests of the development of literature and art, which play an important role in the spiritual life of our society. In literature and art the party supports only such works as inspire the people and unite their forces. Society has the right to condemn works which are contrary to the interests of the people.

All of us exist on means created by the people, and for this we are obliged to pay the people with our own labor. Everyone, like a bee in a hive, must make his contribution to the material and spiritual wealth of society. There may be persons who say that they disagree with this, that this is coercion of the individual, a relapse into the past. To this I reply: We live in an organized socialist society where the interests of the individual are in harmony with the interests of society and not in contradiction with them.

The policy of the party expresses the interests of society as a whole and consequently it also expresses the interests of each individual separately, and the policy of the party is carried out by the central committee, which is vested with the confidence of the party and is elected on its authority by the Party Congress.

On questions of creative art the central committee of the party will demand of everyone — from the most distinguished and famous worker in literature or art to the budding young artist — that he abides unswervingly by the party line.

Thaw or No Thaw?

A considerable number of works on the life of Soviet society in the period of the cult of the individual and nowadays have been printed in recent times in literary magazines and also put out by publishing houses. The efforts of writers to gain an understanding of the difficult and complex phenomena of the past is quite natural. We all know that the central committee has supported a number of works of an extremely sharp, critical character.

But it must be said that books also appear which, in our opinion, give an inexact, or to be more precise, a wrong and one-sided picture, to say the least, of the events and phenomena associated with the cult of the individual, and of the essence of those fundamental changes, based on principle, which have taken place and are still taking place in the social, political, and spiritual life of the people after the 20th Party Congress. I would rank Comrade Ehrenburg's narrative, *The Thaw,* among such books.

Closely associated with the idea of a thaw are times of instability, uncertainty, incompleteness, fluctuations of temperature in nature, when it is difficult to foresee what turn the weather will take or when. It is not possible, by means of a literary image of this kind, to arrive at a correct opinion on the essence of those changes, based on principle, which have taken place since Stalin's death in the social, political, industrial, agricultural, and spiritual life of Soviet society.

The clear, bright prospects of the Communist future have unfolded before our people. The knowledge that the present generation will live under communism fills the hearts of Soviet people with pride in their country and spurs them on to feats of labor for the sake of communism. Today all people in our country breathe freely, regard one another trustfully, without suspicion, and are confident of their present and of their future, which is guaranteed them by the entire system of life.

By eliminating the consequences of the Stalin personality cult, the Communist Party has removed the obstacles which were cramping the initiative and activity of the working people, and has provided the most favorable conditions for the development of their creative forces.

A new period has begun in the life of the party and the people. While overcoming the harmful consequences of the cult of the individual, the party has been vigorously restoring Leninist standards in the life of the party and the state. It has been promoting socialist democracy and rallying all efforts for the full-scale building of a Communist society.

This, however, in no way means that we are letting things take their own course following the denunciation of the cult of the individual; it does not mean that the reins of government have been loosened, that the ship of society is drifting on the sea, or that everyone can be self-willed and behave as he likes. No, the party has pursued and will consistently and firmly pursue the Leninist course that has been charted by it, coming out relentlessly against any vacillations in ideology and any attempts to violate the standards of life of our society.

I should like to touch upon another question, which is connected with the elucidation of the period of the cult of the individual in literature. Magazines and publishing houses are said to be flooded with manuscripts about the life of people in exile, in prisons, and in camps.

I repeat once again that this is a very dangerous theme, and difficult material to deal with. The less responsibility is felt for the present and the future of our country and the party, the more light-heartedly do those who like sensations and "spicy" stuff pounce on this material. [Shouts in the hall: *That's right!*]

A sensation, "spicy" stuff, is produced, and who falls upon it? This "spicy" stuff will, like carrion, attract flies, huge fat flies, and all kinds of bourgeois scum will crawl from abroad.

Anyone who wants to delight our enemies can easily do them a service. Anyone who wants to serve the cause of our people, the cause of our party, will take such a theme, look at it, weigh it up, and if he feels he can cope with this material, he will create a work that is useful for the people and will present the material in such a way that it will strengthen the forces of the people, help our party to rally the people and speed up their advance towards the the great goal. But not everyone can cope with such a task, although, apparently, many people are anxious to take up this material.

One must keep a sense of proportion here. If all writers were to start writing only on those themes, what kind of literature should we have then?

Jews and Anti-Semitism

The central committee of the party is receiving letters in which people express their concern over the fact that in some literary works the condition of Jews in our country is misrepresented. As you know from the exchange of letters between the British philosopher, Bertrand Russell, and myself, the bourgeois press is even conducting a campaign of slander against us.

We already touched on this question at our meeting last December in connection with Yevtushenko's poem "Babi Yar." Circumstances demand that we again return to this question.

What is this poem being criticized for? It was criticized because the author was unable truthfully to show and condemn the fascist, particularly the fascist criminals who were responsible for the mass slaughter at Babi Yar. The poem represents things as if only Jews were the victims of the fascist atrocities, whereas, of course, many Russians, Ukrainians, and Soviet people of other nationalities were murdered by the Hitlerite butchers. The poem reveals that its author did not show political maturity and was ignorant of historical facts.

For whom and what purpose has it been necessary to present things as if someone is discriminating against the Jews in our country? It is not true.

Since the October Revolution Jews have enjoyed equal rights with the other peoples of the Soviet Union in all respects. There is no Jewish question in our country, and those who invent it are slavishly repeating what other people say.

As for the Russian working class, it was a relentless enemy of any national oppression, including anti-Semitism, before the Revolution as well.

In the period before the Revolution I lived among miners. Workers condemned those who took part in the Jewish pogroms which were inspired by the tsarist government, capitalists, landlords, and the bourgeoisie. They needed pogroms as a means of turning the working people away from revolutionary struggle. The pogroms were organized by the police, the gendarmerie, and members of the Black Hundreds, who recruited thugs from among the dregs of society — de-classed elements. In the towns many doorkeepers were their agents.

For instance, the well-known Bolshevik revolutionary N. Baumann, who was not a Jew, was killed in Moscow by a doorkeeper on the instructions of the gendarmerie.

The internationalism of Russia's working class is beautifully portrayed in Gorky's remarkable story *Mother*. The ranks of the revolutionary workers include representatives of different nationalities. Remember, for instance, the Russian worker Pavel Vlasov and the Ukrainian Andrei Nakhodka.

I spent my childhood and youth in Yuzovka, where many Jews were living in those days. At the plant there I worked for some time as assistant to a fitter, Yakov Isaakovich Kutikov. He was a skilled worker. There were other Jews among the workers. I remember that the copper shop's foundryman was a Jew, and his trade was very highly regarded in those days. I often saw that foundryman. He was obviously a religious man and did not work on Saturdays, but since all the Ukrainians, Russians, and others worked, he also spent the entire day at the plant, without, however, doing any work.

Russians, Ukrainians, Jews, Poles, Latvians, Estonians, and people of other nationalities worked at that plant. There were times when nobody knew what nationality this or that worker belonged to. The relations among the workers of all nationalities were comradely.

That is what class unity, proletarian internationalism is.

When I was in the United States of America and rode through Los Angeles in a car, we were joined by the city's Deputy Mayor, as he introduced himself. He spoke Russian, not too clearly, but quite fluently. I looked at him and said:

"How do you happen to know Russian?"

"Oh, I lived in Rostov. My father was a merchant of the Second Guild."

People like that lived in St. Petersburg — wherever they liked.

So you see, it seems that in tsarist times the Jew Kutikov, with whom I worked at the factory, could not live wherever he liked, whereas a Jew like the father of the Deputy Mayor of Los Angeles could live wherever he wanted.

That was how the tsarist government regarded the national question. It approached that question, too, from the class point of view. That is why the Jews among the big merchants and capitalists had the right to live anywhere, while the Jewish poor shared the plight of the Russian, Ukrainian, and other workers. They had to work, to live in hovels and shoulder the burden of forced labor like all the other peoples of tsarist Russia.

Different people also conducted themselves in different ways in the period of the Patriotic War against the fascist invaders. In those days people, including Jews, displayed a great deal of heroism. Those who earned that right were awarded the title of Hero of the Soviet Union. Many were awarded government orders and medals. I can name, for example, Hero of the Soviet Union General Kreizer. He was deputy commander in chief of the Second Guards Army during the great battle of the Volga, and fought in the battles for the liberation of the Donbas and the Crimea. General Kreizer is now commander in chief of our armies in the Far East.

There were cases of treason on the part of people of different nationalities. I can mention the following instance. When Von Paulus' group was surrounded and then crushed, the 64th Army, commanded by General Shumilov, played a part in capturing the headquarters of Von Paulus. General Z. T. Serdyuk, who was a member of the Military Council, rang me up and said that among the prisoners of war captured with Von Paulus' headquarters was a former instructor of the Kiev city committee of the Young Communist League, a man named Kogan.

"How did he happen to be with them?" I asked. "You aren't making a mistake, are you?"

"No, I'm not making a mistake," replied Comrade Serdyuk. "That Kogan was an interpreter with Von Paulus' staff."

Troops of Von Paulus were also captured by the mechanized brigade commanded by Colonel Burmakov, and the commissar of that brigade was Comrade Vinokur, a Jew by nationality. I had known Vinokur since 1931, when I was secretary of the party committee of the Baumann district in Moscow and he was secretary of the party group at the Dairy Plant.

So it seems that one Jew served as interpreter with Von Paulus' staff, while another, serving in the ranks of our army, took part in the capture of Von Paulus and his interpreter.

People's conduct is assessed not from the national but from the class point of view.

It is not in the interests of our cause to root about in the dustbins of the past for examples of disagreement between the workers of different nationalities. It is not with them that the responsibility lay for incitement to national enmity and national oppression. That was the handiwork of the exploiting classes. As for those who betrayed the interests of the revolution, hirelings of tsarism, the landlords and the bourgeoisie recruited them all over the place and found venal creatures among people of various nationalities.

It is absurd to blame the Russian people for the filthy provocations of the members of the Black Hundreds and it is equally absurd to place on the whole Jewish people the responsibility for the nationalism and Zionism of the "Bund," for the provocations of Azef and Zhitomirsky ("Otsov") and of various Jewish organizations associated in their day with the "Zubatovites" and the tsarist Secret Political Police.

Our Leninist party consistently follows a policy of friendship among the peoples and brings up the Soviet people in a spirit of internationalism, of intolerance towards any and every manifestation of race discrimination and national dissension. The lofty and noble ideals of internationalism and fraternity among the peoples are upheld by our art.

An important question is that of the visits paid by our creative workers to foreign countries. The central committee of the party attaches much importance to these visits. It is necessary for Soviet writers to see with their own eyes how the peoples live in different countries, so that they can produce works on the life and struggle of the working people, against imperialism and colonialism, for peace, freedom, and the happiness of the peoples. Works of Soviet literature and art, permeated with the spirit of internationalism, truly reflect the life and struggles of the peoples of the socialist countries.

Visits to the West

But there have also been occasions when visits by writers to foreign countries have not only failed to be of use, but have actually proved to be against our country's interests.

One reads the materials on the statements made by some Soviet writers abroad and wonders what they were concerned with, whether they were concerned with telling the truth about the successes of the Soviet people, or with trying by any and every means to curry favor with the bourgeois public abroad. With amazing irresponsibility, such "tourists" give interviews right and left to various bourgeois newspapers, magazines, and news agencies, including the most reactionary ones — interviews in which they disseminate fairy tales about life in their own country.

An unpleasant impression was left by the visit paid to France by the writers V. Nekrasov, K. Paustovsky, and A. Voznesensky. V. Katayev was also imprudent in his statements during his visit to America.

Abroad, they will flatter an unstable person, they will call him a "symbol of the new epoch" or something in the same vein, and he will forget where he has come from, where he has arrived, and what he has arrived there for, and will begin to talk rubbish.

Quite recently the poet Yevgeny Yevtushenko paid a visit to Western Germany and France. He has just returned from Paris, where he addressed audiences of many thousands of workers, students, and friends of the Soviet Union. Comrade Yevtushenko, it must be agreed, conducted himself in a worthy manner during this visit. But he, too, if the journal *Lettres Françaises* is to be trusted, could not resist the temptation to earn the praise of the bourgeois public.

The poet informed his listeners about the attitude shown in this country towards his poem "Babi Yar," but did this in a strange way, telling them that the poem had been accepted by the people but criticized by the dogmatists. But it is widely known that Comrade Yevtushenko's poem has been criticized by Communists. How can one forget this and fail to draw conclusions for oneself?

The bourgeois press often praises some of our workers in the field of art for the fact that they do not attempt, so the bourgeois press claims, "to go over to the defensive with a covering fire of dialectical tricks," when their observations do not conform to "party doctrine."

Such praise is distasteful to a Soviet person. Vladimir Ilyich Lenin was fond of quoting the fine lines by the poet Nekrasov:*

> *He hears sounds of approval,*
> *Not in the sweet murmur of praise,*
> *But in the wild outbursts of malice.*

This was written, not by this Nekrasov, but by the Nekrasov whom everybody knows.

Everyone should understand the times in which we are living.

Socialism has won once and for all in our country. Today the frontiers of socialism have been greatly broadened. The army of the builders of socialism and communism numbers more than 1,000 million people in its ranks. And there are over 3,000 million living on the globe.

If our forces are growing, the enemy is not sleeping either. Dreading the growing strength of socialism, he is maliciously sharpening his weapons for the war he is preparing against the countries of socialism. The enemies of communism pin their hopes on subversive ideological activities in the socialist countries. You must always remember this, comrades, and keep your arms in complete readiness, prepared for battle.

"We Are Unanimous"

Comrades, we have discussed here a wide range of questions which are of importance to our state and to the ideological work of the party. The fact that we are meeting together in a comradely atmosphere, that we are discussing together problems which are of concern to all of us, is an expression of the new situation that has developed in our country in recent years.

The people and the party are deeply interested in seeing that artistic creation develops here in the right direction. The line of development of literature and art has been defined in the Party Program, which was discussed by the entire people and received the universal support and approval of the workers, collective farmers, and intellectuals.

How to carry out this line in the best and most correct way in artistic creation, each one of you decides in accordance with his understanding of his duty to the people and the special features of his talent, of his artistic individuality.

* Nikolai Nekrasov (1821–1878), the great poet who is frequently evoked for his civic consciousness [P. J.].

The meeting between the leaders of the party and the government and workers in the spheres of literature and art, the criticism of shortcomings, the joint setting of the new tasks posed by life, the frank discussions which have taken place during these meetings — all this shows that we are unanimous in our assessment of the successes and shortcomings of literature and art. I think that today's exchange of views will be of considerable significance for the further development of literature and art.

We call upon the workers of Soviet literature and art, true helpers of the party, to rally their ranks even more closely and, under the leadership of the Leninist central committee, to direct their efforts towards achieving new successes in building communism.

(Pravda, March 10, 1963)

With minor stylistic changes, this is the official Russian-English translation as it appeared in Encounter, *Pamphlet No. 9, "Khrushchev on Culture." Numbered footnotes are from* Encounter.

9

PEAK OF THE CAMPAIGN

The speeches and articles that follow represent the height of the campaign against intellectuals. Only now did writers of the extreme right wing give vent to long pent-up anger and jealousy: jealousy at the vast audiences, the privileges, the talent, the trips to the West of young writers such as Yevtushenko and Voznesensky. Besides the note of vengeance, some of the speeches are remarkable for their chauvinistic overtones. In the passage on Viktor Nekrasov, Podgorny brings to light that spring's boldest example of resistance to demand by the Party that writers engage in self-criticism.

Excerpts from an article by Sergei Pavlov, First Secretary of the Central Committee of the Young Communist League.

The boundless love of Soviet young men and women for their socialist motherland, patriotism — this is what marks the true image of the young generation of our country. At the same time, we do not conceal the fact that there are still fools who are prepared to crawl on their bellies before the foreigner, begging him for foreign rags or chewing gum. There are insignificantly few of these. And everywhere the Young Communist League gives resolute battle to them, since they trample human dignity in the mud.

There is another kind of ignoramus who bites on the shiny bait of bourgeois propaganda. This kind wants the transoceanic "twist," abstract art, and cacophonous music.

Both kinds are loathsome. But even greater indignation is aroused in our young people by those who, pretending to the role of "enlighteners," "talents" or even "spokesmen" of the generation, are prepared to forget about what is most sacred — about the people, who gave them literally everything; about the great achievements of communism; about their motherland, on which all mankind gazes with pride — all, essentially, for the same cheap foreign goods: for a portrait in *Life*, an interview in *Der Stern* or the publication of a book "over there."

.   .   .   .

Under the pretext of the struggle against the consequences of the cult of the individual and dogmatism, certain writers, film makers and artists have begun somehow to "be embarrassed" to speak of lofty ideas, of communism. Juggling with the lofty concept of "truth to life" and distorting this idea, they populate their works with people who stand aside from great public interest and are immersed in a narrow little world of philistine problems. And it is these philistines whom some writers portray with greatest sympathy! . . .

So our educators have to fight the baneful influence of some books intended for young people. Bourgeois propaganda, on the other hand, eagerly arms itself with such works, translates and advertises them extensively. At the Eighth World Festival of Youth and Students, representatives of American, French, Italian, and other delegations told us that the young people of their countries often ask: Why do we meet good Soviet people in real life, but some Soviet books write about utterly different kinds? Indeed, one need merely read I. Ehrenburg's memoirs, A. Yashin's "Vologda Marriage," V. Nekrasov's travel essays, V. Axyonov's "Halfway to the Moon," A. Solzhenitsyn's "Matryona's House," V. Voinovich's "I Want to Be Honest" (and all from the magazine *Novy mir*) — these works breathe such pessimism, mustiness, hopelessness that I fear they could mislead an uninformed person who did not know our life. Incidentally, *Novy mir* prints such works with utterly inexplicable consistency.

Or take the magazine *Yunost* (organ of the U.S.S.R. Union of Soviet Writers), intended, it would seem, for Soviet young people. What does it present to our teenagers as an ideal? The editorial board of *Yunost* very much likes the adventures of notorious "lads" who, if they make an impression on the reader, do so primarily by their tough *stilyaga* slang, their predilection for calvados, which is the word they use for Chechen-Ingush cognac, and their cowboy bravado when it comes to sexual questions.

(*Komsomolskaya pravda*, March 22, 1963. Excerpts.)

Excerpts from Speeches at the Fourth Plenary Session of the U.S.S.R. Union of Writers at the end of March.

ALEXANDER PROKOFYEV

GLORIFY, SING, INCULCATE HEROISM. — The Party calls on us to sing the deeds of the people, the people who by these deeds are amazing the entire world. What the Party asks of us is completely legitimate. In this it is fully empowered by the people, who trust it in everything, seeing it as their leader.

The Presidium of the Central Committee and the Soviet Government have talked with us more than once. I have attended all these meetings. Along with many others, I have in my soul nothing but gratitude to the Party. I, along with many others, am grateful to the Party for its instruction, its exactingness. It would be a bad thing if the Party did not make demands, if it failed to take care of our work, if it thought, "Even this is all right.". . .

We looked with indifference on many things that should not have been permitted in rearing the young, looked with indifference on unrestrainedly laudatory criticism, panegyrics to them; on their genuflections to the West; on the fuss surrounding certain names; on the extravagant interviews; on scandalous verses and scandalous fame. It is not without reason that the people say, "You teach good to a youngster when he is lying across a bench, not when he's sprawled on it."

In my time I have "skirmished," as they say, with S. P. Shchipachev. He told me that one must "educate." Well, the "educational" measures effected by Stepan Petrovich have yielded their fruit! . . .

What I have spoken about above in reference to the Moscow writers' organization is by no means peculiar to the capital. No, life tells us that this is not so, that such phenomena exist in Siberia and other places, and they exist in Leningrad, as well.

Why, for instance, was it necessary to beat the drums immediately upon the appearance of the first book of Viktor Sosnora's poems? The magazine *Novy mir,* for example, announced in its review that "lovers of poetry have been waiting impatiently for this book."

For the artist who serves the people with his art, the concepts of kinship with the people and Party spirit do not present themselves as problems but constitute the very essence of his life in literature or art, an organic element in his world view; they are an expression of the purpose of his creative work, which belongs to the people. . . .

In the concept of kinship with the people I include simplicity — not the kind that is worse than stealing, of course, but another kind. I include in this concept words cut, like diamonds, by the people, the love of the apt phrase, the aphorism, the wit and much else by which the soul of the people lives, that is natural to the people's soul: love for one's native land, loyalty to it, thoughts of happiness. The people do not like pseudo-folksiness, do not like to slobber where some of us slobber. This is why I have protested against such poems as Voznesensky's "One-and-a-Half [-Ton Truck]" and Yevtushenko's "The Bed Was Made." I protest not out of some sort of sanctimonious considerations but because without bragging I may say that I know the people, their likes and dislikes, better than these authors. . . .

I thank the Presidium of the Central Committee and N. S. Khrushchev for having so sharply posed the question of abstractionism and formalism. Even before the conferences in the Kremlin, there was talk in the corridors and in the press about where the young were going and where their patrons were pushing poetry, snubbing those who held different opinions.

The patrons of the arts, of whom there are not a few in our country, have stubbornly continued their patronage. And the recipients of this patronage were getting more and more impudent, and the readers and authors sadly watched this protracted process.

Yet the circle of innovators was expanding. I have been told that some publishers received poems by the pood imitating the "masters." And the "masters" themselves were flattered by the advances of the West, where they were called "grandees." And they would attend interviews, and in these interviews would say devil knows what. . . .

Abstractionism is like cosmopolitanism — it has no native land. It has penetrated and is penetrating into our country like a scout from alien shores. It infiltrates our country like a saboteur, prepared to disrupt the foundations of our art from within. It is alien to our whole tenor of life, to all the bright and beautiful by which we live.

Our enemies are not passive. I remember when we were in Finland and were touring a kindergarten, volumes of *Doctor Zhivago* were lying on the window sills to attract our attention.

All this is despicable provocation. I can imagine what a howl our enemies have raised over the recent meetings of Party and government leaders with writers and artists. But that is no novelty to us: As the proverb says, "The dogs bark, but the caravan moves on.". . .

Too Many Books for Innovators

One more point. Something should be done about book trade policy. Books by the "innovators" are issued in enormous editions of 50,000 to 100,000 copies. Why? Who will answer these questions? Why did Sosnora's first book receive 14 reviews — it was grabbed right away! — while books by those who take a Soviet position receive almost no attention?

And in the provinces? How difficult the situation is with publication in the provinces! How difficult it is there for the young to publish!

People there rejoice endlessly if the central press announces the publication of a local book. But mountains of paper are devoted to the works of Yevtushenko, Voznesensky — this group of four or five persons. There has not been a single magazine, a single newspaper, a single printed publication that did not speak in laudatory tones of anything concerning Yevtushenko, Voznesensky, Akhmadulina, Rozhdestvensky.

The weekly *France Nouvelle* informs us that Yevtushenko, in answer to a question at a Paris press conference as to whether he would revise "Babi Yar" now that the poem had been criticized, said that the Western press's information on this subject did not correspond to the truth. Nobody was forcing him to revise anything. And he added: "Above all, in the Soviet Union they know my character, and no one would think of requiring me to do anything against my wishes."

We do indeed know this character, have known him ever since the time of Gogol's unforgettable Ivan Alexandrovich [Khlestakov, the "Inspector General"].

We are advancing toward communism. We have to be strong, we have to be genuine heroes in peaceful labor, as we were heroes in the days of the war. And here — this is, to my mind, very dangerous — among a part of the young people there are heard complaints that they are bored with these heroics. Revulsion to literary stereotypes cannot be allowed to be confused with what is genuinely high and great in our life, in our goal, in our ideology. . . .

We must glorify, sing, inculcate heroism!

                                        (*Literaturnaya gazeta*, March 28, 1963)

ANATOLY SOFRONOV

HOLD THE COURSE! . . . N. S. Khrushchev and other leaders of the Party and government are always with the people and know by what the people live. Can a writer get along without this? But here you read in the magazine *Voprosy literatury* the questionnaires to which the young writers have responded. What turns out to be the background of these young writers? Ten years of school, a higher educational institution, and then professional literary work. And that's all!

What can such a young man write? For a while, perhaps, his undergraduate impressions will suffice him, but afterwards? Scrivening remains. There is a complete absence of foundation, a complete absence of observation of life. And then certain mentors appear —

In this connection it is necessary to talk about our Moscow organization. We have gathered here in Moscow from various places. Perhaps we have even been abroad, but we do not give and will not give, like some people, vile interviews, insulting to our society, that are simply revolting to read. . . .

I am not saying this out of a desire to offend such poets as, let us say, Andrei Voznesensky and Yevgeny Yevtushenko. Time was when I handed Yevtushenko the card for his candidate membership in the Writers' Union. He was then 19 or 20 years old. I remember that day when I, as an elder comrade, wished Yevtushenko a good journey in life.

And Andrei Voznesensky came to the editorial offices of *Ogonyok*. We printed his work, and we also criticized some poems and advised him not to make them public. He did not, however, listen to us. . . .

A great sin lies upon the Moscow writers' organization. And on its leadership, in particular S. Shchipachev. I respect this good poet, a man who has been in the Party and in literature for many years. But it seems to me that he did not stand up against one human weakness: the flattery with which a group of people surrounded him, encouraging a "kindly," liberal-irresponsible, uncritical attitude with regard to certain phenomena in the life of our Moscow organization, with regard to the creative work and behavior of certain young writers. One example is S. Shchipachev's rapturous appraisal of A. Borshchagovsky's report at the plenary session of the board of the Moscow branch of the Writers' Union, which was devoted to the creative work of young writers. At a meeting of the secretariat of the board of the Russian Republic Writers' Union, S. Shchipachev declared that it was the first time in the history of Soviet literature that he had heard such a wonderful report. And what about Gorky? And Fadeyev? And Sobolev's report to the First Congress of Russian Republic writers? And Korneichuk, who delivered the report on drama to the Second Congress? . . .

.   .   .   .

The Moscow organization of writers is not Yevtushenko, is not Akhmadulina, is not Voznesensky. It is hundreds of really gifted, talented writers who have been with the Soviet power and the Party for all the decades of Soviet rule. They have been, are and will be with the Soviet power and will never depart from Party positions!

(*Literaturnaya gazeta,* March 28, 1963)

TO A YOUNG TALENT

You said that you were
A non-state poet, beyond the pale,
and you squinted into the crystal goblet,
Sitting there dressed like a London dandy.

You said: "You have the medals,
Your work has been recognized by the country,
But I got none, I am beyond the pale;
Such as I do not get awards."

Your irony had the ring
Of off-hand candor;
The onset of unthinking maturity,
No longer childishness.

You've been so long accustomed
To plucking the blossoms of applause
That you can no longer distinguish
Flattery from praise.

The doors to the apartment, both back and front,
You've flung open wide,
And the breeze that stirs your lyre
Has whipped up a chain of turbulence.

And persons to whom your fate, your star
Are matters of indifference
Embrace and kiss you cynically,
Like bosom friends.

"Our progressive! The most honest one!"
We hear their tipsy cry.
But there is also such a thing
As progressive paralysis!

Dressed in modernism, poses and bravado,
As in an opera cape,
What award do you expect,
"Non-state" poet?

My verse is not an epigram
To strike the target.
My only regret now is that
You'll make use of it for publicity.

— SERGEI MIKHALKOV
(*Izvestia,* March 22, p. 3.)

YURY ZHUKOV

RESPONSIBILITY! Creative workers at their meetings are conducting a great discussion on the course of the further development of Soviet literature and art. As always, the foreign spies, sensation lovers, and ill-wishers who dream of finding even the smallest crack in our monolithic society are right on hand. The bourgeois press has already raised an inordinate noise on the subject of our principled creative discussions. It hastens to take "under its wing" the comrades who have been subjected to justified Party criticism.

It must be said that our opponents are very efficient. In London they have already managed to concoct and publish a collection titled "New Voices in Russian Literature," [1] which includes a quite definite selection of authors: There are works by Kazakov, Axyonov, Okudzhava; poems by Voznesensky, Akhmadulina, Vinokurov, Sosnora, Slutsky, and Yevtushenko; and the preface says that the recent "defeat," as they express it, has served to "consolidate the artists" in some sort of "common front" to combat those who have criticized them. . . .

Here is Gleb Struve — the not-unknown successor of the not-unknown reactionary whom Vladimir Ilyich Lenin routed — appearing in the American magazine *New Republic* with an article in which he holds forth on the

[1] *Encounter,* April 1963 [P. J.].

subject of how Soviet literature is going to develop after the meetings of Party and government leaders with people in the arts. In this article he prompts those Soviet writers who he thinks share his views on how they should act: "The representatives of 'avant-garde tendencies,'" he prophesies, "will in all probability once again go underground, and their works will reach the outside world by secret channels. The beginning of an underground literature is one of the most interesting phenomena in Soviet literary life since 1957."

Whom does Struve have in mind as producers of this "underground literature"? Those whose writings are sent abroad secretly and are printed there. We remember the unanimously adverse reaction of Soviet writers to the publication abroad of *Doctor Zhivago*. After that, certain persons who had nothing in common with literature, such as Yesenin-Volpin, also used this route. But now we learn that even among our comrades people are to be found who do not resist the temptation to print their works abroad, bypassing generally accepted channels.

The publication in the French magazine *L'Express* of a "Precocious Autobiography" by someone bearing the name Yevtushenko evoked legitimate indignation among Soviet literary people. This work abounds in untrue assertions and judgments, not only of the literary but also of the social life of our country, that bewilder the reader. It is written in a style uncharacteristic of a Soviet writer, and when I first read it I was actually dubious: It can't be that Yevtushenko wrote this? Can it be a forgery? But it turned out that the manuscript had indeed come from his pen. The editors of *L'Express* announced that they had saved a photocopy of it, in case the author were to try for some reason to repudiate it.

I have before me an issue of the magazine *L'Express* dated March 21. In it is printed the chapter that presents the summing up of the entire work.

I read this chapter, and I thought: Why does Y. Yevtushenko give our ideological opponents an opportunity to conduct speculative discussions about the possibility of an "opposition" of some kind appearing in our country by hinting in the pages of a foreign magazine that some sort of special trend of those who share his views is forming? He writes: "I am finishing these autobiographical notes, still stirred by the reception at the Mutualité Hall and the Palais de Chaillot. I am sorry that my friends, the poets and writers of the post-Stalin generation, were not with me and did not have the opportunity of becoming acquainted with the Parisian public." And further on there is a list of names that coincides almost exactly with the list of "oppositionists" given in the collection published in London, whereupon it is emphasized that the representatives of this trend are waging a struggle with those who, in this "Precocious Autobiography," are called "dogmatists" and "conservatives."

One is alerted also by the fact that Pasternak appears in the "Autobiography" in the capacity of the ideological inspirer of this group.

To the point is Y. Yevtushenko's curious declaration that it is incorrect to think Pasternak lived "outside the times." He continues: "He had to have a lot of courage to play the role he chose. He had to be an extraordinary personality to preserve a carefree smile in our unsmiling age."

In this work Yevtushenko emerges with the point of view of a certain philosophy that is divorced from the one taught us by the Party. He declines to stand on one side of the barricade that divides the two worlds, preferring to "soar above the battle" and defend some sort of abstract "truth." And this is true not of Yevtushenko alone. I like Nekrasov the writer, but I did not like his notes "On Both Sides of the Ocean." In them he stressed that he criticizes the disorders that exist in the West only when he simultaneously criticizes similar disorders existing in the Soviet Union. This is the same philosophy as Yevtushenko's. . . .

A legitimate question arises: Why in general was it necessary to publish memoirs, albeit those of a "precocious man," abroad and afterwards bring them to the notice of the Soviet people? Besides, even if we now desired to publish Yevtushenko's memoirs, we would have to go begging to the weekly *L'Express* and pay it money, since it is their owner! The magazine carries the notice: "Author's rights belong to the weekly *L'Express,* and any republication, even in part, is strictly forbidden."

Someone needs to clear up thoroughly his understanding of the social duty of a writer. I repeat: We should all feel that we are soldiers of our party. I do not wish to say that Yevtushenko is not one. He was a good soldier, we might say, when he wrote the poem "Do Russians Want War?" or the verses on Cuba, or the poems from Helsinki directed against fascism. But why has he now so frivolously shifted to a position of capitulation to our ideological opponents? . . .

(*Literaturnaya gazeta,* March 30, 1963. Excerpt.)

MIKHAIL SOKOLOV

THE PARTY TEACHES EXACTINGNESS. It must be said that we are still managing our literary husbandry poorly, are poorly looking after the correct development of the creative work of some young writers.

I shall cite one example. It throws light on the bumpkins whom we sometimes send to Europe. At some point in one of our conferences we were talking about young literature. Alexander Prokofyev sharply criticized Yevtushenko's creative work, his ideological and artistic immaturity, his ignorance of the life of his people. One wonders, he said, why we should send young people abroad who are still far from having matured either artistically or as citizens, to say nothing of their political maturity. Let them stay home for a while, look at the life of their own people, get a little sense and then go out as prophets of the new world. The head of the Moscow writers' organization, S. Shchipachev, replied: No, let Yevtushenko go and look with his own eyes at the other world, and from this he will better see and understand what kind of life we have. So has Yevtushenko understood what kind of life we have? He has understood badly. He has "understood" in such a way that now one does not even feel like reading Yevtu-shenko's good poems. Comrade Yevtushenko dirtied his hands abroad!

Some comrades have patted similar young "cadres" on the shoulder too often. What did these comrades notice? They noticed a few people in Moscow — Yevtushenko, Axyonov, and others. It can be asked, but where are those thousands of talented young people, living both in Moscow and in other cities, who cannot break through into public notice as these few, who have been elevated almost to Pushkin's fame, are undeservedly break-ing through? Who needs this kind of indoctrination, it is asked? . . .

We have had one writer who has been properly called great within the lifetime of the Soviet people: Mikhail Alexandrovich Sholokhov. It is to this great that we should all be compared. Nikita Sergeyevich has spoken of this more than once.

We Don men, and Muscovite writers too, cannot take a calm attitude to-ward literary manifestations that feed grist not to our own mill but to the enemy's. But many comrades call us "clannish." Why? Because we support Party spirit in literature, the line of the Party and the state, and fight for high civic spirit in Soviet literature. . . .

Our ideals, the ideals of communism, will win sooner or later. And it seems strange when certain leaders of the Writers' Union, whom we trust, say, for example, as Comrade Surkov declared at the meeting of the *aktiv* of Moscow writers, that he wavered and supported the idea of coexistence for exactly nine hours.

This is at once laughable and sad. Comrade Surkov is an experienced literary man, a public official and a Communist. And for a Communist it is not permissible to forget his ideology or propagandize ideological coexist-ence for even nine seconds, let alone nine hours.

There will be no sort of coexistence of ideologies. As for those who have been propagandizing and supporting this "idea," let them state publicly how they came to such a stance, and what they are going to do tomorrow. I address myself, in particular, to Comrade Surkov. . . .

It is impossible to agree with those who claim that we had a period of disorder, of ideological hesitation. There was no disorder whatsoever, no sort of hesitation either among literary people or among others in cultural activities. We went where the Party called us. There were private mistakes. But these mistakes were made by living people. And it is time to inquire about these people, it is time to bring order into our writers' organization.

Why, for example, is it precisely in the pages of *Novy mir* that there appears now one, now another, then a third work upon reading which one can only shrug one's shoulders — Ehrenburg's memoirs, Nekrasov's notes, Solzhenitsyn's stories, and others?

Obviously, all is not well with Party guidance in the magazines and news-papers, or indeed in the union itself.

Recently a working secretariat of the Russian Republic Writers' Union was held. There things were called by their names. Writers of the Don, the

Kuban, Donetsk Province and Ryazan Province criticized certain Muscovites in a comradely way, criticized well, in the name of the cause. But no, certain leaders of the union, including S. Shchipachev and Ye. Maltsev, understood everything topsy-turvy.

May all writers live and thrive, may they work better, and for this, let each of us recognize that he is responsible before the people, before his native land — including Shchipachev, Tvardovsky, Surkov, Maltsev, and so on. . . .

Comrade Ehrenburg is a much respected man, but he needlessly hastens to drag literary corpses out into the light. . . .

Comrade Tvardovsky is an important poet, but Tvardovsky as an editor also makes his mistakes. Let us speak to him about this and hope that he may make them no more.

And here what is striking is that when you criticize Tvardovsky as an editor, he is silent. But why shouldn't he come forward and answer criticism?

We are Communists and should be Communists not only on the public platform but everywhere and under all circumstances.

(*Literaturnaya gazeta,* April 2, 1963)

SERGEI MIKHALKOV

It is no secret, that some people when they go abroad feverishly leaf through encyclopedias to copy out the names of foreign sculptors, writers, poets. If they are asked, they puff up: There, they say, are the ones they studied with. But isn't it better to take in your baggage a sense of political tact, a sense of responsibility for your words and behavior, a consciousness that you are a representative of the advanced Soviet and not some other intelligentsia? And, finally, a sense of citizenly dignity. It is impossible to be both Mayakovsky and Igor Severyanin simultaneously.

(*Pravda,* March 24, 1963)

VASILY SMIRNOV

The overwhelming majority of our young workers of the artistic word (and I mean precisely workers!), in contrast to insignificant groups of spoiled, overpraised, divorced-from-reality producers of 'smelly' literature 'with rot' — I repeat, the overwhelming majority of our young writers and poets live the people's life and see in it the main thing: the bright, the advanced, the Communist, and they write about the main thing." . . . "They bravely combat everything that hinders our movement forward, but they do not exaggerate the bad and present it as typical. For them, the young writers, the major, general task of the artistic word is, as it is for all Soviet writers of the older generation, the creation of a new human character, very wholehearted, truly very close to the ideal of the character of man, a fighter and creator, the glorification for the ages of the legendary acts of this man, true service by the artistic word to the people and the Party in their titanic labors in the construction of a Communist society.

(*Pravda,* March 29, 1963)

LEONID NOVICHENKO

Yevtushenko's case is only one of a number that have come to light. But it is instructive. With all that is good about Yevtushenko and what he has done, he has by his personal example introduced into the poetry of the young a type of poet completely alien to our literature — the troublemaker, the politico, the self-advertiser. Unfortunately, the example has turned out to be infectious; political speculation is no longer peculiar only to Yevtushenko. For us in the Ukraine, it has appeared also in the creative work of Ivan Drach and Vingranovsky.

And one more point: Yevtushenko is a very uneducated man, both generally and in the sense of Marxist education, the Marxist world view. His notes are called "Autobiography of a Precocious Man" — and, I would add, of a man who never seriously studied anything. I will give him his due for tenacity, observation, good 'breakthroughs' into life, into the environment close to him; but still, how often, reading his poetry, I bog down at the places where he begins to philosophize.

All this, combined with the enormous self-confidence that also marks this particular comrade and his friends, makes a literary broth of which it is time to speak in earnest. The advice and instructions of the Party are important and useful for the young poets; they open up a new stage in their lives.

(*Pravda,* March 29, 1963)

Excerpts from the Eighth Plenary Session of the Board of the Writers' Union of the Russian Republic in early April.

THE OFFENSIVE IS ON. . . .

How did it happen that some of our young writers forgot about modesty and disgraced themselves by conceit and vanity, which led them to ideological downfall? . . .

Anatoly Kalinin spoke sarcastically of those "spiritual fathers" who "in a cabal" inflated the undeserved fame of "the talents."

Sergei Baruzdin devoted a considerable part of his speech to an analysis of the reasons for the inflated fame of a small group of young literary troublemakers. He emphasized that the preponderance of Russian writers are fighters, soldiers of the Party, and they did not have to "re-examine their views" after the Kremlin meeting; they know how to argue and take the offensive, but someone in the recent period shirked and abandoned the field of the battle for youth to shortsighted "spiritual mentors" cloaked in "leftist" phrases.

The phrasemongers and poseurs created such a situation in the Moscow writers' organization that, according to *Valery Druzin's* apt description, "It was difficult for people who held correct Party positions to express their views, to criticize what should have been criticized, and possibly to forestall the mistakes that developed without criticism and blossomed in lush flower, and now it is necessary to speak of them in full voice." A number of similar instances were cited by the writers *Vasily Zhuravlev* and *S. V. Smirnov*.

The clique often utilized impermissible methods in their improper activity.

"Any article that appeared in the magazine *Oktyabr*," said *Semyon Tregub*, "even those offered as a basis for discussion, such as, for example, Lyukov's and Panov's articles on films, literally excited hysteria. We (Brovman and I) have been asked how we could belong to *Oktyabr*'s public advisory council for criticism. If we had been on *Novy mir*'s public advisory council, that would have been a different matter. The basis is not *what* is printed, *how* it is written, but *where* it is printed. If it is in *Oktyabr*, then after it! This has determined the attiude toward such comrades as, for example, Pyotr Strokov, Larisa Kryachko, Viktor Chalmayev, Yury Idashkin, Lenina Ivanova, Nikolai Sergovantsev, and others." The poet *S. V. Smirnov* also spoke of the "feeling of defenselessness" in an emotionally stirring speech.

The plenary session participants declared that even the workers of the Bureau for the Propaganda of Artistic Literature labored not a little for hollow fame. One cannot fail to agree, in particular, with the following statement by *Viktor Poltoratsky:*

"They say that the appearances of young writers — Voznesensky, Yevtushenko, Bella Akhmadulina, and so on — at the Polytechnical Museum and at Moscow State University enjoyed great success. But who has even once attempted to arrange an evening of really Russian poetry in these halls? Why not arrange an evening in which there would appear poets from Smolensk, Yaroslavl, Vologda, Rostov, Voronezh (our Russian land has no end of cities!) — after all, the real poets are there. And the listeners would see where the real Russian Soviet poetry is going and what it calls for!

Criticism of the critics resounded strongly at the plenary session. A certain group of critics has concentrated its by no means always objective attention on a specific small circle of writers, at the expense of hundreds and hundreds of gifted writers who are successfully working along the main lines of artistic creation. . . .

.   .   .   .

No compromise with bourgeois ideology. The offensive is on. We have waited for it. An offensive along the whole front — in questions of upbringing, religion, morals, and the family, in questions of art, attitudes to work: a large-scale, prepared, unstoppable offensive! — such was the leitmotiv of all the work of the plenary session of the writers of Russia.

(*Literaturnaya Rossiya,* April 12, 1963)

SERGEI BARUZDIN

THE CAUSE WE SERVE. The meetings between Party and government leaders and workers in literature and the arts have made us think about the fate of our homeland's literature, about our own work, and about our literary world. All of us have been forced to think, not just those who were mistaken. It is true that for the overwhelming majority of us there is nothing in our views to change. We have always stood for Party spirit and kinship with the people in our literature, have always correctly understood the questions of tradition. Finally, we have violated no norms in our own behavior, have not done the things that Ye. Yevtushenko, A. Voznesensky, and V. Axyonov have done, either in our own fatherland or abroad. We have not lost our sense of patriotism, as have some of our young and some of our not-so-young literary colleagues.

All the same, we have shirked our duty. At first we fought, and the literary events of 1956–1957 make it clear that we were capable of arguing and attacking; but then — and especially in the past two or three years — we became either tired or afraid.

What did we fear?

Being voted down by secret ballot? Having labels like "dogmatist," "Stalinist," etc., pinned on us? Or, finally, did we perhaps fear that our activity might have an effect on our own artistic fortunes — that we might not get printed, that we might be ignored, or that we might be bludgeoned with criticism from the noble standpoint of the "fight for quality"?

The chief thing now, however, is not to analyze the past but to try to give some thought to the present and the future.

The first and most important thing we need is a change in the creative situation in the union. We should no longer think only about ourselves, look after only our own affairs. We must think about everyone, about the whole of literature. We should be interested not only in our own books but also in those by our comrades, no matter where they live.

Actually, this has not been the case in the Moscow writers' organization. Many writers have even stopped reading one another's works. When defending or opposing a writer, it was the name that mattered. A great deal has been said among us about five or six fashionable names, but these writers were sometimes discussed even though the speakers had not read them. It sometimes appeared that those writers who praised Axyonov's works had read neither "The Colleagues" nor "Ticket to the Stars"! . . .

At the same time, one heard the word "talent" from all the speakers' platforms. They shouted "talent" when they accepted into the Writers' Union a young critic who was lost in even the most elementary esthetic questions. They used the word "talent" in accepting an immature writer who a week later mounted the platform and said that there are no national traditions in our fiction, that Tolstoy, Hemingway, Chekhov, Remarque, Pasternak, and Yury Kazakov are of equal magnitude both for literature and for the literary education of the young.

What didn't they say!

It is important for us now to think of how to eliminate these excesses on both sides. We must cast out all these sympathies and antipathies, read one another's works, and support everything genuine, everything that works for communism!

(*Literaturnaya Rossiya,* April 5, 1963)

A Key Attack on Yevtushenko

WHERE DOES 'KHLESTAKOVISM' [1] LEAD? By G. Oganov, B. Pankin, and V. Chikin.

Two autobiographies by the poet Yevgeny Yevtushenko are now known to literary history. One was written for the Writers' Union, the other for the Paris weekly *L'Express*. These two documents differ sharply. Among other things, they are of different lengths: The first is a page and a half of modest manuscript, while the other consists of almost a hundred pages of thoughts, predictions, revelations, and frank statements.

The publication of the expanded version might have remained the personal business of Y. Yevtushenko had it contained only information intended to satisfy the curiosity of foreign admirers of talent. However, the work that *L'Express* called la "Precocious Autobiography" was by no means restricted to such a limited aim. The opportunity to write for the reactionary Paris weekly was a great inspiration. As its editors wrote in recommending their author to readers, "the confession of this poet of the new Russia is something more than a document about the brilliant personality of Yevgeny Yevtushenko." In their opinion, "no research, no visit to the U.S.S.R. could throw as much light on the future of this country." . . .

.   .   .   .

The author of the "confession" clearly wishes to steer the reader toward the thought that his own appearance on the literary horizon was foreordained.

> I was oppressed by a sense of a new responsibility that had fallen on my shoulders. Russians have long thought of their poets as spiritual leaders, as keepers of the truth. . . . Nekrasov's famous lines run:
>
> > Perhaps, indeed, you are no poet,
> > But serve as citizen you must.
>
> I was both the former and the latter. . . ,

Are There Two Yevtushenkos?

If we now contrast this dramatic figure of a semiprophet that emerges from the "confession" with the poet Yevgeny Yevtushenko familiar to the Soviet reader, we are confronted with the picture of an unusually split personality. It is as though there were two Yevtushenkos in existence at the same time.

The first, you will recall, wrote in Young Communist League newspapers about the beauty of the everyday labor of the shepherd and the architect, called on the poets of his generation to go to the great construction projects of communism, passionately hailed Glezos and Hikmet, and poured anger on the Parisian imprisoners of freedom who arrested Duclos and Stil. The

[1] From the name of the false inspector-general in Gogol's play. — Trans.

second author, the one who wrote the "confession," now declares in *L'Express*: "I cannot write anything in the style of the epoch. I wrote only intimate verses, considering them to be a protest against official poetry."

The first, like other poets who believed sincerely in Stalin at that time, dedicated his verses to him and linked Stalin's name with our victories, and it would be stupid to reproach him for this. The second heeded an "inner voice" and "whisperings of conscience," and it seems that he began long ago to "understand the responsibility and the guilt of Stalin." "I," Yevtushenko emphasizes, "was vigilant in my own way."

The first joined with thousands upon thousands of young patriots to go to the virgin lands, and from the Altai he sent to *Komsomolskaya pravda* poems singing the praises of the passion, inspiration and enthusiasm of young people. In that same year of 1954, it turns out, the other poet was imagining himself to be "a prophet proclaiming the truth the people awaited, but I had no idea what to write." He left Moscow "hoping to save myself from spiritual torments and to find the peace necessary for thought."

The poetic life of the first turned out very successfully. From the age of 17 on he was published regularly in the central press, including *Komsomolskaya pravda,* and he edited verse anthologies. He was the subject of arguments and he was praised and criticized. One got the impression that he was taking the praise and comment seriously. It seems that the second poet complained to his friends that he was not published. He complained of the "cruel accusations of critics," and he now alleges to his Western readers that it was not until 1957, after "the editors had been bombarded with thousands and thousands of letters from all parts of the country (!), that *Komsomolskaya pravda* opened its columns to my verse."

It is scarcely necessary to clarify which of these biographies corresponds to the truth. But the question is this: Why does Yevgeny Yevtushenko now think it necessary to create this second "I" for himself? What is the purpose of all this romantic window-dressing, the martyr's crown of thorns, the staff of the wandering prophet, the stamp of tragic thoughts upon the brow? We are aided in the search for the answer by the bosses of *L'Express,* who second the author and say literally this: "Yevtushenko quickly acquired the feeling that he was ordained by fate to become, in accord with the great Russian tradition, the lyrical voice of his epoch and his time and the herald of the new generation." But will the herald study grammar assiduously, join all the others in going to the virgin lands, write in the style of the epoch and generally feel himself to be a normal person? The herald has another destiny and other concerns.

After he had decided that "justice is a train that always comes too late," Yevtushenko himself wanted to hurry everywhere, all the more because "there were a great many pressing problems in Russia and no one will solve them if we do not solve them ourselves."

Who are "we" and what do "we" want? . . .

A Victim of West's Propaganda

Apparently Yevtushenko has not yet taken the slightest pains to figure out seriously what is going on. When he spoke at the fourth plenary session of the board of the U.S.S.R. Writers' Union, he did not spare the high-flown words in terming his cooperation with the reactionary bourgeois press "shameful thoughtlessness." However, it is patently clear from this speech that he has not recognized the profundity of his errors. There is no other way to explain the fact that in evaluating his "autobiography" now, he regrets only that it was written "too hurriedly," that it contains "many imprecise phrasings" and that he "forgot about the customs of the bourgeois press."

Soviet writers spoke with anger at the plenary session of the Writers' Union about Yevtushenko's shameful conduct, about political "Khlestakov-ism," civic irresponsibility mixed with self-magnification.

It is high time for him to face the truth, to see what his behavior looks like in reality. This was the reeling in of a thoughtless little fish, who had snapped at the worm of Western propaganda but had not yet felt the barbed hook, and who imagined that it would astound the inhabitants of the ocean with the graceful boldness of the motions of its body. The hook-baiters of the bourgeois magazines and newspapers cannot wait to land their catch. The publishers of *L'Express,* who have not yet published the last pages of the "confession" of this precocious man, have already printed an "Epilogue" in which they clap Yevtushenko on the back in comradely fashion, thank him, encourage him, and urge him on.

We do not wish to ascribe evil intent to Yevtushenko's actions. But he must understand that there are limits to everything, including the state of political infantilism. He must understand that one cannot go on forever falling down, getting up, shaking oneself, and pretending that nothing has happened. One can get a bruise that will leave an indelible scar.

(*Komsomolskaya pravda,* March 30, 1963. Excerpt.)

10

RECANTATIONS

Writers, artists, composers — after the meeting of March 7–8, nearly everyone who had experimented in form or content was under pressure to apologize, to accept the Party's criticism as "correct." As for those who, because of the symbolic value of their work, were under heaviest pressure, some, like Ehrenburg and Nekrasov, were silent. Others left

*Moscow on prolonged trips to the countryside. Even those who chose
to recant made statements that were notable for their ambiguity. (Yevtushenko's statement is known to be incomplete.)*

ERNST NEIZVESTNY

IT IS NECESSARY TO WORK MORE, BETTER, AND WITH BETTER IDEAS.

In these days I have been thinking a great deal about the responsibility
of the artist to society, and also about my own work and my own responsibility. One must strive to make works of art expressive and filled with ideas.
Actually, ideas always constitute the firmest foundation of expressiveness.
It is in the very nature of monumental sculptors to address themselves to
the people and to have a comprehensive world view.

We have the Marxist-Leninist world view, the most comprehensive of all
those existing in the world.

I say to myself once more: One must work more and better, with better
ideas and more expression — only thus can one be useful to the country and
to the people.

(*Pravda*, March 15, 1963)

ROBERT ROZHDESTVENSKY

WE LIVE IN A POETIC TIME.

It is very interesting to live on earth. It is interesting to meet people, to
see the world, to discover it each time anew. It is interesting and joyful to
me to feel that I have friends beside me — friends in life, in work, in the
great idea of communism that unites us.

I say "us," and behind this word I see working people of all the generations of my Fatherland. Those who took the Winter Palace and those who
burst into the Crimea on top of Wrangel's army. I see Party men, men
who cheered Lenin on, and the eyes of those who built Magnitka and
Komsomolsk-on-Amur look straight into my heart. I see men who stopped
the bullets of the fascist hordes and met death at the great Russian river;
men who soaked the flag of victory in their blood; men who saved mankind.
I see my own contemporaries — scholars and cosmonauts, builders and
those who work the virgin lands. I see those who still are only children, only
starting to sing their first song.

Young people in our country have men to learn from, to model their
lives on. We, young writers, with all our hearts accept the advice of the
Party to nurture ourselves on the best revolutionary traditions of the
generations older than we. It is healthy that all the generations of Lenin's
homeland are as one, close as fingers on a fist. All are united by a single
truth, by the one faith, by a common revolutionary banner.

It is interesting for me to be alive on earth. It is interesting to be all the
time checking myself by how much others need me. And it is very interesting
to work for people. For those I know and those I have not yet come to
know.

We live in an astonishingly poetic time, in an astonishingly poetic country. The Communist Party, which leads the country, is the most poetic Party on earth. Poetic in its ideals, poetic in the scope of its plans and achievements, poetic in the grandiose goal it has set our people.

And now, since the meeting of the leaders of the Party and government with the creative intelligentsia, the responsibility which every writer bears the people for his work is growing especially. We ought every hour to measure ourselves by the ideas of the revolution. As Mayakovsky said, "to measure the quality of verses by the commune." To measure both in Party spirit and in quality. And to answer for our every word, our every line, and every page, as if it were our country.

(Pravda, March 18, 1963. In full.)

DMITRY SHOSTAKOVICH

D. Shostakovich, First Secretary of the Russian Republic Composers' Union, told the meeting of the composers' *aktiv* that talent is the property of the people. He emphasized that the Soviet artist must devote his gifts entirely to the people and serve as the Party's first assistant in the formation of the man of the Communist future.

The composer said:

It was my good fortune to be a participant in the Kremlin meeting, and it gave me great joy. I think that even those who were criticized were aware of the fatherly concern of the Party. The criticism was exceptionally benevolent. It is helping all of us to find the necessary direction in creativity.

A great part of D. Shostakovich's speech was devoted to the folk song and to the popular sources of musical creativity. He reported that the Russian Republic Composers' Union will shortly hold ten-day festivals of Soviet Russian songs in Moldavia and Kirgizia.

"Our creativity," said D. Shostakovich, "must take a firm Leninist position, must take the position of Party spirit and kinship with the people. Through our labor we must help to build communism."

(Pravda, March 23, 1963)

YEVGENY YEVTUSHENKO

At the plenary session much attention was devoted to the mistakes of the creative activity and works of Y. Yevtushenko. Yevtushenko's ideological and political immaturity has been made manifest not only in a number of poems but — especially clearly — in the "Autobiography" that he gave to the French bourgeois weekly *L'Express* and that was recently printed in it. This pretentious work contains incorrect evaluations of many important phenomena in our society and literary life, which lead the reader into error; it is permeated with a spirit of irresponsibility, self-advertisement, "Khlestakovism" [untruthful, senseless bragging; derived from the name of Khlestakov, hero of Gogol's comedy "The Inspector General."] Naturally, this work is now being used by bourgeois propaganda for anti-Soviet purposes.

Speaking at the plenary session, Y. Yevtushenko recognized his grave mistakes. In particular, he said:

[The account in *Literaturnaya gazeta* says, in lieu of the above paragraph: "In the first part of his speech Y. Yevtushenko attempted to dispute the sharp criticism directed at him. He also cited tendentiously chosen quotations from his "Autobiography," which do not give an objective representation of it. But under the influence of the exacting, principled atmosphere of the plenary session, Y. Yevtushenko was nevertheless obliged to talk of his mistakes. He declared:]

> In these remarkable days when we are all as never before thinking about the role of art in the life of the Soviet people, I, naturally, would like to impart my thoughts on the subject. Grave charges against me have been heard. Since I am a member of a large writing collective, I consider it my civic duty not to hide in the bushes from responsibility but to give an explanation. . . . In the West I have many times been represented as "the poet cursed by Red Square." In my public appearances abroad I have more than once rebuffed the slanderers. And in the "Autobiography" I wanted to show that I have never been "the poet cursed by Red Square," that the ideology of communism has been, is and will be the basis of my entire life. Now I see that I wrote the "Autobiography" too hurriedly, that it contains many imprecise formulations and unnecessary details, much immodesty.

Yevtushenko declared that he had more than once objected to the fact that some people had begun to call the period after the 20th Party Congress, in Ehrenburg's glib phrase, a period of "thaw"; no, he said, this is a spring, these are years of the country's flowering.

> In my autobiography, [the speaker continued,] there are things that are serious and mature, but on rereading it I now see that there is much in it that is supercilious and often immodest. My most serious mistake was that I forgot about the morals of the foreign press, and I have been severely punished for this.
>
> The French weekly supplied my "Autobiography" with sensational headings, published articles that imparted to the "Autobiography" meanings that I did not intend. From this example I have once again been convinced of where my disgraceful thoughtlessness leads me.
>
> It should also be said that when I saw the French text I was thunderstruck by the distortions and "corrections" made by the editors of *L'Express*. For example, the end of the "Autobiography" had been chopped off. I wrote there: "One student, far from the best grandson of the French Revolution, said to me: 'I am for socialism in general, but I want to wait for the day when you have stores like the Galeries Lafayette; then perhaps I too will fight for socialism.' I was ashamed for this young old man: if you hand him the future on a silver platter, well roasted, nice and brown, and even with a sprig of parsley, then, perhaps he will pick at it with his fork. . . . We have made the future

ourselves, denying ourselves even necessities, we have taken pains over it, we have made mistakes, but all the same we have made it ourselves."

This is what I wrote and what *L'Express* threw out. I will cite an example of an addition to my text. I wrote about a telegram I received several years ago from the sailors of a certain ship, a telegram in which they praised my poetry. I recognize now that it was not necessary to refer to this telegram; this was immodest. For *L'Express* it wasn't enough to rewrite this paragraph so that my immodesty looked like complete hyperbole; they also added something inconceivable: "The telegram was signed by the entire crew. Those who are acquainted with the history of my country know what prestige the Baltic sailors won for themselves. The message from their heirs truly counterbalanced the attacks to which I have been subjected. With head held high, I strode the streets of Moscow as though I had been awarded a gold medal."

I did not write this. *L'Express* wrote it.

I wish to repeat: I have committed an irreparable mistake. I feel heavy guilt on my shoulders. And again and again I think of the great responsibility that each Soviet writer bears. Believe me, this is for me no empty phrase; I have lived through a lot and felt a lot in these days. It is a lesson to me for my whole life. I want to assure the writers' collective that I fully understand and realize my error, and that I will try to correct it by all my future work.

It is necessary to say that Y. Yevtushenko's statement failed to satisfy the plenary session participants: The tone of his speech clearly indicated that Y. Yevtushenko did not realize the crux of his mistakes, either in the matter of the publication of the "Autobiography" or in several of his poems.

(*Pravda*, March 29, 1963)

VASILY AXYONOV

RESPONSIBILITY: I think constantly now about the March meeting in Sverdlov Hall in the Kremlin — the meeting between Party leaders and writers, poets, artists, musicians and film makers.

I can say with complete confidence that this meeting was a turning point in the further development of Soviet literature and art. There was a comradely, impartial, and serious discussion, during which there was debate on the chief and central problems of an ideological and esthetic nature.

All of us who took part in the meeting gained a new and much broader insight into our tasks in the struggle between the Communist and capitalist ideologies, in the struggle against formalist and decadent tendencies, in the struggle for the development of the principles of Party spirit and kinship with the peoples in Soviet art.

I think that it was especially important for us young writers to understand this, not just because some of us (including myself) were subjected to stern criticism at the meeting, but chiefly in order to strengthen our step in the ranks and our vigilance — in brief, in order that we may write better and serve the people better through our work. We have become older and stricter.

I am now thinking about what I have done and what I am going to do in the future, I am thinking about the enormous responsibility that rests on our shoulders.

Very often and very willingly when we are talking about the task of each artist — be he novelist, poet, or painter — we repeat Mayakovsky's famous words "about time and about oneself." We have become so accustomed to these words that we sometimes hear them as if they meant "*both* about time *and* about oneself." One writes a book about the times, another book about one's personal experiences — as if they took place outside of time.

But Mayakovsky expresses this thought, or rather this feeling, in another way. The expression combines precision and economy of phrasing with a striking lyrical tension: "It was something that happened to the army or to the country or in my heart."

Just so: the complete merging of the artist's individuality with the people, with their thoughts, and with the drama of their struggle. No matter what you write about — be it love or about a storm in the Sea of Okhotsk, about dumptrucks making their way along icy Siberian roads, or about the launching of rockets — your heart must take part in it all (otherwise it will come out cold and soulless) and a sense of the life of the whole country must pulse in it (otherwise it will come out petty, which means untrue).

In brief, one must have a constant sense of responsibility. Responsibility to the people, to the Soviet land, to the Communist Party.

A Bookkeeper's Account of the Winged Dream?

To answer to the people and to report to them does not at all mean to draw up some sort of bookkeeper's account saying that one has filled so and so many pages and that so and so many of them are about heroism, so and so many about self-sacrifice and so and so many about the winged dream. In this way one cheapens everything, even the dearest things. It is simply that the conscience of the artist must become a part of the common conscience of the people, of their fate, a part of the people's fate.

As applied to literature, the word conscience has an excellent synonym — happiness. After all, responsibility for people and to them is the same thing as one's feeling that one is needed by them, that one is involved with them. I would say even more than this: One must earn the right to responsibility.

Every writer must think all the time about how difficult it is to win the reader's trust and how easy it is to lose it. How difficult it is to justify the high calling of Soviet writer. The young writer who still has to win the reader's trust must give special thought to this.

The writer's sense of responsibility is becoming especially intense now because of the fierce struggle going on in the world between two ideologies, the imperialist and the Communist. We people who create films, books, and poems must answer for each frame, for each line, for each word. Millions of honest people throughout the world are heeding our every word and our every mistake, and each false word may be seized upon instantly by the malign scribblers of the bourgeois press.

Our word is a weapon in this struggle; each word is like a bullet. Thoughtlessness is for the writer simply amoral.

Because of an urgent travel assignment, I was unable to take part in the plenary session of the U.S.S.R. Writers' Union. At this plenary session there was stern criticism of the incorrect behavior and thoughtlessness of Yevtushenko, Voznesensky, and me. I believe this criticism was correct.

Last autumn at the Writer's Union in Moscow I gave an interview to a correspondent of the Workers' News Service of Poland. Not long ago I read a translation of this interview. My confused and murky phrases made me blush for my professional pride, not to mention other and more important things. It is true that if we are talking about every word for which we bear responsibility, I must reject some of the words, since they do not belong to me. For example, some of the names I mentioned were dropped from the interview for some reason, and other names I had not mentioned appeared in it. I also think that the correspondent who interviewed me made a mistake in not including those points on which I wanted to place political stress. I said some things about what distinguished Soviet young people from Western. I spoke of the naked practicalness that is so natural to Western young people and that is not only alien but shameful to us.

I would not be taking a serious approach if I concealed the most important aspect of the matter behind all these annoying but secondary inaccuracies. I cannot justify my thoughtlessness. I am ashamed to recall the circumstances in which this interview was given. I was in a hurry, on the run. I answered several of the journalist's questions hastily, without thinking my words over very carefully. Of course, Poland is a socialist country, and readers there can figure out what is going on, but the bourgeois hacks are watching the socialist press like hawks.

But it would be still more thoughtless to believe that one may now limit oneself to a recognition of one's errors. This would not be the Communist way or the writer's way. I will never forget Nikita Sergeyevich's stern but kind words to me and his advice at the Kremlin meeting: "Get to work and show through your labor what you are worth!"

During the meeting between Party and government leaders and workers in literature and the arts there was talk of the chief principles of Soviet art and the direction of its development in our times. The direction of my future work, the aim of which is service to the people and to the ideals of communism, became clear to me. I write fiction. To the best of my ability and with full honesty I will attempt to tell about the life around us, about complex and beautiful life.

Like all Soviet writers, regardless of their generation, I am inspired by the optimism of our Marxist-Leninist philosophy. Our philosophy, our bright and bold view of the world, is the chief thing that unites all generations of Soviet people. Our enemies will not succeed in getting us into a quarrel with our fathers. We are one flesh and blood.

Search for a Positive Hero

My last books aroused criticism among literary people. Naturally, I am doing a great deal of agonized thinking about this. But — and I hope that the literary circles will not be offended — what forced me to ponder my work more than did their critical articles was a recent meeting with some young working lads, my readers. They said to me: "Yes, of course, one does meet people like your heroes in life, and one meets them often, you were not lying. But still, we want so much to encounter a hero who would serve as an example to us. You see, we are not specialists. We cannot give you literary advice; we just need this hero very much."

I agree with those who say that we have a great obligation to future generations. But perhaps we have a still greater obligation to our coevals. We have not yet created the positive hero of our days, equal in power to Pavel Korchagin and Pavel Vlasov, those heroes of enormous spiritual power. And we need such heroes, not only for the so-called "literary process" but for people, whom they would help to live.

We are searching, and I, too, am searching to the best of my ability.

The goal and dream of my life is not to create a schematic design of abstract positive qualities (this is easy, but who needs it?) but a character in whose reality the reader would believe unconditionally and whom he would want to emulate. Like all other writers, I am trying to create my own, original positive hero, who would at the same time be a true son of the times, a strong-boned man with a normal circulatory system, a normal and open soul and thoughts that embrace all the magnificence, optimism and complexity of our Communist epoch. After all, every writer has his own vision of the world.

The 30 years of my life have not been all that easy; I have seen some things and met some people, but I am very well aware that I do not yet have enough spiritual and life experience to perform such a responsible and difficult task. I must see a great many more things. I must think over many things and I must do a great deal of studying. I must learn about the various sides of the life of the people, I must overcome the one-sidedness of my observations, look at my contemporary in the many visages of his unity, go more deeply into the guiding ideas of our times and express them to the best of my ability in my work. Of course, this is difficult, but it is in this that one finds the happiness of creativity.

(*Pravda*, April 3, 1963)

ANDREI VOZNESENSKY

Here at the plenary session I have been told that I must not forget Nikita Sergeyevich's stern and severe words. I will never forget them. I will not forget either these severe words or the advice that Nikita Sergeyevich addressed to me. He said: "Work." This word is a program for me. I shall work, I am now working, I am thinking a lot, I have understood a lot of what went on in the Kremlin, of what has been said at the plenary session. I understand my tremendous responsibility to the people, to the times, to the Communist Party. For me this is a most precious understanding.

I am not justifying myself now; I simply want to say: The main thing for me now is to work, work, and work, and this work will show what my attitude is to the country and to communism, will show my nature.

(*Pravda*, March 29, 1963)

11

TVARDOVSKY REAPPEARS

Alexander Tvardovsky, who had been pressing for relaxation of Party policy on literature since 1954, did not speak at the meeting of March 7–8, 1963. However, at the beginning of May, Pravda *published an interview with him by Henry Shapiro, an American correspondent in Moscow. The interview was a discreet defense of the liberal publishing policy which he had followed as editor of* Novy mir.

THE LITERATURE OF SOCIALIST REALISM HAS ALWAYS GONE HAND IN HAND WITH THE REVOLUTION. A. T. Tvardovsky, Editor in Chief of *Novy mir*, Interviewed by H. Shapiro, Moscow Correspondent of United Press International.

Since the days of Radishchev and Pushkin our literature has always had a special historical quality: imbued with the spirit of emancipating ideas and kinship with the people, it has been a powerful factor in the development of progressive public consciousness.

The behests of the great, world-famous figures in our literature and art are not part of the "distant past" for us. Soviet literature in its best examples represents a living bond of succession with its glorious predecessors. The conditions of development and the historical tasks of literature and art have changed, but such distinguishing characteristics as profound humanism, truthfulness in the depiction of life, concern for the interests of the broadest masses of the people, and loyalty to the advanced ideas of the era have remained untouched by time.

To preserve the heritage does not — as we follow Lenin in saying — mean to be limited by the heritage. Soviet literature owes very much to the great literature of the past, both our own and the world's, but it could not but add its own serious acquisitions to this heritage, for it was born of a great revolution that signaled a new stage in the history of human society and its culture.

The chief acquisition of our relatively young literature is its new content, images, and types, revealed and emphasized in the new socialist reality. The new content has brought forth and defined a form of expression that differs from the classical one in many ways having to do with styles, methods, and techniques for embodying the unprecedented life material. Incidentally, it is in this that we find the essence of the phenomenon in literature and art that we call socialist realism.

It is necessary to keep all this in mind when we deal with questions that are directly related to such an important event in the life of our literature as the December and March meetings between Party and government leaders and workers in literature and the arts.

These meetings were not something unprecedented in the life of our creative intelligentsia; such meetings have become a tradition.

The immediate reason for the recent meetings was certain tendencies in present-day art and literature, tendencies that the Central Committee of our party rightly found it necessary to criticize. But the over-all content of the meetings was much broader and deeper. They were a development, a further concretization of the Leninist concept of the tasks of art and literature, a continuation of what had been expressed in previous discussions of this sort and had been elucidated in the press, formulated in Party documents and reflected in the chief among these documents, the new Party Program.

Again and again this document emphasized the special role of literature and art in Soviet society as a mighty educational force, emphasized the need to link literature and art more closely with life and the need for active embodiment of the new reality in artistic images.

The literature of socialist realism has always gone hand in hand with the revolution and has shared with the Soviet people all their hardships and victories. It rears the brave sons of the socialist motherland, its builders and defenders, and inculcates in them the high moral principles of the man of the new society. In addition, it is the duty of this literature to reveal and unmask everything old and stagnant that might impede our progress. Our satire must play a considerable role in this, and it is a good thing that this highly important type of prose and poetic literature is once again relying on the rich traditions of Gogol, Saltykov-Shchedrin, and Nekrasov, and also on the recent experience of Soviet satire — Mayakovsky, D. Bedny, Ilf, and Petrov.

What are the prospects for the development of Soviet literature in the light of recent events in the life of our creative intelligentsia? Naturally, these prospects are defined by the experience accumulated in our art and literature and by each artist's profound awareness of the tasks that were broadly and extensively clarified in the speeches by N. S. Khrushchev and L. F. Ilyichev. Both as a writer and as the editor of one of the country's "fattest" magazines, I have every reason to suppose that Soviet literature will delight its readers with new and remarkable achievements.

In the years that have passed since the 20th Party Congress a number of works have appeared in our literature that have signaled important and promising tendencies. Some of these works I have mentioned more than once in my speeches and articles. They are characterized first of all by a serious knowledge of reality, by truth, by a Party approach to the events of life, and a profound sense of the artist's responsibility to the people. The names of young writers making their first appearance mingle here with the names of writers who have already made themselves known but who have given readers their most significant works in this period. There are Yefim Dorosh, who with his "Village Diary" followed V. Ovechkin and went deeper and more extensively into the rural theme; Vladimir Tendryakov, who was recently a Young Communist League worker but is now a well-known author of incisive and topical tales of our times; Gavril Troepolsky, an agronomist, no longer young, who has brought to the reader from the Voronezh Steppes his original, satirical stories and tales; Vladimir Fomenko of Rostov, a writer of the "Sholokhov region" and a brilliant and altogether original artist who made himself known to the public through his novel *Memory of the Earth*; the very young Vil Lipatov, who lives in distant Chita; his older Siberian comrade Sergei Zalygin, a scholar and teacher who only recently became a professional writer; Yury Bondarev and his new novel *Silence*; and Alexander Yashin, the author of many books of poems, who published the excellent sketch "Vologda Wedding," which is full of poetry. I have named only a few writers, and only ones whose works have appeared in the pages of *Novy mir*.

Solzhenitsyn's Work Phenomenal

A. Solzhenitsyn's *One Day in the Life of Ivan Denisovich,* which first appeared in *Novy mir* — a story by a Ryazan teacher whom no one had heard of until recently — is in my opinion a particularly important and significant phenomenon. This is not only because it is based on specific materials and shows the antipopular character of the phenomena associated with the consequences of the cult of the individual, but also because its whole esthetic structure confirms the unchanging meaning of the tradition of truth in art and decisively counters false innovationism of the formalist, modernist sort.

In my opinion, *One Day* is one of those literary phenomena after whose appearance it is impossible to talk about any literary problem or literary fact without measuring it against this phenomenon.

I will never forget how N. S. Khrushchev responded to this tale by Solzhenitsyn — to its hero, who retains the dignity and beauty of the man of labor under inhuman conditions, to the truthfulness of the account, to the author's Party approach to bitter and stern reality. At the first meeting Nikita Sergeyevich mentioned Solzhenitsyn in the course of his speech and introduced him to all of those present in the Palace of Meetings on the Lenin Hills.

If it were necessary to demonstrate the breadth of the views of our Party's Central Committee concerning literature and art, the sole fact that it approved this story by A. Solzhenitsyn would be more than sufficient. Incidentally, this once again irrefutably proves the complete baselessness of the hostile talk of the "restrictions" and "regimentation" that according to certain people characterize Soviet literature.

Of course, the cult of the individual could not but have had a negative effect on Soviet art and literature. There were certain years when we had a good many books, films, and works of art that bore the stamp of prettification, uninspired illustrativeness, and false monumentality. However, it is completely mistaken, antihistorical, and contradictory to obvious facts to describe all the literature of, say, the 1930's, the period of the Patriotic War and even the postwar years under J. V. Stalin as inaccurate, unoriginal, and falsely ceremonious. Just as the historic creativity of the masses aroused by the Great October Revolution could not be halted in the economic and social fields, so did it continue to make itself felt in the field of the development of the new culture, art, and literature.

I have no intention of listing here all the Soviet writers known to readers throughout the world through works written during precisely these periods. It would be a very extensive list were I to mention only the Russian writers — Sholokhov, Fadeyev, Fedin, Pavlenko, Panova, Kazakevich, Isakovsky, Marshak, Leonov, Pogodin, and many, many others, living and dead, whose works are the glory and pride of our literature. And were I to add the glorious names of the writers and poets writing in other languages of the Soviet Union, the list would be longer still.

The Issue of Fathers and Sons

The so-called "conflict of generations" in our literature, the "conflict between fathers and sons," belongs to the number of invented "conflicts" that are ascribed to us.

The authors of this "discovery" first of all do not know much about the history of our 19th-century literature, whence they have "bought" this problem sight unseen. This expression comes from Turgenev's noted novel *Fathers and Sons*. It deals with the conflict between the "fathers" — the liberal nobles — and the generation of "new people," representatives of the revolutionary democratic intelligentsia of the middle of the last century, who were then appearing on the scene. It is quite clear that the relationships between Turgenev's "fathers and sons" bear not the remotest resemblance to the relations between different generations of our revolution, who have always stood shoulder to shoulder in the struggle for the common cause.

But perhaps if the concept of "fathers and sons" is absurd in relation to the broad historical plan of the life of the people, it does apply to the field of the specifically intellectual, to the present-day life of the scientific and artistic intelligentsia, students, young literary people?

No, here, too, this concept is altogether without basis. Who are the "fathers" here and who the "sons"? If the "fathers" are the honored scientists — the designers of spaceships, for example — and the "sons" are the young officer-pilots who "fly" these ships in space, then there is no antagonism here either. It is not a matter of age at all. For example, when I spoke at the same meeting as Yury Gagarin, I said that as far as years are concerned he could be my son, but in our common goals and desires he and I were coevals in the epoch of socialism. The cosmonaut agreed with me completely.

I could say the same thing to many of our young writers, whose work arouses in me a lively interest and a friendly attitude toward them.

Can we speak of a "conflict" between a venerable poet like S. Ya. Marshak and the young poets, writers, and critics, among whom it would be difficult to name any who have not visited his study — the workshop, as it were, of an artist-teacher, an old friend, and a strict mentor? Where is the "conflict of generations" here? There is none.

The bourgeois press is very undemanding when it comes to the depth of content and esthetic quality of such of our "sons" as Yevtushenko and Voznesensky, for example. This is due to their desire to see in these "sons" the bards of some sort of opposition to the "fathers," their desire to make use of these young people for altogether unliterary purposes. Of course, this tendentiousness can give rise only to cheap sensation, and it is first of all these young poets themselves — young not so much in years as in skill — who suffer from it. I hope that I do not have to emphasize that I am saying this only because I wish them well, because I hope they take a more serious and responsible approach to their calling. I recall that Alexander Blok said a poet should have a destiny, not a career.

The myth of the division of Soviet writers into "liberals" and "conservatives" has also been drawn by the bourgeois press from some broken-down collection of concepts, which are inapplicable to our literary relations. Of course there are disputes among us, and various evaluations of literary phenomena. In other words, we have a normal literary life. It only remains for the Western "connoisseurs" of our literature to learn that our discussions and differences of opinion take place within the totality of our Soviet socialist literature. One can only advise these "connoisseurs" to see reality as it is, and not to substitute for it any illusory constructions or notions.

No Neglect of Western Culture

Won't the denial of peaceful coexistence in the field of ideology have an effect on our cultural ties and relations with foreign countries? Yes, we do reject the theory of peaceful ideological coexistence, but this cannot mean neglect on our part of the advanced, progressive science, culture, and art of the West.

Meetings and personal contacts and deeper study of each other's books is undoubtedly of great mutual interest for us writers. I myself am deeply indebted to Robert Frost's visit to this country for a much closer acquaintanceship with the poetry of this fine master than I had before. The democratic spirit and realism of Frost's poetry, which depicts the labor and everyday lives of the common people of rural America, the pictures of nature that are sometimes so close to our landscapes, the solidity and clarity of form of his tales in verse are all very much to my liking. I was truly pleased and flattered to meet this patriarch of American poetry, to receive him in my house in Moscow, and I am sad to think that if I go to the United States I will only be able to visit his grave.

The traditions of our broad cultural and literary ties and contacts with people of good will, with fighters for peace, with friends of our country speak for themselves. It is hardly necessary to recall that our country holds first place in the world in translations of books from foreign languages. But, of course, a great deal in our cultural relations with the West will depend not only on us but on the West as well. For example, the propaganda of cold and hot war carried on by anti-Soviet circles cannot have a favorable effect on our cultural relations.

Concerning my attitude toward "searches in the field of form": I have never been interested in nor have I engaged in searches for form as such, as though form were something with an existence separate from content. Formalism is profoundly alien to me, and I consider this kind of search generally fruitless. When concern only with form as such begins, art ends. Unfortunately, some of our young artists (and not only young ones!) are not always proof against the seductive temptation of such "searches." But it is something else again to say that everything in art — its principal content, its striking images and characters, the perfection and harmony of its forms — is born only as the result of persistent searching by the artist. Leo Tolstoy once wrote in his diary that if the artist is to affect others, he must be a seeker, his work must be a quest. If he comes to think that he has found everything, that he knows everything and need only teach, then he has no effect, since the reader is not joining in the search but remains a nonparticipant. What can I add to these words? Perhaps only that in our relations with our friends, the readers, we Soviet writers play as little as possible the role of the mentor who knows everything, and intends only to teach. We hold very dear the creative contact with the reader, whom we always consider to be a participant in all our searches in art.

Finally, something about *Novy mir*. In *Novy mir*'s issue No. 4 there is an article in which the editorial collegium gives in considerable detail its views on the present situation in literature and its attitude toward the criticism of certain works printed in *Novy mir*. Specifically, this applies to I. G. Ehrenburg's memoirs *People, Years, Life*, which were seriously criticized by N. S. Khrushchev and L. F. Ilyichev at the March meetings. We take this criticism of Ehrenburg's memoirs very seriously and responsibly, and we are confident that Ilya Grigoryevich will draw the necessary conclusions from it. All the more so because, while subjecting Ehrenburg to strict and demanding criticism, the Party leaders described him as one of the outstanding Soviet writers, a talented publicist and a great public figure. As far as the publication of Ehrenburg's memoirs is concerned, the fifth volume is concluded in *Novy mir*, No. 3.

Our editors will fulfill the obligations to readers they have assumed for 1963.

The other day Chingiz Aitmatov, who was introduced to the Russian reader by *Novy mir,* sent us a new story. Samuil Marshak, one of the magazine's oldest friends, is completing for us the next section of the cycle of article-interviews on the craft of poetry. Rasul Gamzatov, whose work has been appearing in our pages for a long time, has promised a new long poem and some lyrics.

Needless to say, it is very pleasant for the editor to note that these three contributors to *Novy mir* were awarded 1962 Lenin Prizes in literature.

Konstantin Fedin is working on the second part of his novel *The Campfire,* thus completing the famed trilogy by this great master of Russian prose.

The young Georgy Vladimov, known to the reader for his first story "Big Ore," will soon be bringing us a new piece.

Olga Berggolts has reported to us that she has completed the second part of "The Daylight Stars." We are waiting for a new work by Alexander Solzhenitzyn, which will naturally appear in our magazine.

But I am not going to tell you about all the things that will appear in *Novy mir* during 1963. The list includes works by V. Fomenko, V. Nekrasov, S. Zalygin, V. Axyonov, V. Tendryakov, and others.

I have never discussed my own creative plans in the press, and I see no reason to depart from this rule now.

(*Pravda,* May 12, 1963)

12

IDEOLOGY AND THE ARTS AT THE JUNE 1963 PLENARY SESSION

The long-awaited plenary session of the Communist Party Central Committee convened at last on June 18. By now, internal squabbles over the arts were overshadowed by the conflict with Communist China. The question the plenum had been called to discuss, how to ensure the conformity of writers and artists to the ideological line of the Party, remained unresolved.

MARXISM-LENINISM IS OUR BANNER, OUR FIGHTING WEAPON. Speech by N. S. Khrushchev on June 21, 1963, at Plenary Session of The Central Committee of the Communist Party.

The outstanding successes of the Soviet Union and the other socialist countries in building socialism and communism show convincingly that the imperialists have failed in their calculations to undermine us on the economic front.

Our enemies have now concentrated their main efforts on ideological struggle against the socialist countries. The imperialist ideologists entertain the hope of undermining us from within with the aid of hostile ideology. Their thesis is that the more educated people there are in the Soviet Union, the more vulnerable Soviet society is with respect to ideology. They say this frankly in their newspapers and magazines. According to the assertions of imperialist propaganda, as material well-being improves and as the level of culture rises, the Soviet people will come out against the leadership of the Party.

We should know that the opponent is now sharpening his poisoned ideological weapon for an even more bitter engagement with us. This, you know, turns out to be like the Red Army saying during the Civil War: "With the Whites, we have only one question in dispute on which we cannot agree, a very simple question — it is the land question. The Whites want to bury us in the land, and we want to bury the Whites. Who will bury whom first? That is our small dispute." [Laughter in the hall.]

We have the same kind of issue with capitalism. It wants to bury the socialist system, while we want — and not only want, but have even dug quite a deep hole, and will exert further efforts to dig this hole deeper and bury forever the capitalist system, the system of exploitation, war and plunder. And that capitalism will fall — of this there is no doubt. [Stormy applause.] But it will not fall by itself!

Our successes will inspire the working class of all the capitalist countries to more resolute and active revolutionary class struggle. And we have helped and will continue to help them by our own example, by building communism. The peoples of various countries who are struggling for their freedom and independence are receiving our help today, while tomorrow there will be even greater possibilities for rendering assistance of a different character as well.

There can be no doubt that the imperialists' stake in ideological subversion will be lost. Their attempts to undermine the forces of socialism, to halt the development of the revolutionary struggle, will suffer the same defeat as the military campaigns previously undertaken against socialist countries and the perfidious plans to suffocate socialism by economic blockade. [Applause.] . . .

. . . .

It is not only facts and figures that testify to our outstanding successes. We have forced our enemies to acknowledge publicly the great power of socialism, to acknowledge the achievements of the Soviet Union.

Varnishers but not Hoodwinkers

I want to read you excerpts from an article by a certain "varnisher." I don't know why the antivarnishers haven't yet picked on him for it even once. I will tell you the name of this "varnisher" right now.

So malicious a representative of the American bourgeois press as Harry Schwartz, who is considered *The New York Times*'s leading specialist on Soviet affairs, has been obliged to recognize the Soviet Union's outstanding successes. . . .

.   .   .   .

It is possible to cite yet further, even more authoritative admissions.

In his recent speech at American University in Washington, U.S. President J. Kennedy said: "We can hail the Russian people for their many achievements — in science and space, in economic and industrial growth, in culture and acts of courage."

Not badly said! Another varnisher! The President of the United States of America turns out to be a varnisher. [Laughter in the hall.]

But some of our writers and artists want to spit on their own people, the labor of their own people, to dip into the rubbish bin and draw the image of our people in the very darkest shades. Shame on you!

The Party condemns those who hang the label of "varnisher" on our writers and artists. Is a person who writes about everything good that our people and our Party have done a varnisher? Of course not! A writer, an artist who adheres to positions of Party spirit truthfully portrays in his works both positive and negative phenomena in the life of society, and he does this from life-affirming positions. In our life, of course, there are shortcomings, but the new, the revolutionary is being affirmed and grows in the struggle against the old, casting out the survivals of the past. Can it be tolerated that someone calls for writing only about the negative, digging up all kinds of muck about our country, about our people, our reality? The people who adhere to such positions — these are agents of bourgeois ideology in the Soviet midst.

We are most resolutely opposed to hoodwinking. The Party has always called and will call for the exposure of hoodwinking; it has been and will continue to be against embellishing reality. Our Soviet reality does not tolerate falsity.

You remember the film "Kuban Cossacks." As soon as it was shown, we told Stalin that the life of the collective farmers was portrayed untruthfully in this film. In it there was full abundance. Stalin was pleased when the screen showed every collective farmer, sitting at a festive table, dining on a turkey. At the time I told Stalin that those turkeys had been bought by the Minister of Cinematography, Bolshakov, and that it wasn't collective farmers eating them but actors. This wasn't what was happening in real life — the countryside was then experiencing great hardships.

You recall that it was not only into films that hoodwinking penetrated.

Malenkov's report to the 19th Party Congress, in which he said that the grain problem had been solved, that there was an abundance of bread — this was deception of the Party and the people.

The 19th Congress ended and thousands of letters poured in from all over the country. People wrote to the effect that if the grain problem had been solved, why was there no bread? Then Stalin took up the question and all but routed the leaders of a number of provinces because the letters that came from them telling of a bread shortage got into Stalin's hands. Special commissions were sent to these provinces to find out why there was not enough bread there.

Then in a discussion in the Central Committee I said: "Comrade Stalin, the Ukrainians are very dissatisfied that they are not given white bread. At the Party Congress it was said that the grain problem has been solved, but the Ukrainians, who have always eaten white bread, now do not have any of it." Stalin said: "The Ukrainians must be given white bread." This was almost like the French queen who, when told that the people had no bread, said, "If there is no bread, let them eat cake." [Laughter in the hall.]

How could they have been given bread when there was not enough of it in the country? At the September plenary session I could have, like Malenkov, said in my report that we had bread — plenty of it.

Malenkov took the data on the so-called biological yield. But how was this biological yield determined? They took a square meter of sown area, calculated the number of ears on it, then figured how many grains were in an ear — all the grains — weighed them, and then multiplied the figure obtained for this square meter by the entire sown area. This is called the biological yield. But you can't bake any pies and pancakes out of the biological yield. Bread and pancakes are baked from the real harvest, gathered in barns. We severely criticized this declaration about solving the grain problem because it was hoodwinking, deception of the Party and the people.

Unmasking the Stalinist Cult

The Party has done much work in connection with unmasking the Stalin cult and overcoming its harmful consequences. The Central Committee undertook this, showing a sense of responsibility and courage. I remember that when we were discussing this question at the time of the 20th Party Congress we had a very intense struggle in the leadership. We posed the question of the necessity for telling the Party the truth, but some people, who felt much guilt for the crimes they had committed together with Stalin, feared this truth; they feared their own unmasking. After prolonged disputes, they agreed to raise this question at the Congress.

It was a big and complicated question, a question of enormous political importance. Of course, if one were to reason like a philistine, there was no point in raising this question: Stalin no longer existed, many of the people who had been victims of repression no longer existed. The state was growing, the leadership had taken shape, so why rake things up, stir them around, upset everything? But in politics the philistine approach to matters cannot be tolerated. It was necessary to take up and discuss this question not for those who were no longer alive but for those who are living and those who will be living. We were not fighting for our personal interests but for the Party, for the purity of the Leninist Party, because the people regard the Party with reverence, the Party is the highest and greatest truth, it is the brain and conscience of the people, the leader of the people, the organizer of the people! [Stormy applause.]

Some who were then in the Presidium of the Central Committee said, "But how will the Congress take it, how will the Party take it?" We told them: "It will be taken the correct way by the Congress and the entire Party! We must tell the truth about the cult of the individual precisely at the 20th Party Congress, because it is the first Congress since Stalin's death. If we talk about it only at the 21st Congress or later, we may not be understood. At the 20th Congress we will be listened to, and we believe we will be understood correctly. If the mistakes and shortcomings that existed during the period of the Stalin cult are not revealed and condemned, this would mean approving them, legalizing them for the future."

At the 20th Congress our party condemned the cult of the individual and charted a Leninist course for its policy; it undertook work to restore Leninist principles of guidance and norms of Party and state life.

We, comrades, do not deny the importance and role of leaders and managers. But we oppose those leaders who put themselves above the people, above the Party, who think that they are virtually sent by God, while the people are the masses, who must only listen to them and applaud. This was typical of Stalin.

Stalin did not like the people. When did he ever visit plants? Probably the last time was when he went to the Dynamo Plant in 1924. After that he went almost nowhere.

V. I. Lenin constantly maintained the closest ties with the people. In 1918, at the height of the Civil War, when the Soviet state hung by a hair, he went to enterprises, spoke at meetings, traveled to villages, talked to passers-by. Vladimir Ilyich almost paid with his life when an attempt was organized against him at the Mikhelson Plant after a workers' meeting. Lenin had a need for living contacts with workers and peasants, with the people; he was a leader whom all the people loved and love. He was not above the people but always with the people, the recognized leader of the people. [Stormy applause.]

The Central Committee considered it necessary to tell the truth about the Stalin cult and to do everything to prevent its ever being repeated.

Unmasking the Stalin cult gave rise to certain difficulties. But now we are correctly understood, we adhere to a Party, Leninist position, and the people see this, they approve and support our Party's Leninist course. [Stormy applause.]

We were not afraid because some might not understand us, or not understand right away, and our authority and prestige might suffer. We told the

Party everything, brought everything before the Party's judgment, before the court of its 20th Congress. And the Congress said its word, the correct word. The difficulties that existed are now over; the Party has become even stronger and more monolithic, its authority has risen even higher. [Stormy applause.]

The Class Struggle and "Freedom of Creativity"

Consistently carrying out Lenin's behests, the Party is concerned about the correct organization of ideological work and about the translation into life of Vladimir Ilyich's instructions on Party spirit and kinship with the people in literature and art. The assertions that the principle of Party spirit in literature and art fetters the initiative of the creative intelligentsia are profoundly mistaken. There are fairy tales going around to the effect that freedom of creativity and freedom of the press exist in capitalist society. Only people unfamiliar with the mores of the bourgeois world could believe this.

Literature, art, and the press in the capitalist world are the property of the monopolies. I have already described recently an interesting conversation I had with the major British publisher Thomson. He visited Moscow recently as a tourist.

The publisher Thomson has probably not studied Marxism-Leninism, but he has a well-developed class instinct and he has a good grasp of things. He asked me: "Would you not give me permission to sell my newspapers in Moscow?" I answered: "You have raised a very complex question; I must think about it."

"What if I made Adzhubei, *Izvestia*'s editor, the editor of one of these newspapers?" asked the publisher.

"That's a different matter altogether," I answered. "I give you my word, if you make Adzhubei, or the editor of another of our newspapers, the editor of your newspaper, the paper will be sold in all parts of the Soviet Union."

To this he said: "That would not be in my interests."

You see how a capitalist approaches this question. His first concern in this case is not material interest but a purely ideological, class interest.

Or take, for example, such a major center of the American film industry as Hollywood. Is there any freedom of creativity there? Nothing of the sort. Such a world-famous film figure as Charlie Chaplin was thrown out of Hollywood. Although he is no Communist, he is a progressive man, and therefore there was no place for him in Hollywood. That's the kind of "freedom" of creativity, of "free" people they have in the U.S.A.!

The major Hearst newspaper trust in the U.S.A. is well known for its reactionary proclivities. Hearst publishes more than 100 newspapers. It would be naive to think that he is not interested in the ideological and political tendencies of his newspapers and would allow the publication of materials that would go against the interests of his class, against imperialism. If he gets his paws on such a journalist, he'd show him where the crabs spend the winter. No one but naive people and incorrigible simpletons could believe all these maunderings about "freedom" of creativity in the capitalist countries.

Some of our simpletons, who think themselves very smart, do not understand or do not want to understand the class essence in questions of ideology. But Thompson — the old capitalist wolf — understands this very well. Yet there are some people who say that freedom of the press exists in Britain or the U.S.A.

Let these people go to Hearst or Thomson and try to publish an article in their newspapers. How would they look at such an article? Perhaps they would look at it from the point of view of style? They would spit on the style! They would examine it from the viewpoint of politics, the interests of their class, would evaluate it according to whom the article served and what it was aimed at. The chief thing for them is the question of ideology.

In the capitalist countries the ruling classes do a good job of masking their interests behind ideas about the freedom of creativity, the freedom of speech and of the press, and they even write about these things in their constitutions. It would even seem that "freedom of creativity" and "freedom of the press" do exist formally in some bourgeois countries. Everyone is free to write as he pleases, but whether the publishers or owners of newspapers and magazines will want to publish works opposed to their class interests is another question. If a publisher finds that a work is not in accord with the tasks of strengthening the capitalist system, he rejects it, refuses to print it, and it turns out to have been written not for people but for mice.

Why is it that some of our writers and publishers do not understand or do not want to understand this? What do these people want, anyway? Apparently they would like to turn ideological work into a Noah's ark, so that this Noah's ark will contain the aromas of all the ideological tendencies and shadings. No, this will not be! Our Party stands at the head of the people, guides the people, and it has guided and will continue to guide ideological work, it has fought and will continue to fight against all manifestations of bourgeois ideology! [Stormy applause.]

We are using all our opportunities so that our ideological work will develop in the necessary direction, in the spirit of Communist ideology.

It would be a good thing if all our writers, all our workers in the arts took as their point of departure the concept that their activities must strengthen and not weaken the positions of communism. Then they would be able to make higher demands on their own creativity, to keep a stricter check on their activities, and there would be no need for the public to criticize ideologically immature works. It may be asked: "And who is to be the judge, who will decide whether or not ideological work is going in the right direction?" The Party is the judge, the Party and the people; all ideological work, every production of literature and art, must serve their interests, the cause of communism! [Stormy applause.]

Those who want to remain outside the policy of the Party and who deny Party spirit in ideology are as it were setting up a party of non-Party people, are wittingly or unwittingly acting against our party, against our ideology, against our reality.

The policy of the Communist Party and its activities are determined and directed by the Party Congresses and between Congresses by the Central Committee. Our Party is marked by collective leadership, collective guidance of all work. The Party Congress and the Central Committee that it elects determine what is useful for the Party and the people and what is harmful for them. He who denies the Party spirit and collectivity of the leadership wants to decide everything himself. For instance, a writer writes a book or a painter paints a picture, and he says: "There it is — no one has the right to contradict me; I am my own judge!" Who should decide what the artistic value and the ideological tendency of such works is? In the opinion of their authors, they themselves should. They demand that their works be published: "Give me a printshop, ink, paper — give me everything." No, the Party will never go along with this!

Must we dramatize the situation? I think not. We in the Central Committee believe that we have a very small number of people among the intelligentsia who have surrendered to the bourgeois idea of nonpartisan ideology. The absolute majority of our Soviet intelligentsia in general, and of the creative intelligentsia in particular, live by Marxist-Leninist ideas and fight for their victory together with the Party and under the guidance of the Party. [Stormy applause.]

A very important and interesting sector of work for the Party is cinematography. Films are sharp ideological weapons and an easily accessible means of education. For instance, not all people will read a book. Sometimes books are accessible only to the better-educated reader, and more time is needed to read them and understand them. But a film is easily assimilated. Therefore films have the greatest mass appeal of all the arts.

Some workers in cinematography have obsessions, so to speak, incorrect views about the role of films. Specifically, this applies to so famous and experienced a film director as M. Romm. Let us hope that he will think things over and adopt the right positions.

The C.P.S.U. Central Committee has met the cinema workers halfway and has agreed they should have their own creative union. We are in favor of self-administration in the arts and for creative unions, if this helps develop the arts in the right direction. But if some people are thinking of making use of the unions for a struggle against the Party line, they are profoundly mistaken. To these people we say: We recognize a leading role in society for no unions whatever, except for one single union — our Communist Party. [Stormy applause.] All other unions that have attempted to guide their activities against the policy of the Party have inevitably come into collision with the Party and the people. This is said as a warning. It is better to issue a warning ahead of time than to wait until things have gone too far and a warning is no longer enough. Therefore it is better to reach an understanding in advance.

We must give more attention to our intelligentsia — writers, composers, artists, theater and film workers.

Speaking of music, we think that it is now being developed in the right direction. It is true that there have been some obsessions among certain composers, too. We mentioned this at one time, and now things seem to be going well. I admit I have a weakness for music. When I relax I always turn on the radio to listen to music. Some music broadcasts are good. There is less noisy, grating music now.

Some literary broadcasts have become more interesting. Not long ago I had occasion to hear a brief broadcast excerpt from M. A. Sholokhov's *Virgin Soil Upturned*. When the reader finished, I was sorry it was over. I would like to have heard more and more. I asked myself what was remarkable about this. They broadcast the episode in which Davydov, working with bulls, plows a field. This would seem to be an ordinary, everyday affair. But how remarkably it is recounted! You live through it as you listen to it. Davydov finishes his work and sprawls on the grass. You seem to feel yourself the pleasant fatigue, and you stretch out your legs after the hard work. This is the kind of artist Sholokhov is. He knows so well how to tell about simple things expressively and plausibly and to make the reader believe in them.

There are a great many fine artistic works in our literature. Such works as A. Tvardovsky's "Vasily Tyorkin" and "Horizon Beyond Horizon" are worthy of praise. I cannot enumerate here all the fine artistic works of all the poets and writers who are worthy of praise; we have hundreds of them.

Nowhere in the world is there such a mighty, life-affirming literature and art as in the Soviet Union. This is why the ideologists of imperialism are trying so persistently to exert influence on our creative intelligentsia in order to force them off the correct path. They are using various tricks to insinuate among our writers, composers, artists, and theater and film workers a lack of confidence in the great power of their creativity.

The Party is proud of the Soviet creative intelligentsia, is ready to stand behind it and will never let it down. [Stormy, prolonged applause.]

Literary Critics, Art Experts Abuse Trust

Comrades! I would like to recall the demands that V. I. Lenin placed before our agitation and propaganda. "Our main policy," he said, "must now be the economic construction of the state, so that we can harvest additional poods of grain, produce additional poods of coal, so that we can decide how best to use these poods of grain and coal. . . . And all agitation and propaganda should be based on this. We need fewer phrases, since you cannot satisfy the working people with phrases."

V. I. Lenin dreamed about a time when the construction of communism would become the practical concern of all the working people, when all people would understand that our common victory in building communism depends on their labor, on how each person solves practically this or that task in the common effort, be it the smallest and simplest.

We are now living in the time Lenin dreamed about. Everyone must study Lenin's works more, must turn to them more frequently. We must apply Lenin's ideas skillfully in practical work, in agitation, in propaganda, in all our work.

Propaganda and agitation become accessible if one makes skillful use of artistic imagery.

When I was young I read a great many of Rubakin's books. I still remember his story "The Book Peddler." This tale had the purpose of interesting the peasant boy in reading. The book peddler would come to the village in the summer. He had been there many times and they knew him well. The boys would settle down for the night in the hayloft. The book peddler came to them and began telling them various stories. He advised them to read books and told them this was a useful pastime. The boys were interested, and they asked:

"What is written in books?"

"If you read them, you will know."

One lad asked:

"What books should I read? Is it possible to read one book and find out everything so that you don't have to waste time on the others?"

"You have to read a great deal."

"And will I find out how my father is living in the next world?"

"Yes, you will find out everything, but first you must know one word."

"What word is that?"

"I don't know myself what the word is. There was a man who knew the word, and he decided to write a book and put the word down in it. But since then no one has known what the word is or what book it's in. Read all books, one after the other, and you will find out what the word is and what book it's in." [Applause.] Rubakin wrote pretty well!

He wrote some other good stories, "Sparks," for example, or the stories about miners. And all our legal workers should read the lecture he gave in the Northern Caucasus; there is a good description of the old courts.

I would like to say a few words about the state anthem.

A long time ago the question was raised about a new state anthem that would be consonant with our times. We receive a lot of letters on this matter.

Comrade Brezhnev recently showed me a letter in which the writer criticized writers, poets, and composers for not writing a new state anthem. Why is it, he asked, that for so many years they have played only the music of the anthem on the radio? The writer had decided to write some words for the anthem himself, and he sent in his verses.

I think we should return to the question of a new state anthem. Poets and composers can demonstrate their talents and create an anthem that is worthy of our great homeland, which is building communism!

Comrades! We are now working to bring into action all the levers and material means of ideological work and to improve the organization of guidance over this important matter. It must be admitted that ideological work is suffering seriously from the scattering of leadership among various agencies. This is not right. As a result of this practice it often happens that a writer writes a bad book, takes it to a publisher, and if he is turned down takes it to another. If he lives in Moscow or Leningrad and they do not accept his manuscript in the publishing houses there, he sometimes goes off to some distant area. There in some city or other they print it merely because it suits them to publish a book by a writer from the capital.

The necessary order must be brought into the guidance of ideological work. Cadres with a good grasp of the matter should handle the ideological work in the C.P.S.U. Central Committee, the Central Committees of the Union-republic Communist Parties and territory and province Party committees. It is necessary to enlist skilled people who have gone deeply into the work of the press, radio, and television, have read works of literature attentively and become acquainted with the works of composers and film and theater directors, and have correctly evaluated literary and artistic phenomena. To a great extent we have entrusted this work to literary critics and art experts. But experience has shown that they are not on a high enough level and have sometimes approached the evaluation of works of literature and art from factional positions rather than from positions of principle. We must arrange this work otherwise and organize it better.

In recent times we have somewhat reduced our attention to the work of publishing houses, film studios, and theaters, and the result has been the appearance of artistically weak and ideologically feeble works. Therefore things must be corrected.

Ideological work is an important, subtle, complex, and responsible cause. Guidance over it must be exercised with adherence to Party principle and with tact, and the creative intelligentsia must be drawn into it. We cannot allow gross administrative fiat in this.

In her speech to the plenary session Comrade Furtseva told about how one of the abstract sculptors took a spiral metal shaving and passed it off as a piece of sculpture. Apparently they paid him money for it!

Ye. A. Furtseva. — No, he wasn't paid.

N. S. Khrushchev. — Who knows? It would be difficult now to establish whether he got money for it or not. But this isn't even a matter of money, although, of course, that isn't the least important detail.

When you look at some paintings, you don't know what they represent or why they were painted. The trouble is that some artists reason this way: If someone doesn't understand my work, this means he has not attained to a comprehension of this type of art. It seems, then, that the artist is intelligent, while people who don't accept his daubs have not reached his "high level." [Stir in the hall.]

Many people have spoken about the work of the sculptor Neizvestny. I would like to believe that he is an honest and competent man. Perhaps when we talk about the abstractionists we should not mention Neizvestny alone.

Let us see how he carries out his promise, shows by his creative work that he serves the people.

Still, it would seem that we are to blame for not having noticed certain unhealthy phenomena in art in time and not having taken the necessary steps to prevent the spread of these phenomena.

Order must be brought into all this.

I think, comrades, that after this plenary session, after all the work that has been done, we will have a new upsurge on the ideological front. Life has shown that our intelligentsia holds correct Party positions. We cannot, because of two or three or a dozen people who act incorrectly, see some sort of scum in everything and fail to remark the healthy tendency that is characteristic of the activities of our creative intelligentsia. This would be extremely unhealthy for the Party, for the development of our literature and art, for all ideological work. [Applause.]

Our creative intelligentsia is on the correct path, it is guided by the ideas of our Leninist party, the ideas of Communist construction. [Stormy, prolonged applause.] . . .

(*Pravda,* June 29, 1963. Excerpt.)

CURRENT TASKS OF THE PARTY'S IDEOLOGICAL WORK. Report by Comrade L. F. Ilyichev, Secretary of the C.P.S.U. Central Committee on June 18, 1963, at Plenary Session of the C.P.S.U. Central Committee.

The quality of the literature published in our country improves, its ideological-theoretical level rises, year by year. However, there are grave and intolerable shortcomings in the publishing business.

The appearance of a book that raises fundamental questions of modern times and that through the force of its arguments makes a strong impression on the reader, convinces him and leads him forward — the appearance of such a book should be a festive occasion for socialist culture. But do we have many such occasions to celebrate? Too few, very few, if one takes into consideration the fact that we have at our disposal both excellent cadres and comparatively good production potentialities. The cause here lies in the lack of skill, ineptness, and inertia of the organizers of publishing matters. They continue to flood the market with dull, sometimes primitive works that no one needs, to squander paper and manpower on them.

Not only the authors but also the managers of publishing houses bear the responsibility for books containing ideological flaws and defects. They should be penalized not only morally but also materially.

Officials of Mass Media Attacked

The Party has justly criticized the ideological failures in art and literature. But what can be said by the officials of the publishing houses and magazines that have zealously printed and lavished praise upon ideologically defective works? No one must forget that the publishing houses and the magazines are not private enterprises but the fulcrum of the Party's ideological work. Attention must be paid to them, public opionion must be drawn into the work of the magazines, and publishing houses, must be given an opportunity to exert influence on the selection of works for publication in the magazines or as books.

The Leninist idea of the mass nature of radio broadcasting has been implemented in our country. Soviet radio has become a permanent part of the everyday life of Soviet people. Our radio workers have recently enlivened broadcasts somewhat.

But how many dull, thoughtless, and boring broadcasts there still are! Many shortcomings are engendered by the fact that the technical base and the organization of radio broadcasting came into being long ago and do not correspond to the increased demands. The radio is a newspaper without paper and the limitations of distance, it is theater and music for an audience of many millions. The most important task of Soviet radio is to transform broadcasting into a true forum of the masses, to increase its role in the Party's ideological work, in the struggle for communism, to perfect the quality of broadcasts and seek new forms for them.

The radio should enter the home, the family, like a close friend, an intelligent conversationalist and a good adviser.

Our people love the movies. Eleven million people see films every day. But the viewer's encounters with the screen do not always give him joy, do not always enrich him spiritually or make him morally purer and nobler.

Any defective output is unacceptable, and particularly defective ideological output. Such output in cinematographic art leads to consequences that are difficult to correct. Although a number of good films have been made recently, a great many films are issued, unfortunately, that hinder the rearing of the Soviet man rather than help it. At the meeting of Party and government leaders with representatives of the creative intelligentsia, and also in the press, such films, in particular *Ilyich Zastava,* have been justly subjected to stern criticism.

Much of the people's money is spent on the making of unnecessary and, what is more, harmful films.

The film *Lyubushka* has been released. It cost the state more than 400,000 rubles, 70,000 rubles of which was in excess of the plan. Losses from delays during shooting alone amounted to 22,000 rubles. What kind of delays? "A horse didn't go to sleep" — 2,000 rubles; "an actor turned up drunk" — 1,6000 rubles, etc. Note that the state even pays for the consumption of liquor.

The material losses are great. But who can calculate how much ideological harm bad films inflict on people, how many young hearts are poisoned with skepticism and petty-bourgeois ideas? One cannot be reconciled to incorrect tendencies in film art. We cannot allow such a mighty Party weapon to lose its firepower and effectiveness, to shoot at its own people. The Soviet people expect films of great social meaning from our cinematography, films that reveal the spiritual wealth of the builders of communism. We need films that are documents of the epoch, such as the marvelous film epic "The Russian Miracle," made by the German film directors Annelie and Andrew Thorndike.

Television is the most recent member of the family of mass means of communist education. Its development is proceeding at a tempestuous pace. The transmissions from space that have made our country the birthplace of "cosmovision" are a true triumph for Soviet television. We have all seen the exciting shots from space on television. Soviet television, with its many millions of viewers, is becoming a powerful weapon for the political and ideological-esthetic education of the people, for propaganda of the communist way of life. Television is the friend of Soviet art, making it constantly more accessible to millions of people.

Comrades! No matter what new means for ideological work come into being, nothing can replace the living, inspired words of the propagandist, lecturer, and agitator.

The Party has an extensive system of political education. Already there are not merely a few thousand activists but millions of workers, collective farmers, and members of the intelligentsia studying Marxist-Leninist theory. The economic education of the working people has assumed especially broad scope. It is necessary to continue in the future as well to see to it that political education not only contributes a definite amount of theoretical knowledge but is also a factor that actively intercedes in life, that has a practical influence on the affairs of enterprises, collective and state farms, and institutions.

Political education should be so structured that it is based on the principle of the unity of political and technical-economic studies. It is time to shift the center of gravity to political self-education as the basic and most productive method of mastering Marxism-Leninism.

The guiding principle in the organization of political education is voluntariness, a conscious striving for a broadening of outlook, for spiritual enrichment, for a more profound and complete view of the world. Every Communist, every Soviet person must understand that increased political knowledge is necessary above all to himself. It gives a person's life more meaning, content, and interest. Recognition of an internal need for political education is the guarantee of its success.

The propaganda of Marxism-Leninism can be truly profound and effective only when it is constantly enriched by penetrating inquiry, when the best scientific forces take a direct and active part in it.

Lively participation by scientists in the formation of a materialist world view and a Communist morality in the working people is a wonderful tradition of Soviet science that must be developed in every way. The Knowledge Society does great and useful work here. Set up on the initiative of eminent Soviet scientists, this public organization has become an important factor in the cultural life of the country. The society should broaden its activity in every way.

Formalism Most Harmful to Propaganda War

Formalism does more harm in agitation and propaganda work than anywhere else. There was a time when in a village or even a whole okrug only one or two barely literate people could be found. There were not enough newspapers, and radio had just come into existence. A lot of water has flowed over the dam since then. The standards and the very way of life of the Soviet citizen have changed radically.

Meanwhile, in many cases mass political work has taken no account of the changes and is frozen in habitual forms. It is necessary to pursue a course of entrusting propaganda work to the most authoritative people, people who are able to lead the masses, instruct them in the best ways of working, develop creative activity. Life has prompted many new forms of mass political work in recent years. But the soul of political agitation has been and remains individual work with people.

The strength of the agitator, lecturer, propagandist, or cultural-enlightenment worker lies in finding the way to the mind and heart of each person.

The librarian's role is at first glance a modest one. But how greatly people's education depends on him! The kind of book he recommends, what he discusses with readers and how he discusses it, whether or not he holds readers' conferences — all these are not technical questions but large ideological ones. After all, there are more than 100,000,000 library users.

We often hear justified censure of the work of clubs, Houses of Culture, libraries, and museums. In many instances, as the writer of a letter to the C.P.S.U. Central Committee remarked, the ruble remains the commander in chief in cultural-enlightenment work. Is it normal that in several republics the number of clubs is diminishing, and that in some places one club must serve several large communities? Hundreds of clubs remain half-built.

The volunteer principle is being developed extensively in the field of culture.

Two days ago the country learned of the noble initiative of the rural young people of Cherkassy Province, who have resolved to build clubs, kindergartens, and schools in the villages with their own hands and to organize the cultural life in the countryside properly. However, we still have cultural lieabeds. Sometimes the young people of a village or workers' settlement complain and write to all the authorities that the club is in disrepair, the librarian works poorly, etc. They sit and wait for somebody to come and fix the doors, put glass in the windows, sweep the floor, and turn on the lights in the club.

When work in cultural-enlightenment institutions, and ideological-educational work in general, is neglected, the sectarians and clergy step up their activities and drunkenness and hooliganism appear.

Here is what V. A. Lantsova and other collective farm women wrote to the C.P.S.U. Central Committee:

"We live in a remote corner of a district where leading workers very seldom come. We live like some sort of hermits. It is hard to believe that

when people are conquering space we have collective farmers who do not
know what a movie is. Even today it remains a mystery to them. We have no
radio at all. Everyone promises that we will soon get our own radio receiving center, but no one knows when this will be.

"Last year we got good news: A plot was allocated and marked out for
building a club. The women themselves dug and laid the foundation. But
our dream ended there. We sadly anticipate that when winter comes again we
will have to sit at home and play lotto. Lotto bores our men, and they start
to play cards. It is disgusting, and we don't want to play, but we go along
with them, since one wants to be with one's comrades."

Where do you think this letter comes from? From some remote corner
of the Far North, perhaps? No, from Matveyev-Kurgan District in Rostov
Province.

A Crisis in Soviet Culture?

Comrades! The Party has a high regard for the creative activities of
Soviet writers, artists, composers, and theater and film workers, considering
them its loyal assistants. The importance of their creative activities is growing especially rapidly now, when the Communist education of people, the
molding of the new man, has become one of the principal tasks of the Party.

Art and literature deal with subtle spheres of the human consciousness
and psyche, probing into their deepest recesses. They mold the spiritual
aspect of millions of builders of communism. It is therefore quite natural
that the question of the content and direction of artistic creativity is assum-
ing enormous ideological and political significance.

The measures the Party has taken on questions of artistic creativity have
aroused quite a stormy reaction abroad. Not only are the bourgeois ideologists
weeping crocodile tears over an alleged "crisis" in Soviet culture, they
have demagogically assumed the role of uninvited defenders of our artistic
intelligentsia. But from whom is the Soviet intelligentsia being defended?
And what is the real concern of our enemies? Are they actually anxious for
the success of socialist art?

No, their false voices fool no one. Our enemies are not perturbed by an
alleged "crisis of Soviet culture." They would be delighted at such a crisis.
It is something else that has thrown them off balance: the failure of their
vain hopes for a falling out in the ranks of our artistic intelligentsia. They
are maddened by the very unanimity with which the creative forces in our
country have supported the Party's appeal that the mighty weapon of
socialist art be kept clean and in combat readiness. [Applause.]

The turmoil in the camp of our enemies shows that the blow has hit home.

As far as the legend about a "crisis in Soviet art" is concerned, it looks
very stupid. Indeed, how can there be talk of a depression or crisis when
works written by masters of Soviet art of all generations are winning the
hearts and souls of honest people throughout the world? It often happens
that those who howl about the decline of art in the Soviet Union begin to

speak a different language after they have been to one of our best theaters, heard one of our musical organizations, or seen one of our best films.

In evaluating the state of artistic creativity in our country, we must not indulge in self-disparagement. We have things to be proud of. We have a great socialist art and a great socialist literature. [Stormy, prolonged applause.]

What is the essence of the demands the Party makes on literature and art?

It lies first of all in strengthening the ties between art and the life of the people, in the further development and enrichment of the art of socialist realism, and in the Leninist principles of Party spirit and kinship with the people in art. The Party regards art not only as an important means for understanding life but as a factor in transforming it, as a sharp weapon in the struggle against the bourgeois ideology that is alien to us. This is precisely why it has criticized false tendencies and ideological waverings in literature and art. It will not allow the formation of even the tiniest crack through which our enemies might penetrate.

As you know, some cultural workers succumbed to the influence of alien ideas, retreated from the principles of Soviet art that had been won in struggle and tested by life, and slipped into positions of peaceful coexistence with bourgeois ideology.

Ideological instability had a pernicious influence on the work and behavior of some young writers and artists, and not only of young and politically immature ones but of certain self-sufficient and inordinately praised ones as well. They forgot that a fierce struggle is going on in the world between the socialist and bourgeois ideologies. In their creative work they retreated from the principles of Party spirit and kinship with the people, and for high civic enthusiasm they substituted a wallowing in their own petty feelings and experiences.

In depicting Soviet reality some writers were unable to separate the distortions linked with the cult of the individual from the enormous revolutionary and transforming activities of the Party and the people at all stages of the development of Soviet society. Some of them forgot how to joy in the heroic achievements of the people, and they greeted portrayals of the bright side of our life with a sour grimace. There are some people who attempt to assert that art is powerful only through rejection and denial, who allege that the affirmative enthusiasm of socialist realism leads to the varnishing of reality.

There is not a grain of truth in these ideas; everything in them is upside down.

The highest criterion and the very core of socialist realism is the truth of life expressed in artistic images from the positions of the Communist world view. And the truth of life for the builders of communism is the affirmation of the most humane society on earth. In some of its manifestations it may be stern and "bitter." But this is the manly truth of fighters; it strengthens the hearts and souls of people and does not sow philistine panic and confusion in the face of life's difficulties.

True boldness in the artist consists not in seeking out facts big and small, in inventing and painting horrors and shortcomings, but in the civic spirit of his stance, in the consistent and uncompromising affirmation of lofty communist ideals. Individualism and phrase-making, impertinence, the game of ideological giveaways with the bourgeois world, a morbid passion for everything dark and dull, and a spiritual blindness to the bright and triumphant — all this amounts to nothing less than a retreat from the revolutionary traditions of advanced Russian and Soviet literature. Quite often one encounters attempts to substitute skepticism for the joy of creation, deliberately to depict Soviet man as commonplace and ordinary.

At one time in literature, films, and plays one saw miserable, spiritually poor people, characters with narrow minds and primitive feelings and experiences. But are we merely to ignore one-sided works that describe our lives tendentiously, works that offer a profuse description of some tedious little truth while ignoring the great truth? Perhaps I should name some of the works printed in the fat magazines — *Novy mir, Neva, Yunost* and others — that were greeted by the disapproval of the Soviet public, but let the authors and the editors themselves say what they think about this.

The growing *trust* of the Party and the people in the artist presupposes a growing *responsibility* of the artist to society.

The people expect works from the writers and artists that depict all the variety of life, people at various levels of social and moral awareness, but they want the portrayals to be accurate and to emphasize the things in our reality that are basic, leading. The chief heroes of the art of socialist realism are people who are actively engaged in the transformation of life, who are moving forward, who — in V. I. Lenin's words — are "a country's flower, its strength, its future."

The Positive Hero

It is especially important to emphasize the educative role of the positive hero when we speak about art for children and young people.

Only works that vividly reveal the high and noble truth of our life, the heroism and romanticism of the revolutionary struggle of the Soviet people for a new society, can fire young hearts with a desire to accomplish feats, can inculcate a feeling of active and effective love for the great homeland, and can attract the young through the inspiring example of the older generations. Therefore it is necessary to give more attention to the creation of books, plays, and films for children and young people, to the work of children's and young people's publishing houses and magazines, theaters, and film studios.

We live in a period of sharp ideological struggle, of tense class conflicts in the world arena.

Art has been drawn into the maelstrom of the ideological battle, it is on the "barricades of hearts and souls." Here there can be no ceasefires or reconciliations, ideological retreats or compromises. Our ideological adversaries include in their arsenal such weapons as formalism, abstractionism, and decadence, and they are attempting to choke our fields with ideological weeds whose seed was prepared by the ideological selectionists of capitalism.

Our Party is opposed to tendencies that are alien and hostile to socialism; it has fought and will continue to fight on two fronts — both against formalist trickery, and against dullness and hackwork, and for the great and true innovatory art of communism.

The position of our Party on ideological-artistic questions is well known; it is based on the works of our teacher and leader Vladimir Ilyich Lenin, set forth in the Party Program, and concretized and developed in the remarkable speeches by N. S. Khrushchev. The Party has carried out and will continue to carry out the Leninist line of struggle for Party spirit and kinship with the people, for ideological content and high artistry. There is no ground at all for fears that criticism of formalistic and abstractionist tendencies in art might lead to a creative slump, to a revival of the methods of guiding art that were practiced during the period of the cult of the individual, etc. Leninist norms, Leninist principles of guidance have been reestablished in the whole of our life, and this includes the guidance of literature and art. [Applause.]

Literature and art are an integral part of the cause of the entire Party, the entire people.

Let us recall how angrily V. I. Lenin spoke against alien tendencies and ideologies, with what sarcasm he lashed out at philistine drooling and liberal complacency in the guidance of art. The Party, loyal to Leninist principles, takes decisive note of characterlessness and irresponsibility on ideological questions. There must never be an atmosphere of ideological defenselessness among those who are defending correct positions or, on the contrary, an atmosphere of ideological permissiveness for those who propound ideological views that are alien to us.

At one time some creative workers, using the excuse that they were combating the consequences of the cult of the individual, began to express doubts about the need for Party guidance in art and adopted an ironical attitude toward any mention of the public duty of the artist and the educative mission of literature and art.

In their turn, some Party and Soviet officials who had lost their political acuity were reconciled to clearly incorrect tendencies and fled before the demagogues, fearing that they might be labeled retrogrades and conservatives. Things reached the point where some organizations were even afraid to mention the words "socialist realism," "Party spirit," "kinship with the people," "ideological content."

The Party sharply criticizes writers and artists who have made mistakes, who have strayed from the true path. There can be no retreats or compromises in matters of ideology. But all of us remember that we are talking about Soviet artists who are, as a rule, politically close to our people. The task is not to "excommunicate" them but rather to help them understand their ideological and artistic errors, to help them put their talents fully at the service of the people and the cause of communism. It would not be in the spirit of our Party's policy to place creative workers who have made mistakes in the category of hopeless cases and incorrigibles.

We must avoid all prejudice, must remember that the struggle is not against people but for people and against bad ideas. [Applause.]

At the same time, to those people who think that the struggle against ideological waverings and distortions is a temporary campaign which will soon pass and that "all will be forgotten," who believe that they can remain silent and wait it out, we say: "This will not do!" Serious matters are involved here: It is not a campaign the Party is waging but rather a consistent struggle for the affirmation of Leninist principles in all fields of artistic creativity. No honest Soviet artist can today play the role of "bystander," can withdraw into himself or stubbornly persist in his errors and confusions, seek sympathy, appeal to backward and antisocial elements.

The writer or artist is by his very nature a social being, a participant in life, an explorer of hearts and souls.

No Narrow Professional Interests

A situation has developed among us in which writers, artists, composers, and film workers have gathered in unions that are isolated from one another, and willingly or unwillingly they have to stew in the kettles of their narrow professional interests. We should probably give support to the proposals from many workers in culture that the "shop" dissociation of detachments of the artistic intelligentsia be done away with and all creative forces be combined in a single union of creative workers. [Applause.]

The very nature of the creation of artistic values and the unity of basic ideological and creative interests dictate the need to amalgamate our creative forces, which undoubtedly will aid in bringing the arts closer to the life of the people.

Only a little time has passed since the March meetings, but already we see how the situation in the creative organizations themselves has changed, how the activeness of workers in literature and the arts has intensified. Workers in Soviet culture unanimously and warmly supported the criticism of the erroneous tendencies in artistic creativity. They saw in it new evidence of the Party's concern for the multiplication of the spiritual wealth of the people, for the further development of the artistic culture of Soviet society.

The creative intelligentsia is responding with deeds to the Party's concern for a further upsurge in literature and art in our country. On the eve of the plenary session of the C.P.S.U. Central Committee, a hundred Soviet writers wrote in *Pravda* about their work and their creative plans. This was a collective writers' report to the plenary session of the C.P.S.U. Central Committee, to our Party. [Prolonged applause.]

Both old and young writers, composers, artists, and theater and film workers will undoubtedly create new works that are worthy of the great epoch of the construction of communism.

(*Pravda,* June 19, 1963. Excerpt.)

THE STALINIST CULT VS. LENINIST PRINCIPLES

Speech by Comrade A. I. Adzhubei, Editor in Chief of the Newspaper *Izvestia.* Comrades, we are all deeply satisfied that the plenary session of the Party Central Committee is discussing the question of ideological work. This plenary session has coincided with the tenth anniversary of the Party's activity without Stalin. How can one now fail to recall the croakings of the bourgeois press when he died? On that day the National Security Council held a conference in the White House to discuss the question "How can the West best take advantage of this event?" Senator Walter George declared, "Stalin's death will lead to a disintegration within Russia." Kersten, another American Senator [sic], appealed: "Now that Stalin is dead, we must take advantage of this period of internal conflict in the very heart and center of the international Communist organization in order to win the cold war."

We shall be frank: Ten years ago there was much that was very complicated. One recalls what Stalin said shortly before his death: "What will you do without me? You will perish." The situation then, comrades, was not simple! Malenkov announced at the 19th Party Congress that the country's grain problem had been solved. He deceived the Party, deceived the people. It was all the harder for the Party to solve this and many other problems because in words they had already been solved.

We remember how we lived in this decade, how we learned — and we learned much: concreteness, efficiency, truthfulness, boldness. We lived according to Lenin, and it became easier for everyone to breathe. Shall we say once more from whom we learned? We learned from the Party's Leninist headquarters, the Presidium of the Central Committee, from our First Secretary, Comrade N. S. Khrushchev. [Applause.] Our Party has not lived without Party authorities during these ten years, but these authorities have acted with the Party, with the people and in the interests of the people!

When this or that writer tries to assert that the Stalin cult, which actually did leave a heavy imprint on the life of the Party, somehow deprived it of its Leninist fighting potential, that in the Party itself there were no forces that defended the true Leninist principles of Party life, let him read, for example, an extract from the resolution adopted March 17, 1937 — I repeat, 1937 — at the 2,000-strong meeting of the Moscow Party *aktiv,* on the report by Nikita Sergeyevich Khrushchev about the recently completed plenary session of the Central Committee. This resolution says: "The meeting of the Party *aktiv* considers it to be a completely impermissible situation when in a number of the Party organizations of Moscow and the province, general Party meetings and plenary sessions of the district committees cease to be occasions of Bolshevik criticism and self-criticism and become arenas for endless parades, bombastic speeches about successes and completely superfluous greetings to Party leaders."

As you see, there have always been forces in the Party that have acted in the spirit of Leninist principles, and this is precisely why the past decade is so significant in the history of our country and our Party.

One meets people who are inclined to divide the Party's work into the purely economic and the purely ideological. If the Party struggles persistently for an increase in the productivity of labor, for the development of new branches of industry, for an upsurge in agriculture, it seems to such a "theoretician" that it is engaged with purely economic problems at the expense of the development of theory.

Our party has taught and still teaches that the true development of Marxist-Leninist theory occurs only in the concrete transformation into life of the idea of creating a mighty, prosperous, happy Communist society, only in the creation of the material and technical base for communism.

As concerns those sorry theoreticians who engage in writing pompous and plump theoretical works on abstract topics and who at the same time ignore the fact that the life of the people has constantly improved, that they have received more homes, food products, attractive clothes, that the material and the spiritual have harmoniously complemented one another in the life of man — such theoreticians seem important only to themselves. Both Marx and Lenin would turn away from such a theoretical elaboration of Marxism-Leninism.

As is known, words that are not backed up by deeds are in general neither hot nor cold. It is possible, for example, to spout maledictions against capitalism, but if these maledictions are not supported by practical revolutionary construction, you will never succeed in burying capitalism.

The imperialists are in full agreement on the empty maledictions that have been addressed to them. This is shown by the example of the Japanese manufacturer who resorted to the following trick. He made a life-sized stuffed replica of himself and placed it at the entrance to the factory. The workers were permitted to jeer at the replica, to beat it, to spit on it. The factory owner agreed to all this on one condition — that the workers not touch him, the living exploiter, personally. [Laughter.] The case is anecdotal, but it is characteristic; I might even say symbolic. Is it not precisely thus that the bourgeoisie agrees to suffer verbal abuse against capitalism as long as the foundations of capitalism are untouched?

Our ideological opponents are in confusion in the face of the unprecedented growth of the prestige of communism. They are losing the hope of overcoming the Soviet Union and the other socialist countries by force of arms. Whether they want to or not, they see that the Soviet Union is stepping on the heels of the United States in economic competition even today. The victory will also be ours in the battle of the socialist and bourgeois ideologies, between which there can be no peaceful coexistence.

Our ideological opponents know that Communist ideology, our ideological weapon, is an invincible force. Here they prattle, rush about, forget what they said only yesterday. Once the bourgeois ideologists foretold, through the lips of Churchill, the doom of our system, because we were poor, ignorant, and could not even start up the tsarist steam engines. And now the icebreaker Lenin is working with its atomic boilers for communism, while the American ship Savannah for several years has been unable to leave the pier, is laid up, and the American mechanics who work on this vessel complain that "the Savannah is like a man with a bright smile and a sun-burned face. He seems completely healthy and energetic. Then you talk to his doctor and discover that he has diabetes, high blood pressure, and stomach ulcers. It is exactly the same with this ship. Outside it is beautifully built, but inside they have set up obsolete equipment that it constantly going out of whack."

Well, the American mechanics are right! Isn't it thus with capitalism it-self, with its glittering showcases and tempting advertisements — in appear-ance sun-tanned and healthy, but in fact hopelessly ill? [Applause.]

The Party Must Reach Man's Spirit

In the ideological battle that we are waging with the world of capital, we must know the modes and methods of the enemies, as was correctly said in Comrade Ilyichev's report and in the statements of Comrades Yegorychev, Popov and others. We must constantly catch them up in their precarious posi-tions and arguments, we must strike the opponent, giving him no respite.

Much has been said here about the interesting experience and the forms of ideological work. What is delaying us today at the new stage of our ideo-logical struggle, today when all our opportunities have so grown? Primarily it is the elements of bureaucratism, formalism, inattention to man, to his spiritual condition, to what he thinks about, what he has doubts about, what he is searching for during the time of his formation.

Workers of the Central Committee's Ideological Department conducted an interesting investigation in the city of Cherepovets. A major metallurgical plant and many educational and cultural institutions are located here, the city has many educated people and remarkable toilers. If you compare the show-ing of Cherepovets with the average showings of the other cities in Vologda Province, you will find that twice as many people have been reached by the system of political enlightenment in Cherepovets. The number of book buyers and newspaper subscribers among its population shows the same relation to the average for the province. There are three times as many radio receivers and five times as many television sets than in the other settlements and towns in Vologda Province.

And at the same time, right here in Cherepovets there is a much greater demand for liquor, many more people have been to sobering-up stations, three times as many are attracted to petty hooliganism, and more commit various kinds of crimes than anywhere else in the province.

All these acute problems are never off the agendas of the sessions, meetings and conferences of Party and public organizations. But the situation in the city is changing slowly.

What is the matter? This is a very indicative example of the low co-efficient of useful activity in our ideological work. Many comrades in Cherepovets have said that political upbringing work is conducted chiefly at enterprises. When a person finishes work, he is left completely or almost completely to himself. It is right here that we have let people slip out from under our influence.

We must remove all the barriers of formalism from the road of ideological work. Indeed, from time to time we see pointless acts, unneeded by anyone, but we pass them by! Who can object to our need for visual agitation? A bright, expressive poster is a good and necessary thing. But when the slogan "Glory to the Collectives and Shock Workers of Communist Labor" blazes over the building in which is housed the not-unknown Aragvi restaurant — who needs this?

Perhaps these are only details, but they are mordant, unpleasant details.

If you translate such concepts as formalism and bureaucratism into Party language, these signify a poor knowledge of the life and demands of people. The Moscow City Party Committee displayed a good initiative: It adopted a decision to assign Communist writers to various Party organizations, includ-ing those of major industrial enterprises. On the eve of the plenary session, *Izvestia* reporters called ten Party committees at major plants and were told that in recent times not one writer had approached them with a request to be taken on the Party roster. True, Comrade Ryabko, Secretary of the Party Committee of the Second Clock and Watch Plant, said: "Recently one writer came and telephoned the Party committee from the entrance. We received him, prepared to listen, to discuss literature, but he suddenly took a watch from his hand and asked that it be repaired." [Stir in the hall.]

One can hope that this is not all the business Moscow's Communist writers want to transact with the Party organizations of the capital's industrial en-terprises.

But after all, if we speak frankly, the writers not only can give much to plant collectives but — especially young writers — can get from the workers that same wisdom about which the writer V. Nekrasov has spoken so sneeringly.

I will cite only one example. When the young Moscow writer Andrei Voznesensky found himself in Paris, he gave out interviews right and left, quite unintelligible in both their literary and their political concepts. They asked him, "To whom are you giving an interview?" He answered, "I don't know." It was explained that a worker at a fascist radio station in Munich interviewed him and broadcast his interview to the Soviet Union. Here is your lack of political fastidiousness and vigilance. A young Soviet worker, the same age as Voznesensky, also found himself in Paris some time ago. A cheeky journalist talked with him. He asked scornfully: "Tell me, Soviet comrade, here you say that you are well fixed, but how many suits can you buy on your salary?" The young metalworker thought for a second, felt this gentleman's suit and answered: "Such as you have on, three, but such as I have on, one." [Stormy applause.] And this ended the conversation. But, comrades, how much real Soviet pride there is in this answer!

Comrades, the present plenary session is enriching the whole vast experience of the Party in the area of ideological work. Soviet journalists will accept for undeviating execution the decisions worked out by the plenary session and will work in a Communist way, energetically and persistently, helping the Party and the people gain new victories in the glorious name of communism. [Applause.]

(*Pravda*, June 20, 1963. Excerpt.)

13

EHRENBURG AT LENINGRAD

At a meeting of Soviet and European writers held in Leningrad in August, the discussion quickly focused on the modern European literary tradition, exemplified by Proust, Kafka, and Joyce. With nearly all the Soviet speakers attacking this tradition, proceedings became heated. The speech of Ilya Ehrenburg, which was comparatively favorable in its evaluation of Western literary achievements, lowered the temperature of the discussion. (It was Ehrenburg's first public statement since the attacks on him by Khrushchev and Ilyichev at the March 7–8 meeting.)

UPHOLD HUMAN VALUES. By Ilya Ehrenburg.

While listening to some of the speeches during the early days of the meeting I had the feeling I was present at a dialogue of the deaf, when those conversing are talking with great animation but neither can hear what the other is saying.

It seems to me that, having met together, it is possible to choose between two forms of conversation, beginning either with that which divides those conversing or that which unites them. Many of those who have spoken have talked chiefly about what separates us. This applies both to many of our guests and to some of our own writers. Much indeed separates us, first of all the fact that we live in different societies with different ideologies and different mores; but after all, much unites us. There are no enemies of the socialist world here, they did not come. Had it not been writers from Group '47 who spoke here rather than Chancellor Adenauer's ideologists, had it not been leftist French rather than followers of General de Gaulle, then the polemical ardor and anger of certain orators would have been justified.

In the recesses between sessions and in the evenings I have spoken with almost all of our guests, as the other Soviet writers probably have also. Need

I mention that Western society is by no means uniform, and that hardly anyone will take the position of Sartre or Simone de Beauvoir for the position of the *Figaro* staff? Many at our conference have spoken of the French "nouveau roman" group and have argued with the writers from Group '47. But, after all, one can speak of a writer only through knowing his works, and here I have at times heard literary appraisals based not on a knowledge of the literature but only on an acquaintance with literature about the literature. Some writers of the West in speaking about Soviet literature have relied more on reviews of it than on first-hand knowledge of it.

Our guests from the "nouveau roman" group know that I am not greatly enthralled with its literary theory. I have met with them and argued for a long time at the house of that hospitable hostess and good writer Nathalie Sarraute. But I am not going to continue the argument here, for few Soviet writers are acquainted with the works of the "nouveau roman" group. Probably many writers of the West are also little acquainted with the works of Soviet authors that have appeared in recent years. For a person to speak of books he has not read, or of pictures he has not seen, inevitably means for him to fall into scholastic and dogmatic arguments. At present the dogmatism of a certain country in the East is being written about, but dogmatism is also encountered in the West, and it would be better for us writers to renounce it.

It seems to me that we have been incorrect in defining the theme of our meeting as the "crisis of the novel." Every author thinks he writes well, be he a traditionalist or an innovator, that for him there is no crisis of the novel — he'll give the crisis to others. Anyway, "crisis" is in the nature of creative work, and if it were not, that would be the end of art. Any author, when he sits down to write a book, thinks he will communicate what has not been said before him, and that he will say it as it has never been said before. A "crisis" always exists for a writer, artist or composer; this crisis is a pregnancy and a birth that is sometimes difficult.

Art Form Innovators Upheld

I have always opposed those who say that form has self-sufficing significance, just as I have opposed those who say that form is not important; I am convinced that in art form is inseparable from content and content inseparable from form.

Even the French Parnassians spoke of art for art's sake for only a very short time. There cannot be art for art's sake, any more than there can be love for love's sake.

The form of the novel has frequently become enriched and changed. I recall that Zola introduced montage into the novel long before the invention of the film — the alteration of over-all views and close-ups, the swift transition from a historical picture to psychological detail.

Leo Tolstoy said of Chekhov: "It is impossible even to compare Chekhov as an artist with any of the earlier Russian writers, with Turgenev, with Dostoyevsky, or with me. Chekhov has his own peculiar manner, like the impressionists." This is true; Chekhov introduced elements into the short story that are reminiscent of impressionist painting — the awareness of air and light and the depiction of the large through minor detail. This is connected with his approach to man. Chekhov said that it is the duty of the writer to defend man.

Can one reject Joyce and Kafka, two great writers who do not resemble one another? To me this is the past, they are historical phenomena. I do not make banners of them, but neither do I make targets of them.

We had a poet, Khlebnikov; this name says little to our guests — yes, and even contemporary Soviet readers know little about Khlebnikov. He is a very difficult poet; I can read no more than a page or two of Khlebnikov in a sitting. But Mayakovsky, Pasternak, and Aseyev told me that without Khlebnikov they would not have been. Many of our young poets who have never read Khlebnikov have adopted not a few of his poetic discoveries through Mayakovsky, Pasternak, or Zabolotsky.

Joyce found the most minute psychological details, the mastery of the interior monologue, but they do not drink the essence in its pure form, they dilute it with water. Joyce is a writer for writers.

As for Kafka, he foresaw the terrible world of fascism. His works, diaries, and letters show that he was a seismographic station that because of the sensitivity of the apparatus registered the first tremors. They are up in arms against him, as if he were our contemporary and ought to be an optimist, but he was a major historical phenomenon.

Much has been said here about the French "nouveau roman." As though there were no contemporary Spanish, Italian, American, or German novel. I will say that these last are closer to me. But the representatives of the French "nouveau roman" must not be confused with eccentrics, with literature intended for sensation. The authors of the "nouveau roman" work unselfishly; their intentions are honest. I approach their work with respect, although it seems to me that in much they are in error — yet at times they open up what we, for example, opened in 1920. However, we cannot argue here about books that are known only to a few writers of our country; we must become acquainted with their works, and the Western writers must become acquainted with the works of those Soviet authors, old and young, whom they have not read.

But what are we to do right now? It seems to me that we might establish wherein we are all in agreement. For example, we all agree on the fact that writers should uphold human values in the novel. There is literature that is filled with despair. I see nothing reprehensible in this. A man can be in despair, particularly in the environment in which many of our Western guests live. There is, however, a literature that is marked not only by despair but also by antihumanism and scorn or disdain for man. I have not met defenders of such literature at our conference.

One of the finest German poets of our time, Enzensberger, has spoken here; he belongs to Group '47. Angered by something, he made in the heat of the polemics one untrue statement: He attributed to Marxism that which pertains to the vulgarization of Marxism. If one examines the works of Marx and Engels, some of Lunacharsky's articles, the letters of Gramsci, one will see in them nothing in common with that which angered the young German poet. Enzensberger spoke imprecisely about how it is possible to show the internal world of the fascists. I understood him, but some of my colleagues did not. Of course, the political and social nature of fascism has long been clear to Enzensberger, he has demonstrated this in many essays, but he was speaking about something else. During the war I frequently asked myself how people who were not only literate but also frequently had a higher education could be reduced to the superstition and cruelty of primitive beings. Certain books, in particular the books by the German authors of Group '47, have made it possible for me to understand better the distortion of the human creature by fascism. Art does not repeat that which is clear to science, art reveals the world of the emotions. The writer gives keys to understanding people.

When I was arguing in Paris with our friends from the "nouveau roman" group, one writer said to me, "The only good thing in *Crime and Punishment* is the description of Raskolnikov's room." I retorted: "After all, this description had an effect on you only because you knew who Raskolnikov was."

The novelist reveals the inner world of man. Empathy is required for this. Empathy is also necessary in showing bad people, even villains, to the readers. I consider myself an average writer, but when I have succeeded in showing a scoundrel I have hyperbolized that which I myself have experienced. It is impossible to describe a coward if one has never been afraid even for a minute.

There are no novelists who have the keys to all hearts. Chekhov wrote that Tolstoy erred in deciding to include Napoleon in his novel. A poster intruded into a painting because Leo Nikolayevich did not have and probably could not have had the key to the inner world of a conqueror.

But what more do we have in common? The necessity to defend man. We are all against the cold war, against the iron curtain. We joyfully hailed the signing by the three powers of the treaty banning atomic tests. We are all striving for peace and wish to expand contacts with one another, to understand one another better. But there are writers in the world, after all, who wish to deepen the abyss between the socialist world and the West, to wall up all doors.

You have come here in order to deepen friendly contacts with us, and we understand this. Therefore it is out of place to say that socialist realism is bad; after all, many excellent books are connected with it. It is also out of place to reject indiscriminately that which is being written in the West and which one critic or another has not liked. Best of all would be to translate a few more books that stir readers.

We have still more in common. We consider it the task of the author of a novel to show and reveal man. When we succeed in doing this, we do a great deal to strengthen human solidarity and to bring peoples together.

Between the two world wars American literature made a valuable contribution to the development of the novel. Hemingway, Faulkner, Steinbeck, and Caldwell in addition to telling about man began to show man, and this distinguished them from the excellent American novelists of the 19th century.

It seems to me that it is unnecessary to be afraid of experiments. In my book I have quoted the words of Jean-Richard Bloch at the First Congress of Soviet Writers. He said that there must be writers for the millions and writers for 5,000 readers, as there must be pilots "who work on already tested models" and test pilots. Charlatanism can and should be swept aside, but the right of experiment to exist in literature must not be denied.

Writers with Civic Passion

On the other hand, some of our guests are wrong when they think that writers with civic passion, or, as they like to say in France, "les engagés," cannot create truly artistic works. Was not *The Divine Comedy* full of the political passions of the epoch? Many here have mentioned Balzac, but no one has recalled Stendhal. After all, this great novelist also was "engagé." His partiality for describing the political events of the age did not keep him from making of *The Red and the Black* a novel that stirs readers 130 years later.

Dear guests, you must understand that we are living in the first century of socialist society, and that we have more enemies than we know what to do with. I am not speaking about this hall — there are no enemies here. We have not been going along an avenue but across virgin soil, we have frequently made mistakes, but we have moved ahead all the same; most likely we even now are making mistakes now and then, but we are not losing courage, we are going farther.

Our writers at times write poor novels not because they are bound to socialist ideology but because the Lord God has not granted them talent. We have never said that under socialism there would be no mediocrity. We have said that we would have no exploiters, and we have none, but we have enough ungifted writers, I think.

In 1934, during the First Congress of Soviet Writers, one novelist said to me: "I cannot write for such primitive readers." Twenty years later in the club of a Moscow factory I accidentally overheard a conversation about this writer: "Have you read — ?" He named a book by the author who had talked with me in 1934. His comrade replied: "I began it and put it down. Very primitive."

What had happened during that time? A growth of Soviet society and a growth in Soviet readers.

The last thing on which we have all agreed is the responsibility of the writer. There has been much misunderstanding here arising from the interpreting, but in the end we have understood that all who are present consider themselves responsible to the reader.

We have many readers. Don't think I am now going to pull out a piece of paper and begin to tell you how many million copies of the books of Balzac or Dickens have been published since the revolution. Each Soviet prose writer and poet present here has a great many readers. Right now we have neither a Leo Tolstoy nor a Dostoyevsky nor a Chekhov; of this I am convinced. But in Leningrad alone there are now more readers of the average Soviet novel than there were readers of *War and Peace* when this novel was first published. In the beginning the process of expanding culture moved at the expense of depth. This was inevitable. Some people laughed at us: "What readers you have — they don't understand what's what." Then the readers began to understand. At present the process might be called one of deepening.

I have said more than once, and I repeat, that the chief thing in our Soviet literature is not the success of this or that book but the fact that we have created tens of millions of intelligent and politically conscious readers. Now it will be easier for our heirs, for the young writers, to create a genuine, a great literature.

Let us mend friendly relations, make fewer declarations, and converse and explain more! We can reach agreement, in spite of the fact that much separates us. I would like for us to part with the feeling that we have come to know each other better.

(Literaturnaya gazeta, August 13, 1963)

14

TVARDOVSKY IN THIS WORLD— TYORKIN IN THE OTHER

The meeting of writers in Leningrad had a sequel. Khrushchev invited some of them, Russian and European, to visit him in Gagra. On a sunny afternoon, he invited Alexander Tvardovsky to recite his poem "Tyorkin in the Other World," a parable of Stalinist bureaucracy. The poem speaks for itself.

TYORKIN IN THE OTHER WORLD. By Alexander Tvardovsky.

Alexander Tvardovsky's new poem, I think, stands in no need of a special introduction. This prefatory note is not for that purpose. It is neither a literary analysis of the poem nor a critic's comment (poem and author alike still await these), but rather, to speak in the language of journalistic categories, it is a first impression — an account of the thoughts that filled the mind when Alexander Trifonovich had finished reading it to an audience.

This was on the day when members of the European Writers' Association

met with Nikita Sergeyevich Khrushchev on the Black Sea coast near
Gagra. Mikhail Sholokhov, Konstantin Fedin, Leonid Leonov, Alexei Surkov, Boris Polevoi, Mikola Bazhan, Leonid Sobolev, Georgy Markov,
Alexander Prokofyev, Alexander Chakovsky, and Konstantin Voronkov
roared with laughter at times, at others it was evident from their expressions,
their eyes, and the almost tangible silence that they were transported to
distant vistas, following the poet's thoughts and the vein of the story, and
were steeped in Tyorkin's tale. Even the foreign guests, among them many
famous poets and writers, attentively listened or, more accurately, since
some of them did not know Russian, observed this instructive scene, in a
special mood. From the brief explanations of the interpreters, from the
general response, from the sound of the poetry, they too sensed the mirthful
satire of the lines, the witty and lovely flow and the fanciful imagery of the
poet's new work.

I particularly remember how Mikhail Alexandrovich Sholokhov listened.
Naturally, I cannot anticipate his judgment of the poem, but he listened
beautifully, in a special way. It seemed as though he were sharing conversation with Tyorkin about the latter's extraordinary journey, laughing with him,
and bringing to life for himself the scenes of the poem in the penetrating,
wise manner of a man of the pen.

I well remember the time — it was long ago, more than 20 years ago —
when Vasily Tyorkin first announced himself and his front-line experiences.
He endeared himself to millions of readers. At the front there were even disputes as to whether he was an imaginery character or whether Alexander
Tvardovsky was writing about a real soldier. The power of the writer, the
power of his work lay in the very fact that in this dispute both sides were
right.

And here is a fresh meeting with Vasily Tyorkin, and an extraordinary
one — even, one might say, supernatural; the poem is sharply satirical, almost grotesque. No doubt it will arouse debate and objections; and this is
good! But best of all is the fact that Vasily Tyorkin is alive. It is good that
the prominent poet Alexander Tvardovsky took nine years (an example,
this, to some young and immature poets) and did not hasten to present the
tale of Tyorkin's journey "through the other world" before the court of
readers, but labored and labored, not shirking the job of perfecting the lines
and seeking out the most precise words.

Again millions of readers are meeting their old acquaintance, and front-
line soldiers again recall past campaigns. All who remember the start of
Tyorkin's path will be overjoyed, and this new work will set younger folk
to reaching for *Book About a Soldier*.

When Alexander Tvardovsky finished reading the poem, the bright south-
ern sun, reddening, cast a pervasive, happy glow over everything roundabout — the sea, the pine woods, and the silver ribbon of beach. It seemed
as though Vasily Tyorkin, reborn in those minutes, looked at all this power
and beauty of the land, the sea, and the sun, and, smiling widely, like a
Russian, like a master, went striding along, swinging his arms, soldier-fashion,

across our land to choose a town or village in which to live, to choose comrades in work and, of course, to choose the words for new songs about himself and his friends.

A. ADZHUBEI.

Before he reached the age of 30
Tyorkin, willy-nilly,
Checked in at the other world,
Checked out of this one.

Checked out, checked in
Late on New Year's eve,
Gazed about in the underworld
For the first time.

Thus it will go, line after line,
As the picture unfolds.
But the reader's alarmed:
"What deviltry is this?

In the age of space rockets,
Age of scientific discoveries,
It's a peculiar theme, you know —"
"Certainly is!"

"He can't get away with it!"
"There must be some motive
        for it —"
"Something more than
        meets the eye—"
"Exactly!"

Hold on: The mentor's being strict,
He sees through everything from
        the opening lines.

Oh my friend, my know-it-all reader,
Do me this favor:
Be severe, if you will,
But please read it first.

Don't jump to pat conclusions
Like a pedant-critic
Who everywhere sees hints
Of illicit ideas,

Who has a facile way
Of condemning out of hand —
From "harmful" and "decadent"
To "grist for the enemy's mill" —

And exaggerates
Old wives' fears
That Soviet rule is being threatened
With being shaken to its foundations.

Don't suspect traps everywhere,
Don't play scare-pranks from
        behind bushes.
Get out of the habit. The times
        have changed.
Like it or not, they're not what
        they used to be.

Trust me for the sake of our good
        old friendship
Of the terrible years.
I won't tell you fairy tales about
        the nether world
For nothing.

It's not a matter of heaven or hell;
Fiend or devil, what matters it?
There's an old, old saying:
"Cannon ride to battle backwards."

There, in brief, is how the author
Prefaces his tale.
It may take unusual turnings,
It may be strange at times.

But on! Then pen begins to sing;
The story will explain itself.

I repeat: In the flower of his years,
At the prime of his powers,
Inadvertently our Vasily
Passed into the other world,

Looked about, saw
Light, warm passages —
Like Metro stations,
With archways slightly lower.

A shelter reinforced,
Double or triple strong.

The very devil of a bomb
Couldn't crash through this.

(A bomb! Tyorkin, looking
    at the ceiling,
Gauging its strength,
Could not have known then
It would all depend on what kind
    of bomb,

That even in the other world
There'd be no escaping
From a bomb of today,
Scientifically calculated.)

And then — Tyorkin wasn't sure
What was real and what was
    dream —
He saw that his felt boots
Left tracks on the floor.

The place was neat, the place
    was clean —
Not the place to drop a cigarette butt.
The soldier, despite himself,
    was awestruck.
"Ah, this is culture!" he sighed.

If only winter quarters
Were everywhere like this!
Let's look about
And get our bearings now.

An arrow: "Entrance." But
    "Exit"? None.
Clear and obvious:
A warm welcome —
But path of no return.

So be it, then,
Though it be unfamiliar.
Now if only there were somewhere
To get a drink!

His throat was parched
With unexampled heat.
Well, suffer for a bit,
It's not as though it were the
    first time.

The lad saw trains pull up
At the final stop,
Trains from out
The pre-eternal gloom.

Important, poised,
A commandant of the nether world
— A late general —
Came forth to meet the trains.

Not alone: On either side
Stood Military Police, alert.
Not for us to guess why,
Although it was strange:
Whatever one's rank,
Once sent here
There's nothing to run from
Until the terrible judgment.

Stepping forward properly,
Tyorkin then saluted:
So-and-so and thus-and-so,
Reporting to the nether regions.

The general, morose in manner,
Replied in tired accents:
"With which trainload
Did you come?"

Tyorkin stood erect and spoke
Just as straight and stiffly:
"I came myself, on foot,
Comrade General!"

"What do you mean, on foot?"
"Beg pardon, sir."
(Commandants are strict!)
"Confess then, soldier,
That you've lost your unit!"

Whether it be true or not,
There's no use to dispute it.
"All right! It will go into the record.
And it won't happen again.

"Of that, brother, be sure.
Because you don't
Go back
To the other world again."

The general chuckled.
"All right. Register.
There's system here — get that
     straight —
This, brother, is a big job.
Everyone has to be received,
     assigned,
According to his merits.
Who's a coward, who's a hero
Isn't always plain.
Discipline must be
Ironclad:
This isn't the kind of war, brother,
Where you can go off on your own.
Move along, straight ahead —
Right along the platform."
     "Yes, sir!" And Tyorkin
Wheeled smartly.

Hardly had he followed the arrow
Around a turn when,
Between two squat pillars,
He encountered the first checkpoint.
Immediately everything was
     pencilled down:
Name, number, date.
"Present your documents at the
     supply room,"
They told the soldier.

Tyorkin was taken aback.
"Obviously," he said,
"We didn't carry documents
On the field of battle.
And since I've died
They're no concern of mine."

"All of us, brother, are dead.
But regulations are regulations.
That's why we keep the records
Carefully, in numerical order,
So it will be quite clear
That each one died by all the rules.
After all, it's happened:
A wound that isn't mortal,
But the man's sent here —
Then fuss with him separately,

Put him in the detention room — "
(Fleetingly those words
Registered on Tyorkin's mind.)

"You of course are new here,
And so it seems strange.
But just try to register with us
Without the proper papers!"

But Tyorkin had caught on by now
That it didn't really matter:
Papers, shmapers, just you try
To send a person back!

He grew bolder, asked a drink —
Wasn't there a faucet?
Narrowing their eyes,
They looked at him suspiciously.

Smiling crookedly, they said
Into the bargain: "Brother,
When you were in the other world
You should have asked for beer."

All of them were pleased
With the malicious joke.
Tyorkin turned his back.
"Go to the devil," he snorted.

The registration desk behind,
Next an arrow pointing left.
Left he turned and — stop!
Here's the Verification Desk.

Above this desk the vaulting
Seemed a great deal lower,
Here the light was dimmer; all about
Stood shelves, safes, stacks,
Filing cabinets, rotary files,
In back, rows of thick bound books
Like looseleafs filled with papers,
Card files, folders and,
Barrier-enclosed,
The infernal desk,
On it the infernal phone
(Internal line, of course).

Through dead silence came to him,
Like a sigh from beyond the grave:

"Write your auto-bio now,
Briefly and in detail."

Tyorkin started
To protest:
After all, it had been printed,
Must then have been checked before.

"Yes, we know: 'Book About
     a Soldier'."
"What more do you want, then!"
"No beginning — and no end:
Won't do for the files."

"But, since I am dead — "
   "That won't help"
" — isn't the end self-evident?"
"Write the beginning, then."

The soldier tried evading:
"This is all a nuisance.
It's all set forth in rhyme,
The writer's in the Writers'
     Union —"

"That cuts no ice,
It doesn't do. Wait —
Let's check up on
The writer too."

Tyorkin saw trouble
Lurking ahead:
If he didn't write it himself,
They'd make up their own beginning
     for him.

Column by column he wrote in the
     answers, Q. and A.,
Beginning with forebears — Who
     was your grandfather?

"Grandpa planted rye and wheat,
Tilled his plot of land.
Didn't travel overseas,
Had no relatives abroad.
Now and again he drank. Sometimes
     came home
Hatless and roaring, late at night.

Didn't have any reprimands in
     the record,
Except from grandma;
No medals, no awards,
Wasn't a leading worker,
And, for the sake of truth, I add:
Didn't improve his character.
Dodged that duty. And since he
     was nearly 80, didn't mature.
Shirked it."

And so on and so forth. He described
His relatives and loved ones,
All those listed among the quick
And those among the dead.

The Verification Desk cast a glance
At his work:
"Finished? That's the way, brother.
Next! Who's next?

"On second thought, wait." He
     read it over
In case there were blots somewhere.
"Submit photos now
In the required number of copies."

Try to prove to the desk
That you couldn't stock up,
Hadn't been at the rear
A single hour in the whole war.

"I used to carry
A photo from home,
But I had to give it
To a, well, a girl I met."

But the law of the desk was stern.
That deceased voice said:
"That's your personal affair.
The regulations are public."

"Put your finger here,
Press it on the ink pad,
Press it on the paper."
He'd never done that in his life.

Fed up with it all,
He shrugged.

"My finger? Here, take it.
What will they want next?"

Tyorkin emerged into an open space
Beyond the barrier.
One step, a second, and now he faced
The Medical Sanitary Processing
    Desk.

He approached; he couldn't avoid
The predestined reception.
And again, of course,
He hadn't his papers.

When he had hastily stepped forth
He had forgotten
There's no entering eternity
Without a doctor's signature;
That there, too, the doctors
Always check
Soldiers' urine,
Soldiers' blood.

Tyorkin gasped:
"What the hell,
What a way to run things!
You'd think I were trying to get
A medical certificate for a health
    resort cure.
How much red tape there is
Among the doctors!"

Suddenly he was ordered:
"Now breathe deep.
Open your mouth wider.
Did you drink?"
"On the contrary,"
He sighed bitterly.
"I don't understand you people,"
He snorted.

"If I had had a drop or two
When I was wounded,
Maybe I wouldn't have set foot
In your establishment."

But it's the same for a soldier
    everywhere:
Whatever's wrong, it's all his fault.

His fault that in his flask
He hadn't found a drop of moisture.
The sergeant had been too miserly,
Hadn't issued drinks? The
    soldier's fault.
The soldier's fault that the fierce cold
Had tortured him two days.
That a shell fell near —
The soldier's fault,
His fault that in the other world
The dead answer for the living.

But hold your tongue, you're
    just a ghost,
Suffer the procedure:
They put his whole innards
Through the X-ray.

They didn't overlook a thing
And for the sake of science
Filled three fat notebooks
With observations on him.

With rubber mallet, tap, tap, tap
(Although it wasn't painful),
Tapped him here and tapped
    him there.
Dissatisfied with something.

They discussed him. Something
Was wrong: the smell. Why fuss?
The lad smelled of tobacco
And soldier's sweat.

Well, the newly deceased
Barely passed the test,
As though his spirit
Still lingered in his body.

But still the data lacked something;
Maybe the X-ray wasn't clear.
"Prepare for the complete
Procedure."

A bath! He went with joy.
A bath meant —
First and foremost — water.
"No hot water."
"I should have guessed! Just like

Life on earth!
No cold water, either?"
"No. Waterless showers."

"Now that's a new one,"
Protested Tyorkin.
"We have only stump water."
"Let's have stump water, then."

"That's for use if from above
You came in parts. Without, that is,
The full complement of units,"
Explained a voice.
"With stump water then
We'd sprinkle you;
Cement the parts
Precisely,
And there you'd be, as good as new,
Fit for parade.
Get going now. Go on, soldier,
On to the complete procedure."

It's a common saying: When your
        head has been lopped,
You don't mind a small thing like
        having your hair shaved off.
"All right, go ahead, but hurry up.
All I want is to get to a destination."

Since this is the way things went
Through no choice of his own,
Tyorkin sought a corner for rest
In that vale of gloom.

He'd missed sleep on earth,
Now he wanted to lie down
        in warmth,
Even in the clothes he wore —
After all, rest is authorized.

Eternal rest, they say,
And not in jest.
As for him, he didn't care how long,
One night would do.

Ahead into the distance ran
The corridor unending,
Highway of that world it was,
With semaphores, to guide, above.

And visible for half a verst
To keep each man from straying,
Index fingers, arrows,
Pointers and signs.

Sharp light from street lamps,
A dryness in the air
And doors, doors beyond count.
What doors!

All tightly shut, soundproofed
By special device,
They jutted from the walls
Like up-ended caskets.

No matter which you opened
You were met
By a strong, damp, dusty smell
From beyond the grave.

On those who sit behind the doors,
Outwardly like people,
The important look proclaimed:
"Not in. And won't be back."

Tyorkin pondered what to do,
Where to start?
The sign said:
"Executives at Work, Don't Disturb."

What to do? At last
He gathered up his courage.
Zip! — Into an office where a man
Was clipping papers together.

"If you please, I've been assigned
To the eternal reserves here,
And since that's so
I ought to have a billet — "

The man measured Tyorkin
With sleepy gaze and unconcern,
Thumbed past his ear, to indicate
A door
Beyond.
    The soldier went,
Reached for the doorknob,
Heard behind him:
"Oh, the trouble we have
With all this turnover!"

Beyond the door another desk —
Keep right on going to the next,
Said the same gesture
Of thumb past ear.

From one to next
The gestures went,
One after another they passed him on
Without looking up from papers.

At last the answer
Was distinct: "We have no cots,
No bedding.
Only mattress stuffing."

"Stuffing! What good's that?
What am I supposed to do?"
"We're telling you
In plain Russian: No cots in stock.
The sheets are being dried.
We can issue
Wood shavings
    To stuff a pillow."

The words were straight
Out of the old, familiar runaround:
"What do you expect? Do you think
Moscow was built in one day?

"Sign here, sign there,
Let's have your receipt;
The rest of your gear will be
    issued later."
— "Pfui!" Tyorkin spat, but no
    spit came.

It was to laugh — It was to cry!
It would have been easier indeed
To get an apartment — from a city
    housing department —
Than to find rest in the grave.

(And if when alive
I'd heard those words,
That "Moscow" of his,
I'd have shown him what-for.

(For talk like that
I'd have made him go get the
    gear for me,

He'd have learned — but fast! —
How fast Moscow was built.

(Like a true soldier of the Guards,
I'd have made him see stars;
Front and rear —
I'd have taught him which was
    which!)

Tyorkin was on the point of leaving
When he remembered that no doubt
It wouldn't hurt to put an entry
In the complaint book.

But the answer was firm
To this seditious request:
"In this world there are no
    complaints,
Everyone here is contented,

"No reason then to keep a
    complaint book."
This was icy-clear.
"All right. But isn't there a
    newspaper,
Even a wall-newspaper?"

"Why, of course there is. Right
    nearby —
Just around the corner.
Without the press? How could
    we be? —
But you're wasting your time."

Never mind. Tyorkin looked around
The corner; saw the organ of
    that world.
Over the editor's desk
The sign, "Cemetery Gazette."

At the desk sat, if not the editor,
At least the assistant — what dif-
    ference did it make?
"What is your question?" asked he,
Frowning as in pain.

Filled with important cares,
He interrupted Tyorkin:
"It won't do for the paper. Not the
    proper angle

Too trivial a topic."

He twiddled the fountain pen in
     hand.
"Besides, there's no space for it.
On second thought, perhaps it
     could go
In the Unanswered Letters Section."

And plunged his head back into
His sleepless work

Of editing articles: All asweat,
His nose followed the lines, left
     to right;
Now he removed a word, now added,
Crossed out the author's phrase,
Put in his own.
Checkmarks in the margin put,
Himself the *Glav,* himself the *Lit.**
Here he took away the quote-marks,
There he put them back.

It seems that when alive he'd
     warmed a seat
In a newspaper office; prized
     his high position;
And now in the nether world
Fusses just as he used to on earth.

He grew intent and fixed his gaze,
Mouth open, eyes glazed;
Bent forward like a pecking rooster,
Inspected a line through
     a magnifying glass.

Then, the final check applying,
Read the page once more,
Not merely from the top to bottom,
This time from the bottom up.

Faithful to his remembered training,
His brow he wrinkled in doleful
     thought.

If this our tale fell into the hands
     of such
As he, it would be entombed.

With a paternally warm exhortation,
He'd tear it to bits. To ashes
Of the ashes of that world.
"What is *this?*" he'd say.

"What kind of sally or attempt
To resurrect the past,
What revivals of survivals
Or aspersions on our ways?

"Come to think of it, no wonder
That you took this slippery path.
From the collective you're
     separated —
That's the root of it!

"Preening yourself upon your talent,
You were carried away. You wanted
To be proclaimed
A new Dante. But there's a limit.

"Of a certainty you should
Have been hauled before the Bureau,
Called to account
To mend your pen

"So that you
     wouldn't go on wasting
Paper on your own ideas,
Wouldn't write from inspiration,
But submit an outline first

"And without excess pretensions
Then would set to work,
Always keeping in mind the spirit
Of the latest directives,

"Would be guided by that spirit
And wouldn't make any mistakes."

Here, of course, the author
Would object:
"Spirit, yes,
I'm not against the spirit,
I've been versed in the spirit
Since my youth. I'm not lacking
In sense of spirit

----

* *Glav* stands for "Editor in Chief," *lit* for copy editor; together, *Glavlit,* they
mean "Censor."—Trans.

Or of hearing
Or of smell.

"But a question — not an idle one —
Now arises of itself:
There are different kinds of spirits,
Some are living, some are dead.

"For my words I stand in answer,
Not for nothing have I this job:
I can spot a dead spirit
In this world a verst away.

"And isn't your collection
    of dead words
Marked with such a stamp?
Why should I waste time upon
    you? —
There are the living to address!"

Enter now, never fearing,
Across the threshold of the
    opened tale.
Let us follow after my Tyorkin
And see what happens next.

Arcades like GUM's,
    the department store's;
You walk and wander in a daze.
But missing is the noise of people;
Eternal Sunday everywhere.

His bones ached, his feet were weary,
He wanted to find a place to pause.

Splendid balconies
Stretched in endless file,
Offices, a hell of a lot,
But no place for the soldier.

He'd no idea where rest awaited,
Went on in sleepless torment
Like a soldier who'd fallen
'Way behind his column.

Catch up, and there's a load
    off your shoulders,
You'll rest easy then,
But the numbers all about,
    the insignia

And the emblems — they're
    the wrong ones.

So many strange faces,
All at ease among their own,
But the soldier yearned for a glimpse
Of at least one familiar face.

All intent upon their business,
They stared past him unconcerned.
Suddenly — he didn't expect it,
    he couldn't imagine —
He saw a friend. And what a friend!

Two steps ahead and coming
    toward him
His friend, his comrade from
    the front,

A friend he could no longer meet
Among the living. Here, too,
In this other world
It's tough without friends.

And soldier greeted soldier,
The comrade of remembered
    marches,
A man with whom he'd made
    his way,
Fighting the long road east
    from Brest,

With whom he'd parted as a friend
Parts from soldier-friend —
In haste, for lack of a chance
To mark the proper rites.

Don't grieve that you must
    come to anchor
Alone, while I go forward;
Don't be angered, comrade.
(This one was not.)

Perhaps in that moment of
    leave-taking
The living soldier notes
The sadly resigned,
Already far and distant gaze
Stretching forth into eternity

— Notes this in his soul forever
Though their ways already part.

"Comrade, friend, to think we'd meet
In the other world!"

There he stood in weatherbeaten
        uniform
Without epaulets —
The uniform of those days.
And so it's real, and that is that,
Thought Tyorkin: I am where he is,
So this is not a dream.
"Well, brother." Words were
        superfluous.
They greeted one another. Stood.
Tyorkin saw that his old friend
Did not seem overjoyed to meet him.

But why? Had he changed
In this other world?
Or had he risen in rank
Higher than the rank he'd
        held on earth?

"Well then, Tyorkin."
"Well, it's like this:
I can't tell where's the front or rear.
In encirclement, in '41,
There was some way out, at least.

"At least you knew the time of day,
Knew where lay west and
        where lay east,
Had marching rations for the road,
At least had water, at least a drop!

"Slept out the daytime in the woods,
Moved at night. But here?
Let's find a place where we can sit;
My feet are melting in my boots."

They turned off the promenade
Into the depths of courtyards
        'round the corner,
Where empty coffins had been
        stacked
To be chopped up for wood.

Then sat down as for a smoke break,

Not as if they were pitching camp.
"Now report the situation,
As the general used to say.

"Where's the line of the positions? —
I wish I had a map with me.
For instance, tell me in what
        boundaries
Lies this other world we're in."

"To be a general you're not ready:
If you were, you'd first inquire
Which other world. For here as well,
Believe it or not, there are two."

Tyorkin, forgetting the swollen feet
Straining his boots, softly asked:
"What? No kidding?"
The other barely shrugged.

"You couldn't be expected to know:
There's this world where we are
And then there's the other,
The bourgeois one, of course.

"Each has its walls
Beneath a common ceiling:
Two such worlds, two systems,
And the border under lock and key.

"Separate rules for us and them
And, as you'd expect,
Everything different — ways
        and customs."
"Isn't that all immaterial down here?"

"No, brother: Everything of that sort
Is as in life — on our side
        and on theirs."

"But wait: Even in the stillness
        beyond the grave
Do labor and capital exist
And the struggle too, and all
        the rest?"

"No, why? What need of labor
If eternal rest's
The rule on both sides?"

"Then it's like sunbathing
On guard duty — for us and
       them alike?"

"Yes. And of course capital
Doesn't play its former role.

"It hasn't any loopholes
       to get through.
Eternity rolls on eternally.
There's no money, not a kopek.
Capital exists only on paper.

"And as for how things stand,
We're on the upgrade,
       they're in retreat
And there are checkups
       and pep-talks
From time to time — naturally.

"That's the story. Now you know
What's with us and what's
       with them."

Tyorkin plunged into sadness.
"Very, very interesting.

"As for those who came
       at other times
I cannot say, but as for me,
If the choice were mine
I'd have stayed in the war.

"What concerns you in the war?
You seek its fastest end.
What are glory or recognition
To a soldier — without victory?

"Nothing's better for the living
Than to fight for victory,
You pursue her trail
As a thirsty man seeks water.

"One doesn't think of the hour
       of death —
That isn't the important thing.
Death is always there, awaiting;
Life is always short.

"Isn't it so, friend?"

"Be silent, soldier:
The time of life is past."
"But, admit it,
We weren't lucky.

"It's not like me to be lying flat here,
But my ticket is already turned in. —
Well, to hell with that foreign world.
Tell me about ours here."

"That's a big subject.
Here's the chief thing to remember:
In this place beyond the grave,
       our world
Is the best and most advanced.

"And since it has been provided
For all of us thus and so,
It rests on a scientific foundation,
Not on the backs of three big whales.

"Where do you see flames
       or smoke or steam
And the likes of such nonsense?"
"Still, you know, they keep
       the heat up,"
Spoke up Tyorkin, "I can't bear it."

"They're not stoking, don't complain.
It just seems so, just at times,
To those who came here
In winter clothing.

"It's not cold and it's not hot here —
Not a scrap of firewood, see?
In the same way, you won't even find
A street sign saying 'Elysian Fields.'

"It's nothing like the old fables —
Where do you see bowers
       and gardens?"
"But couldn't we find a drop
       somewhere
Of natural water to drink?"

"You forget where you are, Tyorkin.
You'll get off on the wrong foot.
There's no water because
Obviously there's no demand.

"Not far off is that neighboring land.
They run it in the old way —
All those empty fancies
Of fresh-flowing streams
        and fiendish steam.

"Please remember, I repeat:
Our world here is scientific.
We've neither Hades nor Heaven,
We've science here; they've
        superstition.

"Their foundation's shaky,
Ours is solid.
We have shortcomings, of course —
But on the other hand we've system.

"In the first place, the discipline there
Is weak compared with ours.
The picture is:
Over here — a marching column,
        over there — a crowd.

"Our world here is organized
With full precision in everything:
Planned by zones
And divided by departments.

"Perfectly it's organized —
You can go from one end to
        the other.
Look at the military department.
(Of course, it's a model.)

"I'm not in the habit of lying,
And if I've told you false
You'll see for yourself.
Let's go, 'general'."

And in serried supine ranks
Before them arose a solid bank
        of faces —
The Department that is marked
By the Army star.

Calm faces of the soldiers
As though seeing in eternal sleep
That, whatever wars had ever been,
Their war dwarfed them all.

The echoes of their battle front have
        died away,
In the silence of their graves
        they dream
That it was the last
Battle on earth,

That other generations
Of all the future years
Will not be called up to replenish
Their ranks of black-wreathed glory.

"Exact is the dress and distance,
The interval impeccable —
Now take the Civilian Department,
It doesn't form up nearly so smartly.

"A certain slovenliness, not
        to be concealed —
The different ranks and different
        heights mixed up:
Those sent here with orchestra dirges
Mingle with those sent without;
Some sent on a trade union pass,
Others with the cross and candle;
They don't measure up
In drill."

Tyorkin's mind seemed to wander.
Back before the war
He'd had his fill of museum tours
In the tow of a sergeant.

He'd seen wooden plows
        and spinning wheels,
Helmets, bones, an ancient cat o' nine
        tails —
He'd regretted spending Sunday at it.
But here it was a different matter:

Here indeed a rare opportunity
To gaze on everything himself,
Sorry only that there'd be nobody
To whom to report what he learned
        from this reconnaissance.

So the soldier, curious,
Marveling or frowning,
Observed at first hand

The system and the customs.

Here was neither rest
Nor fun, thought Tyorkin.
The ghosts split up by fours
And played dominoes,

This was their one diversion:
Once seated 'round a table
No need there was to talk,
No need to think at all.

With boredom did they dispel
    boredom —
But that's the way it was here:
No matter how they slapped
    the dominoes down,
No sound came;
No matter how they smoked,
    there was no smoke.

O my friends and brothers
Still among the living,
Don't waste precious hours
On that sepulchral game.

Pass up this "entertainment"
In favor of life so fleeting;
There's plenty of time for dominoes
Provided in eternity.

He passed the domino tables,
Next found — also nothing good —
A Bureau of the underworld
Meeting in full session.

Those who'd gathered here, no doubt,
Were persons unable to overcome
The special taste for meetings
That had corroded them when living.

For them neither rest nor food:
No sooner were they seated in rows
Than earth and sky meant nothing —
Just give them a ceiling and walls.

In fair weather or in foul,
They met for hour after hour.
Completely suited to their ardor
Was the eternity at their disposal.

With the majesty of real life
They bent over papers,
Evidently taking up the case
Of an individual at fault — what
    pleasure.

Here were neither jokes nor smiles;
The prevailing tone — solemnity.
A deceased one was confessing errors
(And, of course, he lied).

He lied not simply for the fun of it.
He knew just how far to go,
    and stretched
The facts just so. Listening,
    you might have thought
He deserved at least a medal.

But wait, wait, my fine fellow.
Since matters have taken this turn,
Let's take a deeper look at you,
Look you through and through.

If they can't set your brains aright,
They'll put you through
    the wringer still
And finally issue a reprimand
By all the rules of the game.

Stop — wait! Here's a personage
Of unusual importance,
Telephoning to himself
And answering in another voice.

In the presence of an imaginary
    secretary
He dripped all the more flattery
Because his immediate superior
Was himself.

Reveling in the adulation,
Suddenly he changed his tone,
Addressed himself, the subordinate,
In courteous admonition.

Here was authority beyond compare,
Addressed to a lower being, a cipher.
This favorite of games
Turned him mushy as a drunk.

Their backs to this idiot,
Certain members with proud
And earnest faces gathered
To discuss the draft of a novel.

These members knew all about
What a novel should contain
And how much space is foreordained
To be given to what.

Setting forth the proper outline,
They passed approval on each
          volume,
Instead of having a drink and a snack
Right off and dispersing to their
          homes.

Next — in fierce defence of thesis
A Candidate or Doctor
Of Otherworldly Science
Drew a magic circle,

In prearranged order
Reached for his books,
Slips of paper marking
The quotations all ready,

Interwove them from the books
Into one long thread,
Dangled a thousand dead pages
Down from it.

Scene followed scene
As the friends wended their way.
A man up to his chest in a box
Mumbled on about something.

His eyes were buried in his text.
He didn't raise them from the paper.
On him hung the sign "Fiery Orator,"
Out his mouth stuck a washcloth.

In transitory life my hero
Had disliked such speeches.
Be thou civilian or military,
Give the floor to someone livelier.

The speaker doesn't admit this
          principle,
Insists on holding forth, himself.

But if something turns out wrong
Then — well, someone wrote it for
          him.

Anyway, in that realm of oblivion
This has its own special logic:
These lengthy recitations
Reinforce eternal sleep.

Eternal sleep. The law of nature.
Seeing all this roundabout,
Tyorkin suddenly asked
His guide:

"What kind of work do they do here,
What does our underworld do?
One way or another, someone
Must do some work." "Not at all.

"That's the whole thing,
That's our special way of being:
That everyone here,
From small to great, administers."

"What do you mean — no
          production?"
Objected the newcomer,
"Only administration?"
"No, not only. Also record-keeping.

"The gist of it, dear brother,
Obscure though it be to simpletons,
Is that here there are no sowing
          and reaping,
No factories, no lathes.
All that would be a hindrance —
Coal, steel, grain and herds."

"Ah, so that's it! Then
It's all right,

"It's like the ambulance,
Rushing down the street —
Creates its own accident,
          its own patient,
Then itself provides first aid."

"Soldier, better keep
Those jokes to yourself."
"Jokes? It's no joke

To spend days in this world
Without even arriving at my
        resting place.

"I need so much to sleep,
Not bothering anyone, to sleep
Without bombings — and in warmth.
I missed a lot of sleep on earth."

"You're a strange one. It's so hard
To explain this simple law:
One way or another, you're already
Enjoying endless sleep.

"What do you care for the body's
        habit?
Why do you need bed or cot?"
"Well, why do they need
        Departments
And a whole corps of executives
And all that other red tape here?"

His friend looked upon him dourly,
Bent his head:
"No other way."
"Why?"
"*Nomenklatura.*" *
And the friends fell silent.

Tyorkin was taken aback, stunned,
As though he had heard a nasty word.

Still, he went on,
Developing the theme:
"But what if they tried
To reduce this System?
Lop off a bit
Without any loss?"

"Impossible, friend.
They tried. No luck!

"They're our cadres, don't forget,
Even though they're shades.
The cadres are employed
Not just in the one System.

"It's not a simple matter

When you look into it:
Some are in the System,
Some are in the Network.
(A big Network, too.)

"Then, besides the Network,
Boundless as it is,
There are those in Organs —
        count them!"
"In Organs — yes, I see."

"Then there are all the Desks,
Endless lists of them.
There's the Committee on Affairs
Of the Eternal Reorganization.

"Now just think, soldier,
Try to add it up.
To reduce this staff
You'd need a separate staff.

"It's impossible to tell
Where too few and where too many,
In short, to reduce
You have to increase."

Tyorkin cautiously took his friend
By the elbow.
"But what boredom —
Terrible!
No cares, no work,
Just boredom beyond endurance.
At night — yes. But during the day?"
"Here there's neither day nor night.

"Forget, of course,
Winter and summer."
"Seems as though you and I
Are on another planet!"

"No, brother. You see, this world,
This world of Lethe,
Is beyond the planets
And the universe itself.

"It has another location.
Clear?"
        "Clear enough.

* The lists of executive jobs and of persons qualified and approved for appointment to them—Trans.

It was different under the moon,
In the reserve regiment.

"There, even when we were
        on thin rations
And were being pressed hard,
As long as the war went on
There was a chance of a way out."

"You'll get used to it, young fellow,
It will all be bearable:
After all, you get salary, rations
And smokeless tobacco."

Tyorkin listened in surprise —
Did this mean they'd feed him?
"About this after-life ration —
What do they issue? What
        do they give?"

"A special ration. I'll explain:
It's listed on the menu,
Doesn't exist in fact."

"Oh, I see." The soldier showed
He was still perplexed.
"Well, to be more explicit,
The pay and ration are imaginary.
They record them for you and me
On paper in the records."
"Oh, then it's like the
        workday payment
On a collective farm!"
"Sort of."

All in proper form: Sign the receipt,
And that's that.
"Well, brother, that's no way to live."
"Still thinking about life!
It's strange to hear:
In the world beyond the grave
There should be no life — as
Two and two make four."
And the soldier cast a glance,
Looked at Tyorkin quite askance.

Thus, close or far,
They saw a new block of buildings.
Who was there in the grip of repose,

Confronting eternity?
"Are you curious?"
"Of course. I'm
Exploring another world."
"That's our Special Department.
So — better by-pass it."

"It would be interesting to have
        a look."
"Impossible. It is
Subordinate to neither civilian
Nor military authorities here."

"I guess Special is Special,"
And, sighing, both fell silent.

There — row on row, according
        to years,
Kolyma, Magadan,
Vorkuta and Narym
Marched in invisible columns.

The region of eternal frost
Wrote men off into eternity,
Moved them from the category
        of "living"
To that of "dead" (little difference
        between them) —

Behind that barbed wire,
White and grizzled —
With that Special Article of the
        law code
Clipped to their case files.

Who and what for and by whose
        will —
Figure it out, History.
No bands played, no speeches;
Utter silence here.

Notch it, though it bitter be,
Forever in the memory!
  .   .   .   .

"Who, beyond the grave here,
Directs the Special Department?"

"He who sent both you and me
To this combinat, he

With whose name, soldier,
You died on field of battle.

"You don't remember? The press
Will tell our grandsons
What you were supposed to have
    cried
As you rose up, grenade in hand.
    Now do you know?"

"Without help from the press,
You and I know full well
That, in battle, words are excess;
It wouldn't be battle otherwise.

"We know without the help of print
That in battle the words we use,
The ones that come in handy,
Are mostly the unprintable."

Thus the friends walked on together.
Even under this arched
And gloomy ceiling
There was room for all their thoughts.

Tyorkin grew exceeding sad.
"It never occurred to me
That your Special Department
Was under the Supreme One
    himself."

"Everything is under him, of course;
There is no higher power."
"Yes, but isn't he alive?"
"Alive too. Partly.

"To the living he's the father,
He's the law and he's the banner.
But he's with us as a dead one,
He's among you — and he's
    among us.

"Master of all destinies,
At the same time
While still alive he's been
    building himself
A burial vault in the Kremlin.

"It never occurred to you also
That he rules the living
But has long been erecting
Monuments to himself."

Tyorkin wiped his brow with his
    cap —
Indeed the furnace heat was strong —
But those words sent a shiver
Down his spine.

His mind dwelt upon
How he'd answer for it
That he'd listened to such words
Even in the other world.

And as for us, for the time being
We shall hold our tongue
    about what was,
About the past, so as not to be
Retroactively courageous.

Too sharply etched in memory are
The traits of that unlimited rule.

"Tyorkin, did you know
You've been awarded
    a medal posthumously?

"You came here from the front line,
The medal followed after you.

"Assigned, as you were, to us forever,
Probably you didn't know
What good care is taken here
Of the dead.

"As soon as the report arrived —
    there's system
Here — the medal's ready.
    No delay."

"Yet the award would have been
    better
If I didn't have to get it
    in the other world.

"Better if I'd received it there,
In other days for which I pine.
I would have been happy to go
All the way to Moscow for it.

"So be it. But it would not
   have mattered
How long the road, through snow
Or sand or swamp; I'd have marched
The whole way with full pack.

"How different it would be — to use
The chance to visit Moscow,
To have a holiday among living
   people —
To be, moreover, alive oneself.

"It would be no hardship to wait
A year or even ten years long —
Alive — and let them give me then
A medal of but half the status
   of this one,

"Or even if they said: It's too soon
   for honors,
Your merit remains to be seen.
I wouldn't fuss. That's the way
I am. You know me.

"I do not thirst for honors,
Though pride I do not lack."
"You're carried away with emotion.
All right. But it's been decided
   without you.
However it be, it's still flattering
To wear it on your breast."

"But first I want to get some rest,
Take a nap somewhere."

"How impatient you are!"
"But just think how long I've been
   waiting:
There, at the front, the offensive —
Here the lack of beds."

"Never mind, don't worry,
I'll arrange it. I have pull
With high officials
Here beyond the grave.

"We'll solve the difficulty
   somehow. —
What are you laughing at?"

"Nothing. It seems
That in the nether world too
It makes a difference whom you
   know!"

His former friend shrugged, as if
   to say:
"We have to fight this evil, of course.
You really ought
To look
Through our stereotube."

"What strange marvel is this
That you offer me as consolation?"

"It's only for members of the
   afterworld *aktiv*.
By special permission.

"In the glass before you
You see the whole neighboring world
— Not at all a front line,
Not the smoke of shells exploding,

"But in the precise form of a picture
A direct answer to the question
How degenerate
Their world has become.

"As precisely as in a museum —
What is what and how much it costs.
And such ma'm'selles, brother!
I mean, simply naked."

Tyorkin listened coldbloodedly,
Didn't even raise an eyebrow.
"Yes. But the females are probably
   also intangible,
Fictional as our pay?"

Again his friend, walking with him,
Had a troubled look of concern.

"Unreal? Why, yes.
No one would dispute it.
But let me also
Make an observation.

"More than once I've thought this,
But kept silent, I confess —

Just between us, aren't you
Only fictionally dead?

"No matter what we talk about,
I note you yearn for it:
As if alive, you want a drink,
A nap, or this or that —"

"A smoke!" Tyorkin reached
For his tobacco pouch. Empty, alas!
Not a grain of *makhorka*
Had he carried into the nether
    regions.

Out of the corners of his pockets,
Out of the lining too
He dug the last flakes,
Mixed with bread crumbs and lint.

Drew a deep puff — as though
    alive —
Of that earthly, front-line,
Dependable, inevitable smoke,
The only kind in wartime,
In the hour of thunder or silence —
Like the old and shrewish wife,
Dearer to you than any other,
Though others be pretty,
    others younger
(The others are the more harmful
    kind,
Like the insidious cigarette).

The friends treated each other
To their respective smokes.
They each tried both,
The smokeless and the real.

Tyorkin was strict of taste.
Drew one, two puffs, returned
    the rest
With a wave of the hand:
"Might as well be grass.
Try some of ours."
The friend choked:
"I'm unused to it."
Evidently, in truth, what suits the
    living
Isn't easy for the dead.

"Indeed, though I've checked out
    above
And I am here in my sepulchral sleep,
Hunger and thirst
Give me no peace.

"Such a pity that I left unfinished
A full glass in one place or another.
And the food I might have eaten —
How much I left behind!

"There was the time, in a trench
Across the Ugra River,
    when they shouted:
'To arms!' and I left half a can
    of meat.
I still remember it with longing.

"And there was the pork pie
At the housewife's in Belorussia.

True, other matters
Kept me busy. More exactly,
It was my own fault:
So as not to lose time
I didn't eat the half
Of what I could have licked right
    to the crumbs
To sustain me on the way,
No matter how steep the road;
Yet I knew the good old saying,
'You won't get this in the other
    world.' "

Here his friend, in grave alarm,
Interrupted:
"Just a moment!"

They heard a distant noise.
The walls shook
And the lights flickered;
The howl of sirens grew.

The siren's whine rolled
Through the thick silence,

Then quickly ceased.
"What's that?"

"So it's happened! Let me tell you,

But keep it strictly secret.
This means that an alert's
    been sounded.

"The Verification Desk
Has signaled all detectives:
There's danger that a living man
Has sneaked through from above.

"To prevent trouble —
Urgent orders:
Catch him and place him
In the detention room,

"Lock him under double lock,
Incommunicado,
Make sure that he'll be
Completely dead." "I see."

"Out of friendship, Tyorkin,
You understand,
I do not want
To harm you.

"Friendship is friendship of course,
But it is my duty to report
To the proper authorities" —
"I see" — "that you want to live.

"The slightest thing, and I'd be tried,
Removed immediately."
"So. You're afraid they'll send you
Beyond purgatory?"

"You keep joking, brother,
As you always used to.
There's no front line here,
But there are penal battalions.
The Agencies are well maintained!

"In short, I'll have trouble
    because of you.
Besides, what in hell
Are you wandering around here for
Like a plague, bothering the dead?

"It's not as though you wanted
    to spend
Eternity with us in close
    comradeship;

You keep wanting to live."
"A matter of habit, brother."

"Get rid of old habits.
Try a fresh experience.
Would you say that life on earth
Is heaven?" "Far from it."

"There you are!"
"But — "
"How stubborn you are.
Won't you consider
The detention room?"

"I don't want to."
"Forget wanting.
It won't do you any good, anyway:
You'll still have to retrace
The whole route here
Some day."

"But meantime I would be in action,
On the march or in the fight.

"The time will come, and somewhere
I'll lie under grass.
But, friend of old, forgive the living
Their life.

"A single day of life,
At the rear or at the front,
If it isn't wasted, is dearer to me
Than any or all eternity.

"And, besides, I can confess,
I'm hastening home because
My author has become absorbed
In a new and pressing task.

"He wants my words in full report
To describe the afterworld
All truthfully. And if he gets fanciful
To heighten the effect,
No harm done. On the contrary.

"Truth lives intact
Side by side with good fantasy.
Cannon ride to battle backwards:
Accurately said.

"So brother, I've had enough
Until some future date."
"I see you're terribly smart!"
"Can you say I'm not wise?

"I've no need for false modesty:
Soviet rule taught me wisdom
From my early years.
Where would you be without brains?

"From time to time it tested
How I'd learned my lessons,
Didn't like to wait
If I didn't catch on quickly,

"Encouraged the capacity
To see without eyeglasses.
Nowadays there's no shortage
    of smart people,
You have to look for fools."

"Why look for them? We've plenty.
An abundance.
And what utter fools —
In the System, in the Network —"

"Approximately what do you do
With such an abundance?"
"We're conducting a planned
    program
Here with fools,

"Studying them thoroughly,
Their nature, ways and habits.
We've a special Administration
To direct the task.

"It's busily engaged in shifting
Fools from job to job.
Sending them to lower posts,
Discovering them locally,

"Moving these to here and
    those to there
— A solid program's all lined up."
"And what are the results?"
"Naturally, there are all kinds
    of people.

"Some you ask to move aside

But they won't retire.
These we generally make censors —
With a raise in pay.

"From that job
There's nowhere further
    to move them. —
But what have you decided,
    Tyorkin?"
"Just as I said — I want to live."

"You're only making it hard.
You've seen the trains
Coming here
In a one-way flow?

"All coming here. And you returning.
Just think — by what means? how?"
"The trains come this way;
    I understand.
Do they go back empty?"

"There are no tickets, they take
    no passengers
Surfacing from here."
"They have brake rods,
Platforms, buffers.

"Has your memory failed,
Have you forgotten
How we used to ride into attack
On the rolling armor?"

"It's hard to pass the border, Tyorkin,
The way here is much easier."
"Without an effort, as they say,
You can't reel in a fish.

"To go to the living from the realm
    of the dead
— Riding on the brake rods
Would be traveling in comfort.
Too bad you can't join me,
Drop all this nonsense
And come home to our regiment."

"Yes, but up there I might not
Get in the *nomenklatura*.

"In the afterworld I hold
A very important post now.
Up there what would I be?
All my tenure and rank
Would go up in smoke."

They'd been together just
        a few hours;
They were to be separated
        for all time.
Suddenly out of the tunnel
Came an empty train.

In a flash the roar and clatter
Drowned out everything.
How the handrail wrenched
Out of the living soldier's hands!

How a dead grasp clutched him
With all the force of the grave!
But Tyorkin pulled himself
From the handrail to the
        braking platform.

By a fraction he overcame
The weight dragging at his coat,
Then, lively and happy, flew
Through the tunnel.

The commandant of the other world,
Bustling about his guard duties,
Did not see the passenger
On the braking platform.

Little did he realize!
Empty after empty passed
And Tyorkin quietly waved
Good-bye to him.

I daresay that I know best
What is good for whom;
I'm glad the underworld
Didn't suit our Tyorkin.

Heading directly toward his goal,
Straight up to the wide, wide world,
Upward, upward went the tunnels,
Higher, higher — Ah, but no!

He barely shut his tired eyes

And in a flash there was no more
Brake platform, train —
He was back on his own two feet.

That's what it means to ride sans
        ticket,
The consequences are unhappy.
The road to the upper world
Still stretched a long, long way ahead.

In the dark he flailed his arms
To find the walls by feel
And everything whirled 'round
        and 'round
With pain that makes one cry
        in sleep.

Toiling his way incredibly
Through pitch-black dark,
His mind saw all the terrible winters
And blistering days of the war,

Remembered the steaming rubble
        of ruins
That bombs had piled upon his chest,
The tracers streaking through the sky,
Blotting out the Milky Way.

Waves and billows of wreckage,
Bricks and stones and beams
        heaved up
As the dry and slippery sand
        slipped out
From beneath his helpless feet.

The cold stabbed at his naked flesh
Like an icy knife.
A swallow of water seemed
        more precious
Perhaps than life itself.

Tyorkin was beyond the fringe
Of consciousness that glimmered
On its way — A single
Breath fluttered in his chest.

There was no relief from the pain,
Just heavy, dark agony,
A torment unceasing
That cried for surcease.

The force of life — most faithful
Intercessor and protector —
Perishable life, with her slim
Golden stock of days —
Tugged, tugged the soldier on.

Death grappled for him fiercely
In a shifting battle.
Then came the hour, after long
    days —
The moment came
When he dragged himself to the
    barrier,

To the border. The frontier post!
A pole across the road.
Breathing came easier,
Death herself was tired now
And retreated by one step.

Almost home now — only
To swing his legs across the line.
But the soldier was unable
Without help. Here, at the end
    of the road,
The soldier fell.
Finis, Tyorkin: Die.

How regrettable,
How uncalculated,
When you've nearly escaped
    from death
And all you need
Would be a drop of help.

That's how it is
In the ordinary hurly-burly here:
You do everything you personally
    can,
You just about win out — then
    you're exhausted.

'Tisn't easy to accept
That it will all go for nought —
Years of pain and hope and work.
If God there were, you'd pray to him,
But since there isn't, what then?

What then, in that grim

Dark hour of trial?
A human — not a sepulchral
    bureaucrat —
A human being just like you —
That's whom you need to rescue you.

Death advanced on stealthy feet.
Don't plead with her — she's miserly
    and old.

In this shaky minute now
It's time to turn from fable to fact.

In this world of the living, where now
We carry on our work —

"A rare case in the annals of
    medicine,"
Tyorkin heard through his dream.

His eyes opened in a warm room.
He lay under a sheet, not white snow;

And before him there stood
    in doctor's tunic
Not a ghost — a man.
Although he could breathe easy now,
He couldn't take a deep breath yet.
He sensed he was alive! He had
    dragged
Body and soul up the long road
Out of fever, out of the parched
    darkness. Now
It was as if he had drunk a whole
    kettleful
Of that living, natural, dear
Cold water.

They gave him New Year's greetings.
"So it's the New Year now!"
And outside the walls
The war was going right on
In its usual course.

It's easy to rest in warmth.
Now I'll nap, he said.

Out loud the doctors marveled:
"Some man, Tyorkin! Who could
    have thought it?

"Returned from the other world,
Came back to the sunshine.
It's a sign for sure
He'll live to be 100!"

.   .   .   .

"Put a period here?"
"Your Tyorkin
Got out of that one cleverly,
Out from under the grave."
"A daredevil wind-up."

"No, not a period — a semicolon."

"What do you mean by taking
        Tyorkin to the other world?"
"This was mischief and abuse:
The author sent his hero
Out of the living and breathing
        into the Nothing,
Into the world beyond the grave."

"The question is: Why didn't
        the author
Send him to a construction project
        instead?"
"Or a collective farm?"
"Or state farm?"
"Why not to a motor in the shop?"
"Or blast furnace?"
"Or mine?"
"Or even, say, an office?

He's fit for any job."

"A fine young fellow like that
Shouldn't be in an office. No sense
        in that."
"Then in an ensemble of Georgian
        song and dance.
He'd do well there, too."

"The author missed his chance.
He should have turned the lad
Into a leading cosmonaut."
"He'd be a bit old for a man in
        space."

"But he'd do in courage
And brains."
"For what — a cosmonaut?"
"No, for manager of a store."
"Not that. They'd make a mistake
And put him in jail."

"Tyorkin could go over big
In the Soft Drinks Trust."
"He should be building housing."
"Have you thought of making him
        a policeman in the militia?"
"Or fireman? — Tyorkin should be
        a fireman-hero."

O reader, in this respect
You've forgotten one thing:
You can't count all the roles
That Tyorkin could fit.

The argument as to what our hero
        should be
With so many qualities as he
Possesses — it began long ago
Among our different kinds of troops.

In one way or another,
In his life as a soldier
Tyorkin was close
To the mighty god of war,
        the artillery.
But he also rode along
With the armor of the tanks
— Everywhere he had his friends,
Though in a strict sense
He always favored
The infantry.

Hence, as soldiers saw him,
For his various qualities
Tyorkin was recognized to belong
To all the forces.

And it would be quite irregular
If I were suddenly to enroll him
In one service
Or one job.

I no longer have control of him:

Where he chooses,
There he goes.
It's his right.

And it really doesn't matter
In what post he may be now —
In a ministry
Or co-op —
Storming heights.

Where there's life, he's free,
    untrammeled;
Where there's joy, he's happy too;
Where there's pain, he shares
    the sadness;
Where the battles, he's a soldier,

Though the batteries are different
And new calibers are used
And everything has changed.

The author may grow older;
May his hero never age!

I didn't choose this theme
For my fable just because
I want to do it my way
And reject advice of others.

I pursued my own offensive,
One thought alone possessed me:
If I coped with this one,
I could cope with any.

And in hopes
That I succeeded,
I conclude with the refrain
That began this tale.

I humbly asked you
To read it first.
Now I abdicate my rights;
The judgment's yours.

Don't make a secret of it.
Speak out and to the point.
We're together in this world,
"Eat bread and salt,
    and speak the truth."

Now I've put the task before you,
I'm prepared for any judgment.
"Cannon ride to battle backwards"
Has a meaning of its own.

1954–1963.
                    (*Izvestia,* August 18, 1963)

15

CONTROVERSY OVER SOLZHENITSYN

Because Alexander Solzhenitsyn's first published work, One Day in the Life of Ivan Denisovich, *was known to have the sanction of Khrushchev, it at first evoked little public debate. By Autumn 1963, however, Solzhenitsyn had published three additional stories. These stories, and especially the last, "For the Good of the Cause," provoked an angry discussion which grew more heated still when it became known Solzhenitsyn might be awarded the Lenin Prize for literature. On April 22, 1964, when the list of winners was announced, Solzhenitsyn's name was not among them. He was denied an award which apparently would have meant too much encouragement for the forces of de-Stalinization.*

"SAINTS" AND "DEVILS." By V. Chalmayev.

In the world of A. Solzhenitsyn's characters two ideological and moral poles and two sets of characters corresponding to these poles stand out quite distinctly. In one of them the writer invariably concentrates humility and meekness, righteousness that as a rule is impotent in practice, and in the other he concentrates all-powerful evil, overbearing cruelty, and blind obedience.

In the story *One Day in the Life of Ivan Denisovich* this abstract, non-social, timeless differentiation of the "living stream" was suppressed and some-how disaffirmed by the real picture, by the appearance of characters who lived by a completely different truth and faith (Buinovsky, the old prisoner) and did not gravitate toward either of the imaginary poles. True, they were obviously at the periphery of the author's attention in comparison with Ivan Denisovich and the group of guards, such as Volkov, but their very presence inspired the hope that the author would look closely at them and would discard the contrived scheme to arrive at a living, heroic contemporary. This hope was reinforced by the fact that in Ivan Denisovich himself the abstractly righteous, "Karatayev" qualities were hidden by a vitally active, inspired attitude toward labor. This was the hope-instilling kernel of his character. A new protagonist might mature, living more by civic interests and preaching the lofty ideals of our society.

However, "Matryona's House" convinced us that A. Solzhenitsyn's protagonist is indeed "maturing," but, unfortunately, not in that direction. The rigid confines of the abstract concept have made themselves felt here quite tangibly. The setting in which Matryona passes her life has become completely dismal, but she herself shines the more brightly, shines with a kind of un-earthly, supernatural light. It was labor that exalted Ivan Denisovich. But Matryona is "great," according to A. Solzhenitsyn, for no other reason than her suffering. And this "greatness" is not so much à la A. Solzhenitsyn as à la — F. M. Dostoyevsky! The latter, after all, expressing one of the reactionary sides of his world view, wrote in *A Writer's Diary* in 1873: ". . . the chief thing, the most fundamental spiritual need of the Russian people, is the need for suffering, constant and inconsolable, everywhere and in everything. It seems they have been affected from time immemorial by this thirst for suffering. A stream of suffering courses through their entire history, not be-cause of external misfortunes and calamities alone but welling up from the very heart of the people."

Yes, the "stream of suffering" unfortunately colors A. Solzhenitsyn's artistic perception of the world. He had an opportunity, both at the front and in other situations, to observe how people present a full array of completely different qualities, directly opposed to the sufferer's submissiveness! Why does he artificially archaize his views on the people's character, present this character biasedly and one-sidedly? What result does this archaizing yield in his writings?

In his new story "For the Good of the Cause," published in *Novy mir*, No. 7, A. Solzhenitsyn is completely at the mercy of his own game of abstract concepts. It is as though real life were knocking from outside on its tightly closed shutters.

On the eve of the school year a new building in a province center is taken away from the students of an electronics technicum for the needs of a defense research institute. The bitterness of the wrong is intensified not only because the students must remain cooped up in the old premises, but even more because all the ardent, joyful labor of the summer, when the students voluntarily worked at the construction site, has gone for nought. In this occurrence (as in "An Incident at Krechetovka Station") A. Solzhenitsyn has caught a hint of the collision between the "human" and the "automatic" principles of life.

The incident in itself is isolated from all the rest of the life of our country and is, moreover, placed in opposition to it as the sole truth. It is as though the author did not know that the state is building scores of schools and institutes every year, yet this is far weightier than the ardent altruism that he passes off as the sole "condition" for achieving happiness.

Who are the "righteous" in A. Solzhenitsyn's new story and who are the "devils"? We shall state explicitly once again that the straightforward division of characters into positive and negative, while it sometimes leads to didacticism, is in itself frequently legitimate. And we shall say that even such a writer as M. Stelmakh, who is extremely remote from A. Solzhenitsyn, also divides life into "truth" and "falsehood," into good and evil. But his alignment of forces has real content, expresses the interrelations of the struggling characters, the dynamics of social movement. Such an alignment does not impoverish or emasculate the content of the images but, on the contrary, permits them to be disclosed in all the wealth of their qualities, which express not the subjective antagonistic principles of imaginary life but the actual struggle of ideologies.

For the sake of subjective conceptions of life, A. Solzhenitsyn has sharply deformed the real traits of his character. Let us recall the chief spokesman for the students, Fyodor Mikheyich, the director of the technicum, and his trembling right hand, which — as if to underline this character's utter helplessness — he clasps in the fingers of his left hand in a braceletlike grasp. You think involuntarily: Where did he come from, how was such a character formed?

True, A. Solzhenitsyn does inform us that this man had been a soldier, that he had performed his duties honorably and been wounded, but he tells us this in an aside, casually. In the character of Fyodor Mikheyich there is nothing of the spiritual experience of the soldier, of his military past. The author does not focus on this man's extremely important life history. However, he does find the opportunity to call our attention to everything that is "trembling," "pushed around," and "humiliated" in his character: "Fyodor Mikheyich dipped the pen, grabbed his right hand in a bracelet formed by the fingers of his left, and lifted it to sign his name, but even his coupled hands danced. He tried to sign the paper. The pen began to write something indecipherable, then got stuck in the paper and spattered. Fyodor Mikheyich raised his eyes to the bookkeeper and smiled. The bookkeeper bit her lip, took the checkbook, and hastily left."

We also observe the omission of everything "unnecessary," everything that might not "harmonize" with the character's meekness, in the image of Grachikov, the secretary of the city Party committee, in whom just enough enthusiasm and courage are left to stand up to Knorozov for a little while before he folds his wings. Yet Grachikov had been a front-line soldier and the chief of a factory collective in the past. Apparently, as in the poem of a *Novy mir* contributor, he had been an "imaginary" soldier and Party organizer.

The bookkeeper with the held-back tears, as if the alter ego of the author, looks at all these half-naive, half-comic, martyrlike attempts by Fyodor Mikheyich and Grachikov to defend a just cause. And these tears saturate the entire atmosphere of the wanderings of the "humble" heroes in the sphere of the top executives, who seemingly have been frozen into position "with fangs bared."

In portraying Knorozov, the secretary of the province Party committee, and Khabalygin, the plant director, A. Solzhenitsyn reveals his complete inability to interpret modern, living material. Sometimes it appears that he must have got his information about people occupying important, responsible posts from philistine gossips. The writer draws only the outward, threatening and fearsome appearance of the province committee secretary and the plant director, and reduces the whole sense of their activity to narrow careerism, greed, and automatic performance.

Whereas Fyodor Mikheyich's personal goodness and meekness permit him to live on the fringe of the "kingdom of freedom," the environment of the Knorozovs is a complicated kingdom of iron necessity that drives out everything human or sentimental. "The will and force within him was such that it seemed if he stretched out his hand Grachikov's head would have flown off" — this is how A. Solzhenitsyn presents Knorozov. Khabalygin, the bare-fanged greedy one, gestured so fiercely that it seemed as though "he were chopping not only the air but the land itself," the author says terrifyingly.

But does all this frighten us? The failure of the "saints" and the triumph of the "devils"? Is the reader's mind scalded by the traditional tear that A. Solzhenitsyn has shed (with great delay — some fifty years late!) for the traditional "little" man? Alas, the story does not produce even this effect: Everything in it is toylike, stage setting, borrowed. The naive counter-posing of "bureaucratic" designs to the dictates of personal kindness, of the official to the human, all these contrived constructions crumble to dust upon comparison with modern life, which is filled with a different complexity, rich in other conflicts, and bountiful in true human beauty and courage.

To argue with A. Solzhenitsyn within the frame of the strange world of his strange protagonists is to take his idealistic conception of good and evil seriously. But this cannot be done; it is impossible to do this. And when the ideological bases of the story are rejected, one immediately notices how his whole construction collapses, leaving nothing but the tears the writer sheds for Fyodor Mikheyevich.

Our life itself, in all its richness, takes issue with A. Solzhenitsyn; the contemporary who is creating good in an angry, heroic world refutes him. The writer should go to this "pole," to this element, discarding his archaic conception of the eternal battle between the two principles in human life, of righteousness as a form of moral feat, of the elevating of man through suffering and tears.

(*Oklyabr*, No. 10, October 1963. In full.)

Literary Criticism: IVAN DENISOVICH, HIS FRIENDS AND FOES. By V. Lakshin.

It is difficult to believe that only a year ago we were still unfamiliar with Solzhenitsyn's name. It seems that he has been part of our literature for a long time, and that it would be decidedly incomplete without him. No new story of his leaves the reader indifferent, whether the critics praise or condemn it. It is discussed, quoted, and assessed with the special exactingness, uncommon in our literary debates, that is the first sign that we are really caught up and stirred. Mediocrity evokes mild evaluations, but a writer who excites us on his first appearance cannot count on leniency. And the law of the reader's psychology — of its prejudice, if you wish — is such that no matter what new themes and forms Solzhenitsyn may have developed in "Matryona's House" or in the story "For the Good of the Cause," he cannot escape comparisons, for better or for worse, with his first story. In one way or another the story *One Day in the Life of Ivan Denisovich,* with which A. Solzhenitsyn entered literature, remains for the majority of readers the standard by which all his works are judged. It is all the more useful now, when various points of view concerning Solzhenitsyn's talent have already been expressed by critics, to glance backward at this short story and subject it to closer scrutiny.

One Day in the Life of Ivan Denisovich was read even by those who do not ordinarily read stories and novels. One such "occasional" reader said to me: "I don't know whether this is written well or poorly. It seems to me that it could not have been written in any other way."

The story is striking in the harshness and directness of its truth.

This was that rare instance in literature when the publication of an artistic work rapidly became a social and political event.

N. S. Khrushchev evaluated this story highly, responding warmly to its hero, who even in inhuman conditions preserved the dignity and beauty of the working man; to the truthfulness of the exposition; to the author's Party-like approach to phenomena of such bitter and harsh reality. The very fact of the story's appearance was interpreted by people as the affirmation of the Party's will to be done forever with the arbitrariness and lawlessness that clouded our recent past. And it is understandable that the author's civic courage was noted earlier and more generally than was his artistic courage. . . .

Solzhenitsyn's artistic courage in his first story was already evident in that he did not indulge in our usual concepts of artistic embellishment. Essentially, he did not construct any external plot, did not attempt to develop the action more sharply or to resolve it more effectively, did not stimulate interest in his narrative by contrivances of literary intrigue. His intention was strict and simple, almost ascetic; to recount hour by hour one day in the life of one convict, from reveille to lights out. And this was all the more courageous in that it is difficult to imagine how one can remain simple, calm, natural, almost commonplace when dealing with such a harsh and tragic theme.

Solzhenitsyn disappointed those who expected from him a story of crimes, anguish, bloody torture, excesses of inhumanity in the camp, of martyrs and heroes of penal servitude. It is strange to admit this, but the first impression we experienced on beginning the story was that even there, people live. And they work there, sleep, eat, quarrel, and make up; they are cheered by small pleasures there, hope, argue, occasionally play small jokes on each other.

As if on purpose (and I have no doubt that it was on purpose) the author selected a relatively happy period in his hero's time at camp for the story. After all, it had happened that in the North, in Ust-Izhma, where Ivan Denisovich was first sent, there were no felt boots to wear all winter, there was nothing at all to eat, and Shukhov was "on the verge" of dying of dysentery. And the discipline there was incomparably harsher. "In the Ust-Izhma camp you needed only to whisper that there was a shortage of matches on the outside and you were put in solitary, with ten years added. And here you can shout whatever you want to from the top bunks. . . ." But Ivan Denisovich recalls those times of his life only on occasion, in passing, and usually only in order to emphasize the advantages of the present special camp: "Here it is calmer, I'd say."

The most paradoxical and courageous thing is that from the great number of days spent by Ivan Denisovich behind barbed wire, even in this comparatively easy period of his camp term, the author selects a day that is not merely ordinary but even lucky, "almost happy," for Shukhov. . . .

Were Solzhenitsyn an artist of smaller scale and less sensitivity, he would probably have selected the worst day in the most arduous period of Ivan Denisovich's camp life. But he took a different road, one possible only to a writer who is certain of his own strength, who realizes that the subject of his story is of such importance and gravity that it excludes empty sensationalism and the desire to shock with descriptions of suffering and physical pain. Thus by placing himself in apparently the most difficult and disadvantageous circumstances before the reader, who in no way expects to encounter a "happy" day in the convict's life, the author thereby ensured the full objectivity of his artistic testimony, and all the more mercilessly and sharply struck a blow at the crimes of the recent past. . . .

The story specifies the time of action precisely — January 1951. I don't know about others, but while reading the story I constantly thought back to what I was doing, how I lived at that time. I recall walking along Mokhovaya

Street to the university, through the crunching morning snow, past the Kremlin, liking to look at its beautiful, inaccessible, slightly frost-whitened walls. I attended the winter session, crammed for the just-introduced course "Stalin's Teaching on Language," composed the scenario for a student variety show, attended friendly evening parties. That January the newspapers were writing about the building of the Volga-Don Canal and of the high-speed smelting of steel, the amalgamation of collective farms, and the northward spread of the cultivation of Georgian tea, of the approaching elections and of the Korean War, of Alisher Navoi's anniversary, and of the hockey cup finals. The country lived with its major and minor concerns, and we lived with it in all these things.

But how is it that I did not know of Ivan Shukhov? How could I not feel that on this frosty morning he and thousands of others were led under canine guard out of the camp gate and into the snow-covered field, to the construction project? How could I have lived so peacefully and complacently then? Somewhat like those girl students whom Brigadier Tyurin encountered on the train: "They travel past life, the signal lights are green. . . ."

These are the thoughts that are most difficult to put down.

Critics Master Underhanded Pinpricks

. . . The critical attitude toward the story *One Day in the Life of Ivan Denisovich* did not take shape simply. The story, which was ardently supported in the press (reviews in *Pravda, Izvestia, Literaturnaya gazeta*) at its appearance, later received in a number of magazine articles an evaluation unlike the original one — carefully skeptical and even frankly negative. Incidentally, no one has expressed doubt of the usefulness of an open literary discussion of such a critical theme. Criticism of the story took a different course.

L. Fomenko found, in her article in *Literaturnaya Rossiya* (Jan. 11, 1963) reviewing fiction, that Solzhenitsyn's story "still does not present the whole truth about those times." She wrote that "Solzhenitsyn's story, for all its artistic mastery and harsh, bitter truth, still does not expose the entire dialectic of the time. A passionate 'No!' is expressed here to the Stalinist order. Shukhov and others have retained their humanity. But the story does not rise to the philosophy of the times, to a broad generalization capable of encompassing the antagonistic phenomena of that era." Soon thereafter, in the pages of the same publication (*Literaturnaya Rossiya,* Jan. 18, 1963), this assertion was disputed. G. Lomidze correctly reasoned that it must not be demanded that the author encompass the unencompassable. He pointed out to Fomenko that Solzhenitsyn had not been writing an epic novel but merely a novelette. G. Lomidze objected: "How is it possible to capture in one day of a convict's life the dialectic of all the relations, struggles, and contradictions of an era!"

While one sympathizes with the second critic, it is still impossible to consider his argument a strong one. He has unwittingly assumed a certain apologetic tone and involuntarily resorted to that same normative system of concepts his opponent uses, attempting to establish a certain hierarchy of genres according to which an epic novel is a priori superior to a story when it comes to depicting truth. But is it not possible to "rise to the philosophy of the times, to broad generalization" even in a short story? Is it not an axiom that an artist, if he is a true artist, is able to reflect the entire world in a small drop?

As for Solzhenitsyn's story, in our view what is amazing is not that he "failed to reflect" something or "failed to generalize" but, on the contrary, how broadly he has grasped life, how much he has been able to relate within such narrow bounds as one day in the life of one camp inmate. Indeed, we not only learn the everyday life of the convicts, their forced labor, and their joyless existence. We recognize among them people each of whom evokes something typical, essential to an understanding of the times. . . .

It must also be kept in mind that in an artistic work — unlike, say, a statistical reference book — the merit of completeness and many-sidedness is not determined by the number of themes touched upon but by the quality of the portrayal itself. In a single, fleeting detail dropped in passing a real artist will depict life with more diversity than it can be shown in the hasty "reflection" of dozens of themes in some pudgy illustrative novel.

The authors of the carping, querulous responses to Solzhenitsyn's story that occasionally appear in certain magazines think otherwise. These responses usually have the character of underhanded pinpricks, and they would not be worthy of notice at all had they not recently become excessively importunate. *Ogonyok*'s critic, for example, in heaping praise upon the new novel by I. Lazutin — author of the popular detective story "Sergeant of the Militia" — does not hesitate to remark with infantile literary irresponsibility: "In contrast to A. Solzhenitsyn's story *One Day in the Life of Ivan Denisovich,* I. Lazutin's novel parades many sides of life before our eyes" (*Ogonyok,* No. 39, 1963). Thus it is announced as if it were self-evident that, unlike Solzhenitsyn's story, I. Lazutin's novel is many-sided. If the author of such a statement does not value his critical reputation nothing can be done about it, but why does he place the author of a book he wishes to praise, and the magazine in which he publishes this as well, in an awkward position?

Generally speaking, when Solzhenitsyn is reproached for failing to tell everything in his story that could be told about the camps of those years and about the country's life as a whole, one is amazed at the artificial nature of these demands, a kind of curious ingratitude toward the writer. Instead of marveling at his talent and civic courage, at how deep and truthful everything is in the picture he has drawn — in which, it seems, you cannot find a dot or a line that is contrived or false — the author is reproached for leaving outside the framework of his picture many subjects and characters that are worthy of portrayal. Such insatiable exactingness is understandable when it is part of an appreciation of the artist's work and an encouragement to him to produce new works, but the use of this method is petty and stupid when it is intended to cast a shadow upon the work itself as something inferior and incomplete. And that critic appears in a poor light who, having learned from Solzhenitsyn about the tragedy of Ivan Denisovich's life, having experienced the initial shock and barely allowing it to settle, hastens to teach the writer how the story should have been told in order to satisfy him completely.

A reservation becomes necessary here. We accept as indisputable that the first impulse in the soul of any reader of the story will be a heartfelt sympathy for its hero, a feeling of sorrow and indignation at the sight of innocent people condemned to the cruelest suffering, fury at the crimes of the period of the cult of the individual. And it is difficult to imagine a reader who as the major impression gained from the story will feel dissatisfaction with Ivan Denisovich himself, his character, way of thinking, behavior in camp, etc. It is difficult, but it is not completely impossible, for such a reader exists. This is the critic N. Sergovantsev, who wrote the article "The Tragedy of Solitude and 'the Unvaried Round of Life' " in the magazine *Ogonyok* (No. 4, 1963).

The Simple Man as Hero

After first pointing out that, in his opinion, Solzhenitsyn's story "contains within itself many deep contradictions," N. Sergovantsev hands up against Ivan Denisovich Shukhov a real indictment, compiled according to all the rules of normative criticism and reminiscent of those show trials of the literary heroes Onegin and Pechorin that were held in the schools of our country during the 1920's, when pupils, with the encouragement of their teachers, were learning the art of public defamation. I shall quote N. Sergovantsev's argument as fully as possible, taking the liberty merely of stressing certain passages to which I should like to call the reader's special attention.

> The hero of the story, Ivan Denisovich, is not of an exceptional nature: *He is an "ordinary" person, and "ordinary" in the strictest sense of the word, at that. His spiritual world is quite limited, his intellectual life of no special interest.* But as a whole, Ivan Denisovich is interesting to a considerable degree. Why so?
>
> First of all, because he is precisely an "ordinary," commonplace man placed in the center of tragic events, and because all events are transmitted through the "prism" of his perceptions. It is interesting to know how a simple man, presented by the author as profoundly typical of the people, will interpret the shocking circumstances surrounding him.
>
> And from life itself, as well as from the entire history of Soviet literature, we know that the typical popular character shaped by our entire life is the character of the fighter, active, searching and vigorous. But Shukhov is totally lacking in these qualities. . . .

At this point the critic breaks in on his prosecutor's monologue to inform the reader that he has no intention of "judging A. Solzhenitsyn's hero harshly." It suddenly occurs to him: "My life experience gives me no right to do so." But, having made this curtsey to the literary proprieties, the young critic proceeds with redoubled energy to indict Ivan Denisovich, whose character traits have been inherited, in his opinion, "not from the Soviet people of the 1930's and 1940's" but from the patriarchal peasant. "Not from the Soviet people . . ." is a critical device that is all too familiar but that has not been employed in literature in recent years. N. Sergovantsev reintroduces it in circulation.

Even when N. Sergovantsev recalls that we make Shukhov's acquaintance in circumstances that are unusual, to put it mildly, circumstances in which we have never before seen a hero of Soviet literature, he does so in such a way that all the rocks again land in Shukhov's garden: "That stern reality in which Shukhov lived could mutilate a man in every way." It is striking that in speaking of the "stern reality" in which Ivan Denisovich "lived," the critic chooses words of epic calmness, but with Shukhov himself he deals unceremoniously: Harsh reality has "mutilated" him by — as the critic goes on to say — "systematically obliterating everything human in him."

N. Sergovantsev particularly insists on the "tragedy of solitude," as though it determined the image of Ivan Denisovich. The critic writes that as a result of the "narrowness of Ivan Denisovich's 'daily round,'" he is essentially solitary. Neither Alyosha the Baptist nor Commander Buinovsky nor Tsezar, his barracks neighbors, was able to become close to him. The author repeatedly emphasizes that Ivan Denisovich does not understand many of his brethren in misfortune. Nor does Ivan Denisovich understand the life that still goes on outside the barbed wire. " 'There's no comprehending their lives,' he muses."

And as a final conclusion: "No, Ivan Denisovich cannot claim the role of a typical person of our era."

After going on to evaluate, quite unobjectively, A. Solzhenitsyn's stories "Matryona's House" and "Incident at Krechetovka Station" (in the latter the critic manages to glean the idea of "compassion for the traitor"), N. Sergovantsev relegates the writer's works to those that "leave a feeling of deep dissatisfaction, inasmuch as they recreate life one-sidedly, without historical perspective," and at the same time he denies their artistic merit, since the "truly artistic work opens boundless horizons of life to the reader," but he fails to discover this in Solzhenitsyn's case.

The reader must forgive our quoting and restating N. Sergovantsev's opinions. They are of interest in at least two respects. First, N. Sergovantsev's article is the only one that expresses a direct and absolute condemnation of all Solzhenitsyn's creative work in its entirety. Second, in his attitude toward the character of Shukhov he expresses with the greatest sharpness and certainty what had been more vaguely and circumspectly stated in certain other articles. . . . Thus N. Sergovantsev's viewpoint is not particularly original or subjectively exclusive. And although I do not think that it will find many supporters among the readers, it deserves attention as an expression of a certain position that may not be very secure but that is stubborn in its prejudices inherited from the yesterday of our life.

Perhaps the first thing noticeable in N. Sergovantsev's reasoning is his casually ironical attitude toward the very task of depicting an "ordinary" man of labor whose "intellectual life" holds no interest for the critic. In condescendingly and haughtily speaking of the spiritual world of Ivan Denisovich, he reprimands him for not paying attention to the opinions of "better informed" people. Ivan Denisovich himself appears here as a hopelessly dull and limited creature for whom, because of his peasant ignorance, there is nothing left but to listen to "active" and "keen" people. The critic is annoyed that it never occurs to Solzhenitsyn's hero to demand from these people the necessary information and explanations concerning his lot.

What the "informed people" in the special camp in the winter of 1951 could have answered to Ivan Denisovich's questions might still bear some thought. To us, however, one thing is beyond cavil: It is to the writer's credit that he chose for his hero a man who is, relatively speaking, ordinary and commonplace.

Besides, a person may appear ordinary to those who hurriedly walk past the ranks, without looking at the faces. To someone actually standing in the ranks, his own position appears neither ordinary nor commonplace.

The appearance in literature of such a hero as Ivan Denisovich is evidence of the further democratization of literature following the 20th Party Congress, evidence that it is actually getting closer to the people's life, not just claiming to. Chekhov said that it is easier to write about Socrates than about a young girl or a cook. Experience shows that it is easier to write about Academician-selectionists, district Party committee secretaries, chief agronomists, and directors of Machine and Tractor Stations than about Ivan Denisoviches and Aunt Matryonas. During the years of the cult of the individual, many writers began to show more interest in what takes place in collective farm administrative offices than in what happens under all the other roofs of the village. Is this not the reason why Solzhenitsyn's image of an ordinary, commonplace hero is taken by the critic as a dangerous innovation?

It is beyond argument that the theme of leaders, organizers, and inspirers is important to Soviet literature as to no other. However, if things are to be perceived from the Marxist-Leninist viewpoint, this theme is incomplete, to say the least, without a portrayal of the people who are led and organized, the most ordinary people, those who bear the load of everyday labor, who, as Lenin put it, comprise "the very thick of the broad working masses." Thus irony concerning the "ordinary," commonplace man is out of place here.

Solzhenitsyn's "ordinary" hero appears to N. Sergovantsev to have worked his way into literature illegitimately, and he attempts to blacken him as much as possible in order to deny his kinship with the people. To sum up briefly the critic's judgments about Shukhov, they come to the following:

first, Ivan Denisovich reconciled himself and adjusted to the camp, lost his human traits; second, animal interests conquered him completely and left no room for the conscious and spiritual; and third, he is tragically alone, estranged from other people and almost hostile to them.

Such an interpretation of the story should not be surprising, since N. Sergovantsev, true to the methods of normative criticism, reasons, as it were, independently of the content of the book. As one follows his argument, in which logic is liberally displaced by a peculiar irritation and demagogic zeal, one actually begins to think that he has confused things and by mistake read some other work than the one written by Solzhenitsyn and entitled *One Day in the Life of Ivan Denisovich.* . . .

What Is False Idealizing Worth?

. . . Ivan Denisovich is reproached for allegedly having reconciled himself and become "adjusted" to the camp. But is this not the same thing as reproaching the invalid for his illness, the unfortunate for his misfortune? Certainly, the experience of eight years' penal servitude in Ust-Izhma and the special camp did not fail to affect Shukhov; he developed certain external reactions that were in effect the condition for staying alive: observe camp discipline, bow to the overseer, do not get into squabbles with the guards — after all, "waving one's rights" in front of Volkovoi was not only dangerous but pointless. And one can only wonder at the integrity that his basic moral concepts retain through all this, how little of his pride, conscience, and honor he surrenders. His worldly wisdom and practical guile, his cunning and knowledge of what is worth how much — these virtues that run in the very blood of the Russian peasant, and that are not born in one day's experience, preserve the strength of vitality within Shukhov that helps him to endure the direst suffering and remain human. . . .

And this is so even though Shukhov knows the price of a bread ration and of warm clothing, and is of necessity constantly thinking about how not to lose the piece of bread he had hidden in the mattress, or how to fix up more comfortably a "little rag with eyeholes" for the face in order not to get frost-bite on the march.

Of course, all these concerns can easily be considered mundane, petty, and one can haughtily rebuke Ivan Denisovich for the narrowness of his outlook and for the fact that his interests do not extend beyond an extra bowl of watery soup and the craving for warmth. One can, like the birds of the air that neither sow nor reap but still lack for nothing, scorn in the soul any talk of hunger, cold, bread rations, some kind of little rag with eyeholes, petty bribery. One who has not known such hardships as starvation, lack of sleep, and bone-chilling cold finds it possible to treat them with a certain disdain. Why bring up the unpleasant? Let us talk of lofty things, of spiritual life, of conscientiousness. But what is such false idealizing worth? And does it not seem ridiculous compared with the courageous truth and great ideological content of Solzhenitsyn's story? . . .

There are various methods in literary criticism of expressing dissatisfaction with this or that hero, this or that book, just as in life there are various ways of manifesting one's hostility toward an individual. One can openly condemn a book, but one can also, while pretending to be in complete sympathy with the book's idea, attempt to discredit a character who is close to the author, thereby also casting doubt upon the writer's interpretation of life's phenomena.

As for Ivan Denisovich, a certain pattern formed in that segment of criticism which expressed a skeptical attitude toward Solzhenitsyn's story. The critic approached the story carefully, as though taking aim, deplored the convict's bitter fate, and only then raised the question: But is Ivan Denisovich an ideal hero? He hastened to answer "no" himself, and began to complain about "how great is the self-abasement to which this master of the clever fingers occasionally lowers himself for the sake of an extra bread ration, how the animal instincts of struggle for survival have eaten into him, how terrible, in the final analysis, is his conciliatory thought that concludes this agonizing day . . ." [I am quoting a newspaper review]. Such a willful interpretation of Shukhov's character could be disputed once again, but it is now more important to turn our attention to another matter.

Why, actually, should Ivan Denisovich be an ideal hero? We see Solzhenitsyn's merit as an artist to lie precisely in the fact that he has no pseudo folk sentimentality, does not forcibly idealize even those characters whom he loves, with whose tragedy he sympathizes.[1] If desired, many real rather than

---

[1] The worker V. Ivanov of the Melitopol Plant, with whose letter *Izvestia* (No. 306, 1963) [*Current Digest of the Soviet Press*, Vol. XVI, No. 3, p. 13] recently began the discussion of the story *One Day in the Life of Ivan Denisovich* in connection with its nomination for the Lenin Prize, is correct in pointing out the confusion in the reasoning of several critics, particularly of V. Chalmayev, about A. Solzhenitsyn's creative work. It should be agreed that it would be absurd to see an "ideal hero" in Shukhov. The writer himself did not claim to have created this kind of an "ideal," although he did show in his hero the people's traits of moral fortitude, diligence, comradeship, etc.

It is only surprising that, while admitting that the story is "a work of striking artistry" and "a most valuable book," V. Ivanov at the same time reduces the importance of Shukhov's image to a certain documentation of its truthfulness. It seems to him that the image of Ivan Denisovich is being "generalized and presented as typical"—and falsely, at that—by the critics and not by the creator himself. But this does not happen in literature. Not a single critic has yet succeeded in "making typical" an atypical image. And although V. Ivanov's letter is armed with the terminology of literary criticism as well as with theoretical definitions and stipulations that are professional rather than amateur in their tone, in struggling against critical confusion he has only amplified it.

It is also a pity that the letter under the striking headline "Hasn't the Main Character Been Embellished?" is only to a small degree devoted to Solzhenitsyn's book itself, although after all it is the story that has been nominated for the Lenin Prize, and not the critical articles about it. It is true that V. Ivanov, as he himself reports, learned about the nomination only through a special telephone call from the editorial offices, when he had already completed writing his letter. But the hasty publication and the unfortunate heading increased the ambiguous nature of the letter, since they created the false impression that the subject being discussed was the shortcomings in Solzhenitsyn's story, rather than the blunders of its interpreters.

invented shortcomings could be found in Shukhov. Consider how meekly, with what peasantlike deference Ivan Denisovich treats everything that in his eyes represents "authority" — is there not a dash of patriarchal submissiveness here? Probably other imperfections could be found in Shukhov. But Ivan Denisovich's shortcomings are not such that would warrant shifting the emphasis from his tragic situation to his alleged weakness and spiritual bankruptcy, from his misfortune to his guilt. . . .

The entire system of imprisonment in the camps through which Ivan Denisovich passed was calculated to suppress mercilessly, to kill, all feelings of right and legality in man, demonstrating in matters large and small an impunity for arbitrariness against which any outburst of noble indignation was powerless. The camp administration did not allow the convicts to forget even for a moment that they were deprived of rights, and that arbitrariness was their only judge. They were reminded of this by Volkovoi's lash, which flogged people in the "hole"; they were reminded of this by being deprived of rest on Sunday and forced to work at inopportune times.

People could, like Commander Buinovsky, become heatedly indignant upon arriving in camp, not being immediately aware of the full extent of the arbitrariness and their own defenselessness before it and regarding all that had happened to them as a personal misunderstanding, a mistake. Along with Ivan Denisovich, we sympathize with this explosion of protest by the Commander, who felt the outraged dignity of a Soviet citizen. "You are not Soviet people! You are not Communists!" shouts Buinovsky, vehemently alluding to "rights" and to Art. 9 of the Criminal Code, which prohibits humiliation of convicts. But, together with a feeling of heatfelt sympathy toward this pure, high-principled man, a feeling of sharp pity also arises. . . .

Solzhenitsyn would not be Solzhenitsyn with his harsh, realistic truth had he not told us that the Commander, that authoritative, clear-voiced naval officer, must become a sluggish, wary convict in order to survive the 25-year sentence meted out to him.

Is this really so? How agonizing to believe it! Oh, how we would like to see him protest every day and every hour, tirelessly accusing his jailers, not thinking about the cold or a bowl of porridge, shrinking to a bundle of nerves but keeping up the struggle.

But is this realistic? Isn't it merely wishful thinking?

In order to struggle, one must know for what and against what the struggle is being waged. Senka Klevshin had known against whom he was struggling in Buchenwald when he had prepared an uprising in the camp against the Germans, but what was he to do here, when the administration of the special camp — and herein lies the tragic paradox — represented his own native Soviet regime? How could one untangle this knot of contradictions?

During eight years in camps Shukhov, like his comrades in misfortune, had become convinced that his fate was not an exception, not a chance mistake. Many innocent people sat there next to him: Communists, ordinary workers, people devoted to the Soviet regime. Attempts to achieve the reinstatement of justice, letters and petitions sent by the convicts to higher authorities, all the way up to Stalin himself, failed to ease anyone's fate and remained unanswered. And no one returned home from camp even after he had finished his sentence. Sooner or later it became evident to all the convicts that the law was "twisted," that justice could not be obtained no matter how much one called for it, that evidently there was a system of repressions here rather than isolated mistakes. Thus the question arose: Who was responsible for all this?

The bold guess "Father with the mustache" flashed through some people's minds. Others probably banished such seditious thoughts and found no answer. Did not the chief misfortune of Ivan Denisovich and his comrades lie in the fact that there was no answer to the question about the cause of their troubles? There were guesses, but guesses are not sufficient armament, where knowledge would have been. And therefore, when the first pain of insult and outrage subsided, only a relentless sense of the injustice visited upon them remained.

Critics who would like to have seen Shukhov as "searching" and "active" have reproached him for speaking and thinking little about the causes of his situation. But why should he concoct endless moral anguish for himself after eight years of confinement? What he knew he knew with certainty, and what he did not know he could not know — to our common misfortune.

Certainly, we too would wish that Shukhov and his comrades had realized the nature and consequences of the cult of the individual while sitting in the camp, and had even engaged in a struggle against it. But does this not seem the most baseless wishful thinking when applied to the real conditions under discussion?

This is why it would be — to use Chernyshevsky's phrase — "banal callousness" to reproach Ivan Denisovich for not struggling, not defending his rights, for "reconciling himself" to his situation as a convict and not wanting to think about the reasons for his misfortune.

It is sufficient that in Ivan Denisovich, with his folk attitude toward people and labor, there is a life-asserting force that leaves no room for spiritual devastation and unbelief. And this optimism is all the more mature and real when you consider that the story of Shukhov's fate evokes in us the keenest and deepest indignation at the crimes of the period of the cult of the individual.

The Work a Socialist Landmark

Our image of Ivan Denisovich as a character typical of the people would probably be incomplete if Solzhenitsyn had shown us only what brought Shukhov closer to his comrades in misfortune and had not seen the contradictions and contrasts in the camp environment. . . .

It would be a temptingly simple solution to counterpose Ivan Denisovich, as a person with a modest spiritual life, to intelligent, conscientious people living for the highest goals. I. Chicherov succumbed to such a temptation in his article "In the Name of the Future" (*Moskovskaya pravda*, Dec. 8,

1962). Regretfully noting that "Shukhov fails to understand a great deal," and having pointed out a "conciliatory intonation in the revelation of his spiritual, yet nevertheless poor, world," the critic offered the writer several suggestions on how to improve his story. I. Chicherov wrote: . . . The story would have been even stronger, more important and significant had the characters of the Commander and the 'tall old man' been developed more deeply and in fuller detail. Perhaps this old man was not a Communist. But he was an intellectual." And, shifting from advice to an evaluation of the author's blunders, the critic stated bluntly: "In my view, the essential shortcoming of the story is that it fails to reveal this intellectual and moral tragedy of people who think keenly not only about the fact that a misfortune has occurred but also about how and why all this has come about"!

I do not think that I. Chicherov seriously expected Solzhenitsyn to start adding to and amending the story according to his constructive suggestions. This advice and censure must rather be construed as a rhetorical device, a peculiar method of critical reproach that has not yet become obsolete despite Dobrolyubov's warning a long time ago: "If a work contains anything, then show what it contains; this is far better than launching into observations about what is not in it and what should be there." It is a pity that these words are rarely remembered. This time, too, the critic failed to recall them. It is interesting, however, that in his reasoning about how Solzhenitsyn should have written the story, I. Chicherov clearly expressed his understanding of its conflict, counterposing Shukhov to people who "think keenly." . . .

There is something in this kind of approach to the matter of the old and banal prejudice that "simple people," working people, think and feel less richly than do we ourselves who discuss them with such a confident sense of superiority. It is doubtful that I. Chicherov would have insisted upon his idea had he thought it out to its final conclusion. Moreover, I think that as applied to Solzhenitsyn, the very attempt to search for a counter-position on the level "people-intelligentsia" and to see in Ivan Denisovich a "plow-type" hero whose opinions lend an "anti-intellectual," so to speak, shading to the story is decidedly inappropriate.

Solzhenitsyn's view of things is not simply a different one; it is a view opposed in principle to this one, a view that rises from another level of understanding of life's phenomena, that is based upon another system of measurement than the one used by the critic. For Solzhenitsyn, no division into "simple people" and "intellectual" exists; he sees a more general and important difference in the camp: laboring people, and people who consciously or unconsciously live parasitically on the labor of others. . . .

The heritage of the Russian literature of the last century is dear to Solzhenitsyn — the kinship with the people of Nekrasov and Shchedrin, Tolstoy, and Chekhov. But the view of the people expressed in his story is characteristic precisely of a Soviet writer, and even more so of a writer who has entered literature in the recent years that have been marked by significant changes in our life. . . .

In exposing the crimes that became possible under Stalin and that ran counter to the entire nature of socialist society, the story *One Day in the Life of Ivan Denisovich* also rejects the attitude toward the people that lay at the basis of the ideology of the cult of the individual. Stalin shut himself off from the people with the state punitive organs, and although he often mentioned and praised the people in his speeches, he himself regarded the working people with ill-concealed contempt. At the November, 1962, plenary session of the C.P.S.U. Central Committee, N. S. Khrushchev said: "Stalin did not place his trust in the masses. He was a member of a workers' party, but he did not respect workers. He said scornfully of persons who had come from the workers' milieu: 'This one came out from behind a lathe — where does he think he is climbing?' " The term "the people" when used by Stalin became an empty abstraction. It was as though all together were the people, but each person separately no longer bore any relation to the people.

In reinstating socialist law and the Leninist norms of public life, the Party has also imparted a new significance to the concept of "kinship with the people." From this viewpoint, the appearance of Solzhenitsyn's story in literature was an outstanding event. L. F. Ilyichev said this about *One Day in the Life of Ivan Denisovich:* "Such works foster respect for the working man, and the Party supports them."

Solzhenitsyn wrote this story because it was impossible for him not to write it. He wrote it in the same way that a duty is performed: without any compromise with untruth, with complete honesty and straightforwardness. And this is why his book, for all the harshness of its theme, became a Party book that fights for the ideals of the people and the revolution.

.   .   .   .

Someone may ask us: "And where is your analysis of the author's craft, of the work's form?" Indeed, we have not spoken separately, as is usually done, about the story's "distinguishing artistic features," but we are confident that these were being discussed the whole time, with every mention of Ivan Denisovich, Tsezar, the Commander, of the atmosphere of the "lucky day" itself, or of the scene at the power plant, because Solzhenitsyn's art does not lie in any external embellishment tacked on to the idea and content for effect. No, it lies precisely in the flesh and blood of the work, its soul. It may seem to the unsophisticated reader that he has before him a piece of life torn straight from its depths and left just as it is — alive, quivering, with tattered edges, dripping. But such is only the artistic illusion, which is in itself the result of great mastery, the ability of the artist to see people as they live, to speak of them in unsullied, so to speak new-born, words and in such a way that we can be sure that it could not have been said or written otherwise.

The story *One Day in the Life of Ivan Denisovich* has lived in our literature for only one year, and it has aroused more arguments, appraisals, interpretations than have been aroused by any other book in recent years. But it is not threatened by the fate of fly-by-night sensations, which are discussed for a while and then forgotten. No, the longer this book lives among the readers, the more sharply evident will be its importance in our literature and the more deeply will we realize how necessary was its appearance. The story about Ivan Denisovich Shukhov is predestined to a long life.

[*Novy mir,* No. 1 (January), 1964. Excerpt.]

16

YEVTUSHENKO LOOKS BACK

After the dust had settled, the young poets began appearing in print again, although in some cases with greater difficulty than before. In the first of these poems, which appeared on the journal Moskva, *No. 2 (February), 1964, Yevgeny Yevtushenko reconsiders the uneasy coexistence of the artist and the dictator. In the second, he looks at other poets — who may take his place.*

NEFERTITI

YEVGENY YEVTUSHENKO

Turn as you may,
                    and twist,
Nefertiti did exist.

In this world upon a time
with a pharaoh she lived;
but even though she shared his couch,
to her the future ages laid their claim.

His so manifest possessions
were a source of worry to him.

With dignity he wore his vestments,
and pronounced his condemnations;
he kept strengthening his foundations,
but, as Avicenna once remarked,
when, in nature, authority comes face to face
with beauty, its value depreciates.
And the pharaoh was much tormented
by the complex of depreciation . . . Whenever
he thought of this at dinner,
he dug his heel into the carpet.

He had an army,
                    chariots of war,
but, as for her —
                    she'd a pair of lashes, eyes,
a brow,
          star-resplendent,
and a neck in curved surprise.

When borne on high they floated by,
then the gapers turned
their stares,
                    intuitively,
not toward the pharaoh,
                         but Nefertiti.
The pharaoh was rather grim in his affections,
and even allowed himself rank crudities,
sensing the fragility of a potentate
when compared with the potency of fragility.

Slowly
        the sphinxes
                      crumbled in the breeze,
and beliefs
            in deadly earnest
                               shed their faith,
but right through the ideas and events,
through all those things
                          by which time is fooled,
Nefertiti's neck kept stretching out,
and, stretching, came into our days.

She figures now in some boy's drawing,
and on a woman worker's
                          brooch.
She acts to purify and liberate,
without palling
                 or growing duller,
and some person feels again
his value depreciate
                      when set beside her.
We're often stuck in daily muck . . .
And Nefertiti?
               Nefertiti
through daily muck,
                     through battles,
                                        faces,
                                                dates,
still keeps on stretching somewhere.

Turn as you may,
                    and twist,
Nefertiti did exist.

OTHER TIMES HAVE COME

YEVGENY YEVTUSHENKO

Other times have come.
Other names have risen.

They push and shove and scurry.
Making hard-baked enemies,
they create a lot of difficulties,
and give rise to spite and malice.

That's why they take the lead,
and girls wait for them in the rain,
and, peering through the dusk,
with furtive fingers wet their eyebrows.

Where are your foes, where are they?
You'd have to look for them again . . .
Ah, there they go, so blandly
cordial with their nodding heads.

Where are your girls, tell me where?
The rainy weather's dangerous
for their health, that's the matter —
baby-sitting, they're better off at home.

All your enemies have been stolen.
Stolen, too, the tripping steps,
stolen the whispering of a voice . . .
Only the experience remains.

But why take it to heart and grieve?
Tell me — have you not thieved,
failing to keep accounts,
stealing these things from someone else?

Youth is a form of thieving.
Therein lies all the magic of life.
Nothing passes entirely away,
but is simply a transition.

Be wiser then. Don't fall for envy.
Feel sorry for the lucky thieves.
However much they play the devil,
they'll end by being robbed themselves.

Other times have come.
Other names have risen.

Translated by George Reavey
© Copyright 1964 by George Reavey

Index

293

298

Pervomaisky, Leonid, 73, 76, 82
Petrishcheva, V., 139
Petrov, satirist, 211
Petty Demon, by Sologub, 57n
Picasso, Pablo, 11, 17, 102, 125
Pingaud, Bernard, 65n
Pioneer Palace, 9
Plastov, A. A., 142
Podgoretsky, playwright, 146
Podgorny, Nikolai, 54, 54n, 186
Pogodin, writer, 213
Pokrass, Daniel Y., 174
Pokrass, Dmitrii Y., 174
Polevoi, Boris, 19, 20, 82, 100, 246
Polikarpov, Dmitry, 5n, 7, 46n
Pologova, A., 17n, 107
Poltoratsky, Viktor, 36, 81, 198
Polyansky, Dimitri S., 101
Ponomarev, Boris, 58n
Popov, actor, 96
Popov, G. I., 58, 60n, 238
Poskrebyshev, Alexander, 12, 12n, 25
"Post with Verses," by Voznesensky, 79
Precocious Autobiography, by Yevtush-
    enko, 39–42, 193, 197, 200, 204–206
Pridvorov, E. A., *see* Bedny, D.
Prokofyev, Alexander, vii, 28n, 31, 31n,
    32n, 58, 67, 73, 188–190, 194, 246
"Prometheus," by Serebryakova, 73
Proust, Marcel, 64, 240
Pushkin, Alexander S., 195, 210
Pushkin Museum, 16

Quietude, by Bonderev, 87n

Radishchev, Alexander N., 210
"The Raftsmen," painting by Andronov,
    162
The Railwaymen, by Germi, 99
"Rain," by Akhmadulina, 79
Recantations, 203–210
The Red and the Black, by Stendhal, 244
Reisman, Yuly, 99
Remarque, Erich Maria, 32, 199
Richter, Hans Werner, 65n, 66n
Rivera, Diego, 125
Robbe-Grillet, Alain, 65, 67
Romanov, Alexei, 64
Romanov, M., 112
Romanov, Pavel, 61, 61n
Rome 11 o'clock in the Morning, film by
    De Sica, 99
Romm, Mikhail, x, 9, 55, 62, 223
    attack by *Oktyabr,* 99, 100
    speech, 95–101
Rostotsky, S., 15n
Rousser, David, 40n
Rozhdestvensky, Robert, 14, 29, 38, 50,
    80, 81, 164, 165, 189
    recantation, 203–204
Rozov, Viktor, 16
Rubakin, author, 225
Runin, B., 30n

"Rushnichok," by Maiboroda and Ma-
    lyshko, 174
Russell, Bertrand, 181
The Russian Miracle, film by the Thorn-
    dikes, 163, 229
Rybin, A., 61n
Rylenkov, Nikolai, 50
Ryurikov, Boris, 33, 84

Salinger, J. D., 32
Samoilov, David, 14n, 52n, 81
Sarraute, Natalie, 65, 67, 241
Sartre, Jean-Paul, 83, 241
Schwartz, Harry, 218
"Scorn-Trough," by Shchedrin, 117
The Second Day, by Ehrenburg, 129, 134
Seifullina, Lidia, 127
"Self-Portrait," by Zhutovsky, 108
Semyonov, Nikolai, 9
Semyonov, Yulian, 30, 37n, 80
Serafimovich, novelist, 165
Serdyuk, Z. T., 183
Serebryakov, L. P., 11
Serebryakova, Galina, 11, 12, 19, 22, 25,
    72, 73, 76, 157
"Sergeant of the Militia," by Lazutin, 278
Sergovantsev, Nikolai, 198, 279–281
Serov, Vladimir, 7, 8, 16, 101, 102, 103
Severyanin, Igor, 196
Shapiro, Henry, 10n, 12n, 19, 210–216
    interview with Tvardovsky, 48, 49
Shaumyan, L., 87n
Shchipachov, Stepan, 30, 41, 43, 52n, 80,
    188, 191, 194, 196
Shepilov, Dmitry, 13n
Shevchenko, A., 107
Sholokhov, Mikhail, 23, 25, 32, 32n, 53,
    56, 58n, 73, 95n, 127, 146, 160–
    162, 168, 195, 213, 224, 246
"Short Literary Encyclopedia," 4
Shorts, V., 104, 108
Shostakovich, Dmitry, 9, 12, 13, 102, 175
    recantation, 204
Shterenberg, D., 107
Shumilov, General, 183
Shvarts, Yevgeny, 28
Silence, theory of, 128–137, 144–146
Silence, by Bondarev, 212
Simbirtsev, architect, 171
Simonov, Konstantin, 9, 65, 82n, 87n, 146
Sino-Soviet relations, 2, 6, 45, 47, 58, 62,
    64, 66, 67, 69, 76, 78, 79, 84, 87–
    89, 137
Sivolobov, M., 61n
Sizov, Nikolai, 82, 87n
Skaba, A. D., 54n
Slutsky, Boris, 4, 5, 52n, 81, 192
Smelyakov, Yaroslav, 15n
Smirhov, Sergei V., 30n, 196, 198
Sobolev, Leonid, vii, 2, 3, 28n, 42, 51, 67,
    73, 169, 191, 246
Sofronov, Anatoly, 16n, 30n, 190, 191
Sokolnikov, Grigory, 11